Advances in End User Computing

ISSN: 1537-9310

Series Editor

M. Adam Mahmood

University of Texas at El Paso, USA

Advanced Topics in End User Computing, Volume 4

1-59140-474-6 (h/c) • 1-59140-475-4 (s/c) • copyright 2005

Advanced Topics in End User Computing, Volume 3

1-59140-257-3 (h/c) • 1-59140-297-2 (s/c) • copyright 2004

Advanced Topics in End User Computing, Volume 2

1-59140-065-1 (h/c) • copyright 2003

Advanced Topics in End User Computing, Volume 1

1-930708-42-4 (h/c) • copyright 2002

Visit us today at www.idea-group.com!

IDEA GROUP PUBLISHING

Hershey • London • Melbourne • Singapore

Contemporary Issues in End User Computing

Table of Contents

Preface

The present scholarly book is a collection of some of the best manuscripts published in the *Journal of Organizational and End User Computing* (JOEUC) during last year. This introduction is mainly a collection of abstracts provided by the authors for their manuscripts. The book is divided into three sections: Section I covers Web-based end user computing tools and technologies. Section II addresses end user computing software and trends. Section III discusses end user characteristics and learning.

Section I consists of four chapters. Chapter I, written by Marcolin, Coviello, and Milley, starts the section by introducing a Web-enabled Interactivity Self-Evaluation tool (WISE). Two case studies are used to illustrate how managers can use WISE to develop a thorough, easily communicated profile of their web-enabled interactivity capabilities upon which competitive positioning assessments can be made. The information generated by the audit process is intended to help businesses enhance their interactive communication with Web site users in a market-oriented manner.

Chapter II of this scholarly volume, penned by Larsen and Sørebø, examines Internet use among employees. The results indicate that users perceive differences across various types of Internet use, although no clear distinction is found between organizationally relevant use and personal use. The authors' analyses indicate that personal use is considerably lower than organizationally relevant use of the Internet. Personal IT innovativeness was found to be the best predictor of organizationally relevant use of the Internet. Age contributed negatively to the Internet use. Males appear to use the Internet more frequently than females. Educational level had no impact on the Internet use.

In Chapter III, Ma and Liu, uses the technology acceptance model (TAM) to examine the effect of Internet self-efficacy (ISE) on perceived usefulness (PU), perceived ease of use (PEOU), and behavioral intention (BI) to accept a technology. The authors used a Web-based medical record system and 86 healthcare subjects to investigate the direct and indirect effects of ISE on PEOU, PU, and BI. They found that, using hierarchical regressions, ISE explained 48% of the variation in PEOU; ISE and PEOU together explained 50% of the variation in PU; and the ISE, PEOU, and PU explained 80% of the variance in BI

In Chapter IV, Mao and Brown investigate the effectiveness of online task support (the wizard type in particular) relative to instructor-led training. Also, the underlying cognitive process in terms of the development of mental models is explored.

As stated earlier, Section II addresses end user computing software issues and trends. It consists of four chapters: Chapters V, VI, VII, and VIII. In Chapter V, Foroughi, Perkins, and Jessup compare audio conferencing and computer conferencing in a dispersed negotiation setting. The authors claim that this setting is becoming more and more important as businesses are becoming more and more globalized. Using an empirical study of 128 undergraduate information systems students, the authors established that efficiency aspects of audio conferencing are higher than computer conferencing.

In Chapter VI, Truman empirically evaluates impacts of performance-enhancing software features on user performance. The author puts forth and empirically tests a proposition that states that dyadic procedure is associated with higher levels of user performance when compared to monadic procedure. The author finds that dyadic procedure may decrease the accuracy of users' work. Based on these results, the author questioned the utility and desirability of software design features that are intended to improve user performance.

In Chapter VII, Wang contends that the commercial software industry does not provide a standard format of software specifications for a software package for consumers and, therefore, consumers are unable to judge as to whether software specifications meet the target system requirements. The author proposes a model of commercialized business software specifications for consumers. It suggests that software packages need to provide specifications for consumers in four aspects: business operations, user-computer interfaces, user-perceived inputs and outputs, and business rules. Using an example, the author demonstrates the implementation of the model.

In Chapter VIII, Hazari argues that the behavioral aspects related to maintaining enterprise security have received little attention from researchers and practitioners. The author identified seven behavioral variables from a review of the information security literature. The author conducted an empirical study on the aforementioned variables using students enrolled in a graduate business security course. Based on a Q-sort analysis of these subjects in relation to seven variables identified earlier, three distinct group characteristics emerged. Similarities and differences between these groups are investigated and implications of these results are discussed.

As also stated earlier, Section III addresses end user characteristics and learning. It consists of five chapters: Chapters V, VI, VII, and VIII.

In Chapter X, Kanellis and Brunel uses Global Energy PLC (GE) from the United Kingdom (UK) background to illustrate the vulnerability of information systems in a turbulent environment caused by a series of deregulation of the electricity industry in the UK. The structural changes GE had to go through, because of these deregulations, had a disruptive effect on its enterprise information systems, which were unable to adapt to the new and constantly emerging organizational realities. The authors use GE's experiences to provide for a rich description of the causes of misfit due to contextual change, and establish the ability of a system to flex and adapt to the new environment.

In Chapter XI, Boudreau and Seligman contend that quality of use, instead of the dichotomy of use vs. non-use, is appropriate for understanding the extent to which a complex information technology is being utilized. The authors employed an inductive case study of the implementation of a complex information technology that led to the development of a learning-based model of quality of use. Evidence from the case study along with relationships from the literature are provided to support the model. The model suggests the inclusion of factors relating to training (either formal or informal), learning, and beliefs, their impact on quality of use, and their change over time.

In Chapter XII, Horton and Dewar puts forth the idea of how people can be assisted in learning from practice and how this knowledge can be used in configuring information technology (IT) in organizations. The authors discuss the use of Alexanderian patterns as a means of aiding such learning. The authors then use a longitudinal empirical study that focuses upon practices surrounding IT configuration to derive and discuss three patterns that focus on practices surrounding IT configuration. They also talk about some potential dangers in seeking to codify experience with a patterns approach.

In Chapter XIII, Spitler defines IT fluency first and then contends that it should be an important concern for those who manage workers with jobs that require IT use. The author acknowledges that training is definitely one mechanism to build IT fluency. Using an interpretive case study of junior-level knowledge workers, the author suggests that to use IT in their jobs, these workers relied not only on formal training, but also on on-the-job learning through experimentation; reading books, manuals and on-line help; and social interaction with their peers. Interestingly, the author had identified different types of "master users" who were indispensable for this learning to take place. The author then suggested that managers and researchers interested in training users also devote attention to these other mechanisms for learning, especially the "master user" phenomenon.

Acknowledgments

I wish to recognize contributions made by reviewers and associate editors in bringing this scholarly book to fruition. I thank them for their due diligence in reviewing and critiquing the manuscripts included in this volume. My sincere thanks to the authors for being highly responsive to the reviewers' and associate editors' comments and promptly meeting the deadlines imposed on them. They have made outstanding contributions to this publication.

I express my special thanks to Grace Silerio at the Information and Decision Sciences Department at the University of Texas at El Paso who was instrumental in keeping this project on track. Her effort and dedication to the project are truly appreciated. I also thank Jan Travers and Michelle Potter at Idea Group Inc. for their help towards this project.

M. Adam Mahmood
University of Texas at El Paso, USA

Section I:

Web-Based
End User Computing
Tools and Technologies

Chapter I

Assessing Web-Enabled Interactivity:
An Audit Tool

Barbara Marcolin, University of Calgary, Canada

Nicole Coviello, University of Auckland, New Zealand

Roger Milley, Shell Canada Limited, Canada

Abstract

As business models evolve to integrate technology with organizational strategy and marketing, the application of Web technology to facilitate end-user interactions, or what we call Web-enabled interactivity, *has become increasingly important to customer relationships. This article develops and introduces the* Web-enabled Interactivity Self-Evaluation tool *(referred to as WISE). Two case studies are used to illustrate how managers can use WISE to develop a thorough, easily communicated profile of their Web-enabled interactivity capabilities upon which competitive positioning assessments can also be made. The information generated by the audit process is intended to help firms enhance their interactive communication with Web site users in a market-oriented manner.*

Background

As business models evolve to integrate technology with organizational strategy and marketing, the application of Web technology to facilitate end-user interactions, or what we call *Web-enabled interactivity*, is increasingly important to customer relationship management. Perhaps not surprisingly, recognition of the power of online interaction has been paralleled by growing interest in understanding end-user online behavior (e.g., Hodkinson & Kiel, 2003; Koufaris, 2002), user perceptions of Web site quality (Wang & Tang, 2003), and user satisfaction with Web sites (Huizingh & Hoekstra, 2003; McKinney, Yoon, & Zahedi, 2002; Otto, Najdawi, & Caron, 2000). For example, Otto et al. (2000) examine customer perceptions of Web site download time and their satisfaction regarding site content, format, graphics, ease of use, and responsiveness.

While such research has generated useful insights to a new phenomenon, we believe that it is equally important to assess firm behavior on the Web particularly in terms of organizational efforts to facilitate interactivity with Web site users. This is because the interactive communication process provides the organization with a market-oriented mechanism to uncover and satisfy customer needs. As argued by Min, Song, and Keebler (2002) and Trim (2002), the firm that utilizes tools such as the Web to generate, disseminate, and respond to market information will benefit from improved business performance and enhanced competitive advantage. It is notable, therefore, that in spite of increasing interest in customer-focused research and Web site interactions, as well as the implicit need to be market-oriented in Web site development, we are unable to identify any tool specifically designed to help managers assess their Web site in the context of the processes surrounding interactive communication and market orientation. Rather, tools directed toward internal (managerial) analysis have been focused on either the general functional quality of the Web site (Evans & King, 1999; Selz & Schubert, 1997) or on a more focused topic such as identifying and measuring factors influencing Internet purchases in terms of customer objectives (Torkzadeh & Dhillon, 2002). To link site design with performance, Agarwal and Venkatesh (2002) and Palmer (2002) also examine Web site usability by measuring issues ranging from site content and navigation to the customization and responsiveness possibilities of the site or the extent to which emotional responses are triggered through site use. Again however, while these studies have usefully advanced the variety of metrics available for e-business research (see Straub, Hoffman, Weber, & Steinfield, 2002a, 2002b for a review), their conceptual underpinnings lie outside interactive communication and market orientation.

The purpose of this chapter, therefore, is to introduce a diagnostic audit tool that provides organizations with a mechanism for systematically assessing the Web-enabled interactivity of their site, based on the underlying principles related to interactive communication and market orientation. Specifically, we develop and introduce the Web-enabled Interactivity Self-Evaluation tool (referred to as WISE), in the context of the three critical components of customer interaction: (1) addressing the customer, (2) gathering information from the customer, and (3) responding to the customer. It therefore encourages managers to focus on the firm's interactive communication with end-users in a way that facilitates the implementation of a market-oriented approach to e-business activities. The application of WISE is designed to provide a basis for comparative assessments of Web-enabled interactivity relative to competitor or benchmark organizations and the tracking of changes in Web-enabled interactivity over time. WISE therefore provides information to help managers with various strategic decisions regarding the use of Web technology in creating customer relationships.

As a background to developing and applying the tool, we first provide a brief summary of the nature of Web technology as it pertains to customer relationships. This leads to a discussion linking the principles of interactive communication with Web technology. Finally, we discuss the relevance of market orientation in a Web-enabled environment.

What is the Nature of "Web Technology" in Customer Relationships?

At a minimum, a Web site consists of a home page, but more likely, it also includes a series of other branching pages. Consequently, the site can involve various degrees of complexity for both the firm and the customer. For example, if a business posts a single Web page to promote its offer, the site serves as an advertisement and will require few resources to implement and maintain. Web site complexity increases, however, if the business wants to offer more functionality to its real and potential customers. For instance, to facilitate all stages of the buy-sell process, the system infrastructure could be expanded to include security mechanisms and backend integration for ordering and invoicing capabilities. For sites that foster personalization and community-based knowledge, sophisticated mechanisms for capturing, analyzing, and responding to individual customer preferences are also required (Guay & Ettwein, 1998; Lüdi, 1997; Scharl & Brandtweiner, 1997). Thus, the more relational a firm wants to be with its customers and the more functionality a firm wants with respect to buying, selling, and forming communities, the more complicated the site's technological infrastructure and supporting operations. Also important is that the Web environment is inherently a two-way medium that requires both input and cooperation from the customer (Hoffman & Novak, 1996). This forces the firm to understand issues related to technology-based interaction with buyers in terms of being able to remember and utilize their browsing and buying behavior. Consequently, Web technology is instrumental in enabling interactive communication between a firm and its customers. Given Gammack and Hodkinson's (2003) arguments that the quality of interaction will determine end-user behavior on Web sites, it is therefore important to understand and manage the process of interactive communication.

What Does It Mean to Have "Interactive Communication?"

At a theoretical level, communication through the Web is inherently interactive because it involves being able to address each buyer as an individual, being able to gather (and sometimes remember) that individual's input, and then being able to respond to the individual using their input (Deighton, 1996). While Deighton (1996, p. 151) views such interactivity as "…a tool that allows good marketing to become good conversation," we argue that interactive communication is a process that allows the firm to uncover and satisfy customer needs as they are expressed in the Web environment.

As shown in the left-hand side of Figure 1, the first stage in interactive communication is being able to *address the individual*. As expanded upon in the right-hand side of Figure 1, there are two aspects of the "Address" stage: (1) attracting buyers to the site and (2) engaging them once they are there (Parson, Zeisser, & Waitman, 1998). Attracting buyers to the Web site from *within* the Web environment is facilitated by having links from other sites (e.g., banner advertising, affiliate sites), while attracting buyers from *outside* the Web environment relies on traditional advertising and word-of-mouth to promote the Web site address or a URL (Agarwal & Venkatesh, 2002). Once *at* the Web site, the site's navigational design and systems influence the business's ability to engage the user by guiding him or her to content and functions (Fleming, 1998; Parsons et al., 1998). The Web site can also include communication links such as e-mail or relay chat that start interactive cycles where the buyer communicates with the firm through the Web medium (Hoffman & Novak, 1996). This is an important phase in the interactive communication process as research on human computer interactions suggests that customized navigational functionality must be done well, as partial efforts cause more problems than they solve (Kim, Lee, Han, & Lee, 2002; Lim, Benbasat, & Ward, 2000; Thuring, Hanneman, & Haake, 1995).

The second stage in interactive communication involves *gathering and remembering* the individual's input. As highlighted in Figure 1, there are two broad categories of input in the "Gather" stage: (1) manual input from the buyer and

Figure 1. Stages of interactive communication and related Web-enabled operations

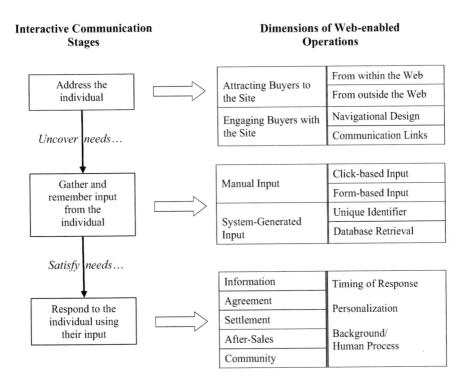

(2) system-generated input, both of which allow the organization to learn about customers (Parsons et al., 1998) while establishing dialogue (Berthon, Pitt, & Watson, 1996). The most basic form of manual input is the "click" on a hyper-link where behavioral data can be logged or remembered for later analysis. Manual input can also consist of that captured in forms, dropdown boxes, Internet telephone, or video conferencing. In contrast, system-generated input may or may not be known to the individual. For example, a unique identifier such as a "cookie" can be passed back and forth between the Web browser and the server without the buyer's knowledge, and database updates/retrievals can be completed through this identifier. As the customer begins to actively input data to the site, the Web site must be both internally stable and externally secure (Kim et al., 2002) in order to reduce frustration and risk perceptions.

The third stage of interactive communication refers to how a business directly *responds* to individual buyers by using their input that was previously gathered and remembered at the Web site. In effect, the "Respond" stage represents what is ultimately offered to buyers. That offering is often available in real-time at the Web site or is initiated as a delayed response such as the delivery of product or a response to an e-mail (Lincke, 1998). The degree of personalization in response can also vary greatly (Lincke, 1998; Parsons et al., 1998), with content and functionality delivered in a manner that is either the same for everyone or modified to reflect individual preferences and experiences as well as status and uniqueness (Holland & Menzel Baker, 2001). The response stage can also trigger a secondary background process where human intervention and action is involved (e.g., a Web site order initiates a telephone call from personnel for order clarification).

One approach to conceptualizing what is offered to buyers is to frame the "Respond" stage in the context of what we call the "buy-sell/community" process. Drawing on the arguments of Selz and Schubert (1997) and Lincke (1998), part of this process captures the exchange relationship between the buyer and the seller and can be broadly described as: (1) providing general *information* with the intention of facilitating a match between the buyer's needs and different offerings, (2) *agreeing* on terms of sale such as pricing, availability, and method of payment, (3) *settling* the transaction through exchange of money for goods or services, and (4) *after-sales* support activities involving the exchange of information (e.g., for product support), money (e.g., a rebate), or goods (e.g., product returned on warranty). Beyond these four stages, Armstrong and Hagel (1996) suggest that online communities are instrumental in facilitating the buy-sell process. Thus, we follow Selz and Schubert (1997) in suggesting that the "Respond" stage also includes the capture, analysis, and use of data for the creation of customer "*community*" and community knowledge as discussed by Lüdi (1997) and Peppers and Rogers (1997). In these communities, "…participants are encouraged to interact with one another to engage consumers in a specific transaction that can be informed by the input of other members of the community" (Armstrong & Hagel, 1996, p. 135). Such activities are also considered to encourage "site stickiness" (Holland & Menzel Baker, 2001, p. 39).

Overall, the Web environment embodies interactive communication and as such, requires input from the user. This input can be interpreted as an expression of buyer needs. Satisfying those needs depends on the firm's ability to gather and interpret user input and to respond either in real-time or by initiating delayed processes. In doing so, the organization can foster interactive cycles of uncovering and satisfying individual buyer needs within the context of the buy/sell process and online community development. As such, Web-enabled operations can be designed to reflect the three stages of interactive communication shown in Figure 1. Importantly, this process of uncovering and satisfying buyer needs parallels the activities underpinning a firm's market orientation.

What is the Relevance of "Market Orientation" in a Web-Enabled Environment?

Being market-oriented requires a firm to possess certain capabilities for uncovering and satisfying customer needs, both now and in the future. Firms accomplish this through participating in a range of activities to generate, disseminate, and respond to market intelligence (Kohli & Jaworski, 1990). Traditionally, firms generate market intelligence by collecting information from customers, suppliers, competitors, and government through market research, competitor analysis, participating in tradeshows, and so forth. Disseminating that intelligence is the second step and involves information exchange through interpersonal contact or organizational systems and processes. This might include cross-functional meetings, management information reports and e-mail, or simple hall talk. Finally, responding to market intelligence requires the firm to interpret and use the information generated and disseminated in earlier steps to plan and create a meaningful market offer for customers.

Both the interactive communication and market orientation processes represent how businesses can interact with their customers. On one hand, the interactive communication created by Web-enabled operations (i.e., Web-enabled interactivity) often occurs in real-time. It is always at the individual buyer level and is mediated by information technology. In the context of Web-enabled interactivity, market intelligence relates to the buyer's input at the Web site, whether it is gathered implicitly through "clicks" or expressed explicitly through typed, audio, or video means. In contrast, classic market orientation activities generally pertain to planning and implementation efforts and are bound by organizational processes and human involvement. Thus, market intelligence pertains to more general buyer needs or characteristics, and anything that impinges upon the buyer, such as competitive activity or government regulation. However, both Web-enabled interactivity and market orientation are cycles of market interaction that can be linked through the collection of Web-based market intelligence that is used in planning and implementation activities. This is represented in the integrated model of "Web-enabled Market Orientation" shown in Figure 2.

As suggested in Figure 2, managing Web-enabled interactivity in a market-oriented manner involves a cycle of continuous change. This represents the idea that Web-enabled marketing efforts should proceed through "thoughtful experimentation" (Parsons et al., 1998, p. 42) with information gathered from Web-enabled operations viewed as a form of market intelligence used in market planning activities. These in turn may result in changes to Web-enabled operations. As such, Web-enabled interactivity contributes to the firm's market orientation efforts, and an enhanced market orientation will reinforce Web-

Figure 2. Conceptual link between Web-enabled interactivity and market orientation

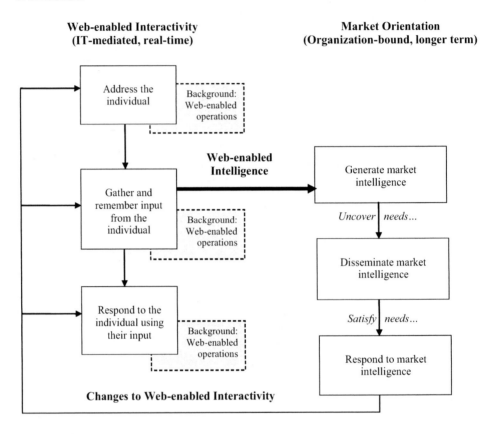

enabled interactivity. For managers then, it is relevant to understand that there is a relationship between interactive communication and market orientation and that market-oriented interactive communication is created by Web-enabled operations. As a consequence, it becomes important to be able to assess the nature and level of Web-enabled interactivity on their sites. This led to the development of a tool for this purpose: WISE.

WISE: A Tool for Auditing Web-Enabled Interactivity

The WISE tool is comprised of 88 items across the three stages of the interactive communication process — a process that contributes to the market orientation of the organization (see Appendix for items). To allow for ease in data collection and analysis, categories are used to group different items within each of the three stages (e.g., the "manual input" category of the "Gather" stage). Furthermore, the "Respond" stage includes indicators to highlight items related to a personalized offering, a delayed IT response (such as system-generated e-mail), or a background process involving humans (such as sending out hard copy information or delivering product).[1]

WISE and its various criteria were initially developed by drawing on the existing literature pertaining to the interactive communication stages and their related Web-enabled operations (previously discussed). To refine the original theory-based criteria, a series of case studies were developed whereby extended depth interviews were combined with content analysis of Web sites. The refinement process began with seven B2C firms that varied in size, product offering, and Web site complexity. This was followed by an assessment of the tool's broader application for B2B operations using six additional case studies representing firms of different size, markets served, and products offered. The overall process, therefore, involved 13 case sites. As it was necessary to allow for WISE to accommodate inapplicable criteria without impacting the integrity of the evaluation process or results, the tool was refined through iterative content analysis, which involved pattern-identification and matching techniques until each test site's functionality was fully represented. This approach to building WISE reflects the essence of comparative case study research as outlined by Eisenhardt (1989) and Yin (1989). It also reflects Parasuraman and Zinkhan's (2002) arguments that qualitative methods such as those used here are useful in gaining a deeper understanding of e-business phenomena.

The process of auditing the firm's Web-enabled interactivity by using WISE was developed through the case research process. The primary activity involves answering a series of questions using data from a range of accessible sources. The seven steps in WISE are:

1. Examine the firm's Web-enabled operations by making direct observations of Web site content and HTML. Use this initial review to identify which items require adaptation and/or deletion. Record all observations on the WISE score sheet, and indicate which items are found on the site.

2. Incorporate participant observation data generated from search engine results and active interaction with the Web site. Add these observations to the WISE score sheet.

3. Interview key personnel to fill any gaps on the WISE score sheet, and probe for further detail and explanation. Key personnel will generally come from marketing, information systems or information technology, Web strategy, and corporate strategy.

4. Throughout the process, acquire additional documents such as Web site statistics and marketing materials for further insight regarding the firm's Web-enabled interactivity.

5.   Go back to key informants and external resources to gather more information, clarify findings, and fully complete the WISE process.

6.   Tabulate and summarize these results in the appropriate format (in time, over time, relative to other sites, etc.).

7.   Discuss the results relative to strategic objectives and planning decisions.

How are WISE Scores Calculated?

As described, information is gathered to complete the WISE tool through Web site observation, interaction, and interviews with company personnel. When an outcome is observed on the tool, a value of 1 is assigned for that item. If it is not observed, a value of 0 is assigned. This approach follows Kim et al. (2002) and Karayanni and Baltas (2003) in that the attributes relate to objective features of the Web site, and as such, their presence (or absence) can be assessed with minimal, if any, ambiguity. The absolute and relative (%) scores are calculated for each category and included in the summary row for each stage. The firm's scores are then graphically illustrated allowing for information to be quickly and easily conveyed to managers. Of note, if a criterion is considered inapplicable to a business, it will receive an "N/A," and the scoring procedure is adjusted by reducing the total number of items evaluated. Overall, the final WISE score indicates the *extent* to which various Web-enabled operations are present at the time of a firm's evaluation and not *how well* the operations work.

WISE in Action: Profiling Companies

To illustrate how the tool exposes the level and nature of a firm's Web-enabled interactivity, two company profiles are now presented, drawn from the 13 cases that were used to build the WISE tool. This maximally different comparison was chosen to illustrate the applicability of WISE across industries, a crucial first step in instrument development.

The first profile is that of GROCER, an organization operating out of two large cities in Canada with two grocery stores, two restaurants, and a wine store. GROCER employs approximately 200 personnel and is positioned as a provider of high quality goods and services. As such, emphasis is placed on using the best supplies, ingredients, and techniques for preparing food. GROCER also maintains a philosophy of educating customers on how to handle, prepare, and enjoy food at home. In this regard, GROCER provides cooking classes and publishes recipes, entertaining tips, product information, and nutritional guides.

The GROCER Web site was launched in 1998 with two major objectives. First, the site was seen as a communications tool for educating GROCER's business and consumer markets about the company, its philosophy of quality, and about food in general. Second, the Web site was seen as a revenue-generating vehicle for capturing orders for its grocery store in one city and catering orders for its two restaurants. Grocery orders come primarily from the consumer market, and catering pertains primarily to corporate clients.

In contrast to GROCER, BANK is a government-owned commercial bank that serves the Canadian small business community. It is a complementary lender to commercial financial institutions and also offers venture capital and consulting services. BANK has a nationwide network of over 80 branches in addition to a virtual branch that provides online services to loan clients. BANK considers e-business a priority, and its Web site has been online since 1996. At that time, the site's primary role was to act as an agent for corporate communications. However, a visitor to the current Web site will now find a substantial amount of information on BANK's various offers, and visitors can apply for financing online, view account information, or send an e-mail to a branch representative. BANK values customer relationships, and it views the Web as a mechanism for extending and improving the level of customer service.

WISE Results for GROCER

The Appendix presents the WISE score sheet in detail, with one column indicating results specific to GROCER. As graphically illustrated in Figure 3, GROCER had 43 observed items out of a total of 88, or 49% of the total criteria. This number is used to gauge the size and complexity of GROCER's Web-enabled operations. On its own, the result suggests a low level of Web-enabled interactivity; however, this number is not particularly revealing. Further insight is offered if the observations are assessed for each of the three stages of interaction. For example, Figure 3 also shows that 50% of the "Address" stage criteria were observed. For the "Gather" stage, GROCER scored 69%, and it received 44% for the "Respond" stage. Therefore, GROCER seems strongest at gathering and remembering buyer input, followed by its ability to direct buyers to the site and once there, aiding them in using the site and accessing staff. GROCER's lowest score is with respect to the information and shopping functionality available to buyers — an interesting result given the retail nature of the business.

Further interpretation of these results involves drawing upon more detailed observations for explanation. In doing so, the Dimensions column in the Appendix can be used as a descriptive guide. For example, GROCER's "Address" results (50%) reveal that the Web site has a help facility, a standard page design, a menu

Figure 3. GROCER's WISE results

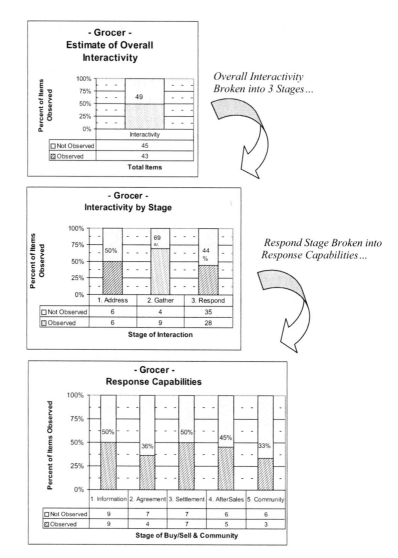

system, and a logon screen. However, GROCER scored only one out of four in "getting to the Web site," and that criterion reflected links to GROCER's Web site, links provided free through other companies. Once on the site, the "communication links" pertain to mechanisms for fostering communication between buyers and grocery store staff. For GROCER, there is evidence of an e-mail link, but no evidence of real-time communication via chat, audio, or video capabilities. GROCER also has a help/FAQ facility available, and navigation is facilitated through a menu system and standardized page design. A logon screen with password is also available. However, there is no site map or ability to customize navigational information.

With respect to the "Gather" stage (69%), several methods of manual and system-generated input are found on the GROCER site. For example, GROCER gathers and uses input from the buyer during each session or visit. The Web site also remembers aspects of a given visit by using forms for user input (such as a personal account, grocery order form, saved grocery lists), and records session and navigational information that is later aggregated and reported. The retrieval of previously stored data specific to the user is enabled through the use of a login screen. This capturing and remembering of information at the Web site indicates that GROCER facilitates a certain level of IT-mediated dialogue with buyers. At the same time, there is no evidence of a "cookie" being employed as the user navigates through the content, and the unique ID for the user is not integrated with transactions or personal information captured outside of the Web site.

Finally, GROCER's component scores for the "Respond" stage are: General Information (50%), Agreement (36%), Settlement (50%), After-Sales (45%), and Community (33%). Thus, GROCER's strongest score is for General Information and Settlement. For example, the General Information functionality of the site provides buyers with information on GROCER's background, philosophy, locations, products, and services. Similarly, the Settlement capabilities of the site are functional in the sense that customers in City A can search for grocery items, place them in a "shopping cart," and collect payment information. The Web site also serves as a conduit for passing payment information to a store clerk, who then processes the payment off-line with a POS/database system. There is also evidence of After-Sales functionality in that buyers can update their personal accounts, view past online transactions, and modify their "saved grocery list." The Web site is not fully utilized for customer self-service, however, as it lacks functionality to help buyers access their user IDs or passwords if forgotten.

The two weakest "Respond" components for GROCER are Agreement and Community — the former a necessary step to precede Settlement, and the latter key in fostering a broader set of relationships. For example, the capabilities of the Web site that address the Agreement component pertain to product pricing, pickup/delivery terms, a secure link, and a brief statement about confidentiality of personal information. The Agreement criteria *not* observed includes product availability, warranty/return policy, a privacy policy, an explanation of security concepts, and personalization of the pricing and terms. Finally, while there is evidence that GROCER fosters Community by providing several types of information of broad interest (recipes, meal plans, and newsletters), and there is also an attempt to better understand the customer through use of a customer survey form, there is no evidence of using transactional data to identify community-based buyer buying behavior. Nor is there evidence of promotions or incentives being used to lure customers back to the site. Consequently, GROCER's efforts to foster a sense of community primarily consist of providing static information of potential interest to its customers.

What Does This Mean for GROCER's Web-Enabled Interactivity?

At first glance, the overall results for GROCER seem to be low at 49%, with particular weaknesses pertaining to the "Address" and "Respond" stages. For example, according to GROCER's Web site statistics, one concern is the minimal traffic attracted to the site from external links (6%). External links are mainly from its Web site developer (which lists GROCER as a client), and general tourism and consumer-related sites, which could generate traffic but have not tapped the broader market. Listing their Web site through search engines, banner advertising, or affiliate programs with other companies would therefore increase the impact in the "Address" stage. In fact, the choice to "not" do this was an early strategic decision, with GROCER's marketing manager stating a preference for targeting existing customers rather than attracting buyers outside their geographic jurisdiction. In recent times, however, customer feedback has shown that customers are frustrated in their efforts to find GROCER's Web site using search engines, and GROCER is now working to register its URL.

This is, however, only one potential modification to the Web-enabled operations that could improve GROCER's "Address" score. Other possibilities include adding a site map, revenue-based affiliated links, or personalized navigation information. At the same time, GROCER may decide that based on corporate objectives and resource considerations, a score within the 50-60% range is optimal, and modifications (and the associated investment costs) are not warranted.

Turning to the "Respond" category again, the component scores appear to be low, although the basic objectives of the organization are met. The General Information section actually supports both of GROCER's site objectives by educating buyers and initiating the buy/sell process for those buyers considering a purchase. The Web site's Settlement capabilities also support the objective of generating revenue online. Similarly, the After-Sales capabilities support the objective of selling groceries online; the Agreement component supports the objective of generating revenue online by giving buyers basic information to facilitate agreement to make a purchase; and the Community function helps meet the objective of educating customers. Thus, while individual component scores might be enhanced through modifications to the Web-enabled operations (e.g., by including online payment to improve Settlement functionality), GROCER's management might determine that the 100% score is not necessarily optimal. Ideally, such a decision would reflect both corporate objectives and buyer requirements.

WISE Results for BANK

To effectively apply WISE to BANK, we recognized that five "Respond" category items are "not applicable" for this B2B service provider. For example, BANK does not sell promotional items (#34), and information on inventory (#45) and merchandise return policy (#47) are not applicable to this business. Also, the site does not sell goods to the public, thus there is no reason for the firm to include shopping carts (#55) or accept credit card payment online (#60). Thus, BANK's Web-enabled interactivity is assessed using 83 items (rather than 88) as shown in the Appendix.

As exemplified earlier with GROCER in Figure 3, BANK's results could be summarized in a tabular format. For the purposes of illustration in this chapter, however, Figure 4 presents BANK's results together with those of GROCER in a graphical format. This comparison, using maximally different organizations, highlights how WISE outcomes can be compared across firms. Normally, such comparisons might be relative to key competitors but could also use other organizations of interest. For example, BANK might benchmark its Web site against that of an accounting firm or management consultancy if both, like BANK, target the small business community. BANK could also compare its own audit performance over time.

Overall, BANK scores 63% using WISE. The "Address" stage shows 50% of the items being observed, with 54% for "Gather" and 67% for "Respond." Therefore, BANK's patterns are quite different from GROCER's as it has a higher total score, with its strongest score in the "Respond" category, followed by "Address," and then "Gather."

The key points flowing from the results of the "Address" stage are that BANK is diligent in registering for search engines. As well, it ensures that it has hyperlinks strategically placed on appropriate sites. While it does not presently purchase banner advertising on the Web, additional information shows that e-mail addresses and the company's URL appear on all business cards and promotional material, including print advertising. At the same time, BANK does not have Internet phone, video, or chat capability. It utilizes traditional telephone, e-mail, and face-to-face contact as primary communications methods. This perhaps reflects its focus on personal customer relationships rather than more arms-length electronic ones. When navigating around BANK's Web site, there is a site-map to help visitors; however, no help facility or FAQ section is available to explain the site.

Figure 4. Graphical comparison of GROCER and BANK

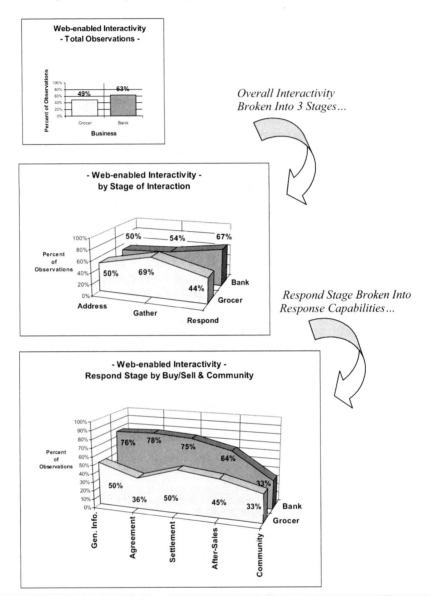

The "Gather" stage results show a 54% score, mostly reflecting the fact that there are numerous forms through which users can manually enter information. Information is entered for a buyer call-back request, online loan applications, and account information viewing. At this time the site does not accept manual input for searching for information or Internet phone/video/chat discussions with personnel. Information is logged as buyers enter the site and navigate around, and some data is passed back to the account viewing option. However, no non-Web-based information is used in these exchanges, although discussions with BANK's key informants indicate they plan to incorporate this function. At this time, BANK chooses not to use cookies, although it has used them in the past.

The "Respond" stage shows a score of 67%. As seen in the Appendix and Figure 4, of the five "Respond" components, the first three (General Information, Agreement, and Settlement) all score over 75%. After-sales is slightly lower at 64%, followed by 33% for Community.

For General Information, BANK provides visitors with a very informative Web site. Detailed information is available about the company's history, philosophy, and products, and contact information is readily apparent. Further research shows, however, that personalized promotions are not employed on the Web site. Regarding Agreement, the site provides buyers with general information on pricing, terms, privacy, and security. Secure exchanges are used at this point. Personalized pricing to an individual online is not provided as it can be facilitated through the Settlement processes. The results for the Settlement category show that BANK's Web site facilitates opening an account online and checking the status of Web-based accounts in a highly secure environment. Personnel are also available to take an order via telephone, e-mail, or face-to-face contact. Account representatives frequently initiate calls to buyers to discuss questions or particulars of financing.

The After-Sales phase of the "Respond" section shows that BANK employs communication mechanisms that reinforce its strategy of personal relationship banking. Telephone, e-mail, and face-to-face meetings are used, and customers can view past Web-based transactions online. Although after-sales service is available by telephone, e-mail, or an online form, customers cannot view external transactions, update past transaction information, update their personal information, or receive after-sales service via Internet phone, video, or chat options.

The Community score is clearly the weak link for BANK (33%), although BANK actively promotes its community involvement and customizes its Web site to each region. For example, a visitor can click on a specific city and be transported to a page that lists local events and discusses BANK's involvement in the community. Survey forms are also provided to collect feedback, and the site contains success stories and testimonials from satisfied clients. However, BANK solicits these testimonials for use as a marketing tool, and so they are perhaps a biased perspective on BANK's offerings. Hence, community aspects are more of a one-way communication to the customer and not the more engaging two-way customer exchanges (e.g., no chat, no online e-mail newsletter).

What Does This Mean for BANK's Web-Enabled Interactivity?

Overall, Web-based initiatives seem to be more of a priority at BANK than at GROCER. The key purpose of the Web-based operations is to facilitate customer interaction, thus increasing BANK's service level. BANK also utilizes the Web to increase its visibility. However, Web-based initiatives are used as a support channel at BANK, and they are not vital to the operations. Indeed, information generated through the WISE interview process confirmed that BANK's operations are quite successful at establishing and maintaining personal relationships through other channels (e.g., phone, e-mail, face-to-face), and the Web site is primarily an extension of that personal contact.

While it is important that BANK not lose sight of its goal of maintaining personal relationships with buyers, several features to further enhance customer service are being discussed. These include the addition of a help/FAQ section, allowing visitors to register for an e-mail newsletter, and allowing customers to view external transactions, update past transactions, and update personal information. BANK might also consider incorporating a pre-screening function into its Web site, allowing the status of non-Web-based orders to be accessed online, offering personalized rates online, and opening chat features. However, the value of these suggestions may be minimal as the account manager and client are in constant contact while an application is being processed, and such modifications may undermine the personal contact within BANK's relationship banking philosophy.

Discussion

If a firm has or seeks an Internet presence, understanding the issues surrounding the creation of Web-enabled interactivity is fundamentally important. As discussed in the literature, e-business success is a function of a number of factors including having both an e-business strategy and a champion (Golden, Hughes, & Gallagher, 2003), as well as technology expertise and knowledge (Savin & Silberg, 2000). However, using the Web-enabled Interactivity Self-Evaluation tool presented here can help firms understand possible gaps in Web site design or an imbalance across the three stages of interactive communication. For example, in the case examples presented here, GROCER focused their Web-enabled operations internally and neglected the early stages of the Address stage and the later community segments of the Respond stage.

WISE is designed as a *self*-evaluation audit tool for any company interested in auditing their internal Web-enabled operations. Some firms will find all 88 items relevant. Others, like BANK, will require simple adaptations to the tool. Regardless, using WISE provides managers with a basis for discussion around targeted or optimal score levels for their organization, given broader objectives and related strategic decisions. This broader context is important because functional and technological integration increases as the WISE score increases. By extension, higher scores reflect higher costs and complexities of operations. Thus, every organization needs to determine a WISE target score appropriate to their situation and competitive context.

Related to this, once an appropriate WISE score is determined, managers can adjust various aspects of their firm's Web-enabled operations. This will contribute to an enhanced market orientation by improving market intelligence. Similarly, an enhanced market orientation will lead to improvements in Web-enabled interactivity. Thus, the two processes are self-reinforcing. This notion is illustrated using the GROCER case (see Figure 5), where the three stages

Figure 5. Illustrative example using GROCER

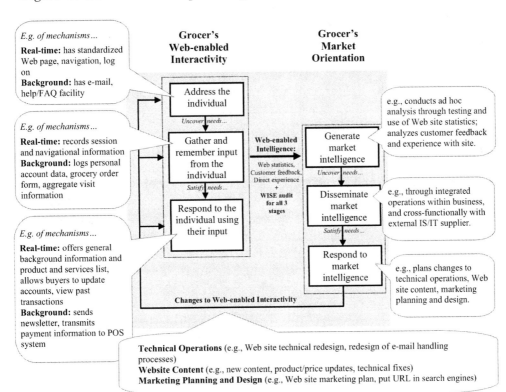

contributing to Web-enabled interactivity facilitate market orientation by generating market intelligence for the organization. For example, the WISE results previously discussed for GROCER identify both existing strengths in interactive communication and opportunities for development. As also identified through the WISE interview process, GROCER already conducts ad hoc analysis of the data generated by its Web site and generates customer feedback on the site through a survey and general e-mail. Therefore, by combining the WISE results with existing efforts to generate market intelligence, GROCER can begin to identify possible changes to their Web-enabled operations. That intelligence would then be disseminated through periodic meetings between GROCER's president and marketing manager, and its external IS/IT developer (including the project manager, site designer, programmers, production artist, etc.). Based on such discussions, GROCER, together with their external developer, could determine a response to enhance GROCER's Web-enabled interactivity by making changes to technical operations, Web site content and design, and marketing planning decisions. These interventions can later be tracked and possibly compared to other sites by a future application of WISE. Consequently, using WISE is a first step in an iterative planning process that encourages market orientation based on a detailed audit encompassing all the stages of interactive communication.

Other Uses of WISE

To implement WISE as we have discussed here requires access to key informants and internal information if all three stages of the tool are to be used fully. We have, however, also found WISE to be a useful mechanism for conducting comparative audits of specific stages of the interactive communication process. For example, a firm's results for the "Respond" stage can be benchmarked against publicly available sites to compare and contrast the firm's buy-sell/community process with that of competitors or other organizations of interest. If the firm has multiple Web-enabled operations across different business units, WISE can also be used to compare different internal operations. Importantly, it became clear in the development process of WISE that managers valued its easy-to-use nature and its ability to provide an objective and structured review of the firm's Web-enabled interactivity. Indeed, one informant commented that, "without the tool as a guide, reviewing our Web site becomes a daunting task mired by the reviewer's subjectivity." Managers also found the WISE process useful in generating thought and discussion around the firm's Web-enabled operations and their efforts to be market-oriented in a Web environment.

Ways to Adapt WISE

Implementation of WISE allows a firm to generate a baseline assessment of its Web-enabled interactivity, and the "baseline" characteristic might be considered one limitation to the tool. That is, the WISE criteria are evaluated using 0/1 (absent/present) scoring, and this does not allow for shades of gray in assessment. Some managers might, therefore, prefer to include a weighting mechanism within the scoring process, as this would allow for WISE to suit a firm's specific strategic and/or tactical emphasis as it regards interactive communication. Of note, while some might suggest that the "absent-present" scoring mechanism might be improved with the use of a five-point scale, for example, such scales are considered less appropriate for the objective attributes assessed by WISE, and more appropriate for measures of perception or satisfaction with a Web site. A second limitation is that the WISE tool does not seek to capture buyer views or experiences. Rather, it was developed to audit internally managed operations. Consequently, some firms might choose to adapt WISE by either complementing the core tool with a matched set of buyer-focused questions to capture user experiences (to allow for gap analysis) or using WISE alongside other evaluation tools that focus on capturing end-user perceptions (e.g., a more traditional assessment of customer satisfaction with Web site quality).

Future Research

Future research on WISE can be undertaken in a multitude of ways to support and extend the current work. The conceptual foundations for WISE are drawn from the existing literature in interactive communication, marketing, and information systems. As we continue to see research integrating these fields, the conceptual base for WISE could be more fully developed by focusing on specific concepts underlying the assessment process. For example, in terms of the address, gather, and respond concepts, researchers might focus on enhancing our understanding and measurement of the real-time buy-sell/community process or personalized interactions. Other emphases could be on the corresponding organizational generation, dissemination, and response processes touched by the interactive customer environments or how feedback loops affect technical operations, Web site content, and marketing planning and design. Ideally, further conceptual refinement would be balanced with empirical data, and implementation of WISE can provide a first step in this process.

Methodologically, the measurements in WISE can be extended from the yes/no assessments toward incorporating weights (as discussed previously). The influence of omitted and added items also needs to be considered, since the meaning of the overall score is determined in relation to the set of items used. Ultimately, common sets of questions will emerge over time to form comparison bases, extending the understanding of Web-interactivity within these boundaries of use. Future research should also seek to move beyond the case method that was employed for this stage of research. While the use of comparative cases was deemed necessary to build a context-free tool, important insight would be obtained if data were collected from many firms in select industries. For example, this would allow WISE to incorporate built-in benchmarks that are industry specific.

Finally, future research might focus on refining the WISE process for application *within* a given firm. For example, a firm can have multiple Web sites catering to different markets. Research could assess how well the tool adapts to those situations and how it should accommodate (for instance) a main Web site that branches into different sites based on market segment. In addition, given business now uses Web technology for a variety of operations, researchers might question how the tool could be adapted for other contexts. Examples include those in the business-to-employee domain such as procurement sites (e.g., online catalogues for ordering) or HR administration sites.

Acknowledgments

The authors would like to thank Rebecca Giffen, Liena Kano, and Connie Van der Byl for their assistance in data collection and analysis. They also thank the three JOEUC reviewers, an associate editor, and Mo Adam Mahmood for their helpful commentary.

References

Agarwal, R., & Venkatesh, V. (2002). Assessing a firm's Web presence: A heuristic evaluation procedures for the measurement of usability. *Information Systems Research, 13*(2), 168-186.

Armstrong, A., & Hagel III, J. (1996, May-June). The real value of online communities. *Harvard Business Review*, 134-141.

Berthon, P., Pitt, L., & Watson, R. (1996). Marketing communications and the World Wide Web. *Business Horizons, 39*(5), 24-32.

Deighton, J. (1996, November-December). Perspectives: The future of interactive marketing. *Harvard Business Review*, 151-152.

Eisenhardt, K. (1989). Building theories from case study research. *Academy of Management Review*, *14*(4), 532-550.

Evans, J. R., & King, V. E. (1999). Business-to-business marketing and the World Wide Web: Planning, managing and assessing Web sites. *Industrial Marketing Management*, *28*, 343-358.

Fleming, J. (1998). *Web navigation: Designing the user experience.* Cambridge: O'Reilly & Associates Inc.

Gammack, J., & Hodkinson, C. (2003). Virtual reality, involvement and the consumer interface. *Journal of End User Computing*, *15*(4), 78-96.

Golden, W., Hughes, M., & Gallagher, P. (2003). Online retailing: What drives success? Evidence from Ireland. *Journal of End User Computing*, *15*(3), 32-44.

Guay, D., & Ettwein, J. (1997). Internet commerce basics. *International Journal of Electronic Markets* [Online], *8*(1), 12-15.

Hodkinson, C., & Kiel, G. (2003). Understanding Web information search behavior: An exploratory model. *Journal of End User Computing*, *15*(4), 27-48.

Hoffman, D. L., & Novak, T. P. (1996). Marketing in hypermedia computer-mediated environments: Conceptual foundations. *Journal of Marketing*, *60*(3), 50-68.

Holland, J., & Menzel Baker, S. (2001). Customer participation in creating site brand loyalty. *Journal of Interactive Marketing*, *15*(4), 34-45.

Huizingh, E. K. R. E., & Hoekstra, J. C. (2003). Why do consumers like Web sites? *Journal of Targeting, Measurement and Analysis for Marketing*, *11*(4), 350-361.

Karayanni, D. A., & Baltas, G. A. (2003). Web site characteristics and business performance: Some evidence from international business-to-business organizations. *Marketing Intelligence & Planning*, *21*(2), 105-114.

Kim, J., Lee, J., Han, K., & Lee, M. (2002). Businesses as buildings: Metrics for the architectural quality of Internet businesses. *Information Systems Research*, *13*(3), 239-254.

Kohli, A., & Jaworski, B. (1990). Market orientation: The construct, research propositions, and managerial implications. *Journal of Marketing*, *54*, 1-18.

Koufaris, M. (2002). Applying the technology acceptance model and flow theory to online consumer behaviour. *Information Systems Research*, *13*(2), 205-223.

Lim, K., Benbasat, I., & Ward, L. (2000). The role of multimedia in changing first impression bias. *Information Systems Research, 11*(2), 115-136.

Lincke, D. M. (1997). Evaluating integrated electronic systems. *Electronic Markets* [Online], *8*(1), 7-11.

Lüdi, A. (1997). Personalize or perish. *Electronic Markets* [Online], *7*(3), 22-25.

McKinney, V., Yoon, K., & Zahedi, F. (2002). The measurement of Web-customer satisfaction: An expectation and disconfirmation approach. *Information Systems Research, 13*(3), 296-315.

Min, S., Song, S., & Keebler, J. S. (2002). An Internet-mediated market orientation (IMO): Building a theory. *Journal of Marketing Theory and Practice, 10*(2), 1-11.

Otto, J. R., Najdawi, M. K., & Caron, K. M. (2000). Web-user satisfaction: An exploratory study. *Journal of End User Computing, 12*(4), 3-10.

Palmer, J. (2002). Web site usability, design, and performance metrics. *Information Systems Research, 13*(2), 151-167.

Parasuraman, A., & Zinkhan, G. M. (2002). Marketing to and serving customers through the Internet: An overview and research agenda. *Journal of the Academy of Marketing Science, 30*(4), 286-295.

Parsons, A., Zeisser, M., & Waitman R. (1998). Organizing today for the digital marketing of tomorrow. *Journal of Interactive Marketing, 12*, 31-46.

Peppers, D., & Rogers, M (1997). *Enterprise one to one.* New York: Doubleday.

Savin, J., & Silberg, D. (2000). There's more to e-business than point and click. *The Journal of Business Strategy, 21*(5), 11-13.

Scharl, A., & Brandtweiner. R. (1997). A conceptual research framework for analyzing the evolution of electronic markets. *Electronic Markets* [Online], *8*(2), 39-42.

Selz, D., & Schubert, P. (1997). Web assessment: A model of the evaluation and the assessment of successful electronic commerce applications. *Electronic Markets* [Online], *7*(3), 46-48.

Straub, D. W., Hoffman, D. L., Weber, B.W., & Steinfield, C. (2002a). Measuring e-commerce in net-enabled organizations. *Information Systems Research, 13*(2), 115-124.

Straub, D. W., Hoffman, D. L., Weber, B. W., & Steinfield, C. (2002b). Toward new metrics for net-enhanced organizations. *Information Systems Research, 13*(3), 227-238.

Thuring, M., Hanneman, J., & Haake, J. M. (1995). Hypermedia and cognition: Designing for comprehension. *Communications of the ACM, 38*(8), 57-66.

Torkzadeh, G., & Dhillon, G. (2002). Measuring factors that influence the success of Internet commerce. *Information Systems Research, 13*(2), 187-204.

Trim, P. R. J. (2002). Corporate intelligence and transformational marketing in the age of the Internet. *Marketing Intelligence & Planning, 20*(4/5), 259-268.

Wang, Y. S., & Tang, T. I. (2003). Assessing customer perceptions of Web site service quality in digital marketing environments. *Journal of End User Computing, 15*(3), 14-31.

Endnote

[1]   All of the dimensions shown in Figure 1 are represented in the WISE tool, with the exception of "From outside the Web" in the "Address" stage. This category is largely associated with mechanisms outside the Web environment and was difficult to operationalize in the tool because of the varied and uncontrolled ways by which a customer might know the URL.

Appendix

WISE Tool Applied to GROCER and BANK

Stage	Dimensions		Question	Grocer	Bank	Item
1. Address	**Getting to the Web site (from within the Web environment)**		URL is registered in search engines.	0	1	#1
			Hyper-links appear on other sites for free (e.g., Associations).	1	1	#2
			Purchased banner advertising appears on other sites.	0	0	#3
			Revenue-based affiliated links appear on other sites (e.g., joint ventures).	0	0	#4
	Within the Web site	**Comm. Links**	E-mail contact or input form is available on the site.	1	1	#5
			Internet phone/video/chat is available on the site.	0	0	#6
		Navigational Design	A site map visually depicts layout of the site.	0	1	#7
			A help facility or FAQ is available to explain the use of the site.	1	0	#8
			Page design is standardized throughout the Web site.	1	0	#9
			Navigation is facilitated through a menuing system.	1	1	#10
			Some navigational information is customized to the user.	0	0	#11
			A logon screen with password is available.	1	1	#12
1. Address Consumer: Total Number of Items Observed:				6/12 50%	6/12 50%	
2. Gather	**Manual Input from User**		Basic hyperlink "click" is accepted (i.e., at least one link available).	1	1	#13
			Personal ID and password is required for authentication.	1	1	#14
			Manual input is in a form for searching information (e.g., read-only).	1	0	#15
			Manual input is in a form for recording information (e.g., account).	1	1	#16
			Manual input involves phone/video/chat with personnel.	0	0	#17
			Manual input is through e-mail.	1	1	#18
	System-Generated Input		Sessional information is logged as the user enters the site.	1	1	#19
			Sessional information is logged as the user navigates the site.	1	1	#20
			Cookies (unique identifiers) are used upon entering the Web site.	1	0	#21
			Cookies (unique identifiers) are used while user navigates site.	0	0	#22
			Database links to user's previous Web-based data.	1	1	#23
			Database links to user's previous non-Web-based data.	0	0	#24
			Hyperlinks from other sites exist with embedded search parameter.	0	0	#25
2. Gather Input: Total Number of Items Observed:				9/13 69%	7/13 54%	

↓

continued on following page

3. **Respond to Input**	Personalize "P" Delay "D" Background "B"	– criteria where information is personalized to the user – criteria where an IT-mediated delayed response is generated – criteria where a secondary process is initiated; likely involving humans			
3.1 **Respond—** **General** **Infor-** **mation**		Company/corporate information explains the business.	1	1	#26
		Copyright insignia is apparent.	1	1	#27
		Statement about copyright and intellectual property is available.	0	1	#28
		Product/service information can be accessed without search facility.	1	1	#29
		Product/service information can be accessed with a search facility.	1	1	#30
		Information is provided on how to use the products/services.	1	1	#31
		Information is provided on where the products/services are available.	1	1	#32
		Information is provided on how to purchase/acquire "core" products/services.	1	1	#33
		Information is provided on how to purchase/acquire "promotional" products.	0	n/a	#34
		Information is provided on how to contact business personnel for information.	1	1	#35
		Homepage reflects up-to-date information.	0	1	#36
	B	Site facilitates product/service information sent later in hard copy.	0	1	#37
	B	Personnel communicate information via Internet phone/video/chat.	0	0	#38
	B	Site conveys phone number/e-mail for general inquiries.	1	1	#39
		Site conveys some information in more than one language.	0	1	#40
	P	Site personalizes promotion based on captured preferences.	0	0	#41
	P	Site personalizes promotion based on previous purchases.	0	0	#42
	P	Site personalizes promotion based on browsing behavior.	0	0	#43
3.1 Respond—General Information Total:			9/18 50%	13/17 76%	
3.2 **Respond—** **Agreement**		General pricing information (e.g., standard prices) is available.	1	1	#44
		General information on product/service availability (e.g., inventory) is available.	0	n/a	#45
		General delivery/access terms (e.g., charges, timing, and location) are available.	1	1	#46
		General terms such as warranty/returns policy, and so forth are available.	0	n/a	#47
		Provides a brief statement about privacy/confidentiality (e.g., one sentence).	1	1	#48
		Provides a privacy policy with details about information usage.	0	1	#49
		Provides a trademark to an independent privacy policy association (e.g., certificate authority, trust network).	0	0	#50
		Link between user's browser and the Web site server is secure.	1	1	#51
		Information to explain security concepts to users is available online.	0	1	#52
	B	Site facilitates mail-out of agreement information (e.g., quote).	0	1	#53
	P	Site personalizes/adjusts terms (e.g., pricing) to the individual.	0	0	#54
3.2 Respond—Agreement Total:			4/11 36%	7/9 78%	

continued on following page

Category	P	B/D	Description			#
			Mechanism is available for online purchase (e.g., shopping cart).	1	n/a	#55
		B	Personnel take consumer order through Internet phone/video/chat.	0	0	#56
		B	Personnel are available via standard phone to take order.	0	1	#57
		B	Web site order initiates call from personnel to clarify order.	1	1	#58
		B	Site accepts order via e-mail or form; to be processed outside Web.	0	1	#59
			Site settles payment directly online (e.g., use of e-cash/credit card).	0	n/a	#60
3.3.Respond— Settlement	P		Site facilitates opening a personal account online.	1	1	#61
	P		Status of Web-based orders can be accessed online (e.g., invoice).	1	1	#62
	P		Status of non-Web orders can be accessed online (e.g., invoice).	0	0	#63
			Site distributes some products online (if it is digitally based).	0	1	#64
		B	Site facilitates distributing product off-line (physical means).	1	1	#65
		D	Delivery/invoicing/receipt documents are sent online (e.g., e-mail).	0	0	#66
	P		Delivery/invoicing/receipt documents are available on the site.	1	1	#67
		D	Delivery/invoicing/receipt documents are sent off-line (e.g., mail).	1	1	#68
3.3. Respond—Settlement Total:				**7/14 50%**	**9/12 75%**	
			General support information for products/services is available.	1	1	#69
		B	Support Information is sent "off-line" because of sale.	0	1	#70
		D	Support Information is sent "online" via e-mail because of sale.	0	1	#71
	P		User can access past Web-based transactions/receipts online.	1	1	#72
3.4 Respond— After-Sales	P		User can access past external transactions/receipts online.	0	0	#73
	P		User can update past transaction information online (e.g., opt-out).	0	0	#74
	P		User can update personal account information online (e.g., address).	1	0	#75
			User can gain online access to ID or password if forgotten (can use e-mail).	0	1	#76
		B	Personnel provide after-sales service via Internet phone/video/chat.	0	0	#77
		B	Personnel provide after-sales service via standard phone.	1	1	#78
		D	Personnel provide after-sales service via e-mail.	1	1	#79
3.4 Respond—After-Sales Total:				**5/11 45%**	**7/11 64%**	
			Promotional incentives exist to encourage customers back to the site.	0	0	#80
		B	Ancillary information of community interest is available online.	1	1	#81
		D	User can register for e-mail (e.g., newsletter) of community interest.	1	0	#82
3.5 Respond— Community		D	User input on core offering is recorded for public viewing.	0	0	#83
			Users can "chat" directly among themselves.	0	0	#84
			User survey/input forms are available.	1	1	#85
			Users can "chat" with or hear from individuals of interest.	0	0	#86
	P		Site personalizes promotion based on community data.	0	1	#87
			Discussion group/news group information can be accessed on the site.	0	0	#88
3.5 Respond—Community Total:				**3/9 33%**	**3/9 33%**	
3. Respond Using Input: Total Number of Items Observed:				**28/63 44%**	**39/58 67%**	
Grand Total			**Total Number of Items Observed:**	43	52	
			Total Number of Applicable Items:	88/88	83/88	
			Percentage of Total Items Observed:	49%	63%	

Chapter II

The Impact of Personal IT Innovativeness on Use of the Internet Among Employees at Work

Tor J. Larsen, Norwegian School of Management, Norway

Øystein Sørebø, Buskerud University College, Norway[1]

Abstract

Examining Internet use among employees, this research investigated the theoretical proposition that personal IT innovativeness will positively impact the use of novel computer technologies. The research model included the individual traits of age, gender, experience with IT, and educational level. The article discusses the categories of organizationally relevant versus personal use of the Internet. Using a questionnaire, data was collected from 328 respondents in one organization. The results indicated that users perceive structural differences across various types of Internet use areas, although no clear support for a distinction between organizationally relevant and personal use was found. Additionally, the analyses indicated that personal use is considerably lower than organizationally relevant use of the Internet. However, employees may not distinguish clearly between these two categories. Personal IT innovativeness was the best predictor of organizationally relevant use of the Internet. Age contributed negatively to Internet use. Males appear to use the Internet more frequently than females. Educational level had no impact on Internet use.

Introduction

A recurring theme within the domain of end-user computing is explaining differences in individual computer use patterns among employees (DeLone & McLean, 1992; Harris, 2000; Powell & Moore, 2002; Seddon, 1997). Recently, Internet usage has emerged as an area of particular importance (Otto, Najdawi, & Caron, 2000; Stanton, 2002). Because of the recent dot-com bubble collapse and numerous e-commerce failures, one would expect the Internet to have less importance to individual users. However, in addition to some dot-com successes, private and public institutions are developing an increasing number of Internet services. Employees of large organizations are active users, and their use is expected to grow (Charlton, Gittings, Leng, Little, & Neilson, 1998; Roberts, 2000). Research addressing differences in personal Internet use patterns has relevance.

Based on the view that change is key, a series of studies has investigated the effect of *personal information technology (IT) innovativeness* on the use of novel technologies. Studies addressing *personal IT innovativeness* often differ from research using the technology acceptance model (Chau, 2001) because the impacts of attitude, beliefs, and intention on behavior (i.e., use) are not the focus. Rather, *personal IT innovativeness* has been viewed as a trait that in its own right may explain use. Hence, the present research builds on the theoretical assumption that *personal IT innovativeness* is positively related to the use of novel technologies regardless of usage area.

The samples used in previous studies addressing *personal IT innovativeness* are users (in general) of the World Wide Web (Agarwal & Karahanna, 2000), online shoppers (Limayem, Khalifa, & Frini, 2000), academicians (Pajo, 2000), and adolescents (Wolfrandt & Doll, 2001). The overall interpretation is that *personal IT innovativeness* has a positive impact on Internet use, yet the relationship between *personal IT innovativeness* and Internet use among the broad population of employees in business organizations has not been directly investigated.

The argument that the present fast-changing business environment requires constant innovation efforts also applies to individual employees. The concept of innovation covers a wide range of issues (Damanpour, 1991; Robey & Boudreau, 2000). Clearly, *personal IT innovativeness* is only a small element within the larger issue of innovation in organizational settings. It has also been argued that there is a difference between change and innovation (Katz & Kahn, 1978; Larsen, 1993). According to these authors, an innovation effort would impact a large part of, if not the entire, organization. Change activities are defined as individual actions taken where the objective is limited to improvements in the individual's own job situation.

However, an information technology that offers a large degree of freedom with regard to its use may leave the responsibility of its use to individual users. In this regard, the degree of *personal IT innovativeness* may play a role. Obviously other socioeconomic characteristics may explain use (Brancheau & Wetherbe, 1990; Rogers, 1983). For these reasons, the present research project focused on the following research question: What are the relationships among employees' degree of *personal IT innovativeness*, other socioeconomic factors, and the use of the Internet at work?

Theory, Hypotheses, and Research Model

IT use (also denoted *system use or utilization*) is one of the most frequently applied concepts of IS-success (e.g., Seddon, 1997; Straub, Limayem, & Karahanna-Evaristo, 1995). Among information systems (IS) researchers, there is a widespread belief that use of IT affects white-collar performance (Davis, 1989; Thompson, Higgins, & Howell, 1991). However, as Guthrie and Gray (1996) and Markus (1994) have observed, IT can be utilized in both appropriate and inappropriate ways. Ineffective or inappropriate use often prevents or undermines positive impacts (Markus, 1994). For example, indiscriminate use of the Internet for personal matters may result in reduced job performance. Because the Internet can be employed for multiple purposes, the issue has been raised that organizations must promote appropriate or organizationally relevant Internet use[2] (Spar & Bussgang, 1996). Conversely, it has also been argued that employees should be allowed to spend time on non-productive tasks since any experience in computer use may increase a person's computer literacy and general ability to take advantage of IT (Guthrie & Gray, 1996).

Based on the work by Guthrie and Gray and Markus, in this research Internet use was conceptualized as a construct including both organizationally relevant and personal use, with use of the Internet as a vehicle for business information search being an example of the former, and use of the Internet for personal banking being an example of the latter. Organizations would obviously promote Internet use that is business related. Consequently, many organizations have established policies that limit or prohibit personal Internet use. Because the information found on the Internet frequently is not organized into clear categories, distinguishing between organizationally relevant and personal Internet use may not be straightforward (e.g., reading news, browsing, and locating home pages). Personal banking and shopping products are examples of personal use. Organizations may not want employees to spend hours on these. Yet, organizations may encourage employees to explore new technologies and new possibilities. Hence, limited personal use of the Internet at work may not be seen as synonymous with inappropriate use. Because of this, employees may not perceive a clear distinction between organizationally relevant and personal use.

In summary, in situations where limited personal Internet use occurs and the organization does not explicitly forbid it or implicitly encourages it to some degree, it may be difficult for employees to differentiate between organizationally relevant and personal Internet use. Also, the information found on the Internet is quite often not presented in clear categories. Hence, the present research anticipated that active Internet users are more active across usage areas than less active users. The argumentation leads to the following hypothesis:

H1.a: Use of the Internet among employees will not exhibit structural differences across Internet usage areas.

It is reasonable to expect that personal Internet use occurs in most organizations and, at least in part, is indistinguishable from organizationally relevant use. As indicated above, reading business news may be a typical example of use that mixes organizationally relevant and personal Internet use. However, shopping and banking are strong personal use candidates, but even these two usage areas may have organizational relevance. For example, filing a business travel compensation request may require access to personal bank and credit card information. Although personal Internet use may be structurally consistent across usage areas (cf. H1.a), we anticipate that Internet use in areas deemed highly organizationally relevant will exceed the use of the Internet in areas deemed mostly personal.

H1.b: Personal use of the Internet in areas deemed organizationally relevant will be more frequent than use of the Internet in areas deemed personal.

As the research question implies, we were particularly interested in exploring the relationship between *personal IT innovativeness* and use of the Internet, the relationship being a well-established research issue (Citrin, Sprott, Silverman, & Stem, 2000; Wolfradt & Doll, 2001). However, recent conceptualization of *personal IT innovativeness* is radically different than that originally defined by Rogers and Shoemaker (1971). They conceptualized innovativeness as an observable phenomenon, the individual point in time of adoption relative to others.

The employment of diffusion theory in organizational settings has been criticized for various reasons, for example, that organizational IT-based innovations in their own right are more complex than Rogers' (1983, 1995) diffusion theory specifies or that organizational IT innovation processes are richer and more diverse than sigmoidal (Larsen, 2001; Lyytinen & Damsgaard, 2001). In particular, the objective of this research was not the investigation of the date of adoption but the level of Internet use. With regard to Rogers' diffusion theory, an employee using the Internet at an early date may not necessarily have maintained that use. Also, an employee having initiated Internet use at a somewhat later date may have become a heavy user, or discontinued that use. Therefore, the date of Internet adoption may not necessarily be correlated with use.

Because of these difficulties and the focus on the amount of use, we turned to Agarwal and Prasad's (1998) conceptualization of innovativeness as a personal trait. Agarwal and Prasad argued that IT innovativeness is a relatively stable descriptor being invariant across user populations. Moreover, they described *personal IT innovativeness* as a general innovative behavior in the context of microcomputer interactions, expressed as "the willingness of an individual to try out any new information technology" (p. 206). The assumption is that individuals scoring high on *personal IT innovativeness* would take advantage of a new technology (Agarwal & Karahanna, 2000; Goldsmith, 2001; Limayem et al., 2000; Pajo, 2000; Wolfradt & Doll, 2001). Based on these findings, we anticipated that *personal IT innovativeness* among employees would influence the level of both organizational and personal Internet use. Although in their work context users may exhibit a willingness to try out new information technology, one cannot infer that the Internet is used for strictly organizationally relevant matters. As discussed previously, it is quite likely that the Internet is used for both organizational and personal purposes. Hence, the hypothesis indicated here is:

H2: Personal IT innovativeness will be positively related to (a) organizationally relevant Internet use and (b) personal Internet use.

Based on earlier articles on individual use (Bannert & Arbinger, 1996; Brancheau & Wetherbe, 1990; Larsen, 1993; Larsen & Wetherbe, 1999; Thompson et al., 1991, 1994), the four socioeconomic factors of experience (with IT), gender, age, and education were included. With regard to experience with IT, Lee (1986) demonstrated that prior experience with computers was correlated with the number of applications used. In a study of the adoption of advanced manufacturing technology, Martin (1988) found that employees who had worked with computers had a more favorable attitude toward complex uses of computers. Based on Triandis' (1971) theory of behavior, Thompson et al. (1994) demonstrated that computer experience has an impact on both attitudes toward use and use. It seems reasonable to assume that experience with IT has a positive impact on Internet use.

H3.a: More experience with IT will be positively related to (a) organizationally relevant Internet use and (b) personal Internet use.

Gender differences are primarily examined outside the specific context of end-user computing. For instance, in a study of secondary school students, Bannert and Arbinger (1996) demonstrated that gender was correlated to differences in attitudes toward computers and actual use of computers. In a study of 202 college students, Shashaani (1993) found that females were less interested in computers and, consequently, that they were low-frequency users. These results suggest that gender differences occur. Although these studies both used students as subjects, we inferred that gender differences might be found in the context of Internet use:

H3.b: Men will be more frequent users of the Internet for (a) organizationally relevant use and (b) personal Internet use than women.

Age and education have served as correlates to a variety of computer-related outcomes. Brancheau and Wetherbe (1990) found that age (negative) and education (positive) were correlated with the early adoption of spreadsheet packages. In his study of middle managers, Larsen (1993) documented a positive correlation between educational level and the use of end-user computing applications, although the relationship disappeared when regression analysis was employed. The result for age was non-significant. Although not clear-cut, these results suggest that age and education may influence user behavior. This might be particularly true when the IT being investigated is new and easy to use. It is expected that the impact of age and education on Internet use may parallel Brancheau and Wetherbe's findings, hence:

H3.c: Older employees will use the Internet less for (a) organizationally relevant use and (b) personal Internet use than younger employees.

H3.d: Educational level will be positively related to (a) organizationally relevant Internet use and (b) personal Internet use.

Items (e.g., age, gender, experience, and educational level) that might be strongly related to the dependent variable are commonly included to ensure that relationships between focused independent and dependent variables are not spurious (Bollen, 1989; Judd, Smith, & Kidder, 1991). A common finding is that the strength of the relationship between focused independent and dependent variables is reduced when other items or variables are included, indicating a spurious relationship. An increase in the relationship between an independent and a dependent variable might indicate a suppressed relation (Judd et al., 1991). Our proposition is that inclusion of the four socioeconomic factors in the research model will reduce the relationship between *personal IT innovativeness* and Internet use. However, we still believe that *personal IT innovativeness* will remain as the strongest predictor of Internet use.

H4.a: Inclusion of age, gender, experience (with IT), and educational level will reduce the relationship between personal IT innovativeness and the use of the Internet for (a) organizationally relevant and (b) personal Internet use.

Figure 1. Research model including hypotheses

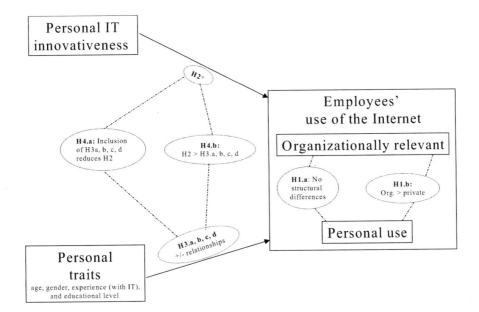

H4.b: After inclusion of age, gender, experience (with IT), and educational level, personal IT innovativeness will remain the strongest predictor of use of the Internet for (a) organizationally relevant and (b) personal Internet use.

The research model is shown in Figure 1.

Methods

Generalizability concerns indicate that a study of employees' use of the Internet should employ a multiple organization data collection design. A particular challenge in general surveys is a low response rate, which may indicate that only subjects with a particular interest in the research issue responded. If so, the collected data may be skewed toward respondents with a particular interest in Internet use and *personal IT innovativeness*. In our research, we were equally interested in collecting data from employees that (1) were infrequent or non-users of the Internet as those that are users, and (2) display a low degree of *personal IT innovativeness* as those that display a high degree of *personal IT innovativeness*. Collecting data from a cross section of employees with these key characteristics may be more likely when a large organization agrees to participate and, hence, encourages its employees to take their time to participate in the research. A large oil company, where the Internet was made available to most employees in April 1997, agreed to participate in the study.

Since our variables and items had been used in previous research efforts and found to be reliable with acceptable validity, a questionnaire (see Appendix A) was developed as the vehicle for data collection. The language of the question-naire was Norwegian. English items were first translated into Norwegian and then back into English by a second person to ensure wording reliability. All items, except for Internet use, were derived from previous research. Agarwal and Prasad's (1998) four items tapping a person's willingness to try out new IT were employed as the measure of *personal IT innovativeness*.

At the time the data was collected, no scale measuring areas of Internet use could be found. Based on 11 semi-structured interviews with selected users, the researchers developed their own. Subjects for the interviews were selected from different departments; they were perceived as conscious users. The interviews questioned the subjects about their own and their coworkers' present Internet use. Based on the interview data, seven items were developed (see Appendix A).

Table 1. Descriptive statistics for the final sample

Women	30%
Men	70%
Age (%):	
< 25	1
25 – 35	29
36 – 45	36
46 – 55	24
> 55	10
Type of education (%):	
Primary school	1.5
College	13
University (≤ 2 years)	13
University (> 2 years)	31
Master degree	34
Doctor's degree	7.5
Job type (%):	
Skilled work	74
Administrative work	16
Other	10
Average computer experience	11 years

The 11 interview subjects then completed a close-to-final version of the instrument without the researchers being present. Subjects were encouraged to write comments if items were found to be ambiguous or difficult to understand.

Using the internal mail system at the company, the final questionnaire was distributed to 500 administrative workers drawn randomly from a pool of 15,000 candidates. Respondents were guaranteed individual anonymity; only aggregated results would be reported. Anonymity was strongly stressed because the company had implemented a no-electronic-games policy. Because of this policy, respondents may have automatically under-reported their real level of Internet use for personal purposes. Returns were by ordinary public mail. By the end of March 1999, 328 usable questionnaires were returned, for a response rate of 66%. Table 1 shows the descriptive statistics of the final sample.

The collected data mirrors Internet use seven years ago and may be dated. However, the research objective was to study the impact of *personal IT innovativeness* on a new technology. In this respect it might be said that data about Internet use in 1999 reflects, to a larger degree, the use of a new technology than would be the case if data were collected today. Also, in 1999 the Internet had been available to respondents for about one year. Hence, although relatively new, the Internet was not a totally unknown phenomenon to the respondents. A somewhat stable usage pattern would have had time to evolve. Additionally, using data from a period where the Internet was relatively new allows for future comparison. For these reasons, we concluded that the collected data has validity.

The recommended two-step procedure of checking item data quality measurement before hypothesis and relationship testing was followed (Anderson & Gerbing, 1988). Items were checked for skewness and kurtosis (see Appendix B for details). The use of the Internet for *personal banking* and *shopping products* yielded, approximately, skewness = 4 and kurtosis = 15, which might indicate a problem (Kline, 1998). However, data representing use of a specific IT type might behave erratically, warranting careful consideration but not immediate deletion. Only one questionnaire in the sample contained missing values for a completion rate of nearly 100%.

The statistical techniques employed were factor analysis, Tukey's follow-up procedure for differences among means, structural equation modeling (SEM) using LISREL, and stepwise regression. Because hypothesis formulations include reliability and validity aspects, these two issues will be discussed in the analysis section.

Analysis

The method employed for testing **H1.a**, that there would be no structural differences among Internet use items, was factor analysis. The maximum likelihood calculation using the varimax and oblim methods documented two factors yielding the similar result of no clear patterns except for *Internet surfing* and *travel information* clearly loading on separate factors. The clearest pattern appeared when using the principal component analysis with varimax methods, as shown in Table 2.

The factor analysis shows that most items load on Factor 1 and that the only item that clearly loads on Factor 2 is *shopping products*. The two items of *information seeking* and *Internet surfing* may load on both factors, although the highest loading values occur for Factor 1. Judging these results conservatively, H1.a, which postulated no structural differences among Internet use items, is rejected.

The one-way Anova test for exploring H1.b, detecting differences among Internet use item means, was significant ($F = 106.64$, $p < 0.01$). The Tukey B follow-up procedure was employed to document statistically significant non-overlapping groupings of areas of Internet use, as shown in Table 3.

As measured in this research, there is a significant difference in Internet use levels among items. The items of *personal banking* and *shopping products*

Table 2. Factor analysis of Internet use items

Items	Factor 1	Factor 2
Information seeking	0.58	0.41
Reading news	**0.62**	0.11
Travel information	**0.80**	0.11
Home page reading	**0.74**	0.22
Internet surfing	0.61	0.51
Personal banking	**0.63**	-0.37
Shopping products	0.06	**0.51**
Percent of variance explained	87.6	12.4
Cronbach's Alpha	0.77	n.a.

Notes: Extraction method is principal component analysis and rotation method is varimax. Numbers in bold represent items that clearly load on one factor — using the rules of item loading ≥ 0.50, no other loading ≥ 0.40, and difference between loadings for one item ≥ 0.20.

Table 3. Groupings of Internet use items

Items	Group 1	Group 2	Group 3	Group 4	Group 5
Information seeking	3.84				
Reading news		3.17			
Travel information			2.60		
Home page reading				2.17	
Internet surfing				2.00	
Personal banking					1.34
Shopping products					1.28

Notes: Follow-up procedure is Tukey B. Numbers represent Internet use mean values.

form a common group. As can be seen in Table 3, the means for these two items are very low, in fact approaching the absolute minimum numeric value of 1. Comparing the two means of *personal banking* and *shopping products* with the other Internet use items, the indication is that H1.b is supported, that is, Internet use that may be *organizationally relevant* is more frequent than *personal Internet use*.

The test results with regard to skewness, kurtosis, factor loadings (Table 2), and means groupings (Table 3) indicate that *personal banking* and *shopping products* are problematic items. Indeed, the initial LISREL model, with all items

Figure 2. Complete structural equation model

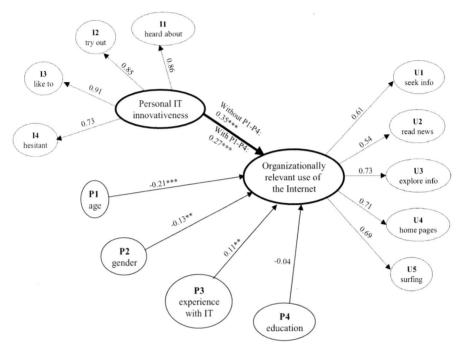

Notes: Asterisks indicate significance levels: *(p<10), **(p<0.05), ***(p<0.01).

Complete model goodness of fit: χ² = 115.30 [p < 0.0, DF = 54]), RMSEA = 0.059 [p (close fit) = 0.15], CFI = 0.96 and NNFI = 0.94. The result of running two models is also indicated on the path between personal IT innovativeness and organizationally relevant use of the Internet. The path coefficient for the full model including personal traits (P1-P4) is 0.27***. The path coefficient for the model without personal traits is 0.35***.

included, confirmed the concern (Model statistics; $\chi^2 = 90.31$ [p < 0.0, Degrees of Freedom (DF) = 43]; Root mean square error of approximation (RMSEA) = 0.06 [p (close fit) = 0.20]; Comparative fit index (CFI) = 0.97; Non-normed fit index (NNFI) = 0.96). In particular, the loadings of *personal banking* and *shopping products* to the latent construct of *organizationally relevant use of the Internet* was 0.12 and 0.09, respectively. Due to their low loadings, both items were dropped from further modeling (see Figure 2 for the final model). Because of this, the remaining hypothesis testing only addresses *organizationally relevant use of the Internet*. That is, for hypotheses H2, H3.a, H3.b, H3.c, H3.d, H4.a, and H4.b only sections (a) *organizationally relevant*, are tested. Sections (b), addressing *personal Internet use*, are dropped.

The redefined model, including *personal IT innovativeness*, individual traits, and *organizationally relevant use of the Internet*, resulted in an improved fit above suggested cut-off levels (Model statistics; $\chi^2 = 49.22$ [p < 0.0, DF = 26],

RMSEA = 0.052 [p (close fit) = 0.41]; CFI = 0.98; NNFI = 0.98). The square of the correlation between the two latent variables is approximately 0.12, which is less than the variance explained between each latent construct and its items, hence discriminant validity is regarded as adequate (Fornell & Larcker, 1981). The composite reliability for *personal IT innovativeness* is 0.91 and for *organizationally relevant use of the Internet* is 0.79. Both are above the recommended threshold of 0.70. The conclusion is that the model can be accepted. The revised LISREL model is shown in Figure 2.

As can be seen in Figure 2, the loading factor on the path between the two latent constructs of *personal IT innovativeness* and *organizationally relevant use of the Internet* is 0.35, $p < 0.01$. Hypothesis 2 is supported. The higher the degree of *personal IT innovativeness*, the higher the *organizationally relevant use of the Internet*.

With regard to personal traits, the results indicate that:

H3.a is supported: The longer the IT experience, the higher the organizationally relevant use of the Internet.

H3.b is supported: Men are more inclined to use the Internet than women.

H3.c is supported: The older the person, the less the organizationally relevant use of the Internet.

H3.d is not supported: In the present sample, a higher degree of education does not result in a higher degree of organizationally relevant use of the Internet.

For hypothesis H4.a, which states that the impact of *personal IT innovativeness* on *organizationally relevant use of the Internet* would be reduced, a separate LISREL model without the trait items of age, gender, experience, and education was run. The model had acceptable fit. The item to latent variable loadings did not change significantly. When introducing the personal traits, the (regression standardized) coefficient between *personal IT innovativeness* and *organizationally relevant use of the Internet* was reduced from 0.35 to 0.27, that is, by 23%. This indicates that H4.a is supported. However, the coefficient is significant $p < 0.01$, with and without these personal trait items. Although a change in the predicted direction, the observed change might be a result of other factors (such as operationalization, measurement method, and sample characteristics). Semi-partial correlations were also investigated, but no major differences between the two models could be found. The major conclusion is, therefore, that

Table 4. Stepwise regression of independent variable and items on organizationally relevant use of Internet

Model #	Variable entering	Adjusted R-square	Unstandardized Regr. Coeff.	Beta at first model entry	Beta at final model entry
1	IT innovativeness	0.10***	0.39	0.32***	0.27***
2	Respondent's age	0.12***	-0.23		-0.17***

Notes: *(p ≤ .10), **(p ≤ .05), ***(p ≤ .01).

The beta value for the path between personal IT innovativeness *and* organizationally relevant use of the Internet *when trait variables are not included is 0.35 in the LISREL model but 0.32 in the stepwise regression analysis. The difference is due to the higher degree of sophistication in LISREL calculations when compared to (stepwise) regression.*

the inclusion of age, gender, experience, and education, although in the predicted direction, do not necessarily significantly reduce the impact of *personal IT innovativeness* on *organizationally relevant use of the Internet*. Our final conclusion is that H4.a is not supported.

Because the two LISREL models did not document any significant change in item to latent variable loadings, stepwise regression was used to explore Hypothesis H4.b, that *personal IT innovativeness* will remain the strongest predictor of Internet use (see Table 4).

In Table 4, we see in Model #1 that *personal IT innovativeness* is the variable that enters first in the stepwise regression. In Model #2, the respondent's *age* enters the equation. The stepwise regression did not find that *gender, experience with IT*, and the level of *education* would contribute to explaining *organizationally relevant use of the Internet* beyond the results documented in Model #2. The conclusion is that H4.b is supported. As measured here, *personal IT innovativeness* contributes most to *organizationally relevant use of the Internet*, that is, *personal IT innovativeness* explains 7% and *age* 5% of the variance in the variable of *organizationally relevant use of the Internet*. The indication is that *age* plays a more decisive role in explaining Internet use than do *gender, experience with IT*, and level of *education*. The partial correlations for *gender, experience with IT*, and level of *education* with *organizationally relevant use of the Internet* are 0.8%, 1%, and 0%, respectively. However, as Table 4 documents, these three items were eliminated from the models generated by the stepwise regression procedure. Hence, among the included personal traits, our data suggest that being younger impacts the use of Internet.

Discussion

Structural differences across various types of Internet use areas were documented, although emerging conceptual categories were somewhat unclear. In the factor analyses, *personal banking* and *shopping products* loaded on different factors. Additionally, the ratio of Internet use in these two areas was very low. Although the reason why personal use is infrequent may be that this type of use is relatively less needed, the explanation may also be that the organizational policy of not using the Internet for personal purposes is understood. Since the present research did not explicitly ask respondents about the reasons why personal use is infrequent, further investigation is needed.

Internet usage areas, at least as measured here, may blend organizationally relevant and personal use. For example, a manager may expect that professionals (say, economists and engineers) read news within their professional field, but would object to having them spend time on news in general. Yet users may not know whether news is relevant until having read it. Given the structure of media news on the Internet, the proportion of general news quite likely is much greater than relevant news. As discussed previously, accessing personal bank and credit card accounts may be a legitimate activity. Increasingly, employees are encouraged to take advantage of Web-based air travel and hotel booking applications. Besides, occasionally business and personal travel are combined. For these reasons, employees might perceive that Internet use by its very nature makes organizationally relevant and personal use indistinguishable. If so, organizational policies that are too strict may discourage desired use (however, some categories of Internet use, for example adult entertainment, would be categorized as unacceptable by all). Given the ambiguities with regard to organizationally relevant and private Internet use discussed here, further in-depth research is needed to develop a deeper understanding of purely organizationally relevant use, acceptable combinations of organizationally relevant and personal use, and obviously unacceptable Internet use. Otherwise concrete advice with regard to appropriate Internet use policies cannot be forwarded.

In our analyses, *age, gender*, and *experience with IT* were significantly related to *organizationally relevant use of the Internet. Age*, as the strongest contributor, was negatively related to Internet use. This finding parallels previous research on innovative adoption, that is, earlier adopters were younger (Brancheau & Wetherbe, 1990). In Larsen's (1993) research with IT, age, and educational level was not related to IT innovation. The reason for the differences in findings may be that the present research and the study by Brancheau and Wetherbe addressed change limited to the respondent's job, while Larsen defined innovation as an effort that would result in improvement for (part of) the organization. The perceived scope of the innovation may, therefore, play a decisive role.

In the present sample, *personal IT innovativeness* was found to have the greatest impact on *organizationally relevant use of the Internet*. This finding supports previous theoretical as well as empirical research stating that *personal IT innovativeness* is a central construct in understanding and explaining innovation adoption (Agarwal & Prasad, 1998; Larsen, 1993) and, hence, the use of Internet (Agarwal & Karahanna, 2000; Goldsmith, 2001; Limayem et al., 2000; Pajo, 2000; Wolfradt & Doll, 2001). The theoretical proposition that *personal IT innovativeness* is positively related to the use of novel technologies across usage areas is supported. Taking Popper's (1959) research objective recommendation into account, further studies aiming at testing this proposition may not be appropriate. Rather, future research efforts may benefit from addressing other aspects, for example the impact of *personal IT innovativeness* on the use of well-established technologies.

With regard to further research within an established theoretical proposition, Popper recommends that the objective should be to test its assumptions. For example, the Agarwal and Prasad instrument may not necessarily measure *personal IT innovativeness* correctly. The four items in the instrument have a strong resemblance to the attitude toward change instrument (Ettlie, 1983; Ettlie & O'Kefee, 1982). The latter instrument includes 12 items divided equally between a factor explaining a person's attitude toward change and a factor representing a preference for the established order. The Agarwal and Prasad instrument may, therefore, not tap the richness of *personal IT innovativeness*. Additionally, Agarwal and Prasad tap a person's willingness to experiment with IT. It is quite likely that the willingness to experiment with IT implicitly includes use. If so, one would expect that the *willingness to try out any new information technology* and use are related. Therefore, the willingness to try out any new IT may be viewed as a dimension of technology use (alongside using the technology for strictly job-relevant purposes, using the technology to staying informed, etc.). In fact, an exploratory factor analysis divides the four items representing *personal IT innovativeness* and the five items representing *organizationally relevant use of the Internet* into two separate factors with no overlap.

It may also be argued that the more a person uses IT, the more he or she would be willing to experiment with it — the causal relationship being reversed when compared to the present research's model (and previous publications utilizing the personal IT innovativeness instrument). Hence, the combined use results presented here may be viewed as a basis for increased understanding of IT use. These arguments indicate that our understanding of IT innovation through *personal IT innovativeness* needs further elaboration.

The present study has other limitations, such as the use of cross-sectional survey data. Correlation designs lack the ability to explicitly test directionality. However, this does not imply that the present research model is invalid. Theories of *personal IT innovativeness* (behavioral, diffusion, and marketing) and the present SEM analyses provide support for causal relationships. Despite this, conclusive statements about causality cannot be made since alternative explanations cannot be ruled out. At the very least, one cannot disregard the possibility of reciprocal interactions among the factors studied. Further research, in particular experimental and longitudinal studies, is clearly needed to address these issues.

Our findings indicate the need for future studies. The relationships in our research model can be moderated by other variables such as organizationally specific Internet use regulations and local managers' statements about appropriate Internet use. The meaning of organizationally relevant and personal Internet use must be investigated. Other constructs and variables representing the use of technology and work content may moderate or intervene between relationships in the research model or demand a research model respecification. The notions of change on the individual level and innovativeness need further elaboration. It seems appropriate to recommend that future research return to the original innovativeness scale (Ettlie, 1983; Ettlie & O'Kefee, 1982) because there the concept of *innovativeness* is defined as a trait regardless of technology content. The importance of innovativeness in research settings exploring our understanding of individual change require simultaneous analysis of similar constructs, for example learning style (Bostrom, Olfman, & Sein, 1990) and personality style (Wolfradt & Doll, 2001).

Implications for Practice

The findings of this study indicate that that the willingness of an employee to try out new information technology may have importance for encouraging increased *organizationally relevant use of the Internet*. Managers should recognize *personal IT innovativeness* as a factor in fostering the use of new applications and IT. Moreover, the construct of *personal IT innovativeness* can be used to identify individuals who can either serve as change agents or be targeted specifically for adoption when resources are limited (Agarwal & Prasad, 1998).

In many areas, the Internet allows organizationally relevant use as well as purely private use, for example reading news, banking, and travel. Therefore, organizational Internet polices that ban Internet use in these areas might be counterproductive. Rather, organizational policies should address the intent of Internet use and not specific usage areas. That is, Internet policies should emphasize organizationally relevant use relative to purely private use across Internet usage areas.

This study also indicated that younger employees and males are the most frequent Internet users. Although older employees and females may learn about the benefits of using the Internet from their peers, organizational polices and incentives should specifically target these user groups. This might be of particular importance in the early usage phase of a new technology or when new major new software functionality is introduced.

Conclusion

Based on a sample of 328 employees within one corporation, the present research found that *personal IT innovativeness* was positively related to the use of the Internet for *seeking information, reading news, travel information, looking up home pages,* and *surfing in general.* The positive relationship between *personal IT innovativeness* and use parallels other research reports in the areas of use of the World Wide Web in general, online shoppers, academicians, and adolescents. Since our sample was limited to only one business organization, this conclusion does not necessarily apply to administrative employees in general. Further studies are required.

The major indication is that *personal IT innovativeness* as a predictor of computer use has validity. In fact, further studies within this theoretical proposition may not be warranted. Future research may benefit from testing under what conditions the proposition does not hold or shifting its focus to other areas, for example, the impact of *personal IT innovativeness* on well-established areas of computer use.

Also, the construct of *personal IT innovativeness* measures an individual's willingness to experiment with new technologies. The wording of instrument items indicates use directly and implicitly. Hence, finding that people who experiment with technology also use it may be viewed as tautological. The instrument for measuring *personal IT innovativeness* may need further development.

Our results indicated that organizational members perceive structural differences across various types of Internet use. However, no support was found for concluding that unequivocal categories of Internet use exist. Use of the Internet in areas that might be viewed as purely personal, for example, *personal banking* and *shopping products,* was significantly lower than for any other category of Internet use. The established literature carries the impression that areas of Internet use can be distinctly divided into the two main categories of organizationally relevant and personal. We anticipate that in many areas organizationally relevant versus personal use is not clear-cut. For example, reading news, making travel arrangements, or filing travel expenses may blend these two main categories of use. Because of this, organizational Internet use policies may benefit from addressing the concept of organizationally relevant versus personal use rather than specifying specific areas of Internet use.

Among the independent variables and items, *personal IT innovativeness* was the strongest predictor of *organizationally relevant use of the Internet*. Age, as the second strongest predictor, contributed negatively to Internet use. The inference is that older employees used the Internet less than younger. This finding parallels previous end-user computing research findings (Brancheau & Wetherbe, 1990). The analysis also suggested that males are more frequent Internet users than females. The indication here is that organizations may need to establish specific policies for these employee categories. The policies would include benefits of Internet use and targeted activities. Previous experience with IT contributed positively to Internet use. As employees gain hands-on IT experience, their use of new applications and new functionality may increase. However, gender and experience with IT may contribute little to explaining Internet use.

Because data was collected from one organization only, our findings are not necessarily generalizable. Further research is needed. We found that *personal IT innovativeness*, as presently operationalized, positively impacts Internet use. The result parallels previous research, lending support to the notion that *personal IT innovativeness* plays a role in determining use of new technologies in organizational settings. It should also be noted that the explained variance (also denoted "R-Square") is about 12%, leaving ample room for inclusion of other constructs that may explain Internet use in future research efforts. Our findings apply to an early phase of Internet use. Obviously, the results may change as use of the Internet becomes mature. The present findings may serve as a baseline for analyzing these changes.

References

Agarwal, R., & Karahanna, E. (2000). Time flies when you're having fun: Cognitive absorption and beliefs about information technology usage. *MIS Quarterly, 24*(4), 665-694.

Agarwal, R., & Prasad, J. (1998). A conceptual and operational definition of personal innovativeness in the domain of information technology. *Information Systems Research, 9*(2), 204-215.

Anderson, J. C., & Gerbing, D. W. (1988). Structural equation modeling in practice: A review and recommended two-step approach. *Psychological Bulletin, 103*(3), 411-423.

Bannert, M., & Arbinger, P. R. (1996). Gender-related differences in exposure to and use of computers: Results of a survey of secondary school students. *European Journal of Psychology of Education, 11*(3), 269-282.

Bollen, K. A. (1989). *Structural equations with latent variables.* New York: John Wiley & Sons.

Bostrom, R. P., Olfman, L., & Sein, M. K. (1990). The importance of learning style in end-user training. *MIS Quarterly, 14*(1), 101-119.

Brancheau, J. C., & Wetherbe, J. C. (1990). The adoption of spreadsheet software: Testing innovation diffusion theory in the context of end-user computing. *Information Systems Research, 1*(2), 115-143.

Charlton, C., Gittings, C., Leng, P., Little, J., & Neilson, I. (1998). Diffusion of technological innovations: Bringing businesses onto the Internet. In T. J. Larsen & E. McGuire (Eds.), *Information systems innovation and diffusion: Issues and trends* (pp. 251-296). Hershey, PA: Idea Group Publishing.

Chau, P. Y. K. (2001). Influence of computer attitude and self-efficacy on IT usage behavior. *Journal of End User Computing, 13*(1), 26-33.

Citrin, A. V., Sprott, D. E., Silverman, S. N., & Stem, D. E. (2000). Adoption of Internet shopping: The role of consumer innovativeness. *Industrial Management & Data Systems, 100*(7), 294-300.

Damanpour, F. (1991). Organizational innovation: A meta-analysis of effects of determinants and moderators. *Academy of Management Journal, 34*(3), 555-590.

Davis, F. D. (1989). Perceived usefulness, perceived ease of use, and user acceptance of information technology. *MIS Quarterly, 13*(3), 319-340.

DeLone, W. H., & McLean, E. R (1992). Information systems success: The quest for the dependent variable. *Information Systems Research, 3*(1), 60-95.

Ettlie, J. E. (1983). A note on the relationship between managerial change values, innovative intentions, and innovative technology outcomes in food sector firms. *R & D Development, 13*(4), 231-244.

Ettlie, J. E., & O'Keefe, R. D. (1982). Innovative attitudes, values, and intentions in organizations. *Journal of Management Studies, 19*(2), 163-182.

Fornell, C., & Larcker, D. F. (1981). Evaluating structural equation models with unobservable variables and measurement error. *Journal of Marketing Research, 18*, 39-50.

Goldsmith, R. E. (2001). Using the domain specific innovativeness scale to identify innovative Internet consumers. *Internet Research-Electronic Networking Applications and Policy, 11*(2), 149-158.

Guthrie, R., & Gray, P. (1996, Winter). Junk computing: Is it bad for an organization? *Information Systems Management,* 23-28.

Harris, R. W. (2000, January-March). Schools of thought in research into end-user computing success. *Journal of End User Computing,* 24-34.

Judd, C. M., Smith, E. R., & Kidder, L. H. (1991). *Research methods in social relations.* London: The Dryden Press.

Katz, D., & Kahn, R. L. (1978). *The social psychology of organizations.* New York: Wiley.

Kline, R. B. (1998). *Principles and practice of structural equation modeling.* New York: The Guilford Press.

Larsen, T. J. (1993). Middle managers' contribution to implemented information technology innovation. *Journal of Management Information Systems, 10*(2), 155-176.

Larsen, T. J. (2001). The phenomenon of diffusion: Red herrings and future promise. In M. A. Ardis & B. L. Marcolin (Eds.), *Diffusing software products and process innovations* (pp. 35-50). Boston: Kluwer Academic Publishers.

Larsen, T. J., & Wetherbe, J. C. (1999). An exploratory field study of differences in information technology use between more and less innovative middle managers. *Information & Management, 36*(2), 93-108.

Lee, D. M. S (1986). Usage pattern and sources of assistance for personal computer users. *MIS Quarterly, 10*(4), 313-326.

Limayem, M., Khalifa, M., & Frini, A. (2000, July). What makes consumers buy from Internet? A longitudinal study of online shopping. *IEEE Transactions on Systems Man and Cybernetics Part A: Systems and Humans, 30,* 421-432.

Lyytinen, K., & Damsgaard, J. (2001). What's wrong with the diffusion of innovation theory? In M. A. Ardis & B. L. Marcolin (Eds.), *Diffusing software products and process innovations* (pp. 173-190). Boston: Kluwer Academic Publishers.

Markus, M. L. (1994). Finding a happy medium: Explaining the negative effects of electronic mail in social life at work. *ACM Transactions on Information Systems, 12*(2), 119-149.

Martin, R. (1988). Attitudes towards advanced manufacturing technology: The role of AMT experience, skill level, and job involvement. *Social Behavior, 3*(4), 297-305.

Otto, J. R., Najdawi, M. K., & Caron, K. M. (2000). Web-user satisfaction: An exploratory study. *Journal of End User Computing, 12*(4), 3-10.

Pajo, K. (2000). Individual characteristics and the adoption of technology in distance education. *International Council for Open and Distance Education Regional Conference for Australia and the Pacific, Distance Education: An Open Question.* University of South Australia. Retrieved from http://www.com.unisa.edu.au/cccc/papers/refereed/paper33/Paper33-1.htm

Popper, K. (1959). *The logic of scientific discovery.* New York: Basic Books.

Powell, A., & Moore, J. A. (2002). The focus of research in end user computing: Where have we come since the 1980s? *Journal of End User Computing, 14*(1), 3-X.

Roberts, L. G. (2000, January). Beyond Moore's Law: Internet growth trends. *Computer, 33,* 117-119.

Robey, D., & Boudreau, M. C. (2000). Organizational consequences of information technology: Dealing with diversity in empirical research. In R. W. Zmud (Ed.), *Framing the domains of IT management: Projecting the future through the past* (pp. 51-63). Cincinnati, OH: Pinnaflex Education Resources, Inc.

Rogers, E. M. (1983). *Diffusion of innovations* (3rd ed.). New York: The Free Press.

Rogers, E. M. (1995). *Diffusion of innovations* (4th ed.). New York: The Free Press.

Rogers, E. M., & Shoemaker, E. (1971). *Communication of innovations: A cross-cultural approach* (2nd ed.). New York: The Free Press.

Seddon, P. B. (1997). A respecification and extension of the DeLone and McLean model of IS success. *Information Systems Research, 8*(3), 240-253.

Shashaani, L. (1993). Gender-based differences in attitudes toward computers. *Computers & Education, 20*(2), 169-181.

Spar, D., & Bussgang, J. J. (1996). Ruling the net. *Harvard Business Review, 74*(3), 125-134.

Stanton, J. M. (2002). Company profile of the frequent Internet user. *Communications of the ACM, 45*(1), 55-59.

Straub, D., Limayem, M., & Karahanna-Evaristo, E. (1995). Measuring system usage: Implications for IS theory testing. *Management Science, 41*(8), 1328-1342.

Thompson, R. L., Higgins, C. A., & Howell, J. M. (1991). Personal computing: Toward a conceptual-model of utilization. *MIS Quarterly, 15*(1), 125-143.

Thompson, R. L., Higgins, C. A., & Howell, J. M. (1994, Summer). Influence of experience on personal computer utilization: Testing a conceptual model. *Journal of Management Information Systems,* 167-187.

Triandis, H. C. (1971). *Attitude and attitude change.* New York: Wiley.

Wolfradt, U., & Doll, J. (2001). Motives of adolescents to use the Internet as a function of personality traits, personal and social factors. *Journal of Educational Computing Research,* 24(1), 13-27.

Endnote

[1] The authors are listed in alphabetical order and have contributed equally to the article.

[2] In the literature, *organizational members' IT use* is denoted as *employees' IT use, end-users' IT use, individual use,* or *personal use.* The terms are used interchangeably, with individual and personal use being employed here.

Appendix A

Questionnaire Items

Personal willingness to try out new information technology — *personal IT innovativeness* (Agarwal & Prasad, 1998) — using a Likert type scale ranging from 1 (strongly disagree) to 7 (strongly agree):

I1 If I heard about a new information technology, I would look for ways to experiment with it.

I2 Among my peers, I am usually the first to try out new information technologies.

I3 I like to experiment with new information technologies.

I4 In general, I am hesitant to try out new information technologies.

The use of Internet technologies. The introduction to Internet use items read:

"Sometimes I use the Internet to:" using a Likert type scale ranging from 1 (not a correct description) to 7 (an exactly correct description):

U1 seek information of interest to me (for example using Kvasir, AltaVista, etc.).

U2 read newspaper headlines (examples of national newspapers provided).

U3 explore information about soon upcoming travel whether business or personal.

U4 look up home pages of areas of interest to me (literature, sports, personal economy, chess, etc.).

U5 surfing the Internet (as time allows).

U6 pay my bills and check account balances.

U7 shop products (for example, books, CDs, or other merchandise).

Personal traits:

P1   Age   A scale: 1 = <25, 2 = 25-35, 3 = 36-45, 4 = 46-55, 5 = >55

P2   Gender   1 = male, 2 = female

P3   Experience Number of years (in absolute figure) respondent has used a
         with IT PC, irrespective of use at work or at home

P4   Educational A scale ranging from 1 (primary school) to 6 (doctoral degree)
         level

Appendix B

Descriptive Statistics

	Mean	Std.dev.	Skewness	Kurtosis	N
Personal IT innovativeness					
I1	3.424	1.742	0.342	-0.879	328
I2	2.960	1.727	0.565	-0.719	327
I3	3.527	1.740	0.245	-0.913	328
I4	3.604	1.859	0.266	-1.092	328
Internet use:					
U1	3.845	2.028	0.016	-1.285	328
U2	3.171	2.126	0.522	-1.216	328
U3	2.598	1.866	0.919	-0.356	328
U4	2.168	1.655	1.363	0.750	328
U5	2.003	1.420	1.582	1.974	328
U6	1.341	1.154	4.009	15.618	328
U7	1.280	0.868	4.199	19.749	328
Age	3.138	0.989	0.295	-0.773	327
Gender	1.275	0.447	1.011	0.994	316
Experience with IT	11.234	4.371	0.089	-0.468	320
Education	4.071	1.177	-0.517	-0.444	324

Chapter III

The Role of Internet Self-Efficacy in the Acceptance of Web-Based Electronic Medical Records

Qingxiong Ma, Central Missouri State University, USA

Liping Liu, University of Akron, USA

Abstract

The technology acceptance model (TAM) stipulates that both perceived ease of use (PEOU) and perceived usefulness (PU) directly influence the end user's behavioral intention (BI) to accept a technology. Studies have found that self-efficacy is an important determinant of PEOU. However, there has been no research examining the relationship between self-efficacy and BI. The studies on the effect of self-efficacy on PU are also rare, and findings are inconsistent. In this study, we incorporate Internet self-efficacy (ISE) into the TAM as an antecedent to PU, PEOU, and BI. We conducted a controlled experiment involving a Web-based medical record system and 86 healthcare subjects. We analyzed both direct and indirect effects of ISE on PEOU, PU, and BI using hierarchical regressions. We found that ISE explained 48% of the variation in PEOU. We also found that ISE and PEOU together explained 50% of the variation in PU, and the full model explained 80% of the variance in BI.

Introduction

Application service provision (ASP) — a model of distributing software services over the Internet — has shown its advantages over the traditional model of information technology (IT) deployment. The expected benefits include the reduced cost of technology ownership, the reduced time to market, and the reduced risks with software deployment. Nevertheless, the growth of the ASP business has been comparatively slow. In response to the situation, many researchers (Jayatilaka, Schwarz, & Hirschheim, 2002; Peterson & Fairchild, 2003; Susarla, Barua, & Whinston, 2003) examined its ensuring factors. Along the same line of inquires, this study attempts to understand the acceptance issue from the end-user perspective and searches for guidance on methods and effective interventions to promote the adoption of the ASP model.

Understanding user acceptance behavior is important for several reasons. First, it is the end users who use the technology in their work on a daily basis. Any decision that changes their work behavior should consider their willingness to adopt the change. Empirical evidence has shown that the technology adoptions involving end users were more successful than those without (Chau & Hu, 2002; Lederer, Maupin, Sena, & Zhuang, 2000). Second, only the end-user acceptance can ensure a potential long-term continuous adoption (Bhattacherjee, 2001). This is particularly crucial to the ASP adoption since most ASPs are operated on short-term renewable contracts.

In the technology adoption literature, the technology acceptance model (TAM) by Davis (1989) is one of the most widely applied models (see Ma & Liu, 2004 for a meta-analytical survey). It has received extensive empirical support through validations, applications, and replications. Compared with competing models, the TAM is believed to be more parsimonious, predicative, and robust (Venkatesh, 2000). However, the TAM has been criticized for being less informative in understanding usage behavior (Taylor & Todd, 1995). Accordingly, researchers have attempted to extend the TAM by embedding it into a nomological network of other antecedents and consequences. To this end, a few researchers appeal to cognition theories and emphasize the importance of self-efficacy.

The notion of self-efficacy refers to beliefs about individuals' capabilities of performing a certain task (Bandura, 1977). Numerous studies have found that self-efficacy is an important determinant of perceived ease of use. For examples, Venkatesh (2000) found that computer self-efficacy was one of the main factors that affect ease of use. Agarwal, Sambamurthy, and Stair (2000) defined software-specific self-efficacy and had a similar finding. However, currently there is no research, to the best of our knowledge, testing the relationship between self-efficacy and behavioral intention (to use an information technology). The impact of self-efficacy on perceived usefulness is also less known, and findings are inconsistent. The goal of this paper is to fill in this gap. In particular, we extend the TAM by considering Internet self-efficacy (ISE) as an antecedent to perceived ease of use, usefulness, as well as behavioral intention in the context of accepting Web-based electronic medical records, and investigate how such an extension affects our understanding about end-user acceptance behavior.

The rest of this chapter is outlined as follows. In the next section, we review the literature related to the TAM. Following that, we present our research model and develop research hypotheses. We then describe our research design, including research methodology, experiment procedure, and instrument validation. Following that, we perform data analysis and show test results. Finally, we discuss the results and draw conclusions.

The Technology Acceptance Model

There are numerous perspectives from which one studies user acceptance and usage behavior of information technologies. Among them the technology acceptance model (TAM) by Davis (1989) is a most popular one. The TAM is grounded in the theory of reasoned action (Fisherbein & Ajzen, 1975). It stipulates a nomological network of three constructs (see Figure 1) — perceived usefulness (PU), perceived ease of use (PEOU), and behavioral intention (BI) — connected by the causal links that both PEOU and PU directly influence BI, and PEOU influences BI indirectly through PU (Davis et al., 1989).

The TAM has been applied to a wide range of technologies, including e-mail, fax, word processors, spreadsheets, and workgroup applications. It has been recently applied to the adoption of e-commerce and Internet technologies (Gefen & Straub, 1997, 2000; Lederer et al., 2000). According to Ma and Liu (2004), there have been over 100 studies applying or validating the TAM. Most of these studies confirmed the reliability and validity of PU and PEOU in predicting BI or technology usage, although conflicting evidence exists.

Figure 1. Technology acceptance model

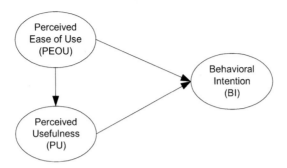

Compared with other competing models, the TAM is believed to be more accurate and parsimonious when it is used to predict adoption. However, its parsimoniousness results in being less informative in understanding usage behavior (Taylor & Todd, 1995) or providing usable results. What IT managers desire to have are implementable prescriptions (Benbasat & Zmud, 1999). It is imperative that researchers equip them with some useful guidance on methods and effective interventions, for example, by augmenting PU and PEOU through manipulating their causal antecedents, to achieve greater technology acceptance or usage. As Gefen and Keil (1998) noted, without a better understanding of the antecedents to PU and PEOU, managers and developers are unable to know which levers to pull in order to affect these beliefs and, through them, technology usage.

Recognizing the necessity of identifying the antecedents to user acceptance, researchers have attempted to extend the TAM by encompassing various constructs such as gender, culture, trust, experience, and social influence (Chircu, Davis, & Kauffman, 2000; Gefen & Straub, 1997; Straub, 1994). Among the constructs, self-efficacy is recognized to be a most important one.

Self-efficacy has been documented to be an important determinant of PEOU (Agarwal et al., 2000; Venkatesh, 2000; Venkatesh & Davis, 1996). However, there is no research examining the relationship between self-efficacy and BI. Also, very few studies have been done to understand the impact of self-efficacy on PU, and their findings are inconsistent. In a study with a sample of 58 participants from the California Network Engineering Center, Lopez and Manson (1997) found that computer self-efficacy was positively related to the PU of the Empowered Desktop Information System. Using 288 junior business students, Agarwal et al. (2000) conducted a similar test within the context of Web technologies. They found a positive effect of self-efficacy on both PU and

PEOU, and a stronger effect on PEOU than on PU. In contrast, Igbaria, Iivari, and Maragahh (1995) found that self-efficacy had an insignificant direct effect on PU. Chau (2000) also found that computer self-efficacy had a relatively small, but negative, impact on PU. Therefore, to understand the exact effect of self-efficacy on PU, additional evidence seems necessary.

Research Hypotheses

The aim of this study is to examine the role of ISE in accepting Web-based electronic medical records. In addition, we want to validate existing findings in the new context. To this end, we extend the TAM by including ISE as an antecedent to the three theoretical constructs: PEOU, PU, as well as BI. We hypothesize that ISE directly influences PEOU and PU, which in turn influence BI (see Figure 2). We also hypothesize that ISE directly influences BI. We justify these hypotheses based on existing theories and findings.

The notion of self-efficacy is due to Bandura (1977). It refers to beliefs about individuals' capabilities to produce designated levels of performance that exercise influence over events that affect their lives. Since its inception, the construct has been widely tested in organizational behavior, education, and human resource management.

In the context of end-user computing, Compeau and Higgins (1995) proposed the concept of computer self-efficacy to refer to the judgment of one's capability of

Figure 2. Research model

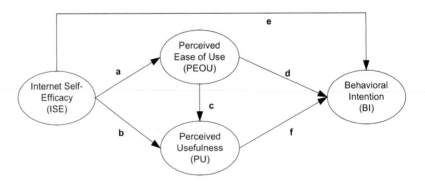

Notes: The paths a, b, and e represent the relationships between ISE and PEOU, PU, and BI respectively. Paths c and d represent the relationships between PEOU and PU and between PEOU and BI. Path f represents the relationship between PU and BI.

using the computer. Marakas, Yi, and Johnson (1998) made a further distinction between computer self-efficacy and task-specific self-efficacy. Following the same distinction, in this study we define ISE as the estimate of one's capability to perform Internet tasks.

ISE is different from general computer self-efficacy in that ISE focuses on what an individual believes he or she can accomplish online now or in the future — the belief that one can establish, maintain, and utilize the Internet effectively over and above basic personal computer (Eastin & LaRose, 2000). It is the judgment of one's capability of applying Internet skills rather than measures of his or her specific skills of using an Internet browser. People who have little confidence in their ability to use the Internet or who are uncomfortable using the Internet may be said to have weak self-efficacy beliefs.

Venkatesh (2000) studied factors that affected PEOU and classified them into two categories: anchors and adjustments. Anchors include computer self-efficacy, perception of external control, computer anxiety, and computer playfulness. Adjustments include perceived enjoyment and objective usability. The general computer self-efficacy turns out to be a strong determinant of PEOU before hands-on experience (Venkatesh & Davis, 1996). Based on this evidence, we expect that ISE has a positive effect on the PEOU of Web-based applications:

Hypothesis 1 (path a): Internet self-efficacy has a positive effect on the perceived ease of use of Web-based electronic medical records.

Self-efficacy is significantly related to end user competence. Munro, Huff, Marcolin, and Compeau (1997) suggested that the construct of user competence is multi-faceted, composed of both *breadth* and *depth* of knowledge on end-user technologies, and one's ability to creatively apply these technologies (*finesse*). Thus, it is reasonable to infer that self-efficacy is also a multi-dimensional construct, with some capability beliefs coming from the breadth of knowledge, some from the depth of knowledge, and some from the finesse of knowledge. Based on this logic, we assume that some aspects of competence or knowledge give a user confidence in using a technology, which contributes to the perception of its ease of use, whereas others give the user confidence in understanding the design logic or objectives of the technology, which contributes to the perception of its usefulness. Therefore, we anticipate that ISE has a direct positive effect on PU:

Hypothesis 2 (path b): Internet self-efficacy has a positive effect on the perceived usefulness of Web-based electronic medical records.

Research has found that self-efficacy is an important determinant of user perception besides PEOU and PU. For example, Levine and Donitsa-Schmidt (1998) found that, as individuals expressed stronger computer confidence, they demonstrated more positive attitudes toward computers and higher levels of computer-related knowledge. According to Bandura (2001), self-efficacy is also a major determinant of intention. Although there is no IT research testing the relationship, studies in other areas confirm its significance. For example, Armitage and Conner (2001) conducted a study testing a model based on the theory of planned behavior in blood donation. They found that self-efficacy accounted for unique variance in behavioral intention. In another extended study with a sample of 172 subjects, they also found that self-efficacy and several other factors were all important independent predictors of behavioral intention. Based on this body of theoretical and empirical evidence, we propose:

Hypothesis 3 (path e): Internet self-efficacy has a positive effect on behavioral intention to use Web-based electronic medical records.

In addition to Hypotheses 1-3, we present the original three hypotheses stipulated by the TAM as Hypotheses 4-6 as follows:

Hypothesis 4 (path c): Perceived ease of use has a positive impact on the perceived usefulness of Web-based electronic medical records.

Hypothesis 5 (path d): Perceived ease of use has a positive impact on behavioral intention to use Web-based electronic medical records.

Hypothesis 6 (path f): Perceived usefulness has a positive impact on behavioral intention to use Web-based electronic medical records.

Research Design

We conducted a controlled experiment using senior clinic trainees and staff members who are responsible for managing patient records. We collected data by means of a survey instrument. We distributed a questionnaire and a cover letter with instructions to selected subjects. In the cover letter, we informed the subjects that the experiment was volunteer-based and they could refuse to participate or quit at any time. In the instruction sheet, we provided an URL to the target system under testing, a test account for using the system, and a link to a quick user guide that details the functionalities of the system.

Target System

According to our research objective, we used a commercial Web-based electronic medical records (EMR) system. We used two criteria in selecting the system. First, the system should be truly Web-based; a subject merely needs a Web browser to load the system and perform record management tasks. Second, the system must be a full-fledged EMR system. It must allow a subject to create, update, delete, and retrieve patient records from anywhere at any time. It must support electronic communication with labs, pharmacies, hospitals, and other service providers. For example, a subject could create and retrieve prescriptions, add and modify medications and pharmacies. The system must support multiple file types including sounds and videos so that a subject can add quick notes to a document, and store and maintain dictation files on the server.

Literally there were hundreds of application service providers who claimed to provide EMR applications. Among them, a few delivered applications that truly worked within a Web browser. Many others employ client/server architecture, that is, a user has to download and install a windows client in order to work with a remote server. After a long process of searching, eliminating, pondering, and many runs of back-and-forth communications with application providers, we decided that HyperCharts™ was the most appropriate for this study.

Subjects

The goal of this study is to understand the end-user behavior in accepting Web-based medical record systems. Thus, the ideal target population should be those healthcare workers who are responsible for managing patient records using the computer. Since these people are typically supportive staff members in clinics, their contact information is often not accessible to outsiders. We assessed that a mail survey is going to be difficult to find its way to a target audience, and the overall response rate would be low. Therefore, in this study, we identified 90 senior healthcare trainees in a large mid-west university as surrogates. These students were majoring in dental hygiene, physician assistant, and radiology. These four-year programs were designed to prepare the graduates to successfully enter healthcare organizations such as hospitals and clinics. Their program curricula included intense problem-based learning modules combined with clinical experience such as internships and externships. All the selected subjects had training and experience in managing patient records and were familiar with the daily operations in hospitals and clinics.

We also obtained 85 clinic e-mail addresses through a medical worker association. We sent e-mail to the candidates requesting their participation. We provided a link to HyperChart system in the message. We assumed they agreed to participate if they did not indicate otherwise. In the following week, we did a Web-based survey. Eventually, we received 11 completed responses. Two candidates refused to participate, and 13 messages were undeliverable.

In total, 86 subjects completed the experiment and returned usable responses. Among them, 75 were senior healthcare trainees, and 11 were staff workers in clinics. The overall response rate is 49%. We did t-test on gender, experience with Web-based medical records, and attitudes toward the Internet; there was no evidence showing any difference between these two groups. Among all the subjects, almost all of them were female, and over 85% of them were at the age of 20-25. Thirteen percent of the subjects reported awareness of some EMR systems, and only 8% of them had hands-on experience with Web-based medical records. The rest of them had used traditional paper-based systems. Based on the five-point Likert scale from very negative to very positive, 69% of them had reported neutral attitudes to their current paper-based systems. With regard to Internet experience, 84% of them had over three years of using the Internet, and 69% of them had positive feelings toward surfing on the Internet.

Instrument

All constructs were measured using multiple scale items. The items underlying each construct were carefully developed according to their respective definitions. Each item was measured using a five-point Likert scale ranging from "low" to "high."

Internet self-efficacy. Research on self-efficacy prescribes that self-efficacy assessment should reflect different facets of the task domain, types of capabilities required, and situational circumstances in which those capabilities are exercised (Bandura, 1997). However, the original computer self-efficacy scales were developed prior to the rise of ubiquitous Internet computing. They do not capture many important skills unique to the Internet (Torkzadeh & Van Dyke, 2002). Existing studies on ISE (Nahl, 1996; Nahl & Meer, 1997) focused on the operations of specific tasks such as entering Web address (URL), creating folders, adding and removing bookmarks, mailing Web pages, and using File Transfer Protocol. Accordingly, Joo, Bong, and Choi (2000) measured ISE based on specific tasks in Internet search such as navigation, printing, and closing the browser. On the other hand, Eastin and LaRose (2000) proposed an instrument based on overall performance of Internet users. In the current study, we took a balanced stand in between these two positions and adapted most of the items from the studies (Dinev & Koufteros, 2002; Eastin & LaRose, 2000; Joo et al., 2000; Torkzadeh & Van Dyke, 2002). We created an additional item for an important skill, which was not addressed in previous studies. Finally we had eight items based on the skills that are required to run Web-based applications (see Appendix A).

Other Constructs. Items for measuring PEOU and PU were originally proposed by Davis (1989) and successively tested and validated in many other studies (Chau, 1996; Gefen & Straub, 1997; Hendrickson, Massey, & Cronan, 1993; Mathieson, 1991; Ridings & Gefen, 2000). We tailored the items so that they were applicable to Web-based technologies. The items for measuring BI were adapted from the studies of Chau (1996) and Venkatesh and Davis (1996).

Task

Due to time limitation, we did not require the subjects to test all functionalities available in HyperCharts™ Instead, we focused on the primary EMR functions as suggested by Waegemann (2002) and required subjects to accomplish the following tasks: (1) Log into the system with the provided user name and password; (2) create, update, and delete a patient record, search for a patient record, and add quick notes to a patient record; (3) search for prescriptions for a patient, add and sign off a new prescription, and add and modify medications on a prescription; (4) upload and download a dictation audio file. These primary functions were also described in the introduction to the system in HyperChart's Web site. All test data were similar to what the subjects are dealing with in their everyday work.

Data Analysis

Analytical Techniques

When deciding on analytical techniques, we considered hierarchical multiple regressions versus structural equation modeling (SEM) techniques like LISREL. SEM has its advantages in assessing both the efficacy of a measurement model and the significance of a structural model in one test, and is becoming popular in IT research in recent years. However, one is advised that SEM has some limitations comparing with other more traditional techniques such as multiple regressions. First, SEM has a stringent requirement on sample sizes. Ding, Velicer, and Harlow (1995) noted that 100-150 subjects is the minimum sample size for SEM, while Hu, Bentler, and Kano (1992) indicated that sometimes 5,000 subjects is insufficient. Second, the goodness-of-fit indices for SEM have no single statistical test of significance that identifies a correct model (Schumacker & Lomax, 1996). The widely cited criteria often falsely accept bad models (Liu, Liping, Li, & Karau, 2003). The problem compounds when the sample is too small or too large.

Therefore, in this study we choose hierarchical multiple regressions as the primary technique for data analysis. The use of hierarchical regression allows us to test recursive models, where a predictor in one model may become the dependent variable in another, and therefore, an antecedent variable may have impacts on a consequent variable in multiple distinct ways, with some direct and some indirect. Our research model is a case in point; each hypothesis stipulates the total effect of a predictor on a dependent variable, including both direct and indirect effects. For example, according to Figure 2, ISE can affect behavioral intention in four distinct ways, and the total effect of ISE on BI is the sum of all these direct and indirect effects:

1. ISE → BI (path e)
2. ISE → PU → BI (path b + path f)
3. ISE → PEOU → BI (path a + path d)
4. ISE → PEOU → PU → BI (path a + path c + path f)

Following the guideline proposed by Hair, Anderson, Tatham, and Black (1998), we assessed the assumptions of hierarchical regressions: The linearity of a phenomenon, the constant variance of the error term, and the normality of the error term distribution. We chose studentized residuals as the measure of the prediction error of each dependent variable. We examined residual scatter plots and partial regression plots. We did not detect any violations of these assumptions.

Scale Assessment

Before the survey was conducted, three PhD students and two faculty members reviewed the survey questions regarding their clarity and face and content validity. Two scale items for ISE were dropped because they were not directly related to Web-based medical record systems. As a result, six items were used

Table 1. Scale reliability

Construct	Number of items	Cronbach's Alpha
Perceived Usefulness (PU)	5	0.94
Perceived ease of Use (PEOU)	5	0.91
Behavior Intention (BI)	5	0.89
Internet Self-efficacy (ISE)	6	0.93

to measure the construct of ISE, while the scales for other constructs remain unchanged (see Appendix B).

Since all research constructs are latent, each one is reflected by a group of measurable items and indirectly measured as the average of their scores. Therefore, before we conduct data analysis on the constructs, we need to ensure the reliability of their scales, which are usually measured by Cronbach's alpha coefficients. The reliability coefficient of each construct is reported in Table 1. In general, a coefficient value of 0.70 or higher is considered acceptable (Hair et al., 1998). As per this standard, the reliabilities of our constructs are very high and comparable to or even better than those in other similar studies (see Appendix A).

To ensure that the items for the same construct measured a single trait, while items for different constructs measured distinct traits, we conducted a principal factor analysis with varimax rotation on 16 items for all independent constructs: ISE, PEOU, and PU. Using the Kaiser Eigenvalues criterion, we extracted three factors that collectively explained 77.28% of the variance in all items. Statistically, to obtain a power level of 80% at significance level 0.05, the significant value of factor loadings with a sample size of 100 is 0.50 (Hair et al., 1998). The rotated factor matrix in Table 2 shows that all the items cleanly load on the correct latent constructs, supporting the factorial validity of the measurement instrument.

Results

In hierarchical multiple regressions, the researcher decides on not only how many predictors to enter, but also the order in which they enter. Usually, the order of entry is based on logical or theoretical considerations. We enter the "most" exogenous predictors first, and the "most" endogenous predictor last. In our case, because ISE is modeled as having a direct influence on PEOU, it is important to statistically control the direct influence of ISE on BI before

Table 2. Factor loadings

	Factor 1	Factor 2	Factor 3
PEOU2	.835		
PEOU1	.813		
PEOU3	.785		
PEOU4	.760		
PEOU5	.627		
PU4		.851	
PU2		.847	
PU3		.840	
PU5		.756	
PU1		.734	
ISE6			.858
ISE1			.802
ISE5			.764
ISE3			.728
ISE2			.697
ISE4			.693
Eigenvalues	9.478	1.540	1.339
% Variance	59.24	68.91	77.28

Note: Factor loadings lower than .50 are not shown.

Table 3. Hierarchical regressions for dependent variable BI

Model	Coefficients			Model Summary		
	Beta	T	Sig.	R^2	R^2 Change	Sig.
1				.548	.548	.000
ISE	.741	10.100	.000			
2				.704	.156	.000
ISE	.363	4.391	.000			
PEOU	.546	6.613	.000			
3				.801	.097	.000
ISE	.162	2.157	.034			
PEOU	.408	5.699	.000			
PU	.441	6.306	.000			

evaluating the independent contribution of PEOU to BI. Failing to control the direct influence of ISE could result in the relationship between PEOU and BI being artificially inflated due to the indirect influences through the perceptual variable. In the same vein, it is important to control the direct influence of PEOU on BI before evaluating the independent contribution of PU. Thus, ISE was entered into the regression model first, followed by PEOU and PU in the second and third step. In this way, we are able to tease out the influence of ISE before considering that of PEOU and PU. The regression results are presented in Table

Table 4. Hierarchical regressions for dependent variable PU

Model	Coefficients			Model Summary		
	Beta	T	Sig.	R^2	R^2 Change	Sig.
1				.451	.451	.000
ISE	.672	8.310	.000			
2				.502	.051	.004
ISE	.455	4.246	.000			
PEOU	.313	2.925	.004			

Table 5. Hierarchical regressions for dependent variable PEOU

Model	Coefficients			Model Summary		
	Beta	T	Sig.	R^2	R^2 Change	Sig.
1				.478	.478	.000
ISE	.691	8.770	.000			

3. We did similar regressions when PU and PEOU were dependent variables, and the results are shown in Table 4 and 5 respectively.

R-square value — the coefficient of determination — represents the percentage of the variance that can be explained by the predictors in a relationship. According to the guideline provided by Hair et al. (1998), the threshold of R-square, for example, with a power of .80 at significance level 0.01 is about 15% for a sample of 100 subjects with four independent variables. In other words, if the R-square value for a relationship is greater than 15%, we will be confident that the effect of the independent variables on the dependent variable is statistically significant. According to this standard, all R-square values are statistically significant.

An R-square change is probably more important than an R-square value itself. A significant R-square change, say at level $\alpha \leq 0.01$, means that an additional predictor can explain a significant amount of the variance in the dependent variable and hence add additional explanation power to the model. For example, according to Table 3, about 80% of the total variance in BI is explained by three predictors: ISE, PEOU, and PU. Besides, all R-square changes are significant, meaning all three predictors exhibited significant positive influences on BI. The three predictors explained respectively about 55% (ISE), 15% (PEOU), and 10% (PU) of the variance in BI. Similarly, according to Table 4, about 50% of the variance in PU was explained by ISE (45%) and PEOU (5%).

In order to test our research hypotheses, we need to calculate the coefficient of each path, called direct effect, as well as the total effect of each predictor. A direct effect represents the change in the dependent variable directly attributable

Figure 3. Direct effects of predictors

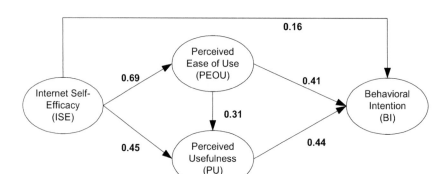

to a standard deviation change in a predictor. A total effect represents the total change in the dependent variable attributable to the direct effect of the predictor, as well as its effects that are mediated through other predictors. Thus, we need to accumulate both direct and indirect effects to compute a total effect. Direct effects are the standardized beta coefficients in the full model. For example, according to Table 3, the beta coefficients in the full model are respectively 0.16 for ISE, 0.41 for PEOU, and 0.44 for PU. Thus, the direct effect of ISE on BI is 0.16. Similarly, the direct effect of PEOU on BI is 0.41 and that of PU is 0.44. Figure 3 shows all direct effects taken from Tables 3-5.

To compute the total effect, we consider all the paths that link a predictor to the dependent variable with or without mediators in between. If a path has no mediator, it carries a direct effect. If a path consists of one or more mediators, it carries an indirect effect, which is the product of all direct effects on the path. For example, the indirect effect of ISE on BI through the path ISE → PEOU → PU → BI is $0.69 \times 0.31 \times 0.44 = 0.09$. The total effect is simply the sum of the direct and indirect effects carried by all the paths. In Table 6, we summarized the total effect for each pair of a predictor and a dependent variable, and the level of support for each research hypothesis. As shown, all hypotheses are strongly supported by the data at the significance level 0.005 or higher.

Discussion and Conclusion

The results of this study indicated that Internet self-efficacy has a significant impact on perceived ease of use, perceived usefulness, as well as behavioral intention to use Web-based electronic medical records. The total effect of

Table 6. Total effects summary

Hypothesis	Relationship	Total Effect	Supported?
H1	ISE → BI	.741	Yes (p<.001)
H2	ISE → PEOU	.691	Yes (p<.001)
H3	PEOU → PU	.313	Yes (p=.004)
H4	PU → BI	.441	Yes (p<.001)
H5	PEOU → BI	.546	Yes (p<.001)
H6	ISE → PU	.672	Yes (p<.001)

Internet self-efficacy on perceived usefulness is slightly weaker than that on perceived ease of use. It indicates that users perceived the system to be both easer to use and more useful when their Internet self-efficacies are higher. This finding is consistent with that of previous studies (Lopez & Manson, 1997; Agarwal et al., 2000). By synthesizing this and other self-efficacy studies (Lopez & Manson, 1997; Agarwal et al., 2000; Igbaria et al., 1995), we found that the impact of self-efficacy on usefulness is significant in Internet or Web related settings but not significant in traditional non Web-based contexts. Of course, this finding needs further investigation before jumping to a firm conclusion.

Perceived ease of use influences both usefulness and intention. However, its total effect on behavioral intention is stronger than that on usefulness. This finding is interesting because the role of ease of use has been found unstable and controversial (Ma & Liu, 2004). Most studies indicated that the impact of ease of use on usefulness is stronger than that of ease of use on behavioral intention, although few other researchers found a much larger effect of ease of use on intention than usefulness (Lim, 2001). In a study with the Internet technology, Gefen and Straub (2000) found that PEOU influences BI when a Web site involves inquiries but does not influence BI when a Web site is used for a purchasing task.

Implications

Theoretically, this study helps understand the antecedents to the key constructs in the technology acceptance model. It confirms the existing findings on the role of self-efficacy in perceiving the usability of an information technology. It adds additional evidence to the conflicting findings on the role of self-efficacy in determining perceived usefulness. Most importantly, it does all these in the context of accepting Web-based electronic medical records, which has not been done yet. Since the software industry is currently undergoing a revolutionary transition from software as products to software as services, a study of how end users respond to such a transition is very important. This paper represents a first attempt in applying the technology acceptance model to the adoption of application services. The result may be generalizable to other emerging e-business technologies such as Web and grid services (Liu & Ma, 2004).

The findings of this study have some important managerial implications in practice. First, cognitive factors have been recognized to be the biggest obstacle for the widespread adoption of electronic medical records (Waegemann, 2002). In fact, the medical informatics community blames physicians for not being ready for a change to the computer. Among others, three critical cognitive factors are recognized (Voelker, 2003): (1) Confidence in computers amongst their users, and especially in the availability, privacy, and security of data made of the electronic medical records; (2) adoption of a positive attitude toward computers in the workplace; and (3) adequate skills and proficiency in the use of the computer application. Our study confirms these general beliefs and addresses these factors using three constructs: Self-efficacy, perceived ease of use, and perceived usefulness. Further research is needed to address other aspects of these cognitive factors. Second, our findings imply that, as for other technologies, enhanced usability and usefulness are a very important step toward the acceptance of Web-based electronic medical records. Third, to achieve end-user acceptance of electronic medical records, healthcare organizations can introduce interventions aimed at improving usability and utility perceptions as well as the end-user's Internet self-efficacy. However, as Table 6 shows, the total effect of self-efficacy on behavior intention is much stronger than that of perceived ease of use and usefulness. The significance of Internet self-efficacy suggests that enhancing self-efficacy may be a more effective option toward technology acceptance than enhancing usability and utility perceptions. After all, enhancing perceived ease of use and usefulness often requires significant effort in modifying the services being provided and is thus more difficult to do.

Note that self-efficacy is not a measure of skills. Rather, it reflects what individuals believe they can do with the skills they possess. As such, it is easy to be manipulated. For example, optimistic outlook, self-deception, heuristics judgments, and excessive wishful thinking can all induce over-confidence (Metcalfe, 1998). Then, will over-confidence bias our findings? In meta-cognition, under-estimation was found to be detrimental to learning outcomes, while over-confidence was found to be beneficial, although individuals with over-confidence tend to over-estimate their knowledge (Gravill, Compeau, & Marcolin, 2002). However, its impact on perceptual and attitudinal variables is not known yet. More research seems necessary to study this phenomenon and examine whether over-confidence enhances one's willingness to accept a technology.

References

Armitage, C. J., & Conner, M. (2001). Social cognitive determinants of blood donation. *Journal of Applied Social Psychology, 31*, 1431-1457.

Agarwal, R., Sambamurthy, V., & Stair, R. (2000). The evolving relationship between general and specific computer literacy. An empirical assessment. *Information Systems Research, 11*(4), 418-430.

Bandura, A. (1977). Self-efficacy: Toward a unifying theory of behavioral change. *Psychological Review, 84*(2), 191-215.

Bandura, A. (2001). Guide for constructing self-efficacy scales. *Measurement and evaluation in counseling and development.* Retrieved from http://www.emory.edu/EDUCATION/mfp/banseg.html

Benbasat, I., & Zmud, R. W. (1999). Empirical research in information systems: The practice of relevance. *MIS Quarterly, 23*(1), 3-16.

Bhattacherjee, A. (2001). Understanding information systems continuance: An expectation-confirmation model. *MIS Quarterly, 25*(3), 351-370.

Chau, P. K. (1996). An empirical assessment of a modified technology acceptance model. *Journal of Management Information Systems, 13*(2), 185-205.

Chau, P. K. (2000). Influence of computer attitude and self-efficacy on IT usage behavior. *Journal of End User Computing, 13*(1), 26-33.

Chau, P. Y. K., & Hu, P. J. (2002), Investigating healthcare professionals' decisions to accept telemedicine technology: An empirical test of competing theories. *Information & Management, 39*(4), 297-311.

Chircu, A. M., Davis, G. B., & Kauffman, R. J. (2000). *The role of trust and expertise in the adoption of electronic commerce intermediaries* (Tech. Rep. No. WP 00-07). Minneapolis: University of Minnesota, Carlson School of Management.

Compeau, D. R., & Higgins, C. A. (1995). Computer self-efficacy: Development of a measure and initial test. *MIS Quarterly, 19*(2), 189-211.

Davis, F. D. (1989). Perceived usefulness, perceived ease of use, and user acceptance of information technology. *MIS Quarterly, 13*(3), 319-339.

Dinev, T., & Koufteros, X. (2002). Self-efficacy and Internet usage — Measurement and factorial validity. In *Proceedings of DSI,* San Diego, CA.

Ding, L., Velicer, W. F., & Harlow, L. L. (1995). Effects of estimation methods, number of indicators per factor, and improper solutions on structural equation modeling fit indices. *Structural Equation Modeling, 2*, 119-143.

Eastin, M. S., & LaRose, R. (2000). Internet self-efficacy and the psychology of the Digital Divide. *Journal of Computer-Mediated Communication, 6*(1). Retrieved from http://www.asusc.org/jcmc/vol6/issuel/eastin.html

Fishbein, M., & Ajzen, I. (1975). *Belief, attitude, intention, and behavior: An introduction to theory and research.* Reading, MA: Addison-Wesley.

Gefen, D., & Keil, M. (1998). The impact of developer responsiveness on perceptions of usefulness and ease of use: An extension of the technology acceptance model. *The Data Base for Advances in Information Systems, 29*(2), 35-49.

Gefen, D., & Straub, D. (1997). Gender differences in the perception and use of e-mail: An extension to the technology acceptance model. *MIS Quarterly, 21*(4), 389-401.

Gefen, D., & Straub, D. (2000). The relative importance of perceived ease of use in IS adoption: A study of e-commerce adoption. *Journal of the Association for Information Systems*, (digital version) *1*(8).

Gravill, J. I., Compeau, D. R., & Marcolin, B. L. (2002). Metacognition and IT: The influence of self-efficacy and self-awareness. In *Proceedings of the Eighth Americas Conference on Information Systems* (pp. 1055-1064).

Hair, Jr., J. F., Anderson, R. E., Tatham, R. L., & Black, W. C. (1998). Multivariate data analysis with readings. Englewood Cliffs, NJ: Prentice-Hall.

Hendrickson, A. R., Massey, P. D., & Cronan, T. P. (1993). On the test-retest reliability of perceived usefulness and perceived ease of use scales. *MIS Quarterly, 17*(2), 227-230.

Hu, L., Bentler, P. M., & Kano, Y. (1992) Can test statistics in covariance structure analysis be trusted?. *Psychological Bulletin, 112*, 325-344.

Igbaria, M., Iivari, J., & Maragahh, H. (1995). Why do individuals use computer technology? A Finnish Case Study. *Information and Management, 29*(5), 227-38.

Jayatilaka, B., Schwarz, A., & Hirschheim, A. (2002). Determinants of ASP choice: An integrated perspective. In *Proceedings of the 35th Hawaii International Conference on System Science.* IEEE.

Joo, Y., Bong, M., & Choi, H. (2000). Self-efficacy for self-regulated learning, academic self-efficacy, and Internet self-efficacy in Web-based instruction. *Educational Technology Research and Development, 48*(2), 5-17.

Keil, M., Beranek, P. M, & Konsynski, B. R. (1995). Usefulness and ease of use: Field study evidence regarding task considerations. *Decision Support Systems, 13*(1), 75-91.

Ketler, K., Willems, J. R., & Srinivasan, M. (2002). The need for training in information technology: A survey of healthcare. In *Proceedings of the Decision Sciences Institute 2002 Annual Meeting.* San Diego, CA.

Lederer, A. L., Maupin, D. J. Sena, M. P., & Zhuang, Y. (2000). The technology acceptance model and the World Wide Web. *Decision Support Systems, 29*(3), 269-292.

Levine, T., & Donitsa-Schmidt, S. (1998). Computer use, confidence, attitudes, and knowledge: A causal analysis. *Computers in Human Behavior, 14*(1), 125-146.

Lim, K.S. (2001). An empirical test of the technology acceptance model.In *Proceedings of the Decision Science Institute Annual Meeting.* San Francisco.

Liu, L., Li, C. C., & Karau, S. J. (2003). *A measurement model of trust in Internet stores.* Akron, OH: University of Akron.

Liu, L., & Ma, Q. (2004). Emerging e-business technologies for electronic medical records. *International Journal of Healthcare Technology and Management, 6*(1/2), 1-22.

Lopez, D., & Manson, D., (1997). A study of individual computer self-efficacy and perceived usefulness of the empowered desktop information system. *Journal of Interdisciplinary Studies, 10,* 83-92.

Ma, Q., & Liu, L. (2004). The technology acceptance model: A meta-analysis of empirical findings. *Journal of End User Computing, 16*(1), 59-72.

Marakas, G. M., Yi, M. Y., & Johnson, R. D. (1998). The multilevel and multifaceted character of computer self-efficacy: Toward clarification of the construct and an integrative framework for research. *Information Systems Research, 9*(2), 126-163.

Mathieson, K. (1991). Predicting user intentions: Comparing the technology acceptance model with the theory of planned behavior. *Information Systems Research, 2*(3), 173-191.

Metcalfe, J. (1998). Cognitive optimism: Self-deception or memory-based processing heuristics?. *Personality and Social Psychology Review, 2*(2), 100-110.

Munro, M. C., Huff, S. L., Marcolin, B. L., & Compeau, D. R. (1997). Understanding and measuring user competence. *Information & Management, 33*(1), 45-57.

Nahl, D. (1996). Affective monitoring of Internet learners: Perceived self-efficacy and success. In *Proceedings of the 59th ASIS Annual Meeting,* Baltimore (Vol. 33, pp. 100-109).

Nahl, D., & Meer, P. (1997). User-centered assessment of two Web browsers: Errors, perceived self-efficacy, and success. In *Proceedings of the 60th ASIS Annual Meeting,* Washington, DC (Vol. 34, pp. 89-97).

Peterson, R. R., & Fairchild, A. M. (2003). Adoption trends in application service provisioning: An exploratory field study of small and medium-size enterprises. In *Proceedings of the European Conference on Information Systems (ECIS).* Naples, Italy.

Ridings, C. M., & Gefen, D. (2000). Applying TAM to a parallel systems conversion strategy. *Journal of Information Technology Theory & Application, 2*(2).

Schumacker, R. E. & Lomax, R. G. (1996). *A beginner's guide to structural equation modeling.* Mahwal, NJ: Lawrence Erlbaum Associates Publishers.

Straub, D. W. (1994). The effect of culture on IT diffusion: E-mail and FAX in Japan and the U.S. *Information Systems Research, 5*(1), 23-47.

Susarla, A., Barua, A., & Whinston, A. B. (2003). Understanding the service component of application service provision: An empirical analysis of satisfaction with ASP services. *MIS Quarterly, 27*(1), 91-123.

Taylor, S., & Todd, P. (1995). Assessing IT usage: The role of prior experience. *MIS Quarterly, 19*(4), 561-570.

Torkzadeh, G., & Van Dyke, T. P. (2002). Effects of training on Internet self-efficacy and computer user attitudes. *Computers in Human Behavior, 18,* 479-494.

Venkatesh, V. (2000). Determinants of perceived ease of use: Integrating control, intrinsic motivation, and emotion into the technology acceptance model. *Information Systems Research, 11*(4), 342-365.

Venkatesh, V., & Davis, F. D. (1996). A model of the antecedents of perceived ease of use: Development and test. *Decision Sciences, 27*(3), 451-481.

Voelker, K. G. (2003). *Primer on electronic medical records.* Retrieved January 3, 2003, from http://www.elmr-electronic-medical-records-emr.com/electronic_medical_record_Primer.htm

Waegemann, P. C. (2002). *Status report 2002: Electronic health records, status report Medical Records Institute.*

Appendix A

Initial Items for Internet Self-Efficacy

Item #:	Item	Source	Construct α	Loading
1	I feel confident to use search engines like Yahoo, Google, and AltaVista.	Joo et al., 2000	.95	NA
2	I feel confident to download necessary material from Internet.	Joo et al., 2000	.95	NA
		Dinev and Koufteros, 2002	.96	.78
		Torkzadeh and van Dyke, 2002	.94	.77
3	I feel confident to search for information on the Internet.	Joo et al., 2000	.95	NA
		Eastin and LaRose, 2000	.93	.65
		Torkzadeh and van Dyke, 2002	.93	.78
4	I feel confident to visit a Web site if I am given a Web address (URL).			
5	I feel confident to log on to a Web site if I have the account information.			
6	Overall, I feel comfortable when I am using Internet.			
7	I feel it is easy for me to learn to use an Internet feature.	Dinev and Koufteros, 2002	.96	.82
8	I feel confident to perform data transactions (e.g., buy a book) on the Web.	Dinev and Koufteros, 2002	.96	.58

Appendix B

Survey Instrument

PU1	Using this system in my job would enable me to accomplish tasks more quickly.
PU2	Using this system would improve my job performance.
PU3	Using this system would enhance my effectiveness on the job.
PU4	Using this system would make it easier to do my job.
PU5	This system is useful in my job.
PEOU1	I found it was easy to do whatever I want.
PEOU2	The navigation on the site is easy.
PEOU3	Learning to operate this system is easy for me.
PEOU4	This Web site provides information content that is easy to understand.
PEOU5	I found this system was flexible to interact with.
ISE1	I feel confident to use search engines like Yahoo, Google, and AltaVista.
ISE2	I feel confident to log on to a Web site if I have the account information.
ISE3	I feel confident to download necessary material from the Internet.
ISE4	I feel confident to search for information on the Internet.
ISE5	I feel confident to visit a Web site if I am given a Web address (URL).
ISE6	Overall, I feel comfortable when I am using the Internet.
BI1	I will support it if my clinic decides to use this system.
BI2	I would like to come back to this site for a second look.
BI3	I do not mind spending some time learning how to use this system for my work.
BI4	I am willing to use the system for my work.
BI5	It would be efficient if we were going to adopt this system.

Chapter IV

The Effectiveness of Online Task Support vs. Instructor-Led Training

Ji-Ye Mao, City University of Hong Kong, Hong Kong

Bradley R. Brown, University of Waterloo, Canada

Abstract

This study investigates the effectiveness of online task support (the wizard type in particular) relative to instructor-led training, and explores the underlying cognitive process in terms of the development of mental models. Ninety-two novice users of Microsoft Access were either trained by an experienced instructor or performed exercises with online task support, and then completed a variety of performance-based tests. Analysis shows that users of online task support tended to outperform instructor-trained individuals on high-level tasks, whereas the performance difference on low-level tasks was not significant. The cognitive processes underlying the difference are also noteworthy. Task support users were more likely to develop conceptual mental models as opposed to procedural ones, which accounted for their better high-level performance. Mental model completeness was also found to be closely associated with performance on both low and high-level tasks. These findings offer support for increased use of online task support.

Introduction

End-user training is a multi-billion dollar business, critical to the successful implementation of systems and the productive use of technology (Compeau, Olfman, Sein, & Webster, 1995). However, spending is no guarantee for success. Traditional training approaches tend to remove trainees from the context of work, provide them with a loaded training program, and then send them back to their jobs. They run the risk of teaching material that would never be transferred to the actual job context. By providing all training in massed sessions, the knowledge acquired might deteriorate over time.

After an initial training, users tend to practice only those procedures that they need to accomplish their most urgent tasks. "As a result, much of what they were initially trained to do but did not continue to do regularly was forgotten" (Bullen & Bennett, 1996, p. 371). Occasional users in particular are not interested in regular training sessions, nor would they benefit from such training (Eason, 1988). According to Eason, what they really need is the "point of need support," which provides specific answers when questions arise from real work. A variety of mechanisms could be used to provide such types of support, including online help facilities.

Advances in information technologies have created both challenges and opportunities for end-user training. On one hand, learning everything in advance has become impossible, and it is difficult to be proficient with many applications or many functions of a single application. End-users must develop the ability of self-learning and support. On the other hand, online task support has become increasingly sophisticated and increased in variety including help and references, examples, wizards, cue cards, and custom-designed job aids. More importantly, online task support has emerged as a potential viable alternative to the conventional training, allowing training to be integrated into working.

The central idea of online task support is embedding training and support functions within an operational system, to enhance knowledge workers' performance by providing access to knowledge, information, advice, and learning experiences in the context of work (e.g., Gery, 1995; Marion, 2002; Masumian, 2000). In other words, online task support is provided to users within the context of work via integrated and on-demand access. Only granular task-specific knowledge is delivered to retain the job context. Rather than lengthy comprehensive lectures on system functionality, sufficiently small task-oriented modules are offered to provide information just enough to complete the task at hand. Training and support are accessed only as required to deal with actual problems arising from work. As a result, the issue of transferring learning from the training environment to the work environment would no longer be a concern, because the training environment would be the work environment. Similarly, rather than massed training sessions, online task support provides ongoing support.

A common feature of online task support is wizard-based scaffolding (Hmelo et al., 1999). A *wizard* in a computer application typically consists of a set of simple dialogue boxes that guide the user through a cognitively complex task. The task is decomposed into multiple subtasks organized sequentially to reduce the cognitive load required to complete the task. There are several benefits of wizards in providing support or scaffolding to a task. A wizard can make the user aware of the expected task components, and necessary parameters to be set. In other words, the user is given a structure and transparency of the task. As a result, the task becomes less cognitively demanding as the user can concentrate on one subtask at a time rather than approaching the task as a whole piece. Navigation from one subtask to another is guided and facilitated. The online task support tool evaluated in this study is primarily based on wizards.

To date little empirical research has been conducted on online task support. Most of the work that does exist is either conceptual or anecdotal in nature (cf., Hudzina, Rowley, & Wager, 1996; Moore & Orey, 2001). One of the few empirical studies investigated the effectiveness of wizards for supporting medical students to design clinical trials (Hmelo et al., 1999). They were asked to design and critique a clinical trial to test a new anticancer drug, assisted by a wizard type of scaffolding tool. Subjects gained a 34% increase in the quality of their group design, and improved by 48% in their individual critiques of flawed designs. In another study, online task support was compared to instructor-led training using a sample of insurance agents (Bastiens, Nijhof, Streuner, & Amba, 1997). Contrary to the hypothesis that online task support would be superior, it was found that there was no significant difference in learning between the two groups of trainees. Moreover, it was found that trainees preferred the instructor-led training due to its social element. The big advantage of online task support in this case was potentially a tremendous cost saving because the number of trainees was large and the costs of instructor-led training were closely related to the number of trainees.

This research intends to fill some of the gaps in the current literature. The research questions are: How effective is online task support relative to instructor-led training in supporting the performance of different types of tasks, and what are the underlying reasons for any performance difference between the two approaches?

The remainder of this chapter is organized as follows. The next section presents several research hypotheses, largely based on the notion of mental models. Then, details of the research method are described, and results of data analysis are presented in the next two sections. Lastly, this chapter concludes with a discussion of the implication and limitations of this research.

Research Hypotheses

Mental models are the internal representations that people have of systems. The conceptual underpinnings of mental models have been prominent in psychology for some time. This paper will not provide a comprehensive review of the literature, as it has been done elsewhere (e.g., Mayhew, 1992; Santhanam & Sein, 1994). According to Johnson-Laird (1980), mental models are knowledge structures that describe the relationships of the various components of a system. Norman (1983) adopted the concept as a cornerstone for human-computer interaction. Through interacting with a target system that people are learning or using, they form their mental model of the system. The model provides predictive and explanatory power for understanding the interaction.

Conceptual models are closely related to, but different from, mental models. Rather, they are often used in the human-computer interaction literature to refer to a model provided to end-users for them to develop their own mental model (Mayhew, 1992; Norman, 1983). Whereas mental models are users' internal representations of a system, conceptual models are invented by the designers, instructors, trainers, or engineers, and can be external training aids that provide a basis for forming mental models (Norman, 1983). Moreover, the provision of an accurate and easy to understand conceptual model is a key factor in determining the ease of learning and use of a system.

There are two types of conceptual models that are used to help users in practice, analogical and abstract (Sein & Bostrom, 1989). *Analogical conceptual models* use metaphorical representations to explain a target system in terms of a system that is familiar (Santhanam & Sein, 1994). This approach allows users to draw upon their existing knowledge, and to apply it to an unfamiliar system. For instance, the "desktop" and "recycling bin" metaphors help novice users handle documents, widely used in graphical user interfaces of computer operating systems. While users might be unfamiliar with the operating systems, the idea of dropping a document into a recycling bin is probably familiar. *Abstract conceptual models* are synthetic representations of a system (Sein, Bostrom, & Olfman,

1987). They depict a target system using only "schematic diagrams, hierarchical charts, or mathematical expressions" (Santhanam & Sein, 1994, p. 381).

Similarly, if a user's understanding of a target system is predominantly analogical or abstract, it is deemed that the user possesses *conceptual* mental models. The other type of mental model is *procedural*, if a user's understanding of a target system is in terms of operational procedures, according to Santhanam and Sein (1994).

As reported in a variety of literature, people do not always form appropriate mental models (cf., Mayhew, 1992). Mayhew concluded that many mistakes by computer users are systematic, and that the mistakes "seem best accounted for by positing an inappropriate mental model from which users are drawing inappropriate inferences and thus making inappropriate predictions" (p. 81). In addition, Norman (1983) observed that mental models are often incomplete, unstable, without firm boundaries, and unscientific. Most people's understanding of the systems that they use is "surprisingly meager, imprecisely specified, and full of inconsistencies, gaps and idiosyncratic quirks. The models ... contain only partial descriptions of operations and huge areas of uncertainties" (p. 9). In this study, mental model completeness is the focus of quality measure based on the work of Santhanam and Sein (1994). It refers to the degree to which a mental model truthfully represents an entire system.

The design and provision of conceptual models through the user interface is a key concern in human-computer interaction (Mayhew, 1992). It is desirable to provide a proactive and "intelligent" help system that reinforces the conceptual model to encourage the development of optimal mental model. There is empirical evidence that such help systems assist users in learning to use systems (Mayhew, 1992). In fact, the online task support assessed in this study features both extensive use of wizards and proactive provision of such support by the system, as illustrated later in the next section.

The authors of this paper believe that a major strength of wizards is its ability to present analogical and abstract conceptual models. Such conceptual models of a system can be purposefully built into wizards and effectively presented to users in the context of their work. In particular, it is natural and convenient to embed conceptual models into wizards; as a complex task is decomposed into simpler subtasks, many mechanisms can be used to present conceptual models such as graphical icons, interface metaphors (such as the "desktop" and "recycling bin"), schematic diagrams, and hierarchical charts.

Moreover, because wizard use is closely tied to the completion of real task as opposed to learning in abstract, conceptual models embedded in wizards are also made available just-in-time or at the "point of need" for task on hand. It is especially the case if wizards are provided to users in a proactive manner initiated by the system. In other words, the wizard type of online task support could also enhance the timing of the delivery of conceptual models, which facilitate the development of conceptual mental models.

Whereas instructor-led training can focus on developing conceptual mental models, for example, through analogies, it is not the case in *typical* instruction-based training. A survey by Bullen and Bennett (1996) found that trainees were often given only basic and mechanic training. Trainees "generally described the training that they had received in the use of their software as directed toward building procedural or mechanical skills — basic instruction in what keys to push to accomplish specific tasks" (p. 370). In addition to the content focus on procedural training, the timing of training delivery is another limitation of instructor-led training. Because training is not at the "point of need," both its usefulness and users' motivation to learn may be reduced (Eason, 1988).

Therefore, online task support has two major advantages over instructor-led training, the ease of presenting conceptual models and the delivery of such models just-in-time. As a result, online task support should be more conducive to the development of conceptual mental models than typical instruction, and with higher quality. The previous discussion is summarized as Hypothesis 1.

Hypothesis 1: (a) Online task support is more likely to lead to the development of conceptual mental models as opposed to procedural ones, and the former type is more likely to be developed with online task support than with instructor-led training. Moreover, (b) online task support will result in more complete mental models than typical instructor-led training.

Mental models are considered one of the key factors in determining users' success with using computer systems (Mayhew, 1992; Shneiderman, 1998). The importance of mental models in assisting system use can be understood from cognitive perspectives. For example, the assimilation theory proposed by Ausubel (1968) explains the cognitive processes underlying learning whereby new knowledge can be committed to long-term memory. According to this theory, learners require a conceptual understanding into which learning can be integrated. A developed conceptual mental model provides this understanding, which outlines how various components of a system work together, thereby providing the appropriate framework upon which learners can anchor and assimilate new information. Indeed, Mayer (1981) found that users who were provided with conceptual models in advance of use were better able to transfer novel tasks to long-term memory.

Prior research has also demonstrated that users with accurate and complete mental models outperform others in terms of task completion (e.g., Mayer, 1981; Borgman, 1986; Sein & Bostrom, 1989; Santhanam & Sein, 1994). In the end-user training literature, Santhanam and Sein (1994) found that users with conceptual mental models performed better than those with procedural ones. Therefore, Hypothesis 2 is proposed to reconfirm the relationship between performance and the presence of conceptual mental models, and to justify the relative advantage of the wizard type of online task support in the delivery of conceptual models.

Hypothesis 2: Individuals with conceptual mental models will perform better than those with procedural ones.

In addition to the benefit of online task support for developing conceptual mental models (Hypothesis 1), which help task performance (Hypothesis 2), the continuous and just-in-time availability of online task support can directly enhance users' task performance (Bastiens et al., 1997; Eason, 1988; Gery, 1995). Wizards can facilitate the execution of otherwise complex tasks (Hmelo et al., 1999), and deal with emerging problems. With a reasonably developed conceptual mental model of a task combined with task-simplifying wizards, users could be in a good position to complete given tasks. In contrast, exposure to instruction alone may not give trainees the necessary and relevant knowledge to complete new tasks. Trainees could be ill-equipped to deal with novel situations, lacking the ability to obtain task knowledge at the point of need. Therefore, Hypothesis 3 posits the expected direct benefit of online task support in terms of task performance.

Hypothesis 3: Online task support will lead to higher performance than instructor-led training.

As discussed earlier, most users lack appropriate mental models, which is a key cause for operational mistakes. Therefore, it is reasonable to expect that the quality of mental models will influence users' performance. In particular, the completeness of mental models is a key aspect of quality, representing the level of comprehensive knowledge about how an entire system should be used and what it is capable of. In fact, a prior study has found that mental model completeness was associated with performance (Santhanam & Sein, 1994). This relationship is to be reconfirmed as Hypothesis 4.

Hypothesis 4: Mental model completeness will be positively related to task performance.

Research Method

Participants and Experiment Procedures

Participants were recruited for one hour of free instruction in the use of Microsoft Access, which is the leading desktop database management system, and an honorarium of $15 for another hour of additional exercises and tests. In total, 92 individuals volunteered to participate in this experiment. They were undergraduate and graduate students with various academic backgrounds in a major Canadian University. The recruitment letter specified that subjects should be Access novices. Subjects were randomly assigned to one of two conditions, the instruction or the online task support condition. Those subjects using online task support were offered the free instruction at a later date. Prizes were offered to the top performer ($50) and the second best performer ($30) in each condition, but the announcement of the prizes were not made until the beginning of the experiment to avoid attracting proficient Access users.

The experiments were conducted in a computer lab with 26 terminals, in five separate group sessions. Each of these sessions lasted for about two hours, one for training and the other for testing. The instructor-led training condition was done in the first two sessions, followed by three online task support sessions. Each session started with a background questionnaire, followed by instruction or exercises with online task support. Then, administered were self-efficacy and mental model measures, and lastly performance tests.

Instructor-Led Training

An experienced professional instructor was hired to conduct the training. This individual had over 20 years of experience as a software instructor, with an extensive background in databases and Access in particular. For the past 10 years she had been working for a local training company, which offered her services to organizations on a contract basis. The design of the instruction condition was left almost entirely to the discretion of the instructor. The intention was to follow the best practice in the training industry. She was simply informed of the duration of the class, that the trainees would be Access novices, that the format and curriculum should be *typical* of what someone might receive in a professional setting, and that the class should not cover the use of wizards or online help.

In a computer lab with a computer for each subject, the instructor introduced the software, and led subjects through a number of hands-on exercises. Subjects were not provided with any guidance in the use of these forms of task support, nor were they prompted to use online task support. The researchers observed the class designed by the instructor, and documented the five main components to follow. (1) General overview — The instructor introduced the class to Access, and briefly explained what the software is used for. She used the analogy of a phone book, and described how the information in a phone book would be stored in a database. (2) Table creation — The first procedural topic was table creation. The instructor described what a table is and what it is used for, and proceeded to walk through the creation of a simple table with the class. (3) Form creation/ Data entry — The instructor explained to students how data is entered into a table. She walked through the creation of a form, and showed students how to enter data using it. (4) Sorting data/Creating filters and queries — After showing students how to enter data, the instructor showed them how to sort it, and organize it in useful ways using filters and queries. (5) Data display/Creating reports — Students were introduced to reports, and briefly shown what is involved in report creation.

Online Task Support

Subjects in the online task support condition had access to pre-installed "Task Advisor" (TA), which was plugged into Access to facilitate the use of Access. TA is primarily a wizard-type of task support tool, assisting novice users in performing basic tasks. It outlines the basic steps to be performed for each task, and provides one-stop access to all relevant task information. In addition to wizards, TA also draws from the online help of Access, but reorganizes the help

Figure 1. TA plugged in Microsoft Access (TA icon appearing in the top right corner)

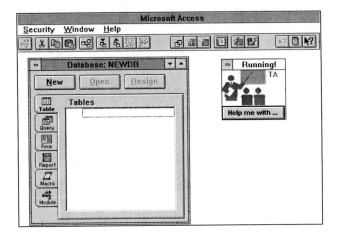

Figure 2. TA's advice on designing one's first table

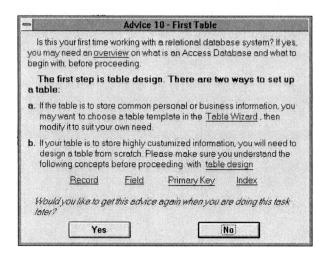

material around common basic tasks. To allow convenient access and to serve as a reminder for the users, a small TA icon constantly appears on the computer screen (see Figure 1). The TA icon can be clicked on with a mouse to open up a window with a menu of help topics available. From this menu users can get an overview of Access, clarification on the meaning of several basic concepts (e.g., tables, fields, relationships), and task-oriented instructions for designing tables and setting up relationships. Figure 2 shows the general procedure for setting up an Access table along with the necessary background knowledge. This wizard can be activated by the user from the TA menu, or by TA proactively when the user attempts a new task. For example, if a user uses the mouse to click on the "Tables" button in the Database window (see Figure 1) and there is no previously defined database table, TA would assume the user is a novice and provide task support as shown in Figure 2.

Figure 3 is an example of how TA provides essential support needed by novices for a task. Note, an abstract conceptual model about the concept of "referential integrity" is provided, and hypertext links can be followed for additional information. TA uses abstract conceptual models extensively to help novices work with Access.

Subjects were given the same amount of time and exposure to similar topics covered in the instruction condition: Based on what was covered in the instruction condition, a paper-based guide was designed accordingly to point subjects in the online task support condition to the appropriate topics. This guide directed subjects to work on specific tasks that were covered in the instruction condition,

Figure 3. TA's advice on the concept of "Referential Integrity

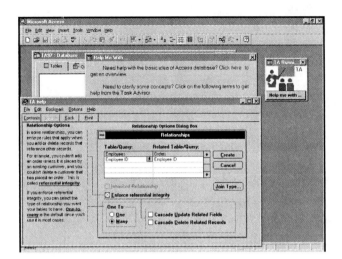

through the use of the Office Assistant, online help, and TA. Care was taken to ensure that the guide did not provide any instruction on the topics themselves. Instead, the guide directed subjects to the relevant task support tools. This approach was to ensure that subjects in both conditions would be exposed to the same material.

In essence, the instruction (control) group received approximately one hour of lecture and hands-on practice. In the same time interval, the online task support (treatment) group was given TA, which featured the wizard type of task support and abstract conceptual models of the system, along with exercises to be completed with the help of other online resources.

Measurement

A set of five Access-based questions was designed as a performance-based test[1]. Three of them required users to perform operational procedures using databases, such as building a table, establishing a series of pre-specified relationships among tables, and extracting information from an existing database. These questions were considered low-level tasks. It was not necessary for the subjects to understand what a table is, what it means that two tables are related, or how the extraction of information might be useful. There were two essay questions, which asked the respondent to describe how various components of a database work together. It was necessary for an individual to have a conceptual understanding of how the entire program is structured, rather than simply a functional knowledge of how it operates. These two essay questions were considered high-level tasks.

Our research identified mental models using an approach similar to Santhanam and Sein's (1994), which had a reasonable degree of success with high inter-rater agreement. Subjects were asked to describe what they understood about the system, and the description was coded as predominantly (conceptual) mental model, predominantly procedures (procedural mental model), or undefined. The question administered was identical to Santhanam and Sein's, although changes in the coding scheme were necessary. A classification scheme was developed, which was intended to identify predominantly mental models or procedures. The coding scheme emphasized the distinction between a procedural focus, which explains "how-to-do-it," and a conceptual one, which describes "how-it-works." While some elaboration on this theme was necessary, the approach basically categorizes "how-to-do-it" answers as procedural, and "how-it-works" ones as conceptual.

Answers to the mental model question were also graded for completeness, based on the approach Santhanam and Sein used. Again, slight changes to the grading scheme were made for our subject domain. For the revised version of this answer key, a list of key aspects of database structure and function was prepared. Mental model completeness was evaluated based upon how many of these aspects were described correctly. Mental model and completeness were graded by one of the researchers first, and then by an independent reviewer. The classifications and scores of the two coders were then compared for inter-rater reliability, and any disagreements were settled through discussion.

Potential covariates were also captured, such as subjects' age, level of education, field of study, computer experience (in years), computer usage (in hours per day), self-reported computer skill, and computer self-efficacy. Self-efficacy was measured using the instrument developed by Compeau and Higgins (1995).

Results

Only 84 complete sets of data were obtained from the 92 subjects for various reasons such as corrupt files on floppy diskette and poor handwriting. Since incomplete sets were used in the examination of some hypotheses, the sample sizes varied and consistently exceeded 84. Before the hypothesis testing, analyses were performed to determine which variables should be included as covariates. As part of these analyses a correlation matrix was calculated (see Appendix). Education, experience, self-reported computer skill, and self-efficacy were all correlated with at least one dependent variable. Therefore, these variables were considered as covariates when the dependent variable with which they were correlated was being examined. However, since our sample size was small, only one covariate with the highest correlation with the dependent variable was included in each ANCOVA.

Chi-square tests were performed for Hypothesis 1(a). As illustrated in Table 1, there was a significant relationship between support medium (instruction vs. task support) and the type of mental model developed (Pearson's chi-square = 5.82, $P = 0.016$). Users of online task support were more likely to develop conceptual mental models than instructor-trained individuals. However, contrary to our expectation, subjects tended to develop procedural mental models irrespective of the support medium. Further chi-squared tests show that this tendency is particularly strong for instruction trainees ($p < 0.001$), but somewhat weaker for online task support users ($p = 0.093$). Therefore, there is partial support for Hypothesis 1(a).

Hypothesis 1(b) predicts the relationship between support medium and mental model completeness. This relationship was tested using ANOVA. The results show that users of online task support achieved a slightly higher score (4.72 vs. 4.56 on average on a 10-point scale), at a statistically insignificant level of $p = 0.781$ ($F = 0.077$). Therefore, although users of online task support were more

Table 1. Effect of support medium on mental model type

	Instruction	Task Support	Total
Conceptual	6 (14%)	16 (37%)	22 (26%)
Procedural	36 (86%)	27 (63%)	63 (74%)
Total	42 (100%)	43 (100%)	85 (100%)

Table 2. ANCOVA: Effect of mental model type on high-level tasks

Dependent Variable: High-Level Tasks					
Source	Sum of Squares	DF	Mean Square	F	Sig.
Corrected Model	392.8[a]	2	196.4	15.5	.000
Intercept	18.1	1	18.1	1.4	.238
Computer Skill	237.4	1	237.4	18.5	.000
Mental Model Type	153.8	1	153.8	12.0	.001
Error	999.6	78	12.8		
Total	7828.0	81			
Corrected Total	1392.4	80			
[a] R Squared = .282 (Adjusted R Squared = .264)					

likely to develop conceptual mental models, their models were not necessarily more complete than those of the instructor-trained users.

Hypothesis 2 was evaluated using ANCOVA, analyzing the relationship between mental model type and performance on both high- and low-level tasks separately. On high-level tasks, subjects with conceptual mental models outperformed those with procedural ones, at a statistically significant level of $p = 0.001$, with self-reported computer skill controlled for, as shown in Table 2. Subjects with conceptual mental models scored an average of 11.2 out of 20 on high-level tasks, compared to 8.1 by subjects with procedural mental models. These results offer strong support for Hypothesis 2. However, in case of low-level tasks, subjects with conceptual mental models appeared to have outperformed those with procedures on low-level tasks (6.19 vs. 5.76 on average), but this result is not statistically significant.

Hypothesis 3 examines the relationship between support medium and performance, and it was evaluated using ANCOVA for both high- and low-level tasks. For high-level tasks, the results summarized in Table 3 show that, with the covariate controlled for, the effect of the support medium was significant ($p = 0.022$). The online task support group's average score was 9.7 out of 20, while the instructor-trained group averaged only 7.8. On low-level tasks, the difference between the two groups is in the same direction as predicted, 6.2 out of 9 vs. 5.5. However, the result is not statistically significance ($p = 0.149$), with the covariate controlled for. Therefore, Hypothesis 3 was supported in the context of high-level tasks, but not low-level tasks.

Note that users of online task support were more likely to develop conceptual mental models (Hypothesis 1), which were associated with increased performance on high-level tasks (Hypothesis 2). Therefore, it is interesting to examine the degree to which the effect of support medium on high-level tasks can be explained by the development of conceptual mental model. Specifically, it is important to ask how much of the effect of support medium on high-level tasks is a direct effect, and how much of it is mediated by mental model type.

As illustrated in Table 3 previously, the independent variable, in this case support medium, does account for a significantly amount of variation in the dependent variable, high-level task. Meanwhile, the potential mediator (mental model type) also accounts for variation in high-level tasks (Table 2). Finally, Table 4 illustrates that the effect of support medium is no longer significant when the mediator is controlled for. These three results satisfy the three requirements to conclude that mediation is occurring (Baron & Kenny, 1986). In other words, mental model type does mediate the effect of support medium on high-level tasks.

By establishing mediation we can conclude that the increased performance on high-level tasks that is associated with the use of online task support is because of the group's tendency to develop conceptual mental models. In other words,

Table 3. ANCOVA: Effect of support medium on high-level tasks

Dependent Variable: High-Level Tasks					
Source	Sum of Squares	DF	Mean Square	F	Sig.
Corrected Model	325.1[a]	2	162.5	11.7	.000
Intercept	12.9	1	12.9	.9	.339
Computer Skill	286.4	1	286.4	20.5	.000
Support Medium	75.7	1	75.7	5.4	.022
Error	1213.0	87	13.9		
Total	8385.0	90			
Corrected Total	1538.1	89			
[a] R Squared = .211 (Adjusted R Squared = .193)					

Table 4. ANCOVA: Effect of support medium on high-level tasks mediated by mental model type

Dependent Variable: High-Level Tasks					
Source	Sum of Squares	DF	Mean Square	F	Sig.
Corrected Model	413.0[a]	3	137.7	10.8	.000
Intercept	4.3	1	4.3	.4	.564
Mental Model Type	122.5	1	122.5	9.6	.003
Computer Skill	245.4	1	245.4	19.2	.000
Support Medium	17.8	1	17.8	1.4	.242
Error	1023.3	80	12.8		
Total	7973.0	84			
Corrected Total	1436.3	83			
[a] R Squared = .288 (Adjusted R Squared = .261)					

online task support had little direct impact on performance, contrary to our expectation.

Hypothesis 4 investigates the relationship between mental model completeness and performance. Because the independent variable, mental model completeness, is in ratio form, regression was used to test the hypothesized relationships on both high- and low-level tasks. Table 5 shows that the relationship between mental model completeness and high-level task performance was significant at a level of $p < 0.001$. Again, the positive value of the standardized beta coefficient ($\beta = 0.453$) suggests that more complete mental models are associated with better performance on high-level tasks. Therefore, Hypothesis 4 is supported.

As illustrated in Table 6, the positive value of the standardized beta coefficient ($\beta = 0.296$) for mental model completeness indicates that low-level task scores increased with more complete mental models, as was predicted. The effect of

Table 5. Regression: Effect of mental model completeness on high-level tasks

Model	Unstandardized Coefficients		Standardized Coefficients		
	β	Std. Error	β	t	Sig.
(Constant)	-.638	1.533		-.416	.679
Mental Model Completeness	.682	.129	.453	5.304	.000
Computer Skill	1.936	.436	.379	4.438	.000
Dependent Variable: High Level Tasks					

Model	Sum of Squares	DF	Mean Square	F	Sig.
Regression	564.2	2	282.1	25.205	.000[a, b]
Residual	973.8	87	11.2		
Total	1538.1	89			
[a] Predictors: (Constant), Computer Skill, Mental Model Completeness					
[a] R Square = .367, Adjusted R Square = .352, and Std. error of the estimate = 3.35					

Table 6. Regression: Effect of mental model completeness on low-level tasks

Model	Unstandardized Coefficients		Standardized Coefficients		
	β	Std. Error	β	t	Sig.
(Constant)	2.043	1.353		1.509	.135
Mental Model Completeness	.242	.080	.296	3.018	.003
Education	-1.040	.593	-.173	-1.754	.083
Experience	.534	.221	.244	2.422	.018
Computer Skill	.609	.293	.210	2.081	.041
Dependent Variable: Low Level Tasks					

Model	Sum of Squares	DF	Mean Square	F	Sig.
Regression	112.8	4	28.2	7.353	.000[a, b]
Residual	302.9	79	3.8		
Total	415.7	83			
[a] Predictors: (Constant), Computer Skill, Mental Model Completeness, Education, and Experience					
[b] R Square = .271, Adjusted R Square = .234, and Std. Error of the estimate = 1.96					

mental model completeness was significant at a level of p = 0.003. These results offer strong support for Hypothesis 4.

To summarize the findings, users of online task support performed better or equally compared to instruction trainees. The underlying reason could be that support medium had a direct impact on the type of mental model developed, and that there was also a mediated relationship whereby support medium affected performance on high-level tasks through its effect on mental model development. There was no evidence of a relationship between support medium and low-level task performance; nor was mental model type significantly related to low-level task performance. However, mental model completeness was significantly related to performance on both low and high-level tasks.

Conclusion and Discussion

Summary of Results

Analysis revealed that the instruction group did not outperform the online task support group on any measure of performance, while the latter did significantly better on high-level tasks. Similarly, subjects with procedural mental models did not outperform those with conceptual ones on any tasks, but the latter group performed better on high-level tasks. Further tests revealed that the superior performance of online task support users could be explained by their increased tendency to develop conceptual mental models. Moreover, as a predictor, mental model completeness was very strongly related to performance on both low and high-level tasks.

Online task support was more likely to lead to the development of conceptual mental models than instructor-led training, although trainees in both conditions were more likely to learn procedures. It is interesting to note that the *abstract conceptual models* of Access featured in Task Advisor (the main online task support treatment) appeared to have helped the development of conceptual mental models, as they were referenced by a number of subjects in their answers. However, there was no significant difference in the completeness of the mental models developed by the two groups. It appears the type training and task support that a user receives does influence the user's knowledge organization and structure about the system, but does not determine the completeness of the knowledge.

Contributions and Implications

The most significant contribution of this research is evidence of the effectiveness of online task support, which is comparable to instructor-led training on every measure of performance and self-efficacy, and sometimes better. This finding is particularly significant when the following points are considered: (1) online task support can be much cheaper to provide than instructor-based training, especially when training large numbers of users and (2) online task support provides ongoing reinforcement of learning, and support in performance. Therefore, while class-room learning deteriorates over time, users of online task support would be expected to build upon initial understanding. Whereas this study found online task support to be equally effective as instruction after less than an hour of exposure, the observed differences could become even greater over time.

The second contribution of this research is an understanding of the underlying mechanism that contributes to the effectiveness of online task support. An increased tendency to develop conceptual mental models accounts for much of the advantage of online task support. This result suggests that it might be time to rethink the focus of online task support. Whereas wizards are typically designed to make complex tasks easy and transparent, this type of task support is also useful for developing conceptual understanding of the application. To our knowledge, this is the first study to examine the potential of wizards for both presenting and just-in-time delivering conceptual models.

This research also has implications for computer training, irrespective of the medium of delivery. For example, the considerable power of mental model completeness in predicting performance indicates that trainers should cover a comprehensive variety of topics, rather than a smaller number in greater detail. Moreover, this research strengthens the arguments of those who have suggested that conceptual training is preferable to procedural training (e.g., Borgman, 1986; Dayton, Gettys, & Unrein, 1989; Santhanam & Sein, 1994).

It is also important to realize that the advantage of online task support did not just materialize automatically. Users were not left alone to complete the task; instead, they were given written instruction to practice using online resources and the wizard type of task support in particular. Therefore, in practice users should be encouraged to use online resources, given the time, specific instruction, tangible learning objectives, incentives, and all necessary resources as in the case of formal classroom training.

Limitations

There are a number of limitations in this study that should be borne in mind when interpreting its results. First of all, a major shortcoming of this study is that the experimental design does not clearly separate the delivery method and content of training. It is assumed that most instructor-led training tends to focus on procedures according to Bullen and Bennett's survey (1996), and that online tasks support is inherently natural and conducive to developing conceptual models. However, in practice, instruction could emphasize conceptual models, and online task support could focus on procedures. A better alternative for future studies would be to have a two-by-two design based on the support medium (instructor vs. online) and content (conceptual models vs. procedures). Unfortunately, our single version of online task support (TA) made it infeasible in this study.

Secondly, there are several factors that limit the external validity of the results, as in other experimental research. For example, despite our best effort to model the best practice in industry with the most experienced professional trainer, it is possible that the performance of the instruction group had more to do with the limitations of the particular instructor than with the instruction method in general. The university student subjects were considerably younger and more educated than the general population, thus they are likely more comfortable with learning from online resources.

Furthermore, although it was clearly stated in our recruitment letter that only novices of Access were invited and no prize was mentioned, there was no guarantee that all participants were truly novices. We expected that the random assignment of subjects to experimental conditions would minimize any chance of bias in the results. Future studies could use a simple test to screen out non-qualifying subjects prior to the experiment or specifically target a known novice population only.

The artificiality of the experimental environment should also be borne in mind as another limitation. The online task support condition directed subjects to use support tools during the software orientation session, although use during task completion was discretionary. Ordinarily it is unlikely that learners would be given this type of direction to use online task support in the real world. Moreover, in an environment where such direction is not provided it is not clear that individuals will take advantage of the tools at their disposal during task completion. On the other hand, most instructors likely would freely use of wizards in their training sessions, as good instructors always use a variety of mechanisms. This constraint, while necessary for the experimental control, could have negatively affected the effectiveness of instructor-led training.

In conclusion, this study shows that online task support can lead to comparable or superior performance than instruction-based training. However, further studies are necessary to establish whether learners will be satisfied with online task support as an alternative to the classroom, and whether they will be confident that they have been sufficiently educated in the absence of structured classes with predefined curriculum. Answers to these questions will certainly be important to the development and adoption of online task support.

Acknowledgments

This research was supported by an operating grant from the Social Sciences and Humanities Research Council (SSHRC) of Canada to the first author when he was a faculty member at the University of Waterloo. The authors thank the associate editor and three anonymous reviewers for their detailed and constructive feedback on earlier versions of this paper.

References

Ausubel, D.P. (1968). *Educational psychology: A cognitive view*. NY: Holt, Reinhart, & Wilson.

Baron, R. M., & Kenny, D. A. (1986). The moderator-mediator variable distinction in social psychological research: Conceptual, strategic, and statistical considerations. *Journal of Personality and Social Psychology, 51*(6), 1173-1182.

Bastiens, T. J., Nijhof, W. J., Streumer, J. N., & Amba, H. J. (1997). Working and learning with electronic performance support systems: An effectiveness study. *International Journal of Training and Development, 1*(1), 73-78.

Borgman, C. L. (1986). The user's mental model of an information retrieval systems: An experiment on a prototype online catalog. *International Journal of Man-Machine Studies, 24*, 47-64.

Bullen, C., & Bennett, J. (1996). Groupware in practice: An interpretation of work experiences. In R. Kling (Ed.), *Computerization and controversy: Value conflicts and social choices* (2nd ed.). San Diego, CA: Academic Press.

Compeau, D. R., & Higgins, C. A. (1995). Application of social cognitive theory to training for computer skills. *Information Systems Research, 6*(2), 118-143.

Compeau, D. R., Olfman, L., Sein, M., & Webster, J. (1995). Issues and challenges in end-user training and learning. *Communications of the ACM, 38*(7), 24-26.

Cohen, J. (1960). A coefficient of agreement for nominal scales. *Educational and Psychological Measurement, 20,* 37-46.

Dayton, T., Gettys, C. F., & Unrein, J. T. (1989). Theoretical training and problem detection in a computerized database retrieval task. *International Journal of Man-Computer Studies, 30*(6), 619-637.

Eason, K. (1988). *Information technology and organizational change.* London: Taylor & Francis.

Gery, G. (1995). Attributes and behaviors of performance-centered systems. *Performance Improvement Quarterly, 8*(1), 47-92.

Hmelo, C. E. et al. (1999). The oncology thinking cap: Scaffolded use of simulation to learn clinical trial design. *Teaching and Learning on Medicine, 13*(3), 183-191.

Hudzina, M., Rowley, K., & Wager, W. (1996). Electronic performance support technology: Defining the domain. *Performance Improvement Quarterly, 9*(1), 36-48.

Johnson-Laird, P. N. (1980). Mental models in cognitive science. *Cognitive Science, 4,* 71-115.

Landis, J. R., & Koch, G. G. (1977). The measurement of observer agreement for categorical data. *Biometrics, 33,* 159-174.

Marion, C. (2002), Attributes of performance-centered systems: What can we learn from five years of EPSS/PCD competition award winners? *Technical Communication, 49*(4), 428-443.

Masumian, B. (2000). Electronic performance support and development for managers. *Journal of Interactive Instruction Development, 12*(3), 19-26.

Mayer, R. E. (1981). The psychology of how novices learn computer programming. *Computing Survey, 13,* 121-141.

Mayhew, D. J. (1992). *Principles and guidelines in software user interface design.* Englewood Cliffs, NJ: Prentice Hall.

Moore, J. L., & Orey, M. A. (2001). The implementation of an electronic support system for teachers: An examination of usage, performance, and attitudes. *Performance Improvement Quarterly, 14*(1), 26-56.

Norman, D. A. (1983). Some observations on mental models. In A. L. Stevens & D. Gentner (Eds.), *Mental models*. Hillsdale, NJ: Lawrence Erlbaum.

Santhanam, R., & Sein, M. K. (1994). Improving end-user proficiency: effects of conceptual training and nature of interaction. *Information Systems Research, 5*(4), 378-399.

Sein M. K., & Bostrom, R. P. (1989). Individual differences and conceptual models in training novice users. *Human-Computer Interaction, 4,* 197-229.

Sein, M. K., Bostrom, R. P., & Olfman, L. (1987). Conceptual models in training novice users. In *Proceedings of INTERACT '87, IFIP Conference on Human-Computer Interaction* (pp. 861-867).

Shneiderman, B. (1998). *Design the user interface: Strategies for effective human-computer interaction* (3rd ed.). Reading, MA: Addison Wesley Longman.

Endnotes

[1]   Interested readers may contact the first author to get a copy of various measures.

This article was previously published in the *Journal of Organizational and End User Computing, 17*(3), pp. 27-46, © 2005.

Appendix A

Correlation Matrix

	Age	EDU	EXP	Use	SKL	SE	SM	MMT	MMC	LL	HL
Age	1	.51*	.11	.37*	.03	.17	.11	.01	.08	.12	.03
Education (EDU)		1	.05	.41*	.11	.20	.08	.04	.17	.22	.16
Experience (EXP)			1	.09	.35*	.17	.07	.04	.02	.32*	.26*
Use				1	.36*	.06	.16	.03	.02	.04	.02
Skill (SKL)					1	.29*	.15	.01	.05	.27*	.38*
Self Efficacy (SE)						1	.02	.00	.15	.22*	.13
Support Medium (SM)							1	.26*	.03	.11	.15
Mental Model Type (MMT)								1	.30*	.11	.34*
Mental Model Completeness (MMC)									1	.38*	.47*
Low Level Task (LL)										1	.70*
High Level Task (HL)											1

* Significant at the level of p < .05

Section II:

End User Computing Software Issues and Trends

Chapter V

A Comparison of Audio-Conferencing and Computer Conferencing in a Dispersed Negotiation Setting: Efficiency Matters!

Abbas Foroughi, University of Southern Indiana, USA

William C. Perkins, Indiana University, USA

Leonard M. Jessup, Washington State University, USA

Abstract

The growing globalization of business is making face-to-face communications, decision-making, and negotiations more the exception than the rule. Internet communication in text-only, audio, and video form are all becoming feasible methods of communication between distantly located parties. However, in order for these new technologies to be used most effectively, more investigation is needed into the impact of various media on decision-making, such as that in negotiation. In particular, negotiators need to have a means of choosing the most appropriate communication medium, based on the amount of richness inherent in the medium, for the particular task at hand. This paper presents the results of an empirical study to examine the effectiveness of a computerized negotiation support system (NSS) in supporting bargaining carried out in a dispersed, but synchronous setting. In the study, pairs of college students, using the NSS, participated in a simulated industrial bargaining scenario that tested the impact of communication media employed and level of conflict on contract outcomes and negotiator attitudes. The subjects, located in separate rooms, played the roles of buyer and seller engaged in negotiations either by telephone (audio-conferencing) or Lotus Notes (computer conferencing). In both low and high conflict, the efficiency aspects of audio-conferencing — a richer medium in which more communication can take place more quickly — overshadowed any negative social cues transmitted.

Introduction

Business collaboration is now possible anywhere in real-time, making it location independent. This trend has brought the management of dispersed decision-making activities to the forefront as a crucial managerial function (Chidambaram & Jones, 1993). Dispersed meetings can now be facilitated by a variety of electronic communication media, such as audio-conferencing, video-conferencing, computer conferencing, and electronic mail. What is the impact of various types of electronic communication in different task environments? Previous communication research has already shown the dramatic effects that electronic media can have on communication in general (Bazerman & Carroll, 1987) and on mixed-motive tasks such as negotiation in particular (McGrath, 1984). Furthermore, the amount of richness inherent in a communication medium is also crucial to understanding its impact on negotiation outcomes (Daft & Lengel, 1986).

Purpose

This chapter presents the results of an experiment that examined the effectiveness of a computerized negotiation support system (NSS) in supporting bargaining carried out in a dispersed, but synchronous setting. The focus of the study was to determine the relative effectiveness of computer conferencing and audio-conferencing — two communication media varying significantly in media richness — when using an NSS in a dispersed setting. The results of the study shed light on the following questions:

1.   Which type of communication medium is more effective when using an NSS in a dispersed setting — computer conferencing or audio-conferencing?

2.   How does the amount of conflict involved in a negotiation impact the effectiveness of a communication medium when using an NSS in a dispersed setting?

The paper is organized as follows. The review of the literature related to this study is divided into three sections, with the first focusing on negotiation support systems, the second on the role of conflict level in negotiations, and the third on the role of media richness in negotiations. The research model that serves as a foundation for the present research is presented, followed by the hypotheses tested in the study, the research methodology, the statistical analysis and results, a discussion of the results, and finally the conclusions reached from the results of the study.

Negotiation Support Systems

Since first being used in the 1960s, computer support for negotiations has been employed in the form of stand-alone decision support systems, used to support either individual negotiators or both sides in a negotiation, and by various forms of electronic communication. NSSs are a category of group support systems (GSSs) designed especially to support decision-makers in non-cooperative, mixed-motive tasks. At a minimum, an NSS includes an individual decision support system (DSS) for each party in the negotiation plus an electronic communication channel between the parties (Lim & Benbasat, 1992-1993). Also suggested is the idea of a full-featured session-oriented NSS (Anson & Jelassi, 1990; Carmel et al., 1993; DeSanctis & Gallupe, 1987; Jelassi & Foroughi, 1989), which offers a structured negotiation process, DSS support, electronic communication, group process structuring techniques, support for a mediator, and documentation of the negotiation. Web-based NSSs are now under development that integrate negotiation software agents with elements of negotiation support systems to facilitate and enhance electronic negotiations (Kersten, 2003; Kersten, Law, & Strecker, 2004).

While DSSs enhance negotiators' information processing, analysis, and decision-making during a negotiation, the communication component of an NSS is meant to enhance communication between negotiators. This communication between negotiators can take many forms. In addition to traditional face-to-face settings (audio and visual), negotiations may be conducted using computer conferencing (text only), a decision room (text and visual), and telephone (audio only). The number of possible negotiation scenarios is growing as technology develops, with an increasing proportion of negotiations today being conducted by audio-conferencing, video-conferencing, or computer conferencing over the Internet.

The Role of Conflict Level in Negotiations

By definition, negotiation and bargaining are characterized by conflict. The intensity of the conflict, however, varies with each negotiation situation. Conflict has been discussed in terms of "level," "size," "degree," "amount," and "intensity." Bargaining research has revealed the importance of conflict intensity in determining the behavior of negotiators and the outcomes they achieve. The amount of conflict in a bargaining situation has been described as an extremely important, if not the most important, factor affecting both negotiator behavior and negotiation outcomes (Hiltrop & Rubin, 1981). For instance, bargainers in high conflict tend to engage in more competitive behavior, perform less effectively, and achieve poorer joint outcomes than those in low conflict (Deutsch, 1969; Rubin & Brown, 1975). Communication between bargainers, including holistic consideration of issues, idea identification, and role reversal, for example, is quite effective under conditions of low conflict, but these approaches have sometimes been found ineffective in a high conflict situation, decreasing the chances of successful conflict resolution (Rubin & Brown, 1975). More recent research, however, has indicated that communication and information exchange in bargaining situations increases the likelihood that bargainers will move from distributive outcomes to integrative, mutually beneficial outcomes (Clopton, 1984; Lindskold & Hans, 1988; Olekalns, Smith, & Walsh, 1996).

Several NSS empirical research studies have used level of conflict as an independent variable. Jones (1988) found that DSS support in the form of joint outcome-maximizing contract suggestions was beneficial for subjects in low conflict of interest treatments, but not for those in high conflict of interest treatments.

Sheffield (1995) manipulated conflict level by instructing some subjects to assume an individualistic bargaining orientation, in which they maximized their own outcome, while others were instructed to assume a cooperative bargaining orientation, in which they maximized joint outcome. The results of Sheffield's study showed that dyads who had been instructed to assume a cooperative bargaining orientation achieved greater joint outcomes than those instructed to assume an individualistic orientation. Cooperative dyads attained more insight into each other's profit tables, perceived the outcome of the negotiation as more profitable for both parties, and perceived the bargaining partner as having a less difficult disposition and as being a more credible source of information than themselves. Bargaining orientation also impacted the effectiveness of communication media. In the absence of visual communication, individualistic and cooperative bargainers achieved similar negotiation outcomes. When visual communication was present, cooperative bargainers maximized joint outcomes. However, for individualistic bargainers, the additional social cues inherent in visual communication increased bargainers' perception that their partner intended to dominate the negotiation, which reduced their motivation and their ability to pay attention to the negotiation process, and led to lower joint outcomes.

Two laboratory studies by Foroughi, Perkins, and Jelassi (1995) and Perkins, Hershauer, Foroughi, and Delaney (1996) operationalized conflict of interest by assigning weights to the issues in a four-issue engine subcomponent contract to create a low conflict of interest treatment, in which mutually beneficial trade-offs were possible, and a high conflict of interest treatment, in which issues for both parties were weighted similarly, creating a zero-sum situation. Both studies found strong evidence for the benefit of DSS support for alternative generation evaluation in both levels of conflict. The Foroughi, Perkins, and Jelassi study (1995) compared NSS-supported dyads to non-NSS dyads, crossed with low conflict of interest vs. high conflict of interest scenarios. They found that NSS-supported dyads achieved higher joint outcomes, greater contract balance, and greater satisfaction, but required longer negotiation time. No differences were found for number of contract proposals and perception of the collaborative climate, but NSS support led to less negative climate in the low conflict scenario. A second similar study by Perkins, Hershauer, Foroughi, and Delaney (1996) reduced the NSS to a stand-alone DSS and employed managers as subjects. As in the first study, the DSS users achieved significantly higher joint outcomes and contract balance in both levels of conflict. Surprisingly, DSS-supported managers took less time to reach agreement than non-supported managers.

The Role of Media Richness
in Negotiations

The increasing frequency of negotiations in dispersed settings has created an urgent need to determine which type of communication medium is appropriate for a given situation. Insight into the impact of various types of media is provided by media richness theory, which argues that the various communication media differ in richness. "Rich" communication media allow the transmission of a multiplicity of cues, provide immediate feedback, allow communication with both natural language and numbers, and facilitate the personal focus of messages (Daft & Lengel, 1986). Existing communication media can be viewed on a continuum of rich to lean, with face-to-face communication being the richest, followed by electronic meeting systems, video-conferencing, and audio-conferencing, with electronic mail, voice mail, and computer conferencing being the leanest (Kydd & Ferry, 1991).

In face-to-face communication, the richest communication medium, close physical proximity enables the communication of many different types of information — visual, aural, and nonverbal (Daft, Lengel, & Trevino, 1987). Negotiators are aware of each other's physical appearance, and they communicate through gestures, facial expressions, eye contact, and body movement. Negotiators communicate information aurally, through pitch, volume and quality of voice, speed of talking, and use of pauses, filler words, and laughter (Baird & Wieting, 1979). Video-conferencing, which links negotiators with televised images of each other's head and shoulders, enables fewer information cues to pass between them. The impact of physical proximity is lost, gestures and postures are not communicated (Drolet & Morris, 1995), real eye contact is not possible (Rose & Clark, 1995), and aural cues are often not communicated. The audio-conferencing mode is often used for negotiations in dispersed settings. Telephone communication is less rich than face-to-face or video-conferencing, because visual clues such as facial expressions, movement, body language, and the impact of physical proximity are not conveyed between negotiators. Aural cues from verbal and nonverbal vocal sounds, such as those possible in face-to-face communication, are available, however. Further down still on the media richness continuum is computer-mediated communication (computer conferencing), which conveys text messages between negotiators, synchronously or asynchronously. Richness is limited to text communication alone, and aural and visual cues are nonexistent.

Daft and Lengel (1986) suggest that organizational decision-making could be improved by matching the decision-making task at hand with the communication medium that best fits the needs and purpose of the task. Equivocality resolution, the basic task in a negotiation, involves the complex task of arriving at a shared meaning of, or agreement on, information. Because a communication medium's richness determines the amount of information it conveys (Poole, Shannon, & DeSanctis, 1992), richness or leanness can impact significantly on the process and outcome of a negotiation (Purdy, Nye, & Balakrishnan, 2000). Because facial and vocal cues may account for more than 90 percent of a message's meaning, negotiators using leaner media may experience a lack of commonality of meaning necessary for successful negotiation (Mehrabian, 1971). The more limited amount and type of information communicated by leaner media can result in a depersonalized, anonymous negotiation environment (Straus & McGrath, 1994) that impacts the rapport between negotiators (Drolet & Morris, 1995), the frequency of impasses experienced (Moore, Kurtzberg, Thompson, & Morris, 1999), and the negotiators' perceptions of power and influence (Hollingshead, 1996).

Communication medium has been used as an independent variable in several NSS laboratory studies. Sheffield (1995) compared the impact of four different communication media — computer conferencing (text only), decision room (text and visual), telephone (audio only), and face-to-face (audio and visual) on negotiator behavior in a bilateral monopoly task, in integrative as well as in distributive bargaining scenarios. This research concentrated on the efficiency (speed of processing information to reach a solution) and the richness (social and emotional information) of the various types of communication media. A cooperative bargaining orientation and/or audio mode of communication led to higher joint outcomes. The results indicated that, for bilateral negotiations, the audio mode was more efficient than the text mode. Richer media helped bargainers reach higher joint outcomes in integrative bargaining settings. However, in distributive situations when trade-offs are not so obvious, the socio-emotional content of the communication that is possible with richer media increased tension and distracted bargainers from their task. Sheffield concluded that decision room settings are more appropriate for more cooperative bargaining, while computer conferencing may be more useful for more distributive negotiation situations.

In an extension of the Foroughi, Perkins, and Jelassi study (1995) described earlier, Delaney, Foroughi, and Perkins (1997) compared the effects of a DSS used in combination with electronic communication with those of DSS support alone. An interactive DSS was used for alternative generation and evaluation. Face-to-face communication was compared to electronic communication between bargainers for inputting their comments and proposals and viewing each other's inputs on a public screen. In both conditions the NSS featured a structured integrative bargaining process, guided by a facilitator, which included a statement of interests, role reversal, searching for common ground, generation and analysis of alternative solutions, and reaching an agreement. The DSS alone brought higher joint outcomes and more balanced contracts, but satisfaction was higher in both low and high levels of conflict with electronic communication.

In a study by Rangaswamy and Shell (1997), pairs of bargainers used NEGO-TIATION ASSISTANT, which employs an Internet connection to link the two parties electronically and provides a DSS which incorporates conjoint analysis to help negotiators prepare for the negotiation by determining their preferences for different settlement options. The study compared four types of communication — face-to-face, e-mail only, DSS used only for preparation, and DSS plus electronic exchange of contract offers and messages during the negotiation (i.e., an NSS). Results showed that the negotiation process was perceived as friendlier for dyads in face-to-face treatments. In a few cases, dyads that communicated electronically failed to reach an agreement, whereas all face-to-face dyads did reach agreements. The researchers concluded that when there is little room for making an integrative agreement, the impersonal quality of electronic communication has the potential to increase tensions, sometimes so much that negotiators reach an impasse and never reach agreement. They found no advantages in electronic communication (e-mail treatment) by itself over simple face-to-face bargaining. The edge for bargainers came, instead, from the structured negotiation preparation process in the DSS and NSS conditions.

Purdy, Nye, and Balakrishnan (2000) compared the impact of four different communication media — face-to-face, video-conferencing, telephone, and computer-mediated communication (computer conferencing) — on objective negotiation outcomes (negotiation time, joint outcomes, and profit inequality) and subjective negotiation outcomes (outcome satisfaction and desire for future negotiation interaction). Subjects, assuming the role of retail store buyer or manufacturer's representative, negotiated a three-attribute sales contract for a men's clothing line. Dyads who bargained integratively could achieve a maximum payoff of $52 million each, and those who bargained distributively could achieve a payoff of $40 million each. Results showed that, although face-to-face negotiators did not achieve higher joint outcomes, they collaborated more, achieved more time efficiency than those using leaner media, and expressed greater desire for future negotiation interaction. Subjects who used richer media achieved greater profit equality in less time. Greater media richness increased satisfaction indirectly by increasing the intent to collaborate and by reducing time to achieve a given profit. The impact of video-conferencing was found to be similar to that of face-to-face communication, in contrast to that of the leaner media — telephone and computer-mediated communication.

As the previous discussion shows, NSS research findings about the role of media richness on negotiation outcomes are somewhat inconsistent. However, in most of the studies, joint outcomes and contract balance were better with richer media. Richer media improved negotiation time and, except for one study, also increased perceptions of satisfaction and positive atmosphere in the negotiation. Interestingly, in one study (Sheffield, 1995), face-to-face communication increased tension in a distributive (high conflict) setting, while Rangaswamy and Shell (1997) found the leanness of computer-mediated communication to be too impersonal in a high-conflict negotiation situation.

Considering the growing frequency of negotiation in dispersed settings, NSS research focused on the use of various communication media is very sparse. The present research will shed more light on the role of media richness in negotiations. It will build on the Delaney, Foroughi, and Perkins study (1997), using the same task, setting, and decision support system, but providing communication in the form of audio-conferencing and computer conferencing. The present study will provide a more comprehensive comparison of these two modes of communication than prior studies, considering two levels of conflict and employing a more complex and more realistic negotiation scenario than prior studies.

Research Framework

The framework for NSS research that serves as the foundation for the present study (see Figure 1) has been adapted from an integrated research framework developed by Dennis et al. (1988). The Dennis et al. framework integrates other causal models that have been used for the study of group processes and outcomes (i.e., McGrath, 1984; Kraemer & King, 1986; DeSanctis & Gallupe, 1987). The framework for NSS research identifies six classes of variables that should be considered in empirical NSS studies. How these variables were operationalized in the present study is described in the discussion to follow (see Figure 1).

Group Variables

Characteristics of the groups and individuals were all controlled. The study used only dyads with zero history of previous negotiating together, and the negotiations were one-time only. All dyads negotiated in a dispersed situation. Subjects were assigned randomly to pairs and to roles within pairs, and pairs were assigned randomly to experimental conditions; gender differences were controlled by assigning subjects to bargain with members of the same sex.

Figure 1. Framework for NSS research

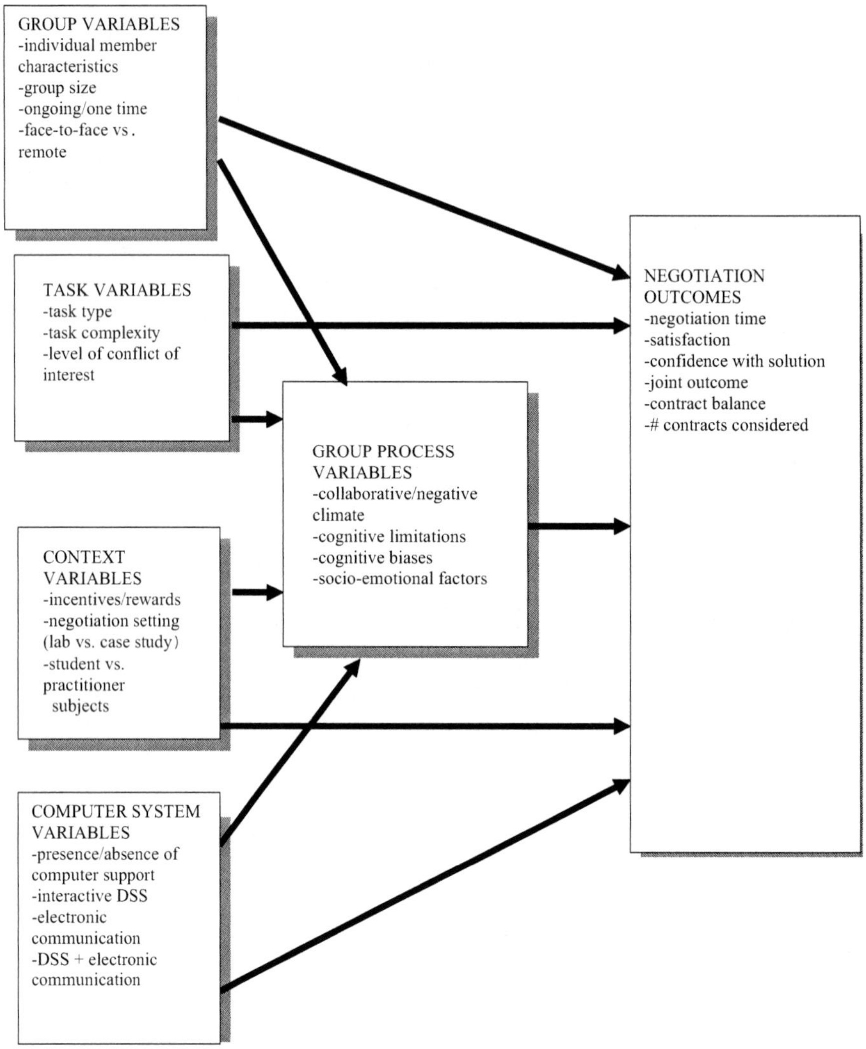

GROUP VARIABLES
-individual member
characteristics
-group size
-ongoing/one time
-face-to-face vs.
remote

TASK VARIABLES
-task type
-task complexity
-level of conflict of
interest

CONTEXT
VARIABLES
-incentives/rewards
-negotiation setting
(lab vs. case study)
-student vs.
practitioner
subjects

COMPUTER SYSTEM
VARIABLES
-presence/absence of
computer support
-interactive DSS
-electronic
communication
-DSS + electronic
communication

GROUP PROCESS
VARIABLES
-collaborative/negative
climate
-cognitive limitations
-cognitive biases
-socio-emotional factors

NEGOTIATION
OUTCOMES
-negotiation time
-satisfaction
-confidence with solution
-joint outcome
-contract balance
-# contracts considered

Adapted from Dennis et al. (1988)

Task Variables

The study used a mixed-motive task (McGrath, 1984), in which group members must resolve conflicts of interest. Pairs of bargainers resolved a manufacturing bargaining problem involving negotiation of four issues of a three-year purchase agreement for an engine subcomponent. The amount of conflict of interest between the bargainers was manipulated to create high and low conflict situations. Equal weights were assigned to the negotiation issues in the high conflict condition to create a win-lose, conflict-laden situation. Different weights were assigned to the issues in the low conflict condition, so that there was room for trade-offs and a win-win solution beneficial for both sides was easier to achieve.

Context Variables

Context variables were controlled. All subjects were chosen from the multiple sections of the same School of Business course, with experimentation taking place in the same three small rooms in the same behavioral laboratory. All subjects were given the incentive of earning class credit for participation in the study; they were also given a chance to win a monetary reward presented to the dyads with the highest joint outcomes in each condition at the end of the study.

Computer System Variables

Communication medium was used as an independent variable. Computer conferencing treatments featured communication using Lotus Notes on personal computers connected via a local area network. Audio-conferencing treatments featured communication via telephone lines. All other computer system variables were controlled, with subjects using the same type of decision support software for alternative generation and evaluation.

Group Process Variables

Several group process variables were controlled. All experimental bargaining conditions were supported by a human mediator and were one-time sessions, and all used the same structured, integrative bargaining process.

Negotiation Outcome Variables

Outcome measures of several dependent variables were collected. Objective outcomes included joint outcome, contract balance, negotiation time, and number of alternative contracts proposed. Subjective outcomes included post-bargaining measures of negotiator satisfaction, the amount of negative climate (suspiciousness, inflexibility, difficulty of resolution), and the amount of collaborative climate (cooperativeness and consideration) perceived by the negotiators.

Hypotheses

The hypotheses examined in the present study are listed next. After each grouping of hypotheses is presented, the rationale for the hypotheses, including the relevant literature, is provided.

Joint Outcomes

H1: In the low conflict treatments, there will be no significant difference between the joint outcomes achieved by dyads using audio-conferencing and dyads using computer conferencing.

H2: In the high conflict treatments, dyads using audio-conferencing will achieve higher joint outcomes than dyads using computer conferencing.

In the low conflict treatments, mutually beneficial trade-offs are relatively easy for the bargainers to achieve. The benefits of the additional information exchange possible with audio-conferencing as compared to the leaner computer conferencing mode should not make a significant difference on joint outcomes. In contrast, the high conflict treatments presented a negotiation task that was more difficult for the bargainers, in which one party's gain was essentially equal to the other's loss. The richer medium of audio-conferencing should enable bargainers to engage in the "give and take" that is necessary for reaching a negotiation solution. The support for collaborative problem-solving behaviors should enhance the bargainers' discovery of a mutually acceptable negotiation solution that matches their expectations and maximizes high joint outcomes (Pruitt & Carnevale, 1993). Thus, for high conflict treatments, audio-conferencing dyads should achieve higher joint outcomes than dyads using computing conferencing.

Several empirical studies have provided evidence of the positive relationship between media richness and integrativeness in a negotiation (Drolet & Morris, 1995; Morley & Stephenson, 1997; Williams, 1977). Compared to audio-conferencing, computer conferencing lacks social context cues that would help convey the meaning of messages (Rice & Love, 1987; Sproull & Kiesler, 1986). The leaner computer conferencing would tend to make negotiators in high conflict feel frustrated and alone in their task, a type of social anonymity that can encourage uninhibited behavior (Kiesler, Siegel, & McGuire, 1984) and less cooperation, and often leads to impasses in contexts with little integrative potential (Rangaswamy & Shell, 1997). With computer conferencing, bargainers show less accuracy in judging bargaining partners' interests, often obtaining lower, more unequally distributed joint outcomes (Arunachalam & Dilla, 1995; Eliashberg, Rangaswamy, & Balakrishnan, 1987).

Contract Balance

H3: In the low conflict treatments, there will be no significant difference between the contract balance achieved by dyads using audio-conferencing and dyads using computer conferencing.

H4: In the high conflict treatments, dyads using audio-conferencing will achieve more balanced contracts than dyads using computer conferencing.

In the low conflict treatments, as described earlier, mutually beneficial trade-offs are relatively easy for the bargainers to achieve. Therefore, just as for joint outcomes, the richer audio-conferencing mode should not make a significant difference on contract balance. However, because the high conflict treatments presented a zero-sum situation, the richer medium of audio-conferencing should better facilitate the bargainers' engagement in the "give and take" integrative behavior that is necessary for reaching a mutually agreeable result with balance in the joint outcomes achieved. The social cues conveyed through audio-conferencing should tend to motivate negotiators away from trying to divide the pie to their own advantage (Kiesler, Kiesler, & Pallak, 1967). Previous studies have shown that the lack of social cues and the social isolation of bargainers in computer conferencing often result in less contract balance, in addition to lower joint outcomes (Arunachalam & Dilla, 1995; Eliashberg, Rangaswamy, & Balakrishnan, 1987).

Negotiation Time

H5: In both low and high conflict treatments, dyads using audio-conferencing will have shorter negotiation times than those using computer conferencing.

Less information can be conveyed in a given amount of time with the text-based exchanges of computer conferencing as compared to the aural exchanges of audio-conferencing (Heid, 1997). Negotiators who use computer conferencing tend to use fewer words, but inputting them into text form takes a longer time than aural communication (Sheffield, 1995). Computer conferencing also increases the amount of time needed to understand the structure of a negotiation task

(Sheffield, 1995). The inefficiency of computer-mediated communication compared to aural communication is thus expected to yield increased negotiation times for both low and high levels of conflict.

Number of Contracts Proposed

H6: In both low and high conflict treatments, dyads using audio-conferencing will propose more contracts than those using computer conferencing.

As argued previously, the spoken word is faster than typing and aural communication enables negotiators to understand the negotiation task faster and interact more efficiently. For these reasons, audio-conferencing is expected to facilitate the conveyance of more proposed contracts than computer conferencing.

Collaborative Climate

H7: In the low conflict treatments, there will be no significant difference between perceived collaborative climate for dyads using audio-conferencing and dyads using computer conferencing.

H8: In the high conflict treatments, perceived collaborative climate will be higher for dyads using audio-conferencing than for those using computer conferencing.

Negative Climate

H9: In the low conflict treatments, there will be no significant difference between perceived negative climate for dyads using audio-conferencing and dyads using computer conferencing.

H10: In the high conflict treatments, perceived negative climate will be less for dyads using audio-conferencing than for those using computer conferencing.

Satisfaction

H11: In the low conflict treatments, there will be no significant difference in satisfaction for dyads using audio-conferencing and dyads using computer conferencing.

H12: In the high conflict treatments, satisfaction will be greater for dyads using audio-conferencing than for those using computer conferencing.

Because low conflict dyads will encounter a minimal amount of conflict in their task, the wider range of information conveyed through the richer audio-conferencing medium, compared to the leaner computer conferencing medium, should not make a significant difference on collaborative climate, negative climate, and satisfaction in low conflict treatments.

In high conflict, however, audio-conferencing is expected to be more beneficial to the negotiation process by enabling bargainers to interact more fully and engage in fruitful problem solving (Kydd & Ferry, 1991). In turn, the outcome measures are expected to be more favorable for audio-conferencing, which also impacts the attitude measures. Thus, in high conflict, audio-conferencing is expected to result in greater collaborative climate, less negative climate, and more satisfaction than in the computer conferencing mode.

Research Methodology

Research Design

The research design included two independent variables (level of conflict and type of communication media), each with two treatments (high or low conflict, computer conferencing or audio-conferencing), thus necessitating a two-by-two random factorial design (CRF-22) with fixed-effects.

Figure 2. Audio-conferencing and computer conferencing

Audio-Conferencing: Bargainers communicated via telephone connections. Each had an individual decision support system to use for alternative generation and evaluation.

Computer Conferencing: Bargainers communicated on personal computers via Lotus Notes. Each had an individual support system to use for alternative generation and evaluation.

Independent Variables

Level of Conflict of Interest

Bargaining research has revealed the importance of the amount of conflict of interest inherent in a negotiation situation as a determinant of negotiator behavior as well as of the outcomes achieved (Rubin & Brown, 1975). Level of conflict of interest was chosen as an independent variable for this study in order to examine the effectiveness of an NSS in two different bargaining situations (low and high conflict of interest). These two treatments represent two extremes of conflict of interest that are encountered in real-world negotiation situations.

The bargaining task chosen for this research involved negotiation between a buyer and a seller over four issues of a three-year purchase agreement for an engine subcomponent (Jones, 1988). The issues were unit price, purchase quantity, time of first delivery, and warranty period. Low conflict treatments were simulated by assigning different weights to the issues, creating a bargaining situation in which mutually beneficial trade-offs were possible between the buyer and the seller. In the high conflict treatments, issues for both parties were weighted similarly, creating a zero-sum situation in which one party's gain was equal to the other one's loss. For both low and high conflict levels, point sheets of outcomes were constructed for buyer and seller using these weights (see Appendices A and B).

Communication Medium

Two types of communication media were used in the study — computer conferencing and audio-conferencing (see Figure 2). In the computer conferencing treatments, bargainers were located in two different rooms, so that visual and verbal communications were not possible. They communicated by using personal computers (PCs) connected via a local area network (LAN) using Lotus Notes. A three-PC computer conferencing system was designed on a LAN so that the negotiators could communicate with each other in real-time from their own PCs and the experimenter (acting as a mediator) could monitor the communication and intervene when necessary from the experimenter's PC[1]. Lotus Notes was used as the vehicle for computer conferencing. During the computer conferencing, the negotiators identified themselves as the buyer (Roberts) or seller (Simo) before giving input so that the experimenter could follow the online conversation.

In the audio-conferencing treatments, subjects were also in different rooms, but these bargainers communicated via telephone lines, and the experimenter could also monitor and intervene when necessary from a third telephone instrument on the same line. During the telephone-mediated communication, negotiators also identified themselves as buyer (Roberts) or seller (Simo) before giving input so that the experimenter could follow the conversation. The experimenter always identified himself (orally in audio-conferencing, in text in computer conferencing) before giving any instructions to the bargainers.

In both computer conferencing and audio-conferencing treatments, each bargainer was provided with a Negotiation Decision Support Tool (NDST), the DSS that was developed for use in this series of NSS studies to support alternative generation and evaluation. The NDST consisted of a spreadsheet with two windows, running on a stand-alone microcomputer. Window #1, the Decision Tool, was used by negotiators to input their own priorities for the issues as well as their perception of the other party's priorities based on what they learned about the other party during the statement-of-interests stage of negotiation. Based on the priorities input by the subjects, the Decision Tool estimated the point structure of the other party, generated all the possible contract alternatives (748 altogether), and ranked them in descending order according to the joint outcome they would give. The Decision Tool then displayed — for the user only

— the three contract alternatives that would give the highest joint outcome. The Decision Tool was designed to display only these three contract alternatives in order to avoid the possibility of information overload that might result from displaying too many contract options. Window #2 contained a Contract Point Evaluator, which was used for alternative evaluation. It incorporated the complete point structure of the negotiator. The negotiator plugged in alternative contracts, and the algorithm determined the total score (for the user only) that could be achieved with each one.

Dependent Variables

Joint outcome was measured by adding buyer and seller points on the final agreement. *Contract balance* was the absolute value of the difference between the outcomes of the two bargainers in each negotiating pair. *Negotiation time* was measured as the time needed to reach an agreement or deadlock, with no time limit placed on negotiators for reaching an agreement. The *number of contracts proposed* was determined from the computer records in the computer conferencing treatments; in the audio treatments, the experimenter used a third telephone instrument on the same line to listen to and record the number of contracts offered.

Post-bargaining negotiator attitudes (perceived collaborative climate, perceived negative climate, and satisfaction) were measured by a questionnaire administered at the end of the bargaining session. The subjects responded to each item in the questionnaire by circling a number from 1 to 7 on a 7-point Likert scale. Based on factor analysis on the questionnaire data collected in the initial study in this program of research (Foroughi, Perkins, & Jelassi, 1995), the items were condensed into a set of three factors that we have named perceived collaborative climate, perceived negative climate, and satisfaction. Davis' Technology Acceptance Model questionnaire (1985) was also administered to measure overall evaluation, perceived ease of use, and perceived usefulness of computer conferencing or audio-conferencing and the DSS.

Control Variables

Group structure was controlled, with each negotiating side consisting of one person, and with each person in the dyad having zero history in negotiating with the other. Subjects were randomly assigned to the role of buyer or seller and to dyads, and dyads were randomly assigned to experimental treatments. The same task type was performed by all treatment dyads, with the only difference being the assigned weights to the issues. The physical environment was essentially the same for all treatment dyads, with each bargainer located in a separate room and supplied with an individual DSS. The only difference was in the communication medium, computer conferencing or audio-conferencing, that was used.

Experimental Procedures

This experiment was conducted during the spring semester, using three small adjacent rooms in a behavioral laboratory in a School of Business building, with communication provided via telephone lines or a data communications network (LAN). During the experiment, the experimenter was in the middle room directing and monitoring the negotiators, who were junior or senior students majoring in information systems or accounting. The two negotiators were located in the rooms on either side of the experimenter, entering their individual rooms before the beginning of the experiment and leaving the rooms only after completing the post-bargaining questionnaires.

The experiment was conducted in three phases. During Phase 1, subjects filled out a consent form and were given a printed outline of the procedures for the entire experiment and a listing of the rules to be observed. Next, subjects were assigned randomly to the role of buyer or seller, to an experimental treatment, and to a room from which they would negotiate. They were given a 10-minute training session on the use of the communication medium to which they had been assigned. Then they were given the case materials and a page of confidential information about their company. After these materials had been read by the subjects, they were given point sheets for their respective companies. Next, subjects completed a Point Sheet Exercise in which they were asked to add up the points for each issue of the alternative ("third party") contract and verify that the score given at the bottom of the point sheet was correct. This was done to make sure that the subjects understood the task. At this time, ten minutes of software training on the NDST was given to all dyads. Subjects then filled out a pre-negotiation questionnaire that provided demographic information about themselves as well as information about their typing ability, experience with Lotus Notes, and experience with computers.

During Phase 2, subjects were given a final instructions sheet with an outline of the negotiation process. They then proceeded to negotiate, beginning with a statement-of-interests phase to share what factors were important to each party. Each negotiator stated which of the four issues — unit price, purchase quantity, time of first delivery, and warranty period — were most important to the company that he or she represented. When an agreement was reached, they signed a final agreement form.

During Phase 3, all subjects answered a post-bargaining attitude questionnaire, as well as Davis' Technology Acceptance Model questionnaire.

Subjects

One hundred and twenty eight student volunteers from an undergraduate information systems course (all information systems and accounting majors) at a large Midwestern university served as subjects for this experiment. All of the subjects had used e-mail before, making it easy for them to master the use of the computer conferencing software in the 10-minute training session. In addition, all these students had used Microsoft Excel in their classes, making it easy for them to learn how to use the NDST, which was itself an easy-to-use Microsoft Excel-based tool, in the ten-minute training session. Furthermore, the NDST had been successfully used in three previous studies (Foroughi, Perkins, & Jelassi, 1995; Perkins, Hershauer, Foroughi, & Delaney, 1996; Delaney, Foroughi, & Perkins, 1997) and had received a favorable technology evaluation in each of these studies. To provide an incentive for subjects to participate and to perform well, course credit was offered to all participants and a monetary reward ($100) was given to the top pair of bargainers (in terms of joint outcome) in each of the four experimental cells.

Task

The bargaining task used in this study involved negotiation between a buyer and seller over four issues of a three-year purchase agreement for an engine subcomponent. The issues were unit price, purchase quantity, time of first delivery, and warranty period. Low conflict treatments were simulated by assigning different weights to the issues, creating a bargaining situation in which mutually beneficial trade-offs were possible. High conflict treatments featured issues for both parties being weighted similarly, creating a distributive bargaining, zero-sum situation in which one party's gain was essentially equal to the other one's loss.

Statistical Analysis and Results

The SPSS statistical package was used to perform statistical analysis of the experimental results, using a fixed-effects two-way analysis of variance (2-way ANOVA) model for *joint outcome, contract balance, negotiation time, number*

Table 1. Hypotheses and results (sample size: four cells, 16 dyads per cell, total of 64 dyads, total of 128 subjects)

Hypothesis	Mean Audio-conferencing	Mean Computer Conferencing	Level of Significance (p)	Hypothesis Supported
Joint outcome				
H1: low audio = low computer	128.75	129.00	N.S.	YES
H2: high audio > high computer	101.50	99.88	p<.005	YES
Contract balance				
H3: low audio = low computer	8.00	10.63	N.S.	YES
H4: high audio > high computer	4.38	4.88	N.S.	NO
Negotiation time				
H5.1: low audio < low computer	20.31	43.75	p<.005	YES
H5.2: high audio < high computer	30.31	57.13	p<.005	YES
Number of contracts proposed				
H6.1: low audio > low computer	3.81	6.00	p<.02	NO
H6.2: high audio > high computer	13.13	9.81	N.S.	NO
Perceived collaborative climate				
H7: low audio = low computer	6.02	5.64	p<.05	NO
H8: high audio > high computer	5.69	5.57	N.S.	NO
Perceived negative climate				
H9: low audio = low computer	2.51	3.13	p<.10	NO
H10: high audio <high computer	3.04	3.19	N.S.	NO
Satisfaction				
H11: low audio = low computer	5.83	5.50	p<.07	NO
H12: high audio >high computer	5.06	5.16	N.S.	NO

of alternatives, and *post-bargaining negotiator attitudes*. See Table 1 for a summary of these results. t-tests were used to analyze the results of the technology evaluation questionnaire; these results are reported in the text but not in tabular form.

Joint Outcomes

No significant difference was found between joint outcomes for audio-conferencing and computer conferencing in low conflict, but joint outcomes for audio-conferencing were significantly higher in high conflict. Both hypothesis H1 and hypothesis H2 were supported.

Contract Balance

No significant difference was found between contract balance for audio-conferencing and computer conferencing in low conflict, thus supporting hypothesis H3. No significant difference was found between contract balance for audio-conferencing and computer conferencing in high conflict, and thus hypothesis H4 was not supported. However, although not statistically significant, the results do indicate better contract balance for audio-conferencing dyads than for computer conferencing dyads.

Negotiation Time

Negotiation time was significantly greater for computer conferencing dyads at both low and high conflict levels. Hypothesis H5 was supported.

Number of Alternatives

In low conflict dyads, significantly more alternatives were generated with computer conferencing than with audio-conferencing. In high conflict dyads, there was no difference in the number of alternatives generated with audio-conferencing and with computer conferencing. Hypothesis H6 was not supported.

Collaborative Climate

Perceived collaborative climate was significantly lower for computer conferencing dyads than for audio-conferencing dyads in low conflict, and there was no difference in collaborative climate for the two communication media in high conflict. Neither hypothesis H7 nor hypothesis H8 was supported.

Negative Climate

In low conflict dyads, there was a significantly greater amount of negative climate for computer conferencing dyads than for audio-conferencing dyads, whereas in high conflict dyads there was no significant difference in the amount of negative climate for the two communication media. Again, neither hypothesis H9 nor hypothesis H10 was supported.

Satisfaction

In low conflict dyads, satisfaction was significantly lower for computer conferencing dyads than for audio-conferencing dyads, whereas in high conflict there was no difference in the amount of satisfaction for the two communication media. Again, neither hypothesis H11 nor hypothesis H12 was supported.

DSS Evaluation

In terms of evaluating the DSS using the technology acceptance model, the means for both low and high conflict treatments in both computer conferencing and audio-conferencing were all above the midpoint (4.0) on the Likert scale (in fact, all means were above 5.0), indicating a favorable evaluation of the DSS under all conditions. In both low and high conflict treatments, the DSS was rated as having higher perceived usefulness by the audio-conferencing dyads than by the computer conferencing dyads ($p < 0.005$ for low conflict, $p < 0.03$ for high conflict). There was no difference across communication media in terms of overall evaluation and ease of use of the DSS.

Communication Media

In terms of evaluating the communication media using the technology acceptance model, the means for both low and high conflict treatments in both computer conferencing and audio-conferencing were all above the midpoint (4.0) on the Likert scale, indicating a favorable evaluation of the communication media under all conditions. In low conflict dyads, audio-conferencing was rated as having higher perceived usefulness than computer conferencing ($p < 0.05$), whereas in high conflict dyads there was no difference in perceived usefulness ratings for the two communication media. There was no difference across communication media in terms of overall evaluation and ease of use of the media.

Discussion

The hypotheses had predicted that audio-conferencing would enhance negotiation outcomes and attitudes in high conflict treatments, and this was partially substantiated by the results. Audio-conferencing was shown to help high conflict dyads achieve *greater* joint outcomes than did computer conferencing. While contract balance in high conflict was better with audio-conferencing than with computer conferencing, the difference was not statistically significant. Surprisingly, audio-conferencing did not increase the number of alternative contracts proposed in high conflict. There were no differences between the two communication media in terms of perceived collaborative climate, perceived negative climate, and satisfaction. In summary, audio-conferencing *did* enhance negotiation results and *did not* negatively impact attitudes in high conflict. The key result is that joint outcomes were higher with audio-conferencing. As expected, negotiation time was greater with computer conferencing than with audio-conferencing.

In the low conflict treatments, it was expected that there would be no differences between the two communication modes except for the negotiation time (expected to be greater for computer conferencing) and the number of contracts proposed (expected to be greater for audio-conferencing). These expectations held true for joint outcome, contract balance, and negotiation time, but not for number of contracts proposed or for the attitude measures (collaborative climate, negative climate, satisfaction). These are very interesting results; when there is little conflict, it appears as though computer conferencing (e.g., the mechanics of using the system and the impersonality of communicating via the computer) just got in the way, while the audio-conferencing let the bargainers get the job done quickly and easily. Or, to phrase this conclusion another way, *efficiency matters* to the bargainers! They were able to achieve outcomes that were just as good, with less time and fewer proposed contracts, with audio-conferencing, and thus their attitudes towards audio-conferencing were more favorable than towards computer conferencing.

This same "efficiency matters" argument also applies to the high conflict results. Here the bargaining task was much more difficult, and it was possible that the transmission of negative social cues via audio-conferencing might result in less favorable outcomes and attitudes. But it appears as though the efficiency aspects of audio-conferencing — a richer medium in which more communication can take place more quickly (people can speak faster than they can type) — overshadowed any negative social cues transmitted. The result was improved joint outcomes, using less negotiation time, with audio-conferencing, and no significant differences in the attitude measures.

Of course, there is more than one possible explanation for the poor showing of computer conferencing. For example, the results may be explained by the novelty of the communications software and the fact that this was a "one-shot" performance. Subjects in computer conferencing dyads used two types of software (the DSS and Lotus Notes) for the first time. The novelty of both may have combined to hamper their potential performance in the negotiation as opposed to the audio-conferencing dyads, which also used the unfamiliar DSS but communicated over the telephone, a familiar means of communication. The implication of these results is that longitudinal testing of computer conferencing versus audio-conferencing might provide a more accurate comparison of the two communication media. Such testing would overcome the "novelty effect," if any, of both the DSS and computer conferencing.

Conclusion

The results of this study — as well as earlier studies by Sheffield (1995), Rangaswamy and Shell (1997), and Purdy, Nye, and Balakrishnan (2000) — tend to provide support for media richness theory. High conflict dyads, whose task was more equivocal than that of low conflict dyads, achieved higher joint outcomes with the richer audio-conferencing mode of communication than with the leaner computer communications mode. Whereas audio-conferencing provided two types of cues (voice and voice inflection), computer communication provided only one type of cue (text). The leaner mode of communication appears to have hindered successful problem resolution rather than facilitating it. The implication is that in certain task settings where cooperation between parties is essential for conflict resolution, the impersonal, rational atmosphere created by computer communication may not create a beneficial atmosphere.

Computer conferencing might prove to be more advantageous in dispersed bargaining involving multiple members on each bargaining side. Whereas several bargainers speaking in an audio-conference might have difficulty in distinguishing each other's voices, the written text of computer conferencing, which identifies the inputs of bargainers, might help to keep bargainers' inputs straight. The written text would also provide bargainers with an ongoing log of what had transpired thus far in the negotiation.

The implications of the results of this research project are, of course, limited by the use of student subjects in a simulated bargaining situation, where real-life bargaining conflict was not possible. Future research in the area of communication media for computerized negotiation support systems should include longitudinal testing, the use of real-life bargaining situations containing actual conflict of interest (but this will be very difficult to do except in a case study setting), and the use of multiple members on each bargaining team. Further experimentation into the value of a DSS for dispersed negotiators should also be conducted. Do dispersed negotiators really achieve better results with a DSS? What difference does it make if only the buyer, or only the seller, has access to a DSS?

References

Anson, R., & Jelassi, M. T. (1990). A developmental framework for computer-supported conflict resolution. *European Journal of Operational Research, 46*(2), 181-199.

Arunachalam, V., & Dilla, W. N. (1995). Judgment accuracy and outcomes in negotiations: A causal modeling analysis of decision-aiding effects. *Organizational Behavior and Human Decision Processes, 61*(3), 289-304.

Baird, J., & Wieting, G. (1979). Nonverbal communication can be a motivational tool. *Personnel Journal, 19*, 637-654.

Bazerman, M. H., & Carroll, J. S. (1987). Negotiator cognition. In L. L. Cummings & B. M. Staw (Eds.), *Research in organizational behavior* (Vol. 9, pp. 247-288). Greenwich, CT: JAI Press.

Carmel, E., Herniter, B. C., & Nunamaker, Jr., J. F. (1993). Labor-management contract negotiations in an electronic meeting room: A case study. *Group Decision and Negotiation, 2*, 27-60.

Chidambaram, L., & Jones, B. (1993). Impact of communication medium and computer support on group perceptions and performance: A comparison of face-to-face and dispersed meetings. *MIS Quarterly, 17*(4), 465-491.

Clopton, S. W. (1984, February). Seller and buying firm factors affecting industrial buyers' negotiation behavior and outcomes. *Journal of Marketing Research, 21*, 39-53.

Daft, R. L., & Lengel, R. H. (1986). Organizational information requirements, media richness and structural design. *Management Science, 32*(5), 554-571.

Daft, R. L., Lengel, R. H., & Trevino, L. K. (1987). Message equivocality, media selection, and manager performance: Implications for information systems. *MIS Quarterly, 11*(3), 354-367.

Davis, F. (1985). *A technology assessment model for empirically testing new end-user information systems: Theory and results.* Unpublished doctoral dissertation. Cambridge, MA: Massachusetts Institute of Technology.

Delaney, M. M., Foroughi, A., & Perkins, W. C. (1997). An empirical study of the efficacy of a computerized negotiation support system. *Decision Support Systems, 20*(3), 185-197.

Dennis, A. R., George, J. F., Jessup, L. M., Nunamaker, Jr., J. F., & Vogel, D. R. (1988). Information technology to support electronic meetings. *MIS Quarterly, 12*(4), 591-624.

DeSanctis, G., & Gallupe, B. (1987). A foundation for the study of group decision support systems. *Management Science, 33*(2), 589-609.

Deutsch, M. (1969). Conflicts: Productive and destructive. *Journal of Social Issues, 25*, 7-41.

Drolet, A. L., & Morris, M. W. (1995). *Communication media and interpersonal trust in conflicts: The role of rapport and synchrony of nonver-*

bal behavior. Paper presented at the Academy of Management meeting, Vancouver, Canada.

Eliashberg, J., Rangaswamy, A., & Balakrishnan, P. V. (1987, June). *Two party negotiations: A theoretical and empirical analysis*. Paper presented at ORSA/TIMS Marketing Science conference, Jouy-en-Josas, France.

Foroughi, A., & Jelassi, M. T. (1990). NSS solutions to major negotiation stumbling blocks. In *Proceedings of the 23rd Annual Hawaii International Conference on System Sciences,* Kailua-Kona, HI (Vol. IV, pp. 2-11).

Foroughi, A., Perkins, W. C., & Jelassi, M. T. (1995). An empirical study of an interactive, session-oriented computerized negotiation support system (NSS). *Group Decision and Negotiation, 4,* 485-512.

Heid, J. (1997). Face-to-face online. *Macworld, 14*(1), 146-151.

Hiltrop, J. M., & Rubin, J. Z. (1981). Position loss and image loss in bargaining. *Journal of Conflict Resolution, 25*(3), 521-534.

Hollingshead, A.B. (1996). Information suppression and status persistence in group decision making: The effects of communication media. *Human Communication Research, 23,* 193-220.

Jelassi, M. T., & Foroughi, A. (1989). Negotiation support systems: An overview of design issues and existing software. *Decision Support Systems, 5*(2), 167-181.

Jones, B. H. (1988). *Analytical negotiation: An empirical examination of the effects of computer support for different levels of conflict in two-party bargaining*. Unpublished doctoral dissertation. Bloomington, IN: Indiana University.

Kersten, G. (2003). *E-negotiations: Towards engineering of technology-based social processes*. InterNet Working Paper, Concordia University, University of Ottawa, and Carleton University.

Kersten, G., Law, K. P., & Strecker, S. (2004). *A software platform for multiprotocol e-negotiations*. InterNet Working Paper, Concordia University, University of Ottawa, and Carleton University.

Kydd, C. T., & Ferry, D. L. (1991). Computer supported cooperative work tools and media richness: An integration of the literature. In *Proceedings of the 24th Annual Hawaii International Conference on Systems Sciences* (Vol. III), (pp. 324-332). Los Alamitos, CA: IEEE Society Press.

Lim, L. H., & Benbasat, I. (1992-1993). A theoretical perspective of negotiation support systems. *Journal of Management Information Systems, 9*(3), 27-44.

Lindskold, S., & Hans, G. (1988). GRIT as a foundation for integrative bargaining. *Personality and Social Psychology Bulletin, 14*(2), 335-345.

McGrath, J. E. (1984). *Groups, interaction and performance.* Englewood Cliffs, NJ: Prentice Hall.

Mehrabian, A. (1971). *Silent messages.* Belmont, CA: Wadsworth.

Moore, D. A., Kutzberg, T. R., Thompson, L. L., & Morris, M. W. (1999). Long and short routes to success in electronically mediated negotiations: Group affiliations and good vibrations. *Organizational Behavior and Human Decision Processes, 77*(1), 22-43.

Morley, I. E., & Stephenson, G. M. (1997). *The social psychology of bargaining.* London, UK: Allen & Unwin.

Olekalns, M., Smith, P. L., & Walsh, T. (1996). The process of negotiating: Strategy and timing as predictors of outcomes. *Organizational Behavior and Human Decision Processes, 68*(1), 68-77.

Perkins, W. C., Hershauer, J. C., Foroughi, A., & Delaney, M. M. (1996, Spring). Can a negotiation support system help a purchasing manager? *International Journal of Purchasing and Materials Management, 32,* 37-45.

Poole, M.S., Shannon, D.L., & DeSanctis, G. (1992). Communication media and negotiation processes. In L. Putnam & S. Rolloff (Eds.), *Communication and negotiation: Sage annual reviews of communication research* (Vol. 20, pp. 46-66). Newbury Park, CA: Sage Publications.

Pruitt, D. G., & Carnevale, P. (1993). *Negotiation in social conflict.* Pacific Grove, CA: Brooks/Cole.

Purdy, J. M., Nye, P., & Balakrishnan, P. V. (2000). The impact of communication media on negotiation outcomes. *International Journal of Conflict Management, 11*(2), 162-187.

Rangaswamy, A., & Shell, G. R. (1997). Using computers to realize joint gains in negotiations: Toward an electronic bargaining table. *Management Science, 43*(8), 1147-1163.

Rice, R. E., & Love, G. (1987). Electronic emotion. *Communication Research, 14,* 85-108.

Rose, D. A. D., & Clark, P. M. (1995). A review of eye-to-eye videoconferencing techniques. *BT Technology Journal, 13* (4), 127.

Rubin, J. Z., & Brown, B. R. (1975). *The social psychology of bargaining and negotiation.* New York: Academic Press.

Sheffield, J. (1995). The effect of communication medium on negotiation performance. *Group Decision and Negotiation, 4,* 159-179.

Sproull, L., & Kiesler, S. (1986). Reducing social context cues: Electronic mail in organizational communication. *Management Science, 32*(11), 1492-1512.

Straus, S. G., & McGrath, J. E. (1994). Does the medium matter? The interaction of task type and technology on group performance and member reactions. *Journal of Applied Psychology, 79*(1), 87-97.

Williams, E. (1977). Experimental comparisons of face-to-face and mediated communication: A review. *Psychological Bulletin, 84,* 963-976.

Endnote

[1]   Interventions by the experimenter were rare in both the computer conferencing and audio-conferencing modes. Interventions were employed only when the bargainers did not appear to know what step to take next (no more than four instances) or when one of the bargainers raised a procedural question (approximately 20 times).

This article was previously published in the *Journal of Organizational and End User Computing, 17*(3), pp. 1-26, © 2005.

Appendix A

Point Sheets for Low Conflict Treatments

ROBERTS' POINT SHEETS (BUYER/LC) possible terms for the contract

Possible terms for the three-year contract

QUANTITY UNITS=POINTS	WARRANTY PERIOD YEARS=POINTS	$PRICE $ = POINTS	DELIVERY TIME MONTHS=POINTS
5000=39	4-years=16	$200=16	5-months=29
5500=33	3-years=10	$204=13	6-months=16
6000=27	2-years=5	$208=11	7-months=10
6500=20	1-years=0	$212=8	8-months=0
7000=13		$216=5	
7500=7		$220=3	
8000=0		$224=0	

The total points on your alternative contract is 44.

SIMO'S POINT SHEETS (SELLER/LC) possible terms for the contract

Possible terms for the three-year contract

QUANTITY UNITS=POINTS	WARRANTY PERIOD YEARS=POINTS	$PRICE $ = POINTS	DELIVERY TIME MONTHS=POINTS
8000=15	1-year=28	$224=37	8-months=20
7500=13	2-years=19	$220=31	7-months=13
7000=10	3-years=9	$216=24	6-months=7
6500=8	4-years=0	$212=18	5-months=0
6000=5		$208=12	
5500=3		$204=6	
5000=0		$200=0	

Appendix B

Point Sheets for High Conflict Treatments

ROBERTS' POINT SHEET (BUYER/HC) possible terms for the contract

Possible terms for the three-year contract

QUANTITY UNITS=POINTS	WARRANTY PERIOD YEARS=POINTS	$PRICE $ = POINTS	DELIVERY TIME MONTHS=POINTS
5000=29	4-years=15	$200=39	5-months=17
5500=25	3-years=10	$204=32	6-months=11
6000=20	2-years=5	$208=26	7-months=6
6500=15	1-years=0	$212=19	8-months=0
7000=10		$216=13	
7500=5		$220=6	
8000=0		$224=0	

The total points on your alternative contract is 44.

SIMO'S POINT SHEET (SELLER/HC) possible terms for the contract

Possible terms for the three-year contract

QUANTITY UNITS=POINTS	WARRANTY PERIOD YEARS=POINTS	$PRICE $ = POINTS	DELIVERY TIME MONTHS=POINTS
8000=29	1-year=19	$224=35	8-months=17
7500=24	2-years=13	$220=29	7-months=11
7000=19	3-years=7	$216=23	6-months=6
6500=14	4-years=0	$212=17	5-months=0
6000=10		$208=12	
5500=5		$204=6	
5000=0		$200=0	

The total points on your alternative contract is 46.

Appendix C

Screen Shot of Negotiation Decision Support Tool (NDST): NDST Software for Simo

```
|A   B   |C  D  |E   F   |G  H  |I   J  |K   L   |M   N  |O  P  |Q    R   |S   V   |W|X|Z  AA    AB

 1
 2  |  ************************ SIMO'S(SELLER) DECISION TOOL (LC)        *************************
 3  |  Input Your Priorities & Estimated      |       ------------------- SUGGESTED OFFERS ---- |
 4  |  Priorities for Your Opponent           |                    BEST  SECOND  THIRD           |
 5  |  PRIORITY 1 is highest                  |  QUANTITY          5000   5000    5000           |
 6  |  PRIORITY 4 is lowest       Your        |  WARRANTY            1      1       1            |
 7  |                 YOURS   Opponent's      |  PRICE             224    224     220           |
 8  |  QUANTITY        4          1           |  DELIVERY            5      6       5            |
 9  |  WARRANTY        2          4           |  YOUR POINTS        65     72      59           |
10  |  PRICE           1          3           |  Your Opponent's Points  65  56    69           |
11  |  DELIVERY        3          2           |  JOINT POINTS      130    128     128           |
12  | After you enter your priorities & estimates    PUSH
13  | of your opponent's priorities click on push
14  | ****************************         CONTRACT POINT CALCULATOR          ***************************** |
15  | QUANTITY : PTS | WARRA.: PTS | PRICE : PTS | DELIV.: PTS |  TOTAL                                    |
16  | --------- : ----- | --------- : ----- | ------- : -------- | ------ : ------ |: --------               |
17  |   7000 :  10 |    2 :  19 |  216 :  24 |   7 :  13 |:  66                                              |
18  |   5000 :   0 |    1 :  28 |  224 :  37 |   5 :   0 |:  65                                              |
19  |   6000 :   5 |    1 :  28 |  220 :  31 |   6 :   7 |:  71                                              |
20  |      0 : #### |  0 : #### |  0 : ##### |  0 : #### |: #####                                            |
21  |      0 : #### |  0 : #### |  0 : ##### |  0 : #### |: #####                                            |
22  |      0 : #### |  0 : #### |  0 : ##### |  0 : #### |: #####                                            |
```

This screen shot shows the NDST for Simo (the seller) after it has been used in a negotiation. Window #1, the DECISION TOOL, is the top half of the screen (down to the CONTRACT POINT CALCULATOR heading). The negotiator playing the role of Simo enters his/her priorities under the YOURS column (originally containing four zeros); these priorities would be known from the confidential information sheet distributed to Simo at the beginning of the negotiation. For instance, price might be most important (a "1" has been entered under YOURS next to PRICE), warranty might be second most important (2), delivery third most important (3), and quantity least important (4). In the Your Opponent's column, the negotiator playing the role of Simo enters his/her best estimates of the opponent's priorities, as identified during the statement-of-interests stage of negotiation. Simo will not know these priorities for certain, but he/she should have a reasonably good idea of them after the statement-of-interests. For instance, quantity might be most important for the opponent (a "1" has been entered under Your Opponent's next to QUANTITY), delivery second most important (2), price third most important (3), and warranty least important (4). Then the negotiator presses the PUSH button, and the NDST computes the three contract alternatives that provide the highest joint outcome (130 points, 128 points, and 128 points in our example) and places them in the columns on the right-hand side of Window #1. Please note that if the priorities for both parties are accurate, these three contract alternatives are the best available from the standpoint of maximizing joint outcome.

Window #2, the CONTRACT POINT CALCULATOR, occupies the bottom half of the screen. This is a very simple tool designed to make the calculation of Simo's contract points from any alternative contract very easy. The negotiator replaces the zeros in any line (we will start at the first line, as is usual) with the values of a possible contract — for example, 7000 for quantity, two years for warranty, 216 dollars for price, and seven months for delivery. The spreadsheet translates these values to points (see Appendices A and B) and then provides the total number of points to Simo in the right-most column — in this case, 66 points in the low conflict situation. The second and third lines show alternative contracts worth 65 and 71 contract points, respectively.

Chapter VI

Software Use Through Monadic and Dyadic Procedure:
User-Friendly or Not-So-Friendly?

Gregory E. Truman, Babson College, USA

Abstract

Our research objectives are to provide a theoretical discussion on how software may impact user performance in ways contrary to designers' intentions and users' desires, and to empirically evaluate user performance impacts that derive from ostensibly performance-enhancing software features. We propose that dyadic procedure is associated with higher levels of user performance when compared to monadic procedure. Using word-processing software utilization as the research context, we test the proposition on data from 46 participants. Contrary to expectations, the results suggest that dyadic procedure may decrease the accuracy of users' work. We conclude that software design features that are intended to improve user performance may have opposite effects, which raise questions about these features' utility and desirability.

Introduction

Users' access to and utilization of computers have become widespread due in part to developments surrounding graphical user interfaces, multifaceted packaged software, the Internet, and electronic commerce. However, there are indications that suboptimal utilization persists (Brynjolfsson, 1996; Marcolin, Compeau, Munro, & Huff, 2000), which challenges a frequent assumption that unqualified utilization is positively related to performance (Thompson, Higgins, & Howell, 1994). Thus, it may be that users do not know how to carry out effective and efficient computer use, which may potentially have adverse consequences for individual and firm-level performance.

Partly in response to this situation and partly due to competitive necessity, software vendors have continually improved their products to increase ease of use and to enhance user performance outcomes. Despite these advances, we contend that software innovations do not uniformly produce favorable performance impacts. Moreover, we argue that a critical examination of software innovations' impact on user performance is needed for two related reasons. First, the various ways that users apply an innovative feature do not always coincide with developers' intentions, therefore the effects of any feature cannot be fully predicted. Second, while a software designer may *intend* that an innovative feature enhance user performance, the feature may *actually* bring about reduced performance.

Research Objective

Our research objectives are to provide a theoretical discussion on how software may impact user performance in ways contrary to designers' intentions and users' desires, and to empirically evaluate user performance impacts that derive from ostensibly performance-enhancing software features.

Research Scope

Our characterization of computer use relates to software that end users typically utilize in the workplace. End users include workers whose formal role designation lies outside the IS area (McLean, Kappelman, & Thompson, 1993) and who commonly use software referred to as productivity software. Productivity software includes Microsoft Office, Corel WordPerfect Office, Lotus SmartSuite, and the like.

A focus on this type of software is particularly relevant because it is pervasive in the workplace. Among U.S. workers who use computers, about 63 million employees or about one half of the U.S. workforce as of October 1997, 57% use word- or document-processing programs, 41% use spreadsheet or analysis programs, and 26% use desktop publishing or graphic programs (U.S. Census Bureau, 1998-2001)[1]. Moreover, it is estimated that there are approximately 300 million Microsoft Office users worldwide ("WordPerfect," 2002). Within the productivity-software market segment, Microsoft's increasingly dominant share is exemplified by cessation of market-share tracking efforts since 2000 ("Microsoft," 2002).

Theoretical Perspective

In his seminal work on decision-support systems (DSSs), Silver (1990) identified two conceptually distinct ways that computer-based DSSs may change decision-making processes — nondirected and directed. The nondirected view specifies that any direction of change in decision-making processes is determined solely by the decision maker and is, therefore, relatively independent of the computer-based DSS. In contrast, the directed view specifies that a DSS will force a direction of change in the decision-making process that may or may not be consistent with the decision maker's preferences. Under this view, while not entirely subjugated to the computer-based DSS, the human decision maker's discretion over decision making is limited or reduced by the computer-based DSS.

Where DSSs manifest directed change in decision-making processes, Silver (1990) identified *system restrictiveness* and *decisional guidance* as two system-level attributes that may possibly influence decision-making behavior. System restrictiveness is defined as "the degree to which and the manner in which a DSS limits its users' decision-making processes to a subset of all possible processes" (p. 52). Decisional guidance is defined as "the degree to which and the manner in which a DSS guides its users in constructing and executing decision-making processes, by assisting them in choosing and using its operators" (p. 57). In summary, DSSs may effect directed or nondirected change in decision-making behavior. Where the DSS is directive, it may either restrict or guide.

While these attributes are not entirely independent, Vessey, Jarvenpaa, and Tractinsky (1992) adopt them as two categories among three that together form a CASE tool classification framework. The third category conceptually overlaps with Silver's (1990) concept of nondirected change — "A flexible CASE tool is designed to allow the user complete freedom in using it" (p. 92). They assess 12 commercial CASE products on various design features in order to categorize each one as restrictive, guided, or flexible in terms of dominant design philosophy for systems development methodology support. They conclude that, while their study suggests some validity to the view that the theoretical principles may be usefully applied for CASE tool classification, no tool offered an entirely consistent design philosophy for methodology support in that each inhered features of multiple design philosophies.

While Silver (1990) and Vessey et al. (1992) apply this conceptual distinction to the specific system types of DSS and CASE, respectively, Orlikowski and Robey (1991) draw this conceptual distinction more generally. They convincingly argue that any IT-based system may concurrently assume a constraining (restrictive) or facilitating (guidance) role in its mediation of human action. Thus, we find that these theoretical premises have been applied to specific yet different IT-based systems, and that these premises can be extended to apply to any IT-based systems including word-processing ones.

Word Processing as Context

We assume that end users' word-processing efforts proceed toward some identifiable goal and can be divided into discrete actions. Although end users have control over most of their actions while using word-processing software, there may be occasions where the software controls user actions. Some examples include tasks that are *presumably* made easier or more efficient through programmed procedures, including those that are explicitly embodied in wizards and others of a more implicit and hidden nature. We refer to actions that are performed by the user without any software control as *user directed*. Actions that are initiated by a user *and* controlled in any way by the software are referred to as *computer directed*.

Our theoretical view informs us that computer-directed action may either restrict or guide. We define restrictive computer-directed action as *the degree to which the software hinders, impedes, or reduces the user's advancement toward some identifiable goal.* We define guided computer-directed action as *the degree to which the software furthers, promotes, or increases the user's advancement toward some identifiable goal.* Where restrictive or guided computer-directed action occurs, we argue that the system occupies a constraining or facilitative role, respectively. We summarize these conceptual distinctions in Table 1.

On a conceptual level, a user's actions in any word processing program involve text entry and text-formatting efforts on some document. Framing our arguments on these two general efforts, we describe specific examples to further elaborate on these theoretical distinctions. In these examples, computer-directed actions intervene by guiding or restricting users' actions as they work toward identifiable goals. While each example illustrates either a facilitative or constraining role, we note that the specific role played out is *context dependent*. Thus, any example illustrating a facilitating (constraining) role may invoke a constraining (facilitating) role in a different use context.

Text Entry Actions

For text entry, user-directed action largely manifests in typing text into a document. Alternatively, a user may use clipboard features or drag-and-drop capabilities in order to edit and refine the document's content. These features relieve the user from having to retype text and generally facilitate more efficient text entry actions. Computer-directed action manifests in various ways, including actions carried out by the spell check, grammar check, and the autocorrect features among others.

The spell check is useful to many users for correcting spelling errors. While spell check guides users' actions in most cases, there may be limited instances where spell check invokes computer-directed action that restricts. The automatic substitution of capital *I* for lowercase *i* when the user types *i.e.* is one example. On the other hand, some users may inadvertently type lowercase *i* when they intend uppercase *I* for the first-person singular pronoun in the nominative case. In this event, computer-directed action will make the appropriate correction, and the system takes on a facilitating role.

The grammar check is useful for alerting the user to various grammatical errors, and it optionally provides for error correction. This feature may improve grammatical quality for some users by applying grammatical rules in a consistent way. However, there may be valid exceptions to grammatical rules due to the complex nature of language. For example, consider the phrase "...many IS organizations try to...," where *IS* is an acronym for information systems. The grammar check feature may substitute the phrase "...many are organizations try to..." because *IS* is interpreted as the singular form of the verb *to be* and the proximal noun is in plural form. In this case, the computer-directed action is restrictive and the computer takes on a constraining role. On the other hand, there are numerous instances where grammar correction is guiding — substituting "The parents encourage their children..." for "The parents encourage there children..." In this last example, the computer's role is facilitating.

While the autocorrect feature may be applied in various ways, including typing correction and pseudo electronic shorthand, it is fundamentally based on character substitution. Another use of character substitution is to substitute several consecutive keyboard characters with nonkeyboard characters that are used in correspondence (e.g., ellipse, dash, copyright and trademark characters). For example, an ellipse character may be substituted for three consecutive periods or the copyright symbol for *(c)*. When the copyright symbol is appropriately substituted for *(c)*, the user is guided toward the desired goal and the system is facilitating. On the other hand, the autocorrect feature may substitute a copyright symbol for *(c)* when the user wants to express the latter, and the system becomes restrictive and assumes a constraining role.

Text-Formatting Actions

Users' actions involving text-formatting goals largely rest on using format properties and styles on text blocks such as words, sentences, and paragraphs. Some common format properties include bold, italics, underline, justification, numbering, bulleting, tabs, and indentation. Representative of relatively more advanced text-formatting skills, styles provide the ability to define, apply, and modify groups of format properties as a unit. Generally speaking, styles facilitate the efficiency of the formatting task and the uniformity of the formatting outcome.

In applying format properties, a user may italicize a word or sentence in order to create emphasis, or may simultaneously use bold and underline on several words that form a book title. Contrasting left and right indentation along with justified alignment to offset a paragraph as a quote provides another example. In most cases, the use of format properties is wholly user directed.

Other formatting properties such as bulleting and numbering paragraphs may occur through computer-directed actions. For example, computer-directed action may intervene to alter the numbering or bullet format property such that ⇒ appears rather than •, or *(II)* appears rather than *(2)*. Where these substitutions are consistent with user preferences, the computer-directed actions are guiding. In contrast, where the user enters a desired bullet symbol or number type that is replaced with another, computer-directed action becomes restrictive because it hinders the user's advancement toward the text-formatting goal. Thus, we see that there are instances where the system's role is guiding, and other instances where it is constraining.

Styles may be used to streamline the text-formatting effort, and possibly to extend into other uses like the generation of a table of contents and table of figures. When using styles, a user may experience that a reserved style like Normal or Heading[1] is automatically substituted for a user-defined style when the set of format properties to be applied is comparable to an existing style's set. Similar substitutions may occur during style definition or modification, and all are examples of computer-directed actions. While these computer-directed actions may produce results consistent with user desires, the result may vary from the desired goal. Thus, computer-directed action may be either guiding or restrictive based on whether its outcome conforms to user preference. Where conformance (nonconformance) occurs, the system assumes a facilitating (constraining) role.

Monadic and Dyadic Procedures

We assume that actions carried out pursuant to some identifiable goal may be logically combined into procedures. For any identifiable goal that is attained *solely* through user-directed actions, we say that the user follows *monadic procedure*. Where any identifiable text entry or text-formatting goal is reached through joint user-directed and computer-directed actions, we say that the user follows *dyadic procedure*.

Including computer-directed action, dyadic procedure allows for the concurrent existence of restricting and guiding system roles. In predicting what role has dominance, there are several considerations. Addressing IT generally, Orlikowski (1992) states, "Which (role) dominates depends on multiple factors including the actions and motives of designers and implementers, the institutional context in which technology is embedded, and the autonomy and capability of particular users" (p. 411). In formulating our proposition, we assume that software designers' design objectives and the institution's use imperatives combine to implement word-processing software so as to exact enhanced user performance. We further assume that users' decision making is rational, and that they have intrinsic motivation to perform well. Thus, it seems reasonable to argue that under dyadic procedure where computer-directed action occurs, a guidance role will dominate and effect enhanced user performance. Consequently, we propose that dyadic procedure will be associated with higher levels of user performance when compared to monadic procedure.

Table 1.

Actions		Goals	
Action Definitions		Text Entry	Text Formatting
User-directed Action: Actions that are performed by the user without any software control.			
Computer-directed Action: Actions that are initiated by a user and controlled in any way by the software.			
Restrictive Computer-directed Action: The degree to which the software hinders, impedes or reduces the user's advancement toward some identifiable goal.		Theoretical Focus	Theoretical and Empirical Focus
Guiding Computer-directed Action: The degree to which the software furthers, promotes or increases the user's advancement toward some identifiable goal.			

Proposition 1: Dyadic procedure will be associated with higher levels of user performance when compared to monadic procedure.

Empirical research that falls in the realm of end-user computing frequently operationalizes user performance in terms of time and error. We operationalize user performance in similar ways.

Proposition 1a: Dyadic procedure will be associated with lower time requirements when compared to monadic procedure.

Proposition 1b: Dyadic procedure will be associated with greater accuracy levels when compared to monadic procedure.

Research Methodology

While we developed our theoretical arguments on text entry and text-formatting actions, our empirical focus is on text formatting. We begin with a discussion of the research design, follow with a description of the research and data analyses procedures, and close with identification of variables and measures.

Research Design

We use a paired-sample research design to test our propositions on 46 cases. After participating in a 2.5-hour training session on the use of styles in Word, participants were required to format a four-page document using 12 prescribed styles during a 30-minute testing session. Of the 12 prescribed styles, 9 and 3 were defined through monadic and dyadic procedures, respectively (Table 2). Data were aggregated across styles grouped by procedure and compared through a mean difference test.

Research Procedures

The training session involved several activities that placed emphasis on reading about styles and practicing their use. Read independently by all participants, a training session document instructed participants on the use of styles in Word[2]. The training session document presented a three-step general procedure for

Table 2. Prescribed styles

Prescribed Style	Style Name	Format Property Specifications	Procedure
1	course	Font: Times New Roman, font size:14 pts, italic, alignment:left, center tab at 3".	Monadic
2	course option	Font: Times New Roman, font size:12 pts, alignment:left, right tab at 3", decimal tab at 3.5".	Monadic
3	direction	Font: Arial Black, font size:14 pts, alignment:left, bullets, left border and right border .	Dyadic
4	direction heading	Font: Arial Black, font size:18 pts, alignment:center, space before, top border and bottom border	Monadic
5	heading	Font: Times New Roman, font size:14 pts, italic, alignment:left, outside border .	Monadic
6	item	Font: Times New Roman, font size:14 pts, italic, numbering	Dyadic
7	main info	Font: Arial Black, font size:18 pts, alignment:left, space before.	Monadic
8	name	Font: Times New Roman, font size:12 pts, italic, bullets, increase indent.	Dyadic
9	subitem	Font: Times New Roman, font size:12 pts, italic, increase indent.	Monadic
10	title1	Font:Arial, font size:16 pts, bold, alignment:center.	Monadic
11	title2	Font: Arial, font size:16 pts, bold, alignment:center, outside border .	Monadic
12	title3	Font: Arial, font size:16 pts, bold, underline, alignment:center.	Monadic

participants to follow when working with styles, including style definition, style application, and style modification. These procedures were presented in the context of a practice exercise, which the participants were instructed to do as they read through the training session document.

Each step of the general procedure was broken down into a more detailed procedure. The style definition procedure was used to define a style on one paragraph, and it conceptually consisted of two parts — *format group specification* followed by *style naming*. Format group specification involved specifying one or more format properties on a paragraph (Step 1). Style naming involved specifying a style name on a paragraph (Steps 2 through 4). The style application procedure was used to apply a style to paragraphs. The style application procedure could be applied to either one paragraph or to multiple adjacent paragraphs. The style modification procedure was used to modify a style. In the practice exercise, the modification procedure was set up to reinforce the advantages of using styles. All procedures are shown in Table 3.

Following the training session, all subjects participated in a testing session under timed conditions. All participants were provided the same test task, and they

Table 3. Style procedures

General Procedure
1. Define the style.
2. Apply the style.
3. Modify the style.

Definition Procedure
1. Format the paragraph by applying one or more format properties.
2. Position the insertion point in the paragraph that was just formatted.
3. *Select* the style box, which is the far left combo box of the formatting toolbar. The current style name will appear highlighted.
4. Type the name for the style and then press enter. Style names are not case sensitive.

Application Procedure
1. Position the insertion point in the paragraph where you want to apply the style. You may select multiple adjacent paragraphs in order to simultaneously apply the same style to several paragraphs.
2. *Open* the style box.
3. Select the style by clicking on it. You may need to scroll through the style box in order to find the desired style.

Modification Procedure
1. Reformat any paragraph that is assigned the style that is to be modified.
2. Select the reformatted paragraph.
3. *Open* the Style Box.
4. Select the style that is to be modified — the one that is already applied to the reformatted paragraph.
5. The Modify Style dialog box will ask you to indicate one of two choices. When modifying styles, you select the first choice — Update the style to reflect recent changes?, and click OK.

were informed that their performance was weighted equally on accuracy and completion time. Shown in the Appendix, the testing session documentation included the same style procedures that were provided during the training session, and formatting specifications on a test task that involved using 12 styles in a four-page document. Participants were instructed to define all styles first, and then follow by applying all styles. When finished applying all styles, they were instructed to signal the trainer in order to obtain further formatting specifications for modifying some styles.

Participants' performance data were compiled from two computer files. A Word document file captured the outcome of each participant's work on the test task. From the Word document we had record of accuracy, which we separately assessed for format group specification and style naming. A computer-monitoring log file recorded and time-stamped user's keystrokes during the test task. The log file facilitated analysis of the time required for format group specification *and* style naming. A tiered incentive scheme rewarded subjects based on equal consideration of their performance on accuracy and completion time. The participants who performed in the top quartile received $60. Those who performed in the middle-two quartiles received $50 and the lowest performing quartile received $40.

Data Analyses Procedures

From the two computer files, we obtained objective measures of participant performance. With regards to format group specification accuracy, our analyses proceeded by comparing the actual set of format properties to the prescribed set. There was no allowance for partial accuracy, therefore a subject had to specify the format group exactly as prescribed in order to be judged correct. For each style, we coded format group specification accuracy with a binomial variable — 1 if specified correctly, otherwise 0. Concerning style-naming accuracy, the test instructions identified a paragraph on which the subject was to name the style. We judged style-naming accuracy according to whether the style name was assigned to the designated paragraph[3].

The computer-monitoring log files were examined to determine the amount of time that was required to define each prescribed style. Since work activity was time-stamped to precision in seconds, we could identify the start and end times for each style and compute the difference as time duration in seconds. Thus, each time figure reflects the amount of time in seconds for performing the style definition procedure.

From 99 participants, 4 had either a corrupted Word document file or computer-monitoring log file, yielding 95 usable cases. For these 95 cases, accuracy assessment was straightforward, but time assessment was not interpretable in some cases for two reasons. First, while most participants followed the specified procedure by completely defining all 12 styles before proceeding to the style application procedure, some did not. Some participants defined *and applied* the first style before proceeding to the second style, and a few iterated the style definition and application procedures four times according to a page[4]. Consequently, style definition time included the application time for these subjects, which yielded noncomparable style definition times across participants. Thus, we omitted 39 who did not follow the specified procedure, so time duration for remaining cases includes *only* time spent on the style definition procedure. Second, although we could discern the start and end points for *each* style definition procedure in most instances, in some we could not and therefore we recorded zero for time duration. Ten cases had at least one style showing zero

Table 4. Time and accuracy statistics by style (means and standard deviations)

Style	Time (in seconds)		Accuracy Format Group Specification (%)		Accuracy Style Naming (%)	
	Mean	Std. Dev.	Mean	Std. Dev.	Mean	Std. Dev.
course	79	63	72%	46%	100%	0%
course option	106	68	61%	49%	100%	0%
direction	71	53	24%	43%	98%	15%
direction heading	64	31	80%	40%	100%	0%
heading	58	37	59%	50%	98%	15%
item	49	28	96%	21%	98%	15%
main info	81	43	65%	48%	100%	0%
name	66	36	50%	51%	100%	0%
subitem	51	30	93%	25%	100%	0%
title1	68	38	89%	31%	100%	0%
title2	69	31	85%	36%	100%	0%
title3	70	33	98%	15%	100%	0%

time duration, and these were removed from our analyses. The final sample contained 46 cases.

Variables and Measures

Table 4 shows descriptive statistics for time completion, format group specification accuracy, and style-naming accuracy on *each* style. The time figures represent the average time (in seconds) that was required to perform the style definition procedure — including both format group specification and style naming. For the course style, users completed the format group specification and style naming in 79 seconds on average with a variability of 63 seconds. The accuracy figures represent the proportion of users who accurately performed the respective format group specification or style-naming procedure. For example, the prescribed format group for course was accurately specified by 72% of the participants with a variability of 46%.

While format group specification accuracy and completion time showed variability, practically no variance occurred in style-naming accuracy. For 9 of 12 styles, all participants accurately performed style naming. The lowest mean accuracy was 98% on three styles. Due to the lack of variability in style-naming accuracy, we omit these data in subsequent analyses. Therefore our subsequent discussion on accuracy relates only to format group specification.

For each subject, we computed two accuracy measures and two completion time measures. One accuracy measure shows average accuracy on format group specification of styles defined under monadic procedure ($accuracy_{mona}$) and the second measure shows average accuracy under dyadic procedure ($accuracy_{dyad}$). Similarly, for completion time, one measure shows the average completion time

Table 5. Time and accuracy variables (means & standard deviations)

Variable	Mean	Std. Dev.
Time (in seconds)		
$time_{mona}$	72	19.6
$time_{dyad}$	62	29.5
Accuracy (%)		
$accuracy_{mona}$	78%	21.5%
$accuracy_{dyad}$	57%	23.2%

Table 6. Time and accuracy variables (correlations)

	Correlations			
	$time_{mona}$	$time_{dyad}$	$accuracy_{mona}$	$accuracy_{dyad}$
$time_{mona}$	1.00			
	--			
$time_{dyad}$	0.29*	1.00		
	0.05	--		
$accuracy_{mona}$	(0.21)	0.08	1.00	
	0.16	0.62	--	
$accuracy_{dyad}$	0.19	0.02	0.15	1.00
	0.20	0.90	0.31	--
** p<.01; * p<.05				

for styles defined under monadic procedure (**timemona**) and a second measure shows completion time under dyadic procedure (**timedyad**). To test the propositions, we used a one-tailed paired-sample mean difference t-test.

Results

The means and standard deviations of the time and accuracy variables are reported in Table 5, and the correlations are reported in Table 6. The mean difference between monadic procedure and dyadic procedure on time and accuracy was significant at $p < .05$ and $p < .01$, respectively. The average time to define styles under monadic procedure was 72 seconds, compared to the significantly lower 62 seconds under dyadic procedure. Thus, dyadic procedure yielded significantly better performance with respect to time, and Proposition 1a is supported. The average accuracy for format group specification under monadic procedure was 78%, compared to the significantly lower value of 57% under dyadic procedure. Thus, monadic procedure yielded significantly better performance with respect to accuracy. Proposition 1b is not supported, and this result is contrary to expectations.

Discussion

Users were significantly less accurate in performing text-formatting tasks under dyadic procedure when compared to monadic procedure. Thus, where joint user-directed and computer-directed actions were used pursuant to the goal of defining prescribed format group specifications, users tended to create more error on average. Examination of computer log files suggests that some users made repeated unsuccessful attempts to override or work around computer-directed actions, however, many remained unsuccessful in the end. These efforts mostly consisted of varying attempts to specify the bullet symbol and left-indentation distance as prescribed in the test task instructions, only to have their efforts reversed or overridden by the system.

Our theoretical framework helps us to explain *how* performance degradation may occur on occasions where computer-directed action intervenes. In this particular use context, the user's advancement toward the intended goal of defining a prescribed set of format group specifications was impeded through repeated override and reversal by the system. Consequently, these computer-directed actions were restrictive in terms of facilitating the users' work and effectively reduced accuracy. This calls into question the desirability of com-puter-directed actions where prescribed format group specifications are used.

While users required less time to create format group specifications under dyadic procedure as expected, it is interesting to note that the variability was signifi-cantly higher under dyadic procedure (29.5) than under monadic procedure (19.6) (Table 5). An F test on the difference between two variances was significant at $p < .05$. This result shows that users were much more varied in terms of completion time under dyadic procedure than under monadic procedure. One interpretation of this result is that users varied in their ability to comprehend, react to, and work with computer-directed action, which did not come into play under monadic procedure.

While high completion time variability under dyadic procedure is not necessarily detrimental, there may be business processes that involve word-processing tasks where consistent performance is desirable. For example, publishing firms or certain retail establishments may have an interest in creating a relatively standard throughput rate on word-processing tasks. As a specific example, consider a retailer that offers fast and convenient printing and reproduction services. It seems reasonable to argue that service turnaround time would be a significant factor affecting customers' perceptions of service quality, and that *consistent* service turnaround time would be an important performance objec-tive. Our results would suggest that the potential for greater turnaround time variability is increased to the extent that text formatting occurs under dyadic procedure[5]. This would increase the probability of *inconsistent* customer

Figure 1. Word use frequency responses

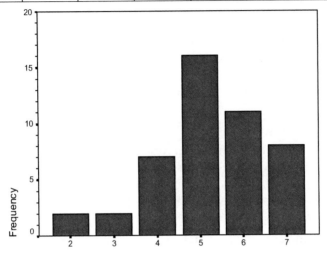

Within the last year, how frequently have you used Word software?						
Not at all	Less than once per month	About 1-3 times per month	About once per week	About 2-4 times per week	About once per day	More than once per day
1	2	3	4	5	6	7

Table 7. Time and accuracy results by experience group (means & mean differences)

	Time (in seconds)			Accuracy (percent)		
	$time_{mona}$	$time_{dyad}$	Difference	$accuracy_{mona}$	$accuracy_{dyad}$	Difference
Less Experience	78	56	22*	72%	61%	11%
Medium Experience	78	66	12	70%	50%	20%*
More Experience	63	62	1	88%	60%	28%*
* significant at p<.05						

experiences for the repeat customer, which may result in degradation of perceived service quality in the long run. Thus, under certain circumstances, the desirability of computer-directed actions under dyadic procedure may be called into question due to potential for greater completion time variability.

Research shows that the efficacy of computer-assisted design features varies according to user experience (Gay, 1986; Steinberg, Baskin, & Matthews, 1985; Taylor, 1987), which may inform this study. In general, the cumulative empirical research shows that less experienced users perform better with computer-assisted design features, and that more experienced users perform better without computer-assisted design features. In the context of this study, consistent findings would show that less experienced Word users perform better under dyadic procedure, while more experienced Word users perform better under monadic procedure. We decided to probe whether our data were consistent with the cumulative findings, therefore we looked at performance outcomes under monadic and dyadic procedures across Word experience levels.

One measure asked participants to specify their use frequency in Word on a Likert scale of 1 to 7, which we use as a surrogate measure for experience. The measure's scale and resulting frequency distribution are shown in Figure 1. No participants specified "Not at all." In order to equalize the number of subjects across groups to the extent possible, we combined response categories 2, 3, and 4, and categories 6 and 7. This yielded experience groups that we identify as Less Experience (11 responses), Medium Experience (16), and More Experience (19).

Table 7 shows time and accuracy performance results between monadic and dyadic procedures across experience levels. For the Less Experience participants, dyadic procedure provided benefit in that completion time requirements were *significantly* reduced when compared to monadic procedure. While differences between monadic and dyadic procedure for the More Experience and Medium Experience participants are not significant, the results do show dyadic procedure leading to less advantage on completion time for subjects at greater experience levels. Thus, although these results across experience groups do not conclusively show that the efficacy of dyadic procedures varies across experience levels, these findings are consistent with this notion.

The accuracy results by experience levels provide a less clear pattern. While the More Experience and Medium Experience group performed *significantly* better on accuracy under monadic procedure than under dyadic procedure, this also holds true for the Less Experience group. While this latter result is not significant, the 11% difference suggests that monadic procedure had some advantage over dyadic procedure nonetheless. Thus, the accuracy results across experience levels are less consistent with the contention that the efficacy of dyadic procedure varies across experience levels.

The pattern of completion time performance differences across experience groups suggests that software design features may beneficially adapt to experience level. In general, it may be that dyadic procedures should be reduced as the user gains experience, and possibly should be eliminated for very experienced users. For example, a behavior-based adaptive mechanism could cease automatic substitution of capital *I* for lowercase *i* in *i.e.* where a user consistently changes it back to *i.e.* Alternatively, a time-based adaptive mechanism could gradually reduce the occurrences of dyadic procedure as usage hours are accumulated.

While the notion of adaptive software design is not new, the software design features that are conceptually characterized here under dyadic procedure are adaptive neither to user behavior nor over time. This suggests that a critical review of existing software design features in this and other widely used software programs may be warranted, with a specific focus on incorporating more extensive adaptive design features.

Limitations

During the test period, users were instructed to define, apply, and modify a *prescribed* set of styles to format a four-page document. While this is representative of some real tasks, such as producing government control and compliance reports or writing various legal briefs and other documents, users do not always work under prescribed formatting conditions. Where prescribed formatting is not required, users may find a variety of formatting outcomes acceptable. Thus, the notion of correctness (or accuracy) is significantly broadened, and dyadic procedure will not yield inaccurate results per se. Consequently, the context of users operating under prescribed task conditions significantly limits the generalizability of these findings to situations where prescribed formatting is required.

The styles that were used under monadic procedure were different from those used under dyadic procedure. While the number of format properties varied across styles (Table 2), which could potentially explain accuracy and required time differences, there was no systematic difference in the number of format properties between monadic and dyadic styles. An alternative research design might include a set of styles that were identical in format properties, but were defined, applied, and modified under both procedures. However, this design would require modification of the Word software program in order to suppress computer-directed actions where dyadic procedure would normally invoke, thereby mimicking monadic procedure. Obviously this is not currently possible provided Word's proprietary status.

Conclusion

We found that dyadic procedure decreased the accuracy of users' word-processing formatting tasks under prescribed conditions. Therefore, we find instance where ostensibly performance-enhancing software design features lead to *reduced* user performance. Thus, we conclude that software design features that are intended to *improve* user performance may have contrary effects, which raise questions about these features' utility and desirability.

Consequently, these features' practical usefulness and benefit should not be presumed nor taken for granted, but rather questioned, examined, and evaluated from a critical disposition supported through empirical inquiry. We believe that this is particularly true provided that several hundred million people worldwide use word-processing software, which *increasingly* exhibits design features that embody computer-directed actions under dyadic procedure.

References

Askenas, L., & Westelius, A. (2000). Five roles of an information system: A social constructionist approach to analyzing the use of ERP systems. *International Conference on Information Systems,* Brisbane, Australia (pp. 426-434).

Brynjolfsson, E. (1996). The contribution of information technologies to consumer welfare. *Information Systems Research, 7*(3), 281-300.

Gay, G. (1986). Interaction of learner control and prior understanding in computer-assisted video instruction. *Journal of Educational Psychology, 78*(3), 225-227.

Marcolin, B. L., Compeau, D. R., Munro, M. C., & Huff, S. L. (2000, March). Assessing user competence: Conceptualization and measurement. *Information Systems Research, 11*(1), 37-60.

McLean, E. R., Kappelman, L. A., & Thompson, J. P. (1993, December). Converging end-user and corporate computing. *Communications of the ACM, 36*(12), 79-92.

Microsoft reports weaknesses in office software. (2002, August 23). *Washington Post.*

Orlikowski, W. J. (1992, August) The duality of technology: Rethinking the concept of technology in organizations. *Organization Science, 3*(3), 398-427.

Orlikowski, W. J., & Robey, D. (1991, June). Information technology and the structuring of organizations. *Information Systems Research, 2*(2), 143-169.

Poole, M. S., & DeSanctis, G. (n.d.). Understanding the use of group DSS: The theory of adaptive structuration. In J. Fulk & C. Steinfield (Eds.), *Organizations and communication technology* (pp. 173-193). Newbury Park, CA: Sage Publications.

Robey, D., Vaverek, K. A., & Saunders, C. S. (1989). *Social structure and electronic communication: A study of computer conferencing.* Hawaii International Conference on Social Sciences.

Silver, M. (1990, March). Decision support systems: Directed and nondirected change. *Information Systems Research, 1*(1), 47-70.

Steinberg, E. R., Baskin, A. B., & Matthews, T. D. (1985, Spring). Computer-presented organizational/memory aids as instruction for solving Pico-Fomi problems. *Journal of Computer-Based Instruction, 12*(2), 44-49.

Taylor, R. (1987). Selecting effective courseware: Three fundamental instructional factors. *Contemporary Educational Psychology, 12*, 231-243.

Thompson, R. L., Higgins, C. A., & Howell, J. M. (1994). Influence of experience on personal computer utilization: Testing a conceptual model. *Journal of Management Information Systems, 11*(1), 167-187.

Trauth, E. M., & Cole, E. (1992, March). The organizational interface: A method for supporting end users of packaged software. *MIS Quarterly*, 35-53.

U.S. Census Bureau. (1998-2001). *Statistical abstract of the United States.*

Vessy, I., Jarvenpaa, S. L., & Tractinsky, N. (1992, April). Evaluation of vendor products: CASE tools as methodology companions. *Communications of the ACM, 35*(4), 90-105.

WordPerfect wins an office battle. (2002, August 27). *ZDNet.*

Endnotes

1   These data are consistent with earlier data reported in McLean et al (1993) and Trauth & Cole (1992).

2   The training documentation on Word styles may be directly obtained from the author.

3   We allowed for minor misspellings or typos, such as transposing two characters. For example, 'cuorse' would be judged as accurate for the 'course' style.

4   As noted above, style modification specifications were given to the subject *after* the style definition and application procedures had been completed for all styles, therefore any modification time occurred separate from definition and application time.

5   We assume that customers provide content on a diskette or as e-mail attachment. The customer service personnel provide finishing touches that would mostly involve text formatting tasks.

This article was previously published in the *Journal of Organizational and End User Computing, 17*(1), pp. 1-22, © 2005.

Appendix

Test Task

Instructions

You will find two versions of several documents on the following pages. These documents include a memorandum (lines 1-19), an agenda (lines 20-36), a menu (lines 37-51) and some driving directions (lines 52-60). Section A shows the documents such that they appear similar to those in Section B. Section D summarizes the procedures discussed during the training session (p. 12).

Your overall performance will be computed from two criteria, which are equally weighted: (1) the amount of time that you require to complete to test task; and (2) the number of errors that you make. Generally speaking, there is a trade-off between time are error. Thus, you will have to strike a balance that is right for you. There is an incentive scheme designed to motivate you to perform as fast and accurately as possible, however. The top 25% performers will receive $60, the middle 50% will receive $50, and the bottom 25% will receive $40. Your overall performance will be used to place you into one of these three categories in order to determine the amount of reimbursement.

1	**Section A**
2	MEMORANDUM
3	TO: Board of Directors
4	FROM: Michael Brown, President
5	RE: Notice of Board of Directors Meeting
6	DATE: November 7, 1999
7	The next regularly scheduled meeting of the Board of Directors of the Seattle area Teachers Federal
8	Credit Union will be held on Wednesday, November 30, 1999, at 7:00 p.m. in the conference room of the
9	Credit Union. Dinner will be served prior to the board meeting at 6 p.m. Please notify Cheryl Sears at
10	ext. 324 by November 23 of your plans for attending the dinner and the meeting.
11	As a result of the recent elections, we will be welcoming three new board members at this meeting.
12	Below I have listed their names, school district, and business telephone. If you plan on attending, please
13	take some time at the meeting to extend a special welcome to them. Also, please return the menu form by
14	November 25 to the address indicated.
15	Teresa Markowitz, Seattle ISD, 747-0005
16	Gilbert Crowley, King Country ISD, 283-9214
17	Ed Newell, Bellevue ISD, 637-7389
18	I look forward to seeing all of you at the meeting.
19	Enclosure
20	Seattle Area Teachers Federal Credit Union
21	Agenda for the Board of Directors Meeting
22	November 30, 1999
23	Call to Order: Otis Johnson, Chairman
24	Approval of Minutes: Sharon DiMarco, Secretary
25	Committee Reports
26	Treasurer's Report: Julius Knebel, Treasurer
27	Last Quarter's Spending Report
28	Next Quarter's Spending Report
29	President's Report: Michael Brown, President
30	New Business: Otis Johnson, Chairman

31	Unfinished Business: Otis Johnson, Chairman
32	Existing Delinquent Rescue Plans
33	Credit Enhancement Project
34	Special Repayment Plan
35	Online Account Management System
36	Adjournment
37	Menu Form
38	Appetizer
39	Pork egg roll	$0.95
40	Steamed Bum	$2.50
41	Entree
42	Egg Foo Young	$8.95
43	Peking Duck	$12.95
44	Dessert
45	Fresh Fruits	$4.95
46	Ice Cream	$4.95
47	Beverage
48	Sparkling Water	$2.00
49	Fruit Juice	$2.95
50	Beer (Glass)	$3.95
51	Wine (Glass)	$3.95
52	Address: 1234 Kennedy Avenue, Beunell
53	Telephone: (555)237-8392
54	Direction information
55	Take freeway I-1 to exit 34
56	Turn Right to West Avenue (North bound)
57	Go straight for about 3 miles, turn left at Kennedy Avenue.
58	Go straight for two blocks, Building is at your left side between State Street and Forest Street.
59	Add additional direction information below.

Section B

MEMORANDUM

TO: *Board of Directors*

FROM: *Michael Brown, President*

RE: *Notice of Board of Directors Meeting*

DATE: *November 7, 1999*

The next regularly scheduled meeting of the Board of Directors of the Seattle area Teachers Federal Credit Union will be held on Wednesday, November 30, 1999, at 7:00 p.m. in the conference room of the Credit Union. Dinner will be served prior to the board meeting at 6 p.m. Please notify Cheryl Sears at ext. 324 by November 23 of your plans for attending the dinner and the meeting.

As a result of the recent elections, we will be welcoming three new board members at this meeting. Below I have listed their names, school district, and business telephone. If you plan on attending, please take some time at the meeting to extend a special welcome to them. Also, please return the menu form by November 25 to the address indicated.

Teresa Markowitz, Seattle ISD, 747-0005

Gilbert Crowley, King Country ISD, 283-9214

Ed Newell, Bellevue ISD, 637-7389

I look forward to seeing all of you at the meeting.

Enclosure

Seattle Area Teachers Federal Credit Union

Agenda for the Board of Directors Meeting

November 30, 1999

Call to Order: Otis Johnson, Chairman

Approval of Minutes: Sharon DiMarco, Secretary

Committee Reports

Treasurer's Report: Julius Knebel, Treasurer

> *Last Quarter's Spending Report*

> *Next Quarter's Spending Report*

President's Report: Michael Brown, President

New Business: Otis Johnson, Chairman

Unfinished Business: Otis Johnson, Chairman

> *Existing Delinquent Rescue Plans*

> *Credit Enhancement Project*

> *Special Repayment Plan*

> *Online Account Management System*

Adjournment

Menu Form

Appetizer

Pork egg roll	$0.95
Steamed Bum	$2.50

Entree

Egg Foo Young	$8.95
Peking Duck	$12.95

Dessert

Fresh Fruits	$4.95
Ice Cream	$4.95

Beverage

Sparkling Water	$2.00
Fruit Juice	$2.95
Beer (Glass)	$3.95
Wine (Glass)	$3.95

Address: 1234 Kennedy Avenue, Beunell

Telephone: (555)237-8392

Direction information

- **Take freeway I-1 to exit 34**
- **Turn Right to West Avenue (North bound)**
- **Go straight for about 3 miles, turn left at Kennedy Avenue.**
- **Go straight for two blocks, Building is at your left side between State Street and Forest Street.**

Add additional direction information below.

Section C

Styles apply to paragraphs on these lines*

title1 — 1
heading — 2-5
name — 15-17
title2 — 20-22
item — 23-26, 29-31, 36
subitem — 27-28, 32-35
title3 — 37
course — 38, 41, 44, 47
course option — 39-40, 42-43, 45-46, 48-51
main info — 52-53
direction heading — 54, 60
direction — 55-59

* Dash (-) means consecutive line numbers, while comma (,) means nonconsecutive.
For example, 5-8 means lines five, six, seven and eight, while 5,8 means only lines five and eight.

Section D

Three-step Procedure

1. Define the style.
2. Apply the style.
3. Modify the style.

Style Definition Procedure

1. Format the paragraph by applying one or more format properties.
2. Position the insertion point in the paragraph that was just formatted.
3. Select the style box, which is the far left combo box of the formatting toolbar. The current style name will appear highlighted.
4. Type the name for the style and then press enter. Style names are not case sensitive.

Style Application Procedure

1. Position the insertion point in the paragraph where you want to apply the style. You may select multiple adjacent paragraphs in order to simultaneously apply the same style to several paragraphs.
2. Open the style box.
3. Select the style by clicking on it. You may need to scroll through the style box in order to find the desired style.

Style Modification Procedure

1. Reformat any paragraph that is assigned the style that is to be modified.
2. Select the reformatted paragraph.
3. Open the Style Box.
4. Select the style that is to be modified — the one that is already applied to the reformatted paragraph.
5. The Modify Style dialog box will ask you to indicate one of two choices. When modifying styles, you select the first choice — Update the style to reflect recent changes? — and click OK.

Chapter VII

Business Software Specifications for Consumers:
Toward a Standard Format

Shouhong Wang, University of Massachusetts Dartmouth, USA

Abstract

Commercialized business application software packages have been widely used to implement business information systems. In order to determine whether a software package meets the system needs, consumers must check the software specifications against the target system requirements. Since the commercial software industry does not have standard format of software specifications for consumers, free-formatted descriptions of application software and ad hoc demos are commonly used in marketing software products, but are often too ambiguous for consumers to uncover the implemented capacity. This chapter proposes a model of commercialized business software specifications for consumers. It suggests that software packages need to provide specifications for consumers in four aspects:

business operations, user-computer interfaces, user-perceived inputs and outputs, and business rules. Using an example, the chapter demonstrates the implementation of the model.

Introduction

Information systems analysis and design lies in the core of the information systems discipline. The techniques and approaches of information systems analysis and design are continually renovated. About 15 years ago, systems analysis and design projects were more likely to place the focal point on the use of databases and fourth generation languages to implement real business information systems. Gradually, systems users and consultants found that commercialized business application software packages were readily available in the software market. According to the author's observations over the past decade in supervising 428 real-world MIS (Management Information Systems) systems analysis and design projects, the percentage of business applications that can be implemented by using commercialized software packages has dramatically increased since 1994 (see Figure 1). Clearly, the phenomenon and the trend observed are based solely on the author's personal experience, and the

Figure 1. Increasing commercialized business software

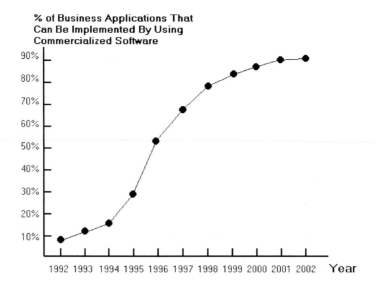

claim may not be generally valid. Nevertheless, the observed real-world cases indicate that about 90% of small or middle-size business applications can be implemented by using off-the-shelf software packages. One can do shopping online to find a low priced and well designed laundry management system, salon management system, and flower delivery management system, to name a few.

As a result of the proliferation of commercialized business application software, for most business information technology professionals, the tasks of system design and implementation have been shifted from software construction to software system adoption. Nowadays, assessment of strategic values of software systems has become the central issue of systems development (Jurison, 2000). In this view, the theme of systems analysis and design for business enterprises has been shifted from system *construction* to system *acquisition*. In the traditional systems analysis and design cycle, system specifications are used for software development. However, in the system acquirement analysis cycle, specifications of software systems are needed for software consumers in choosing commercialized software packages that best match their system

Figure 2. Comparison of the two systems analysis cycles

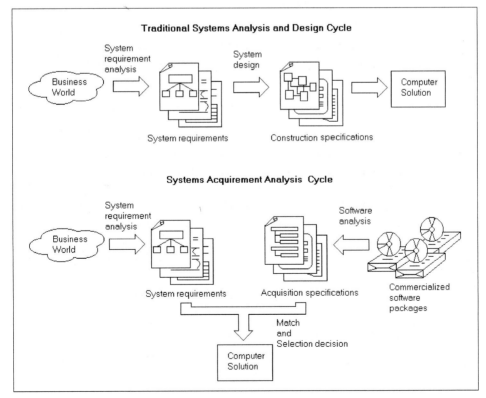

requirements. Accordingly, specifications for software construction and specifications for consumers, which are so called *acquisition specifications*, play different roles, as depicted in Figure 2.

The software industry has various specification instruments with *de facto* standards for business software development, such as data flow diagrams (DeMarco, 1978; Gane & Sarson, 1979), UML (the Unified Modeling Language) (Rumbaugh, Jacobson, & Booch, 1999), and entity-relation diagrams (Chen, 1976). These instruments are used to describe the deep structures and system components for software construction, but are not meant for software feature description. Consumers of a commercialized business software package would like to have explicit specifications about the business process that can be carried out by the software package, rather than the specifications for the construction of the software system (Wang, 2002). This is similar to the fact that consumers of computer hardware or cars never want to review the manufacturing blueprints in making a purchase decision. Since nowadays there is no commonly applied format of business software specifications that can be used for conveying the software features to consumers, sellers of commercialized business software packages use free-format descriptions and *ad hoc* style demos to market their products. Consumers have few guidelines for examination of software system utilities. Although this issue has been standing for some time (Trauth & Cole, 1992), few practical techniques of software specifications for consumers have been reported in the literature.

To facilitate consumer-centered system acquirement, a standard structure of acquisition specifications is imperatively needed. In this chapter, we propose a model of business application software specifications for consumers to meet this challenge. This model formalizes the major aspects of business application software that have been identified in the literature as the most important factors for consumers. To focus on the primary issue of software specifications, this model excludes environmental requirements, such as minimal requirements for hardware and operating systems. The rest of the paper is organized as follows. The section on business application software describes the major aspects of business software packages that are important to consumers and the structure of these aspects. The case study presents the implementation of this model structure through the use of XML (Extensible Markup Language). The final section, the summary, summarizes this study.

Major Aspects of
Business Application Software

In formalizing the structure of business application software specifications for consumers, the first step is to identify the aspects of software systems that are most important for consumers in choosing packaged software. The second step is to integrate these major aspects into a structure that software consumers can easily understand and analyze. The third step is to implement the structure using the uniform data exchange language XML so that consumers can readily access acquisition specifications.

Business Operations: Tasks, Processes, and Steps

Business operations implemented by the application software package are the major concern for organizations (Kendall, 1994). In the view of the traditional structured modeling approach (e.g., DeMarco, 1978), which is simple and commonly adopted, a business operation is a hierarchy of sub-operations. Using simple terminology for consumers, a business operation supported by a software system can be decomposed into three levels of sub-operations: tasks, processes, and steps, which are corresponding to group and individual activities in business, as proposed below.

1. **Task:** A business task is a set of business processes performed by a group of actors through the interaction between the actors and the software system to accomplish a specific outcome.

    The specifications of a task shall describe the business functionality of the system in accomplishing the task and the type of the actors. Here, actor is referred to a particular role played by the user(s).

2. **Process:** A business process is a set of steps performed by a single actor through the interaction between the actor and the software system to carry out the associated task. The specifications of a process shall describe the accomplished functionality for the particular actor.

3. **Step:** A specific action performed by an actor through the interaction between the actor and the software system in carrying out the associated process.

Figure 3. Specifications of business operation

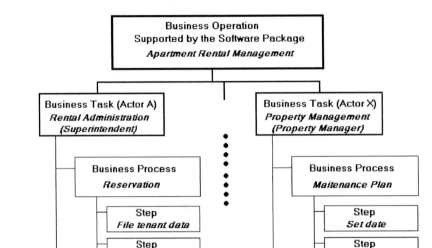

Business operation specifications can be organized in a tree, as shown in Figure 3. As a practical example, segments (in italic) of an apartment rental management system are included in the figure.

Note that the tree structure represents the hierarchical relationships between the tasks, processes, and steps, but not necessarily the sequence of the business operation. Here, the tasks, processes, and steps in a business operation tree may not be independent. Many real-world operations would involve complex interactions resulting in network structures. The use of dependent trees to describe network structures usually brings about redundant descriptions. Nevertheless, the tree structure of business operation specifications is easy to understand and is in compliance with XML that is used to implement the model.

User-Computer Interfaces

As application software became widespread, the human-computer interaction is one of the most important aspects in software specifications (Diaper & Addison, 1992). It is so important because systems development specifications, such as the data flow diagram and UML, emphasize descriptions of functional and data requirements within the context of software engineering, but not within the context of software usability (Sutcliffe, 1989; Wang, 1995). To determine whether an application software package fits the business task requirements, one must specify user-centered cognitive aspects of usability (Anonymous, 1993; Benyon, 1992; Diaper, 1989; Harrison & Monk, 1986). Accordingly, the second aspect of acquisition specifications for commercial software packages is the user-computer interfaces.

A user-computer interface is the part of the software system that allows the user to interact with the system in carrying out the tasks. It includes the screen

Figure 4. Specifications of user-computer interfaces

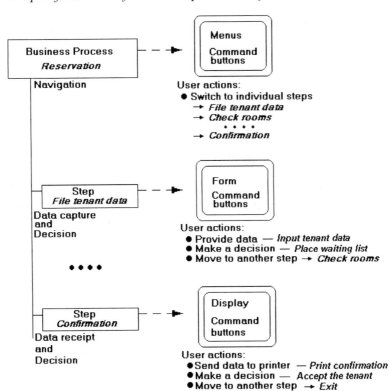

displays that provide navigation through the software system, as well as the screen displays that capture or generate data (Wang, 1995).

In specifying a software system, a user-computer interface is associated with a process or a step, as illustrated in Figure 4. Again, a practical example in italic is included in the figure.

Conceptually, there are three basic types of user-computer interfaces: Navigation, data capture coupled with decision, and data receipt coupled with decision (Dennis & Wixom, 2003). A navigation interface is associated with a business process. It provides menus and command buttons that allow the user to proceed through the subsidiary steps. An interface for data capture coupled with decision provides forms and command buttons that allow the user to input data and make a business decision or move to another step. An interface for data receipt coupled with decision displays or prints data for the user and allows the user to make a decision or move to another step.

User-Perceived Inputs and Outputs

Originally, inputs and outputs of processes were considered to be central components of systems analysis and design in almost every systems analysis and design approach (Ballou & Pazer, 1985; Carey & McLeod, 1988). HIPO (hierarchy plus input, process, output) (Stay, 1976) is a typical example of input and output driven approaches. Later, research (Srinivasan, 1985) indicated that user-perceived inputs and outputs, not system internal inputs and outputs, are the major measures of effectiveness of systems. For example, in evaluating a payment system, the user is interested in the receipt for a payment rather than the payment history data written to the disk. Research of contemporary object-oriented systems analysis (Wang, 1996) and information system planning (Li & Chen, 2001) has also confirmed this finding.

User-perceived inputs and outputs are associated with a business process, as illustrated in Figure 5. The specifications of a user-perceived input or output shall provide summarized information of the input and output contents.

Business Rules

Business rules are constraints or guidelines for business operations. They specify the relationships between an anticipated condition and expected actions/ outcomes. Using the currently available computer techniques, business rules are implemented through coded decision procedures or data models. Yet, there is a lack of systematic techniques for mapping business rules and the software

Figure 5. Specifications of user-perceived inputs and outputs

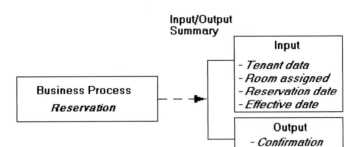

system onto each other (Amghar, Meziane, & Flory, 2000). As the perspectives of business rules are crucial for software systems acquirement, important business rules implemented in the software system must be described in an explicit way (Hale, Sharpe, & Hale, 1999).

In this proposed model, workflows are specified in the business operation and interface specifications, and are not considered to be business rules. Here, business rules are referred to those constraints associated to a task or a process. Software specifications for consumers shall describe two types of business rules implemented in the software system: User-defined and built-in.

1. **User-defined business rules:** The specifications of a user-defined business rule shall describe the general formula of the rule and how the user can define his/her own parameters during the installation of the software system. The specifications shall also indicate the default settings for those user-defined business rules.

2. **Built-in business rules:** The specifications of a built-in business rule shall describe the formula of the rule that has been implemented in the software system.

Discussion

The above model of application software specifications for consumers de-emphasizes several aspects of design specifications for software construction, as discussed next.

Figure 6. Specifications of business rules

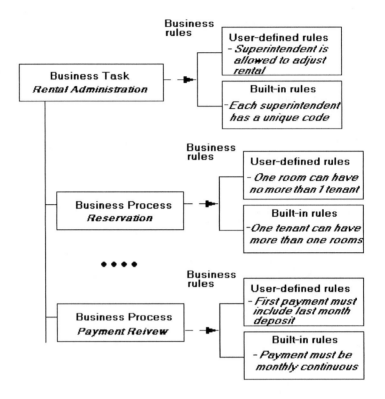

1. **System decomposition:** In systems analysis and design, system decomposition is one of the important issues. This is because the system modules are the construction units for the software development. On the other hand, the software users are not particularly concerned with these construction units, as long as the system supports the required business operation. For instance, in object-oriented systems analysis and design, objects are the system modules. However, few software companies specify the objects of their systems for consumers.

   In this proposed model, the structure of specifications is generally not a system decomposition solution, although it could be a start point for structured systems analysis and design. Specifically, the structure of business operations provides a user's view of the system instead of the designer's view of the system. The definitions of business tasks, processes, and steps, as well as the relationships between them, are not necessarily corresponding to the system modules. The issues of module coupling (how modules are interrelated) and cohesion (how the lines of programming code are related to each other) in the structured systems analysis and design are not relevant here.

2. **Data modeling:** Data models are certainly important for systems construction and software implementation. However, reviewing data model would involve excessive efforts for a consumer. Also, conceptual data modeling techniques vary depending upon systems development tools (Topi & Ramesh, 2002). For instance, the traditional entity-relationship model and object-oriented models use different semantics at the conceptual level. Consumers may not be familiar with the particular data modeling method used for a software system. In fact, few software producers provide data models for their consumers while marketing their products.

3. **Internal states of processes or objects:** In designing a software system, states of a process or an object are used to describe the dynamic aspects of the process or object and specify the instances that evolve over the time. However, compared with industrial control engineering systems, business information systems use less states descriptions because business rules and operation structures describe system states in an intuitive way (Wang, 2002).

Implementation of the Specification Model: A Case Study

To experience a practical application of the proposed model, a pre-commercialized software system with a reasonable scale was specified using the method. It is the Apartment Rental Management System developed by a small real estate and software company in southern New England, where the author was a project consultant for the software development. One of the company's founders was a fairly sophisticated computer end-user, but was not a system developer. He was leading the software development team. The other founder was a real estate and rental businessman and was familiar with the rental management software market, but had little computing background. He played the role of marketing manager and facilitated the software development team to fully understand consumers' requirements.

The system was implemented in Microsoft Access. Using it, the user was allowed to perform various tasks on apartment rentals, including property management, tenant record maintenance, reservation, billing and payment, damage and property maintenance, and cash flow management. The company reviewed several competitors' software products and found that the current diversified forms of specifications do not describe their products to consumers adequately. The work team felt that a formalized structure was needed to specify the software system, and decided to use the proposed model.

One guiding principle of the proposed user-centered acquisition specification model is to standardize the specification forms for software consumers. XML (W3C, 2003) enables software companies to develop consistent specification documents with a common format across the application domain. XML documents are flexible for customization. Software specifications encoded in XML are easy for consumers to retrieve specification information and compare components of various software systems. Thus, XML was used for documenting the acquisition specifications for the Apartment Rental Management System.

The XML document of the software system acquisition specifications presents a structure tree with actualized data elements and hyperlinks between these elements. For an intuitive presentation, the data tree represented by the XML document, instead of the XML Schema or DTD (document type definition), is depicted in Figure 7 using the common convention of notations in the XML field. Here, a rectangle represents an element, an ellipse represents the attribute of the element, and a plus sign symbolizes multiple entries of the element.

In Figure 7, each of the four aspects of acquisition specifications has its branch in the data tree, and can be easily presented to the user through XSLT (Extensible Style Language Transformation). As discussed in the previous section, there are connections between those elements in different aspects, which are not shown explicitly in the figure. For instance, a process can have its user-computer interface and its business rules. These connections are presented in Figure 7

Figure 7. The data tree represented by the XML document of acquisition specifications

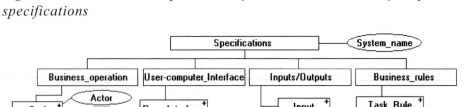

Figure 8. XLink implements the hyperlink connections

```
<?xml version="1.0"  ?>
...
<Process      ProcessName = "PaymentReview"
              ProcessDescription =
              "1. For each unit
                  1.1. Review outstanding payment.
                  1.2. Specify an extension if there is a reason
                       of the late payment.
                  1.3. Print a late payment notice to the tenant.
               2. Print all records of outstanding payment." >
    <Link  xlink:type = "simple"
           xlink:href = "#UCI_PaymentReview" >
           User-computer interface for this process
    </Link>
    <Link  xlink:type = "simple"
           xlink:href = "#BR_PaymentReview" >
           Business rules for this process
    </Link>
    ...
    <Step ... >
    ...
</Process>
...
<UserInterface   UCI_ProcessName = "UCI_PaymentReview"
                 Screen = "UCI_PaymentReview.gif"   >

    <StepUCI ...>
    ...
</UserInterface>
...
<ProcessRule   BR_ProcessName = "BR_PaymentReview"
               Description =
               "1. A due date is set for monthly payment.
                   The default due date is 15th of the month.
                2. Payment for the final month of the lease
                   is the one-month deposit."   >
</ProcessRule>
...
```

implicitly through common attribute names (e.g., process name) for the associated elements (e.g., process and its user-computer interface). XLink was used to implement these implicit connections through hyperlinks. Figure 8 shows a small portion of XML segments that illustrate the hyperlinks between the payment review process and its associated user-computer interface and business rules. The XML document of the software specifications allows consumers to download from the Internet and is more flexible to use than documents with other formats. To compare two or more software systems, one can develop an alternative matrix for these systems, and evaluate them based on the hierarchical specifications. Using the well established analytic hierarchy process (AHP) (Saaty, 1980) method, for instance, an adoption decision can be derived based on the conceived alternative matrix.

The proposed model provides a template for the company in specifying the features of the Apartment Rental Management System for potential consumers. It helps the company in two aspects. First, this specification structure is used as a marketing tool that clearly documents the product for consumers. It is also used as an internal communication tool that bonds the marketing side and the development team side in the company. As a result, the company now has a clear vision of its product. Second, the company is now using this specification model to compare the product with its competitors' products. This allows the company to have a better understanding of the strength and weakness of the product in order to penetrate the market. The company has found that the software system is well documented for consumers using the organized acquisition specifications. It has highlighted the features of the software system that are unique to other competitors' products. The specification model is easy to implement. However, the company has found that there are needs for integration of the acquisition specifications and users' manuals, which would make consumers easier to learn the system. Currently, the company is undertaking further analysis on this issue.

It is our experience that this model offers a pragmatic and useful structure of software specifications for consumers. Clearly, more experiments need to follow in order to make further validation.

Summary

The proliferation of business application software packages has introduced new tasks of acquirement analysis for the systems analysis and design field. To facilitate the communication between software consumers and software builders, application software specifications for consumers must be users-centered instead of builders-centered. This paper proposes a model of software acquisition specifications for consumers. It suggests that business operations, user-computer interfaces, user-perceived inputs and outputs, and business rules are the four essential aspects of acquisition specifications. The four aspects are organized into a static tree, and can be hyperlinked into a complex network for the consumer to examine.

In the history of management information systems, methods for systems specifications have been dominated by computer software builders-centered approaches. On the other hand, the fast growth of the commercialized business software packages on the market demands concise and precise consumer-centered specifications of business software. The proposed acquisition specification model is to bridge the gap between the business requirement definitions and the software implementation descriptions for consumers. Compared with the current system specification techniques such as data flow diagrams and UML, the proposed acquisition specification model is easy to understand for consumers; yet, it mirrors the utilities of application software packages explicitly for consumers. Once the structure of acquisition specifications becomes standardized, it will be possible to investigate the general mapping relationship between acquisition specifications and software construction specifications.

Acknowledgment

The author is indebted to the associate editor and three anonymous referees for their valuable comments for the revision of this paper.

References

Amghar, Y., Meziane, M., & Flory, A. (2000). Using business rules within a design process of active databases. *Journal of Database Management, 11*(3), 3-15.

Anonymous (1993). Two communities, two languages. *Communications of the ACM, 36*(4), 113.

Ballou, D. P., & Pazer, H. L. (1985). Modeling data and process quality in multi-input, multi-output information. *Management Science, 31*(2), 150-162.

Benyon, D. (1992). The role of task analysis in systems design. *Interacting with Computers, 4*(1), 102-123.

Carey, J. M., & McLeod, Jr., R. (1988). Use of system development methodology and tools. *Journal of Systems Management, 39*(3), 30-35.

Chen, P. P. (1976). The entity-relationship model: Toward a unified view of data. *ACM Transactions on Database Systems, 1*(1), 9-36.

DeMarco, T. (1978). *Structured systems analysis and design.* New York: Yourdon.

Dennis, A., & Wixom, B. H. (2003). *Systems analysis and design* (2nd ed.). New York: John Wiley & Sons.

Diaper, D. (1989). The discipline of HCI. *Interacting with Computers, 1*(1), 3-5.

Diaper, D., & Addison, M. (1992). Task analysis and systems analysis for software development. *Interacting with Computers, 4*(1), 124-139.

Gane, C., & Sarson, T. (1979). *Structured systems analysis: Tools and techniques.* Englewood Cliffs, NJ: Prentice-Hall.

Hale, D., Sharpe, S., & Hale, J. E. (1999). Business: Information systems professional differences: Bridging the business rule gap. *Information Resources Management Journal, 12*(2), 16-25.

Harrison, M. D., & Monk, A. F. (Eds.). (1986). *People and computers: Designing for usability.* UK: Cambridge University Press.

Jurison, J. (2000). Perceived value and technology adoption across four end user groups. *Journal of End User Computing, 12*(4), 21-28.

Kendall, J. E. (1994). End user reengineering: Breaking the rules systems developers wrote. *Journal of End User Computing, 6*(2), 24-26.

Li, E. Y., & Chen, H. G. (2001). Output-driven information system planning: A case study. *Information & Management, 38*(3), 185-199.

Rumbaugh, J., Jacobson, I., & Booch, G. (1999). *The unified modeling language reference manual.* Boston: Addison-Wesley.

Saaty, T. L. (1980). *The analytic hierarchy process: Planning, priority setting.* New York: McGraw Hill.

Srinivasan, A. (1985). Alternative measures of system effectiveness: Associations and implications. *MIS Quarterly, 9*(3), 243-253.

Stay, J. F. (1976). HIPO and integrated program design. *IBM Systems Journal, 15*(2), 143-154.

Sutcliffe, A. (1989). Task analysis, systems analysis and design: Symbiosis or synthesis? *Interacting with Computers, 1*(1), 6-12.

Topi, H., & Ramesh, V. (2002). Human factors research on data modelling: A review of prior research, an extended framework and future research directions. *Journal of Database Management, 13*(2), 3-19.

Trauth, E. M., & Cole, E. (1992). The organizational interface: A method for supporting end-user of packaged software. *MIS Quarterly, 16*(1), 35-53.

Wang, S. (1995). Object-oriented task analysis. *Information & Management, 29*(6), 331-341.

Wang, S. (1996). Toward formalized object-oriented management information systems analysis. *Journal of Management Information Systems*, *12*(4), 117-141.

Wang, S. (2002). Teaching the object-oriented approach for business information systems analysis and design. *Journal of Informatics Education and Research*, *4*(1), 17-26.

W3C, Extensible Markup Language (XML). (2003). Retrieved November 2, 2003, from http://www.w3c.org/XML/

Chapter VIII

Perceptions of End Users on the Requirements in Personal Firewall Software:
An Exploratory Study

Sunil Hazari, University of West Georgia, USA

Abstract

Information security is usually considered a technical discipline with much attention being focused on topics such as encryption, hacking, break-ins, and credit card theft. Security products such as anti-virus programs and personal firewall software are now available for end-users to install on their computers to protect against threats endemic to networked computers. The behavioral aspects related to maintaining enterprise security have received little attention from researchers and practitioners. Using Q-sort analysis, this study used students as end users in a graduate business management security course to investigate issues affecting selection of personal firewall software in organizations. Based on the Q-sort analysis of end users in relation to seven variables identified from review of the information security literature, three distinct group characteristics emerged. Similarities and differences between groups are investigated, and implications of these results to IT managers, vendors of security software, and researchers in information security area are discussed.

Introduction

Information must be readily available in organizations for making decisions to support the organizational mission. Murphy, Boren, and Schlarman (2000) state that due to increased connectivity and the urgency to exchange information and data among partners, suppliers, and customers on a real time basis, the need to protect and secure computer resources is greater than ever. As a result, this has created the possibility of exposing sensitive corporate information to competitors as well as hackers who can now access organizational computer resources from remote sites. The potential loss of such information to an organization goes beyond financial losses and includes the possibility of corrupted data, denial of services to suppliers, business partners and customers, loss of customer confidence, and lost sales. Security in business processes (i.e., maintaining proper authentication, authorization, non-repudiation, and privacy) is critical to successful e-business operations. Enabling business functions over the Internet has been recognized as a major component for the success of businesses, and by mitigating risks in a cost-effective manner, security is now being viewed as a component of business operations (Deise, Nowikow, King, & Wright, 2000). Decisions about information systems made by managers are vital to the success, and even survival of a firm (Enns, Huff, & Golden, 2003).

Despite increased security threats, organizations have traditionally allocated very little of the total IT budget to information security. Forrester Research estimates that in Fortune 500 companies, the average amount of money as a percent of revenue that is spent on IT security is .0025 percent or slightly less than what they spend on coffee (Clarke, 2002). Organizations must evaluate and prioritize the optimum mix of products and services to be deployed for protecting confidentiality (maintaining privacy of information), integrity (maintaining information is not altered in transit), and availability (maintaining access to information and resources) of corporate assets. The decision to deploy certain technology is based on variables such as the organizational business model, level of risk, vulnerability, cost, and return on investment (Highland, 1993).

There are several ways in which information can be protected. One method to safeguard information is by using controls. The concept of controls can be applied to financial auditing as well as technical computer security. General controls include personnel, physical and organizational controls, as well as technical security services and mechanisms (Summers, 1997). Computer security controls can be hardware or software based and may include biometric devices, anti-virus software, smart cards, firewalls, and intrusion detection systems that can be used to build the enterprise security infrastructure. Additionally, these controls may be preventive, detective, or corrective. This paper will focus on one such computer security control — personal firewalls. Firewalls intercept traffic and make routing and redirection decisions based on policies. Some firewalls can also inspect packets and make transformation and security decisions; therefore, they are critical components in maintaining security in organizations. There are different types of firewalls such as hardware, software, enterprise, and personal firewalls. Personal firewalls are client-based solutions that are installed on desktop/laptop computers and may be administered individually from a central location. Successful selection and adoption of firewalls (enterprise as well as personal) is based on various factors, some of which are technical, while others may be behavioral. This exploratory study looks at the new genre of personal firewalls, and based on review of the literature attempts to identify factors that could result in successful selection of personal firewalls in organizations and further provide empirical evidence to support deployment of firewall software.

The purposes of this chapter are to investigate self-referent perceptions of end users and use Q-Sort analysis to investigate factors affecting deployment of security firewall software in organizations. The chapter is organized as follows: Review of research on information security is presented to the reader along with extraction of variables from the literature that may determine firewall deployment in organizations. The Q-Sort Factor Analysis method used for the study is explained, and the research design is provided. Along with data analysis, results of the study are then explained, which is followed by discussion and applications to practice. Due to the nature of research design used in this study, limitations are also explained. The study also sheds light on behavioral aspects of information security, which may be tied to perceptions of end users who may influence technology selection in their organization. This will provide empirical evidence to an area that has been identified as lacking in research (Dhillon & Blackhouse, 2001; Troutt, 2002) and provide direction and guidance for future studies.

Information Security Research

In the area of information security, research has often lagged practice. Dhillon and Blackhouse (2001) have stressed the need for "more empirical research to develop key principles for the prevention of negative events and therefore to help in the management of security." Despite known vulnerabilities in applications and operating systems, companies continue to deploy software to stay competitive, and steps taken to secure products and services are knee-jerk reactions to media stories that are more reactive than proactive in nature. Most IT managers lack a coherent framework and concrete methodology for achieving enterprise security. A security plan that includes technology, personnel, and policies would be a much better approach to developing an enterprise security strategy. One such model is the Enterprise Security Framework Price Waterhouse Coopers (PWC) model. The PWC model is comprehensive because it addresses the entire enterprise of security architecture. The model emphasizes information security strategies within the organization using a holistic rather than a piecemeal approach. The framework is based on four pillars: Security Vision and Strategy, Senior Management Commitment, Information Security Management Structure, and Training and Awareness. Within the pillars are Decision Drivers, Development, and Implementation phases. Firewalls are placed in the Development phase since they are used to provide interpretation of corporate standards at the technical level. For a detailed discussion of the PWC model, the reader is referred to Murphy, Boren, and Schlarman (2000).

Firewalls can be considered a last line of defense in protecting and securing information systems. Wood (1988) provided a context for information security systems planning and proposed that reactive and incremental improvement approaches to address security are harbingers of a more serious problem. Other factors identified in Wood's model are the lack of top management support, information overload, insufficient staffing, and limited resources. Straub and Welke (1998) advocate using deterrence, prevention, detection, and recovery security action cycle to mitigate systems risk and use prioritized security controls. Data on computer crimes is often underreported because companies are not willing to risk public embarrassment and bad publicity. Most companies choose to handle these incidents internally without keeping documentation or reporting to local, state, or federal authorities (Saita, 2001). There is a need for un-biased empirical studies in the information security area that will provide insight into problems affecting today's technology dependent corporations and industries. With a strong need to collect and analyze computer security data, the CSI/FBI Computer Crime and Security Survey is published yearly (see http://www.gocsi.com). This study provides descriptive statistics but does not attempt to identify relationship between variables as is expected in analytical surveys.

Also, results reported in this annual survey have been identified by the publishers themselves to be potentially misleading due to the limited number of respondents and their accuracy as a result of the anonymous nature of the surveys. These results have also been called into question because of lack of statistical or scholarly rigor and self-serving interest (Heiser, 2002). Despite these limitations, the CSI/FBI survey provides a useful role in comparison of yearly data for similar parameters.

To provide better evidence of factors that affect deployment of technology tools that create awareness of security issues and produce better informed employees, research into behavioral factors also needs to be conducted to gain insight into programs and processes that will lead to the development of a robust enterprise security strategy. Information security awareness research has been mostly descriptive and has not explored the possibilities offered by motivation/behavioral theories or the related theory of planned behavior and the technology acceptance model, specifically in the information security domain (Legris, Ingham, & Collerette, 2003; Mathieson, 1991; Siponen, 2000). Since security has been deployed at the perimeter of electronic network and on servers by system administrators, the area of information security has ignored users of information systems since software developers are far removed from how the user will interact with security software. Human compliance with information security rules requires an understanding of how people work and think (Highland, 1993). Lane (1985) considers the human factor to be the first and most important component of security and a critical part of the risk analysis process. This is especially true in personal firewall software since the burden of maintaining a secure environment is being shared by the user and the system administrator.

The area of human computer interface provides a link between the user and software applications. User satisfaction is a function of features, user interface, response time, reliability, installability, information, maintainability, and other factors. "If a product's user interface catches a user's attention and is simple to learn and use, and has the right price and features, then the product may gain competitive advantage" (Torres, 2002a, p. 15). The theory of user interface design and user involvement in completing tasks based actions related to Internet and security software has been substantiated by two studies in which user interaction with peer-to-peer software (Good & Kerkelberg, 2002) and PGP software (Whitten & Tygar, 1999) were examined. Good and Krekelberg (peer-to-peer study) found that applications connecting to the Internet need better usability and software design to maintain integrity of information stored on a user's computer. In this study, individuals assumed responsibility of keeping firewalls operational at all times. This contributed in large part to maintaining effective enterprise security. Whitten and Tygar (PGP study) found that user errors are a significant portion of computer security failures, and further concluded that user interfaces for security programs require a usability standard much different from other consumer software. (Although this study is not directly concerned with user satisfaction, but is more focused on factors that affect deployment rather than development of end-user software in a specific area, some factors may be directly tied to user satisfaction as will be shown by correlational analysis.)

An important reason to look at end user perceptions is that it may affect how well the user does his or her part in staying vigilant to combat threats posted by hackers to organizational assets. The end user may be a conduit to organizational data being compromised. Proper software selection as well as positive user attitude and motivation for using the software are therefore important to ensure ongoing use of personal firewall software. Kettinger and Lee (2002) address the fact that the proliferation of personal computing and individualized software and popularity of the Internet in organizations have resulted in users playing an important role in driving IT implementation. Their study found that for users selecting their own IT applications (such as desktop software programs), there is greater user satisfaction after implementation. Grantham and Vaske (1985) also state that positive user attitudes are important predictors in continued system use. This is especially important for personal firewall use because computers are at risk at all times when connected to the Internet. In reference to software selection, Chiasson and Lovato (2001) emphasize, "Understanding of how users form perceptions of software innovation would help software designers, implementers and users in their evaluation, selection, implementation and ongoing use of software. However, with the exception of some recent work, there is little research examining how a user forms his or her perceptions of innovation over time" (p. 16). The area of information security as it relates to maintaining confidentiality and integrity of data stored on personal computers can benefit from identification of factors that would make it possible to safeguard corporate assets that are at risk as a result of remote data access by employees. Software selection for deployment on company computers cuts across different user levels in terms of knowledge and level of expertise of the user. Selection of software therefore must be done to accommodate all types of users ranging from novices to experts. The latter category of users may have higher tacit knowledge of tasks to be able to compensate for the interface without realizing it (Gery, 1997).

Due to increasing mobile and off-site access by employees using cable modems, DSL connections, and wireless devices to access corporate resources, personal firewalls are a necessary component to maintain overall enterprise security in an organization. Because of the nature and availability of personal firewall software, most companies choose to acquire it rather than develop it in-house. Software acquisition that results in productivity gains and strategic advantage is of critical concern to organizations, and factors that relate to these benefits must be correctly identified and understood for software acquisition decisions (Nelson,

Richmond, & Seidmann, 1996). Purchase of commercial software includes identifying requirements, evaluating packages from different vendors, configuring, installing, and evaluating it either as a server or client-based solution. This may further involve requirements acquisition that leads to product selection (Maiden, Ncube, & Moore, 1997). As a method of selection, professionals in charge of evaluating personal firewall software could draft a feature requirements document, and evaluate vendor products by comparing available features as well as using demonstration versions of software. This would be followed by user experience with the software. As mentioned earlier, the need for user involvement in information systems has been considered an important mechanism for improving system quality and ensuring successful system implementation. It is further believed that the user's satisfaction with a system leads to greater system usage (Baroudi, Olson, & Ives, 1986). The requirements for software, though, must be as measurable as possible to enable product selection and may also use repertory grids in which stakeholders are asked for attributes applicable to a set of entities and values for cells in an entity-attribute matrix. This would produce representation of requirements in a standardized, quantifiable format amenable even to statistical analyses (Maiden, Ncube, & Moore, 1997). In relation to the security area, Goodhue and Straub (1991) found company actions and individual awareness to be statistically significant in a study of perceptions of managers regarding controls installed in organizations.

Research Design

Subjects in this exploratory research study were 31 MBA students enrolled in a Security and Control of Information Systems course. The students came from different backgrounds such as finance, liberal arts, nursing, and computer science. From a business perspective, the course examined implications of information security risks faced by organizations. Although technical issues of security such as authentication, authorization, and encryption that make electronic commerce sites successful in processing business transactions securely were also explored in the course, the primary focus in the course was from a business perspective. There was no structured lab work during class, but to gain a better understanding of security issues, students were expected to complete hands-on exercises outside of class. During the initial weeks, topics covered included the PWC model, TCP/IP vs. OSI models, network, e-mail, database security, digital certificates and signatures, risk assessment, and privacy issues. Also, during Week 5, students had been previously tested on the above topics using short-answer type questions to determine learning competency of factual information and applications related to information security in organizations. The test score counted towards 15% of overall course grade. With coverage of above topics, it was safe to assume that students had knowledge of current security issues facing organizations in today's economy. Because there is no consensus on the Common Body of Knowledge acceptable for all security professionals, and since this was an exploratory study, the study was conducted in a controlled environment with a homogenous population of students to minimize confounding by extraneous variables. Using MBA students as surrogates for professionals or executives in reference to use and evaluation of technology has also been found to be acceptable (Briggs, Balthazard, & Dennis, 1996).

The hands-on firewall assignment in this course covered installation, configuration, and use of one standard personal firewall software (ZoneAlarm). After students had a chance to use the software, they were asked to participate in the study. No class discussion was conducted on results of the firewall tests in case it affected students' perceptions about the software, which could have influenced their response. Therefore, the data reflected individual student perception without class discussions. Students were given instructions to visit a Web site that explained the nature of the study and provided information on how the Q-sort statements should be sorted. This was important since students are more used to completing questionnaires in a survey format that uses Likert scale, open-ended, or close-ended questions (such as those used during end of term class evaluation of instruction), but may not be familiar with the peculiarities of the Q-sort procedure. To reduce data errors and extract usable data, instructions were presented in detail before the respondents were shown the statements for the study. This was an exploratory study for the purpose of investigating and contributing to research in the relatively new domain of user-centered security products that are being deployed by businesses to increase enterprise security.

Q-Sort Analysis

Q-sort analysis uses a technique for studying human subjectivity (Brown, 1980; McKeown & Thomas, 1988; Stephenson, 1953). It is useful in exploratory research and a well-developed theoretical literature guide and supports its users (Thomas & Watson, 2002). Q-sort methodology is suited for small samples and relies on theories in the domain area being researched to develop items for analysis. Disadvantage of the Q-sort methodology are that it is not suitable for large samples, and it forces subjects to conform to certain expectations (such as fitting responses within a normal distribution). Brown (1986) suggests that 30 to 50 subjects are sufficient for studies investigating public opinion. Q-sort uses an ipsative (self-referenced) technique of sorting participants' statements about subjective conditions. It is a variation of the factor analysis technique that uses Q-methodology theory to analyze correlation measure (Brown, 1980). Respondents to Q-sort studies are required to sort statements into predefined normal distribution type scale in which a fixed number of items fall under each category. The rankings provide clusters of perceptions of individuals' consensus and conflict, which can be used to place individuals with similar characteristics into groups for further study. In the past, the

Q-sort technique used index cards for sorting, but now Web based data collection programs (such as WebQ) are common. Initially the statements are presented to respondents in random order, and each respondent organizes statements into predefined categories. To view entered data, the respondent also can update statement rankings to see where the statements fall under each category. One advantage of using the WebQ method is that data submission errors are reduced since the program verifies that the statements are sorted according to predefined requirements.

In this personal firewall study, the statements were to be classified by respondents as "Most Important" (+2), "Important" (+1), "Neutral" (0), "Less Important" (-1), and "Least Important" (-2). To provide a forced distribution that is expected in the Q-Sort methodology, respondents were given instructions to

Figure 1. WebQ questionnaire

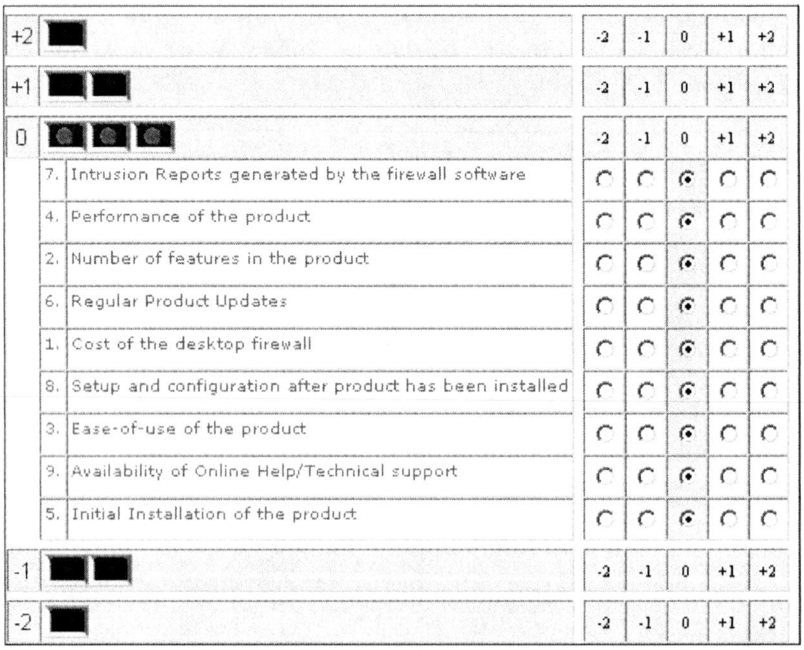

identify one statement as "Most Important," two statements each as "Important" and "Less Important," and three statements as "Neutral." The instrument used is shown in Figure 1.

Data Analysis

Q-Sort analysis is a type of inverse factor analysis in which the cases (subjects) rather than statement variables (features) are clustered. As recommended by Brown (1980), a procedure that arranged statements based on responses of a single individual was used for data analysis. The responses involved statements of opinion (also called Q-sample) that individuals rank-ordered based on the feature requirements in personal firewall software. The arrayed items (Q-sort) from the respondents were correlated and factor-analyzed. The factors indicated clusters of subjects who had ranked the statement in the same fashion. Explanation of factors was then advanced in terms of commonly shared attitudes or perspectives.

A review of security literature (Hazari, 2000; Northcutt, McLachlan, & Novak, 2000; Scambray, McClure, & Kurtz, 2001; Strassberg, Rollie, & Gondek, 2002; Zwicky, Cooper, Chapman, & Russell, 2000) was used to extract the following statement variables relating to requirements in personal firewall software: Performance, ease of use, updates, features, reports, cost, configuration, and support. Operational definitions of these variables as they relate to the study are provided below:

- **Performance [PERF]:** Refers to how well the software operates under various conditions (such as high traffic, types of data, port scans, etc.)
- **Ease of Use [EOU]:** Refers to usability of the product (such as screen design and layout, access to features using tabs, buttons, etc.)
- **Updates [UPDTS]:** Refers to product updates at regular intervals after product has been installed and used
- **Features [FEATR]:** Refers to the number of program options and features available in software
- **Reports [RPORT]:** Refers to Intrusion Reports and log files generated by the firewall software
- **Cost [COST]:** Refers to price paid for the product (either as shrink wrapped package or as a download)

Table 1. Participant ranked scores

Variable	Mean	SD
PERF	4.45	0.77
EOU	3.39	1.08
UPDTS	3.23	0.88
FEATR	3.06	0.93
RPORT	3.00	1.03
COST	2.97	1.20
CONFIG	2.55	0.85
SUPPRT	2.35	0.98
INSTLL	2.00	0.89

- **Configuration [CONFIG]:** Refers to setup and configuration after product has been installed
- **Support [SUPPRT]:** Refers to availability of online help and technical support either by phone or e-mail
- **Installation [INSTLL]:** Refers to initial installation of the product

Prior to conducting the Q-sort analysis, ranked scores of all participants (before identifying factor groups) on each statement variable were calculated for preliminary descriptive statistics. These are shown in Table 1 (Mean Score: 5= Most important, 0= Least important).

Correlation between the nine feature variables shows a low level of correlation between statements. This indicates there is a high degree of independence between the statement categories as used in the analysis. This finding is important since it supports the assertion that the statements represent relatively independent factors obtained from the review of the literature.

In the correlation matrix shown above, Table 2 shows significant correlation ($p<.05$) between cost and updates, cost and reports, ease-of-use and performance, ease-of-use and updates, and installation and support.

As mentioned earlier, in Q-factor analysis, the correlation between subjects rather than variables are factored. The factors represent groupings of people with similar patterns of response during sorting (Brown, 1980; Thomas & Watson, 2002). Following guidelines for Q-factor analysis, eight factors were initially identified with eigenvalues >1 (eigenvalue is the amount of variance in the original variable associated with the factor). These factors and their percentage of variance are shown in Table 3.

Factors selected were rotated to maximize the loading of each variable on one of the extracted factors while minimizing loading on all other factors. Factors

Table 2. Correlation matrix between variables

	COST	FEATR	EOU	PERF	INSTLL	UPDTS	RPORT	CONFIG	SUPPRT
Cost	1.00	-0.21	0.27	-0.18	-0.13	-0.43*	-0.49*	-0.08	-0.10
FEATR		1.00	-0.29	0.35	-0.16	0.06	-0.17	-0.13	-0.25
EOU			1.00	-0.44*	0.00	-0.37*	-0.27	-0.20	-0.04
PERF				1.00	-0.10	-0.11	-0.13	0.13	-0.14
INSTLL					1.00	-0.13	-0.04	0.18	-0.53*
UPDTS						1.00	0.26	-0.30	0.17
RPORT							1.00	-0.15	0.03
CONFIG								1.00	-0.24
SUPPRT									1.00

Table 3. Eigenvalues of unrotated factors

	Eigenvalues	%	Cumul. %
1	11.56	37.28	37.28
2	6.03	19.45	56.73
3	3.91	12.61	69.34
4	2.98	9.61	78.95
5	2.14	6.92	85.87
6	1.93	6.23	92.10
7	1.43	4.61	96.71
8	1.02	3.29	100.00

selected for rotation are usually identified by taking those with eigenvalue greater than one (Kline, 1994). However, in this study, the more rigorous Kaiser rule of selecting factors whose eigenvalue is at or above the mean eigenvalue (in this case 3.85) was used. Factors 1, 2, and 3, which represented almost 70% of total variance in data, were then subjected to principal component analysis with varimax rotation.

Following rotation, a factor matrix indicating defining sort (i.e., respondents in agreement) identified three factor groups with similar pattern of responses. The correlation of individual respondents with factors is shown in Table 4.

From Table 4 it can be observed that for Factor 1, respondents 4, 12, 13, 15, 18, 20, 22, and 27 were in agreement and are highly loaded on this factor. Similarly, respondents 6, 10, 14, 16, 21, 24, 26, 29, and 30 were in agreement in Factor 2, and respondents 5, 7, 8, 9, 11, 17, 19, and 23 were in agreement in Factor 3.

The statements in which these three factor groups were ranked are shown in Table 5.

Table 4. Factor matrix of respondents (indicates defining sort)*

	Factor Loadings		
Q-Sort	1	2	3
1	0.2386	-0.0398	0.8988
2	0.0227	0.1971	0.8158*
3	0.4975	-0.3790	0.5458
4	0.8575*	-0.2912	0.0811
5	-0.2639	0.0196	0.7993*
6	-0.0614	0.7524*	-0.2289
7	0.4014	-0.1587	0.4678*
8	0.1367	0.0728	0.9054*
9	0.5351	0.1183	0.6886*
10	0.5065	0.5665*	0.1764
11	0.5351	0.1183	0.6886
12	0.8192*	0.3263	0.1035
13	0.6495*	0.3357	-0.0844
14	-0.0464	0.7321*	0.5845
15	0.6535*	0.3450	0.3053
16	0.2052	0.8598*	0.2453
17	-0.1340	0.0127	0.9512
18	0.7553*	0.2324	0.2987
19	0.2431	0.4049	0.6946
20	0.5983*	0.5865	-0.0334
21	0.4660	0.6533*	0.4573
22	0.5672*	0.1057	-0.3342
23	0.3501	-0.1001	0.8185
24	0.1008	0.9240*	0.0038
25	0.3329	0.0999	0.2194
26	0.2254	0.6545*	0.1329
27	0.7660*	0.1246	0.5677
28	-0.1210	-0.3611*	0.2307
29	0.3850	0.7032*	0.0144
30	0.4656	0.5605	-0.3196
31	-0.1987	0.8988*	0.2470
% explained variance	21	22	26

Table 6 shows correlation between the factors. Similar to the findings earlier about variable independence, the factor groups also show a high degree of independence.

The normalized factor scores for each factor were examined next. This provided a measure of relative strength of importance attached by a factor to each

Table 5. Ranked statement totals with each factor

No.	Statement	Factor 1		Factor 2		Factor 3	
1	COST	0.31	5	0.91	2	-1.45	9
2	FEATR	-0.45	7	0.10	5	0.70	2
3	EOU	0.91	2	0.63	3	-0.55	6
4	PERF	1.26	1	1.72	1	1.80	1
5	INSTLL	-1.92	9	-0.31	6	-0.63	7
6	UPDTS	0.52	3	-0.54	7	0.61	3
7	RPORTS	0.03	6	-1.28	8	0.55	4
8	CONFIG	-1.07	8	0.12	4	-0.17	5
9	SUPPRT	0.41	4	-1.34	9	-0.87	8

Table 6. Correlation between factors

Factor	1	2	3
1	1.0000	0.3218	0.2970
2	0.3218	1.0000	0.2298
3	0.2970	0.2298	1.0000

statement on the scale used during sorting. Tables 7a, 7b, and 7c show these scores.

From Table 7a it can be seen that adherents of Factor 1 feel strongly in favor of statement 4 (Performance) and oppose statements 8 and 5. This indicates for Factor 1 group, performance is preferred over initial installation, setup, and configuration of the product.

The results of Factor 2 group are consistent with Factor 1, that is, Performance of the product is the highest rated criterion. Ease of use also rated highly in Factors 1 and 2. Perceived ease of use in an information systems product has been shown to play a critical role in predicting and determining a user's decision to use the product (Hackbarth, Grover, & Yi, 2003). The largest dissension between Factor 1 and 2 groups involved statements 9 (Availability of online help), 7 (Intrusion reports generated), and 6 (Regular product updates).

The results of Factor 3 are consistent with Factors 1 and 2 with Performance criteria once again being highly rated. The most dissension between Factors 2 and 3 involved statements 1 (Cost) and 3 (Ease of use). The most dissension between Factors 1 and 3 involved statements 1 (Cost), 3 (Ease of use), and 9 (Availability of online help).

Table 7a. Normalized Factor 1 score

No.	Statement	z-score
4	PERF	1.258
3	EOU	0.910
6	UPDTS	0.524
9	SUPPRT	0.409
1	COST	0.314
7	RPORT	0.032
2	FEATR	-0.454
8	CONFIG	-1.071
5	INSTLL	-1.922

Table 7b. Normalized Factor 2 score

No.	Statement	z-score
4	PERF	1.717
1	COST	0.905
3	EOU	0.626
8	CONFIG	0.116
2	FEATR	0.102
5	INSTLL	-0.313
6	UPDTS	-0.535
7	RPORT	-1.276
9	SUPPRT	-1.343

Table 7c. Normalized Factor 3 score

No.	Statement	z-score
4	PERF	1.805
2	FEATR	0.702
6	UPDTS	0.606
7	RPORT	0.553
8	CONFIG	-0.170
3	EOU	-0.547
5	INSTLL	-0.632
9	SUPPRT	-0.872
1	COST	-1.446

Discussion and Applications for Practice

The Q-sort analysis classified subjects into three groups. Eight subjects were classified under Factor 1, and 10 subjects each were included in Factors 2 and 3. There were three subjects in the study that were not distinguished in any group. These subjects were excluded from further analysis. The classification into factors gave a better idea of group characteristics. Since Factors 1 and 2 were similar and shown to include subjects who considered performance, ease of use, and availability of online help as the most important characteristics, this group can be considered to be comprised of non-technical users who place more emphasis on the product performing as expected in achieving goals for security. Factor 3 subjects emphasized technical characteristics and were more interested in number of features in the product, updates to the product on a regular basis, intrusion reports generated by personal firewalls, and setup/configuration of the product after installation. This group had characteristics of technical users.

The normalized factor scores provided a measure of relative strength of importance attached by factors to each statement on the scale used during sorting. As mentioned earlier, adherents in Factor 1 felt strongly in favor of statement 4 (Performance) and opposed statements 8 (Setup/configuration) and 5 (Installation). The results of Factor 2 are consistent with Factor 1, that is, Performance of the product is the highest rated criterion. Ease of use also rated highly in Factors 1 and 2. The largest dissension between Factor 1 and 2 groups involved statements 9 (Availability of online help), 7 (Intrusion reports generated), and 6 (Regular product updates). The most dissension between Factors 2 and 3 involved Statements 1 (Cost) and 3 (Ease of use). Results of Factor 3 were consistent with Factors 1 and 2, with Performance criteria once again being highly rated. The largest dissension between Factors 1 and 3 involved statements 1 (Cost), 3 (Ease of use), and 9 (Availability of online help). Extreme differences between all factors appeared in Cost, Intrusion Reports generated, and Availability of online help. There was only one statement, Performance of the product, that showed consensus among all factors, that is, it did not distinguish between any pair of factors, which indicates Performance of the desktop firewall software is an agreed upon criterion irrespective of group characteristics.

The managerial implications of this study can be assessed at the level of selecting appropriate software for use on computers in organizations to maintain security. There is evidence of user satisfaction being a useful measure of system success (Mahmood, Burn, & Gemoets, 2000). While the end user may not purchase individually preferred software for installation on company owned computers, the user can influence decisions for selection by making known to IS managers the features that would contribute to regular use of security software such as personal firewalls. Given access of these machines to corporate resources, appropriate and regular use of software would contribute to maintaining enterprise security. For technical professionals (e.g., programmers) who install firewalls on their desktop, programs could emphasize the statements that are defining characteristics shown in Factor 3. For an industry that has non-technical professionals (such as Factor 1 and 2), other non-technical characteristics of the product could be emphasized thus achieving maximum effectiveness in program deployment. Increased awareness should minimize user related faults, nullify these in theory, and maximize the efficiency of security techniques and procedures from the user's point of view (Siponen, 2000).

The results of this study could also benefit vendors who develop software for end users. In this study it was found that performance of the software is the most important factor that affects selection of software, irrespective of group characteristics. Due to project deadlines and market competition, software is often shipped without being fully tested as secure, and standard industry practice is to release incremental service packs that address security issues in the product. In a case of security software, this may adversely affect the reputation of a vendor once its products have been shown to have high vulnerability to being compromised. The findings of this study could provide a better understanding of importance of personal firewall security software on organizational client computers. The decision to install an information system necessitates a choice of mechanisms to determine whether it is needed, and once implemented, whether it is functioning properly (Ives, Olson, & Baroudi, 1983). More research needs to be done in the area of selection of software for implementation on users' computers that are owned by corporations and given to employees for off-site work. This can include regular employees versus contractors, who may connect to employer and client networks from the same computer. If the findings are to have wider applicability, qualified industry professionals and security officers responsible for maintaining secure infrastructure in corporations should be included in the analysis. The study provides management and security professionals a basis for making decisions related to enterprise security. It provides personal firewall vendors an insight into feature requirements of the personal firewall market and provides academic researchers interested in security a more focused approach on various dimensions of security software from the behavioral perspective. Future studies could be industry and product specific in order to assess differences in selecting general-purpose software versus security specific products.

In many cases, management has looked at the need for implementing information security programs and products as a necessary encumbrance, something akin to paying taxes or insurance premiums (Highland, 1993). But organizations are increasingly becoming aware of the potential for legal exposure via lawsuits and are deploying countermeasures (e.g., personal firewalls) to reduce vulnerability and mitigate risk. The chief information security officer in today's organizations should have the responsibility of managing organizational risks by using empirical models and analysis to determine strategies for protecting corporate assets. Firewalls are the last line of defense in the corporate network and therefore play a critical role in information security. With personal firewalls being a new product genre, this study was conducted since there is no research available that specifically looks at determinants for selection of security software in a corporate environment to protect organizational assets. As the information security field evolves further, decisions for security software acquisitions need to be researched further. Selection and deployment of appropriate firewalls can make a significant difference in an organization's enterprise security strategy. It is therefore also important to understand the variables (as shown in this study) that may affect decisions to select and deploy personal firewall software in a corporate environment.

Limitations of the Study

Due to the exploratory nature of this study, there are several limitations. The sample used in the study was comprised of all students enrolled in a security course at the same university and was further limited to the firewall topic among a wide range of technical and behavioral information security topics. Students worked with only one type of firewall software, and characteristics of this particular program may have heightened their awareness of certain strengths and weaknesses in the software. Since the purpose of information security implementation in an organization is to support business objectives of the organization, information security departments are sometimes placed under the chief financial officer recognizing the direct relationship between information assets and monetary assets. Software acquisition decisions may therefore be made by the finance department with limited input from the IT department. The purpose of this study was to explore an important topic for research on information security and determine operant subjectivity in a field where empirical research is severely lacking. The Q-sort technique itself is suitable for small sample populations (Thomas & Watson, 2002), but the correlations obtained in smaller samples tend to have considerable standard errors (Kline, 1994). The exploratory nature of this study was not intended to prove some general proposition but to seek a better understanding of group characteristics that directly relate to maintaining a secure network environment (in this case by deploying personal firewalls to plug possible vulnerabilities that might exist in a network through use of computers by employees either on-site or at remote locations). The perceptions of end users will therefore guide the selection and deployment of security technologies in an organization to provide a secure corporate environment.

Conclusion

In this study, Q-methodology was used to define participant viewpoints and perceptions, empirically place participants in groups, provide sharper insight into participant preferred directions, identify criteria that are important to participants, explicitly outline areas of consensus and conflicts, and investigate a contemporary problem relating to desktop firewalls by quantifying subjectivity. Similar to other IT areas, security software selection and deployment in today's environment faces many challenges such as staying current with new threats, project deadlines, implementation issues, and support costs. Quality drives customer satisfaction and adoption of software. Human factors are important in contributing to successful software deployment in organizations, especially when it relates to desktop software applications. Organizations are now viewing security and controls as business enablers, and desktop firewall technology plays a critical role in safeguarding corporate assets. In a fast-paced area where the new generation of applications and services is growing more complex each day, it is critical to understand characteristics that affect selection of end user security products in enterprises.

This study addresses a small but important area of safeguarding enterprise information security by using personal firewalls. As has been previously noted, limited research exists beyond the current study that explores behavioral aspects of information security. This study holds importance for professionals tasked with evaluating and selecting security products for companywide deployment. As the area of information security gains increased importance due to the strategic role of technology in organizations, and current events impact areas such as disaster recovery and enterprise continuity planning, a study of end users to determine their perceptions about selection of technology controls in organizations is critical for protecting organizational assets. More research needs to be done in the area of perception of users toward other security software (e.g. anti-virus, intrusion detection, virtual private network software, and encryption products), and due to varying security needs in different industries, studies could also be industry and product specific. While the findings should be considered preliminary, the results raise interesting observations about issues uncovered regarding security perceptions of feature requirements in personal firewalls. Information security is a dynamic area, and in this environment, this exploratory study contributes to evolving research by identifying variables from theoretical literature and using an empirical technique to study issues that affect safeguarding vital assets of an organization from internal and external threats.

References

Baroudi, J., Olson, M., & Ives, B. (1986). An empirical study of the impact of user involvement on system usage and information satisfaction. *Communications of the ACM, 29*(3), 785-793.

Briggs, R. O., Balthazard, P. A., & Dennis, A. R. (1996). Graduate business students as surrogates for executives in the evaluation of technology. *Journal of End User Computing, 8*(4), 11-17.

Brown, S. R. (1980). *Political subjectivity: Applications of Q methodology in political science.* CT: Yale.

Brown, S. R. (1986). Q-technique and method: Principles and procedures. In W. D. Berry & M. S. Lewis-Beck (Eds.), *New tools for social scientists: Advances and applications in research methods.* Beverly Hills, CA: Sage Publications.

Chiasson, M., & Lovato, C. (2001). Factors influencing the formation of a user's perceptions and use of a DSS software innovation. *ACM SIGMIS Database, 32*(3), 16-35.

Clarke, R. (2002, February). *Forum on Technology and Innovation: Sponsored by Sen. Bill Frist (R-TN), Sen. Jay Rockefeller (D-WV), and the Council on Competitiveness.* Retrieved October 28, 2003, from http://www.techlawjournal.com/security/20020214.asp

Deise, M., Nowikow, C., King, P., & Wright, A. (2000). *Executive's guide to e-business: From tactics to strategy.* New York: John Wiley & Sons.

Dhillon, G., & Blackhouse, J. (2001). Current directions in IS security research: Toward socio-organizational perspectives. *Information Systems Journal, 11*(2), 127-153.

Enns, H., Huff, S., & Golden, B. (2003). CIO influence behaviors: The impact of technical background. *Information and Management, 40*(5), 467-485.

Gery, G. (1997). Granting three wishes through performance-centered design. *Communication of the ACM, 40*(7), 54-59.

Good, N., & Krekelberg, A. (2002). *Usability and privacy: A study of Kazaa P2P file-sharing.* Retrieved November 12, 2003, from http://www.hpl.hp.com/shl/papers/kazaa/

Goodhue, D. L., & Straub, D. W. (1991). Security concerns of system users: A study of perceptions of the adequacy of security measures. *Information & Management, 20*(1), 13-27.

Grantham, C., & Vaske, J. (1985). Predicting the usage of an advanced communication technology. *Behavior and Information Technology, 4*(4), 327-335.

Hackbarth, G., Grover, V., & Yi M., (2003). Computer playfulness and anxiety: Positive and negative mediators of the system experience effect on perceived ease of use. *Information and Management, 40*(3), 221-232.

Hazari, S. (2000). *Firewalls for beginners.* Retrieved December 17, 2003, from http://online.securityfocus.com/infocus/1182

Heiser, J. (2002, April). Go figure: Can you trust infosecurity surveys? *Information Security*, 27-28.

Highland, H. J. (1993). A view of information security tomorrow. In E. G. Dougall (Ed.), *Computer security.* Holland: Elsevier.

Ives, B., Olson, M., & Baroudi, J. (1983). The measurement of user information satisfaction. *Communications of the ACM, 26*(10), 785-793.

Kettinger, W., & Lee, C. (2002). Understanding the IS-User divide in IT innovation. *Communications of the ACM, 45*(2), 79-84.

Kline, P. (1994). *An easy guide to factor analysis.* London: Rutledge.

Lane, V. P. (1985). *Security of computer based information systems.* London: Macmillan.

Legris, P., Ingham, J., & Collerette, P. (2003). Why do people use information technology? A critical review of the technology acceptance model. *Information and Management, 40*(3), 191-204.

Mahmood, M. A., Burn, J. M., Gemoets, L. A., & Jacquez, C. (2000). Variables affecting information technology end-user satisfaction: A meta-analysis of the empirical literature. *International Journal of Human-Computer Studies, 52*, 751-771.

Maiden, N., Ncube, C., & Moore, A. (1997). Lessons learned during requirements acquisition for COTS systems. *Communications of the ACM, 40*(12), 21-25.

Mathieson, K. (1991). Predicting user intentions: Comparing the technology acceptance model with the theory of planned behavior. *Information Systems Research, 3*(2), 173-191.

McKeown, B., & Thomas, D. (1988). *Q Methodology.* CA: Sage Publications Inc.

Murphy, B., Boren, R., & Schlarman, S. (2000). *Enterprise Security Architecture*, CRC Press. Retrieved November 2, 2003, from http://www.pwcglobal.com

Nelson, P., Richmond, W., & Seidmann, A. (1996). Two dimensions of software acquisition. *Communications of the ACM, 39*(7), 29-35.

Northcutt, S., McLachlan, D., & Novak, J. (2000). *Network intrusion detection: An analyst's handbook* (2nd ed.). IN: New Riders Publishing.

Saita, A. (2001, June). Understanding peopleware. *Information security*, 72-80.

Scambray, J., McClure, S., & Kurtz, G. (2001). *Hacking exposed* (2nd ed.). CA: Osborne/McGraw-Hill.

Siponen, M. T. (2000). A conceptual foundation for organizational information security awareness, *Information Management & Security, 8*(1), 31-41.

Stephenson, W. (1953). *The study of behavior*. Chicago: University of Chicago Press.

Strassberg, K., Rollie, G., & Gondek, R. (2002). *Firewalls: The complete reference*. New York: Osborne McGraw-Hill.

Straub, D. W., & Welke, R. J. (1988). Coping with systems risk: Security planning models for management decision making. *MIS Quarterly, 22*(4), 441-469.

Summers, R. (1997). *Secure computing: Threats and safeguards*. New York: McGraw-Hill.

Thomas, D., & Watson, R. (2002). Q-sorting and MIS research: A primer. *Communications of the AIS, 8*, 141-156.

Torres, R. J. (2002a). *Practitioner's handbook for user interface design and development*. NJ: Prentice-Hall.

Torres, R. J. (2002b). Why Johnny can't encrypt: A usability evaluation of PGP 5.0. In *Proceedings of the 8th USENIX Security Symposium*.

Troutt, M. D. (2002). IT security issues: The need for end user oriented research. *Journal of End User Computing, 14*(2), 48.

Wood, C. (1988). A context for information systems security planning. *Computers & Security, 7*(5), 455-465.

Zwicky, E., Cooper, S., Chapman, D., & Russell, D. (2000). *Building internet firewalls* (2nd ed.). CA: O'Reilly.

Section III:

End Users Characteristics and Learning

Chapter IX

The Changing Demographics:
The Diminishing Role of Age and Gender in Computer Usage

Michael B. Knight, Appalachian State University, USA

J. Michael Pearson, Southern Illinois University at Carbondale, USA

Abstract

As the changing demographics of the workplace influence how organizations operate, the need to reexamine relationships between these demographic variables and their effect on the organization continues. This study provides an empirical examination of the effect of two demographic variables, age and gender, and any moderating impact anxiety, enjoyment, and/or peer pressure may have on computer usage. Based on our analysis of 292 knowledge workers, we identified no significant difference between men and women and/or young and old regarding their computer usage in the workplace. Therefore, the findings from this study do not seem to support earlier research regarding age and gender, which indicated that these variables did impact computer usage. However, the moderating construct (anxiety) did appear to be significant in the employees' computer usage.

Introduction

The use of information technology within an organization can have a dramatic effect not only on the success or failure of the organization, but also on the overall work life of its employees. There are at least two issues associated with organizations investing in information technology. The first issue is whether employees will accept the technology. The second issue is whether employees will be more productive with the new technology. While many studies have examined technology acceptance (Davis, 1989; Gefen & Straub, 1997; Szajna, 1996) and have attempted to focus on how particular variables impact technology acceptance, few have looked at the implications concerning the changing demographics (i.e., age, gender, education level, position, organizational training, and organizational pressure to use technology) in the U.S. workforce.

As the workforce has changed over the past decade, so has the use of computers (Igbaria, Parasuraman, & Baroudi, 1996) and the level of sophistication embedded in their software applications. However, only limited research has been conducted to examine how the changing demographics of the workforce have affected computer usage within the organization. As the number of women in the workforce has increased and the average age of workers has also increased (Census, 2000; Greco, 1998), earlier studies may no longer accurately reflect the current dynamics within the modern organization. With the proliferation of computers into the home, older employees may have become more comfortable with basic software packages (White, McConnell, Clipp, & Bynum, 1999). Therefore, by looking at the changes that have occurred in the workforce demographics and the current usage of information technology in the workplace, we should be able to develop a better understanding of what is currently affecting the usage of information technology within the modern organization.

The following study examines data collected using multiple validated instruments, compares the results to current literature, then attempts to show the effect of age and gender on the usage of technology and the modifying effect of perceived pressure and enjoyment. The perceived pressure to use technology may be best explained, from Compeau, Higgins, and Huff's (1999) work, as the social influences of encouragement by others, others' use of IT, organizational support, and personal anxiety.

Literature Review

Traditionally, research in the information systems and/or information technology areas have focused on the technology (the system) being implemented (Brown, 2001; Yang & Moore, 1995). Individual studies have looked at the user regarding perceived satisfaction in the use of IT (Robie, Ryan, Schmieder, Parra, & Smith, 1998; Simmers & Anandarajan, 2001), acceptance of technology (Davis, 1989), learner behavior (Brown, 2001), gender and discriminatory practices (Truman & Baroudi, 1994), gender and learning (Arbaugh, 2000), age and the use of the Internet (White et al., 1999), previous computer experience (Thompson, Higgins, & Howell, 1994), and motivational factors to use computers (Pintrich & Schunk, 1996). While not all of the previously mentioned articles are exclusive to the IS and IT arena, they all hold relevance to the current research project due to the findings that each study has provided.

Brown (2001) found, through a study of technical employees at a Fortune 500 manufacturing firm, that age is a factor affecting the speed at which computer training can be presented and the quality of its retention. Older employees were found to exhibit less interest in and have a less positive attitude toward computers than younger employees. Additionally, Brown found older employees had lower learning outcomes than younger employees do. Brown concluded that an increase in age may be associated with greater resistance to computer usage. However, the Brown study did not use a control group and did not report separate findings for its male and female subjects.

Progressively over time the workforce has changed (e.g., a greater number of women, a higher average workforce age, and a higher level of education; Census, 2000); the sophistication of IT has increased as has the demand placed on the end user. Simmers and Anandarajan (2001) found that age is an important factor in user satisfaction and that younger workers generally had higher satisfaction than older workers. Therefore, due to these findings by Simmers and Anandarajan, the limitations expressed by Brown (2001), and age emerging as a barrier to the placement of individuals who are looking for employment (Gibson, Zerbe, & Franken, 1993), age is an important and viable variable for further research to see if there is a correlation with computer usage.

Gender no longer seems to be a factor in job placement or level of placement (Truman & Baroudi, 1994). However, once an employee is placed into a position, gender differences can be noted in the social setting of the organization. Women may favor computer collaboration and networking, while men may see computers more as a tool to obtain and evaluate content (Gefen & Straub, 1997). Gefen also reports that gender could affect the diffusion of IT use in the workplace. This is based on findings from a study conducted by Gilroy and Desai (1986) that is presented as an extension of the technology-acceptance model (TAM; Davis,

1989). The TAM, however, attempts to predict and explain system and/or computer use by stating that perceived usefulness and ease of use are of primary relevance in computer-acceptance behavior. In the original form, TAM defined the construct of perceived usefulness as the degree to which a person believes that using a particular system would enhance his or her job performance, and perceived ease of use as the degree to which a person believes that using a particular system would be effortless.

Attempts to explain the predictive powers of the technology acceptance model have not specifically included age or gender. Attempts to describe demographics regarding end-user computing (EUC) have concluded that women generally have less skill with computers and that women therefore may have restricted access to higher positions within an organization (Harrison & Rainer, 1992). However, considering the more equal representation in the workforce of men and women (Census, 2000), the proliferation of computers into the home, and the reduction of anxiety regarding computer usage (Thompson, Higgins, & Howell, 1994), the findings of Harrison and Rainer (1992) may have to be revisited. Additionally, the 2000 census estimated a 30% greater enrollment of women in higher education than men. This census information is almost a reverse image from what was reported in the 1970 census. Moreover, in 2000, there were almost 3% more women in the workforce holding a college degree than men. With the increase in college enrollment reported for women and the current change in workforce demographics, organizations must reconsider what age and gender dynamics in their workplace are currently and how they may be changing in the future.

More recent literature by Pearson, Crosby, Bahmanziari, and Conrad (2003) empirically investigated age and gender as moderating variables to end-user computer efficacy. They found that age and gender did not seem to impact how organizational culture influenced computer efficacy. However, they did report age and gender as direct predictors to computer efficacy and that older employees and females in general were not as confident about learning new computer applications. Additional research has provided evidence that the workforce has more computer experience and a continued narrowing of the differences between males and females regarding software use, anxiety, and enthusiasm (Rainer, Laosethakul, & Astone, 2003). As found in the literature, these conflicting reports seem to demonstrate the need for further investigation in the gender and age dichotomies in organizations and the role these dichotomies play in end-user computing or the training organizations implement to educate these dichotomous groups.

Organizations, as they attempt to implement new technologies into their workplaces, continually need to upgrade the computer skills of their employees and may have to invest in ongoing training programs for the workforce (Igbaria,

Parasuraman, & Baroudi, 1996). This perceived need by organizations, to have a more computer-literate workforce, may lead employees to feel pressure to use computers and/or to gain acceptable computer knowledge. Additionally, this may affect older employees more than younger employees (Gibson et al., 1993). Gibson et al. found that employers generally considered younger employees' training a better investment, but that hiring older employees would allow more security for the organizations because older employees were more likely to have long tenure with the company. With this evident conflict in perceptions noted, clearly organizations, whether training young or older employees, are expecting a return on their training investment. This expected return on investment may be considered or be perceived by the employee as a pressure to use the implemented technology (Bolt, Killough, & Koch, 2001). Furthermore, Caputo and Cianni (1997) found that the average age of women participants in on-the-job training programs increased steadily between 1970 and 1991, and that older women more often completed training programs than their younger counterparts did.

We first propose a model that shows the relationships between age and gender with computer usage, and the modifying effects of social influences. Second, we will develop a set of research questions to be tested. Third, we will analyze the survey data and discuss the results.

Research Questions

Literature contends that older workers find the use of computers more difficult than younger workers. The workforce has increased in average age and has been exposed to information technology through the proliferation of computers into the home and workplace. For more than a decade, computer-usage requirements by employers have also increased.

RQ1: With the changing demographics in the workplace and the proliferation of computers into the home, does age still affect computer usage?

While in previous studies gender was found to have an effect on computer usage, increased educational levels for women and the proliferation of computers into the home may have caused gender to have less of an effect on computer usage within the organization. Additionally, with the increasing number of women in the workforce and the continued growth of computer usage required by employers, questions arise as to whether gender affects computer usage. Studies from the 1980s and 1990s have typically concluded that gender does affect computer usage.

Figure 1. Proposed research model

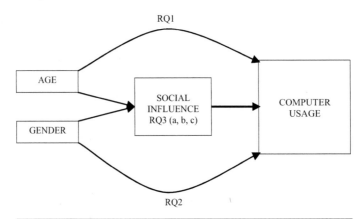

The proposed model incorporates three research questions. RQ1 investigates the effect age
has on computer usage. RQ2 asks the effect gender has on computer usage. RQ3 (a, b, c)
tries to determine the moderating effect of social influence between age and computer usage,
and gender and computer usage.

*RQ2: With the changing demographic in the workplace and the proliferation
of computers into the home, is gender still affecting computer usage?*

The workforce has increased in average age, changed its composition
regarding men and women, and has been exposed to computer technology for
many years. Also, computer usage may now be expected and/or required by
employers (i.e., there is increased pressure). Compeau et al. (1999) studied
the perceived pressure to use technology and found there are three perceived
social elements that should be considered in the implementation and intended
use of a computer technology by an end user. Just as Compeau et al. looked
at the dynamic social pressure and measured it as a perceived social
influence, we consider the same three elements of social influence and how
the workplace perceives these influences through three research questions.

*RQ3a: Does internal peer pressure moderate the impact of age and gender
on computer usage?*

*RQ3b: Does anxiety moderate the impact of age and gender on computer
usage?*

*RQ3c: Does enjoyment moderate the impact of age and gender on computer
usage?*

Research Method

Participants

The target population for this study was knowledge workers: specifically, individuals whose primary work involved the use of computer technology in their daily work activities. Representatives from 20 companies were identified and asked to participate in this study. The companies were large multinational organizations that represented a diverse group of industries including agriculture, oil refining, insurance, retail, consulting, transportation, and finance. Each representative was asked to distribute 20 questionnaires to a randomly selected group of knowledge workers throughout their organization. Individuals were identified for participation based on their job description and a short interview to determine the extent to which they utilized computer technology in their daily activities.

Instrument

The survey package contained a cover letter from the organization's representative, a letter from the researchers explaining the purpose of the study, and the questionnaire. All respondents were guaranteed confidentiality of their responses. This study utilized three sections of a multipart questionnaire: 10 questions were included to solicit information about the respondent and his or her organization, six questions were to determine the extent of computer usage, and 10 questions were designed to measure the items that make up social influence in this study. As a follow-up, after two weeks the company representatives contacted those individuals who had not completed the survey instrument.

Results

A total of 352 employees voluntarily participated in this study. Gender was split equally with 50% male and 50% female. Fifty-nine percent were college graduates with 54% citing business as their primary educational background. Seventy-one percent of the respondents were employed in a functional area other than information systems. Sixty-eight percent of the participants were middle management, first-line management, or professionals. Almost all (99%) responded that they used a computer at their place of work several times a day. Obviously, the use of computers is an integral part of their jobs. In fact, 92% of the respondents reported that the use of a computer was required at their jobs. Therefore, the participants of this study were predominantly knowledge workers. A summary of the key demographic characteristics is presented in Appendix A.

Before starting the analysis, we decided that there might be issues that arise when separating young respondents from older respondents. Therefore, to eliminate any confusion regarding proximity to the median age, we decided that a clean dichotomy could be made by not including respondents that were between the 40th and 60th percentile for age. This study produced a minimum age of 21, a maximum age of 57, and a median age of 29. Therefore, 60 respondents between the ages of 27 and 31 were removed from all calculations.

Analysis

When addressing the research questions, we focused on computer usage first by age, then by gender, and concluded with the moderating influence social pressures have on computer usage. Table 1 lists the pertinent descriptive statistics of our respondents.

Table 1. Descriptive statistics for sample

Younger Males (n = 79)	Min	Max	Mean	Std. Dev.	Younger Females (n = 63)	Min	Max	Mean	Std. Dev.
Age	21	27	24.65	1.68	Age	21	27	24.95	1.78
Hours of Use per Day	1 hr	11 hrs	5.63	1.86	Hours of Use Per Day	2 hrs	9 hrs	5.67	1.75
Peer Pressure			4.35	0.77	Peer Pressure			4.52	0.76
Anxiety			1.45	0.53	Anxiety			1.83	0.82
Enjoyment			3.89	0.69	Enjoyment			3.94	0.80
Older Males (n = 71)	**Min**	**Max**	**Mean**	**Std. Dev.**	**Older Females (n = 79)**	**Min**	**Max**	**Mean**	**Std. Dev.**
Age	31	56	35.32	6.00	Age	31	57	39.14	6.72
Hours of Use per Day	0 hrs	8 hrs	5.22	2.02	Hours of Use Per Day	2 hrs	9 hrs	5.61	1.77
Peer Pressure			4.48	0.61	Peer Pressure			4.61	0.65
Anxiety			1.46	0.63	Anxiety			1.41	0.48
Enjoyment			4.07	0.69	Enjoyment			4.11	0.68

Likert Scale (1 = Strongly Disagree, 5 = Strongly Agree)

Direct Predictors

To investigate further, a t-test was conducted on age as a predictor of the self-reported usage of computers. As shown in Table 2, age is not a significant factor (t-score = 1.012) affecting computer usage. Although research looks for significance, the lack of significance in this case is in itself very important. While past research has indicated that age may be an issue affecting computer usage (Brown, 2001; Simmers & Anandarajan, 2001; White et al., 1999), this study suggests that age is no longer a factor in computer usage. Therefore, according to these results, we suggest that age may no longer have a significant effect on computer usage.

A t-test was also conducted on gender as a predictor of the self-reported usage of computers. As shown in Table 3, gender, male or female, is not a significant factor (t-score = 0.949) affecting computer usage. As stated in the discussions leading to RQ1, research looks for significance; the lack of significance for gender in this study is again important. As with age, past research regarding gender has typically indicated that gender may be an issue affecting computer usage (Arbaugh, 2000; Gefen & Straub, 1997; Harrison & Rainer, 1992; Truman & Baroudi, 1994). This study finds that gender by and of itself is not a factor in computer usage. Therefore, according to these results, we suggest that gender does not have significant effects on computer usage.

To analyze the data further, we separated the data into a simple matrix of younger employees, older employees, male, and female as seen in Figure 2. We found that younger females use computers only slightly more (5.67 hours) than the other groups. After conducting a one-way analysis of variance, we found $F = 0.91$ and that there is significance of only 0.438 for the grouped sections with regard to computer usage. As stated previously, this is significant in and of itself because of the findings of past research stating there was a difference for age, gender, and computer usage. This provides additional evidence of nonsignificance regarding computer usage being affected by age and gender.

Moderators: Social Influence

The third research question, RQ3, addresses the perceived social influences of peer pressure, anxiety, and enjoyment, and any moderating effect they may have on computer usage. Peer pressure was measured by one item utilizing a 5-point Likert-type scale ranging from *strongly discourage use* to *strongly encourage use*. The measures for anxiety and enjoyment are constructs relying on multiple items derived from Compeau et al. (1999). The construct for anxiety has five questions and provides a standardized reliability alpha of 0.8014. The

Table 2. Age as predictor of computer usage

Age	N	Mean	Std. Dev.	Std. Error
Younger	142	5.65 hrs	1.808	0.152
Older	150	5.43 hrs	1.895	0.155

	T-Test for Equality of Means			
Age-Usage	t	df	Sig. (2-tail)	Mean Diff.
Usage	1.012	290	0.312	0.22

Table 3. Gender as predictor of computer usage

Gender	N	Mean	Std. Dev.	Std. Error
Female	142	5.64 hrs	1.756	0.147
Male	150	5.44 hrs	1.941	0.159

	T-Test for Equality of Means			
Gender-Usage	t	df	Sig. (2-tail)	Mean Diff.
Usage	0.949	290	0.344	0.21

construct for enjoyment has three questions and provides a standardized reliability alpha of 0.7839. Details for the confirmatory factor analysis are found in Appendix B. Composite measures were calculated for both the anxiety and enjoyment constructs and can be found in Appendix C.

To address RQ3a, we looked at peer pressure. When examining Figure 3, we see that older women perceive the strongest pressure to use computers (mean = 4.608), while younger men perceive slightly less pressure to use computers (mean = 4.354). Also clear is that women in general feel more pressure to use computers than do men (t = 1.923, 0.055). However, peer pressure appears not to moderate the impact of age or gender on computer usage at a significant level.

When examining Figure 4 and considering RQ3b, older women in this study are found to have the lowest anxiety regarding computer use. Interestingly, the younger women have the highest levels of anxiety (statistically significant relative to the other groups). The overall low anxiety level in this study supports the findings of Thompson, Higgins, and Howell (1994), which suggested that there has been a lowering of anxiety levels in the use of computers. Additionally, Figure 4 reveals that this research potentially could support Gefen and Straub's (1997) position that gender does play a role in computer usage. While Gefen and Straub's work has findings that gender does play a role in computer

Figure 2. Age and gender relating to computer usage

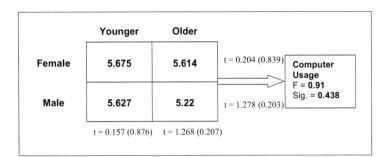

Figure 3. Peer pressure as moderated by age and gender

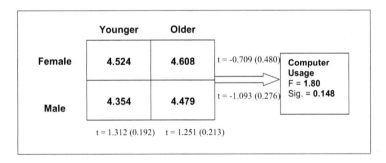

usage, we find that the only time there is a significant difference between the genders or the ages is when the anxiety levels are examined. Therefore, we can only substantiate Gefen and Straub when considering the modifying effects anxiety has on age and gender in computer usage.

The last research question, RQ3c, regarding enjoyment, also fails to provide significance at any level. However, in Figure 5, it is interesting to see that older individuals in this study perceived greater levels of enjoyment from using the computers (t = -1.948, 0.052). This is contrary to what Simmers and Anandarajan (2001) found. In this study, older women more strongly look forward to using computers on the job than any other group. While earlier studies may have found men and women significantly different in their computer use (Arbaugh, 2000; Gefen & Straub, 1997; Truman & Baroudi, 1994), we believe that the differences are no longer as dichotomous (distinct) as they once were.

Figure 4. Anxiety as modified by age and gender

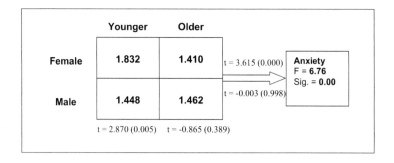

Figure 5. Enjoyment as modified by age and gender

Conclusion

Having identified the change in U.S. social demographics, we went into this research project anticipating that there would be limited, if any, change in the role that traditional usage predictors have on computer usage, namely, that age and gender would influence the acceptance and/or degree of usage of computers by employees. We expected that social influences (peer pressure, anxiety, and enjoyment) would have significant impacts on computer usage amongst the different age and gender groups. These expectations were based partly on the limited published research that would predict or document a change in the acceptance or use of computers by different genders and age groups. Previous research would lead us to expect male and younger employees to more readily and more often use computers in the performance of their work.

However, based on the results of this study, it now appears that differences in age and gender no longer predict computer usage among knowledge workers. Being that this research found no significant differences between younger and older employees, and/or between males and females in their usage of computers, it is our opinion that computer skills and the accompanying usage of computers have reached a level of maturity in our domestic corporate culture equivalent to an employee's ability to read and write: It is expected and, therefore, any employable person has it.

If the moderating effect of peer pressure, anxiety, and enjoyment are examined for effects on age and/or gender in computer usage, only anxiety moderates, that is, causes changes in usage to be significant. It would appear that organizations should undertake programs that reduce or remove those elements of computer usage that can cause anxiety about computer usage within the organization. This may take the form of additional training or possibly allowing the workforce alternative methods of completing certain computer-based tasks.

Before we can generalize our findings to the general population, future research should examine computer-usage rates to see if those effects were caused by the changing workforce demographics itself, some precedent or posterior condition to the change in workforce involvement, or possible opportunities emerging (arising) from the years of economic growth, a large but unnoticed change agent to computer usage. Will these changes in computer usage be sustained in a lower (slower) economy? This must also be evaluated to uncover possible predictors and/or conditions that would enable predictors to influence computer usage.

Limitations

While our findings suggest that age and gender are no longer significant influences in computer usage, there are limitations to this research that must be presented. While we tried to create a separation within the age variable by removing 10% of the respondents on either side of the median, our separation between young and old was only four years (27 to 31). Future research should investigate a group in which there is a greater dichotomy between young and old.

Another limitation of this study is that we focused on knowledge workers, that is, people who use computers as part of their jobs. By focusing on individuals who may be required to use computers (92% of our respondents were required to use computers to complete work assignments), the findings may not be indicative of the situation where computer usage was voluntary. Also, by focusing on knowledge workers, we excluded individuals who do not use the computer on a regular basis. Again, future studies should investigate whether mandatory computer usage vs. voluntary computer usage would significantly change the findings of this study.

The last significant limitation was how the construct of peer pressure was measured. This construct was measured via a one-item question that asked respondents if "peers within [the] organization encouraged or discouraged the use of computers." Future research should investigate other items that could be used to measure the peer-pressure construct. These limitations must be considered when extending the findings of this research to the general population. The results of this study, based on a limited sampling frame, suggest that changes are occurring in the impact the variables studied have on computer usage.

References

Arbaugh, J. B. (2000). An exploratory study of the effect of gender on student learning and class participation in an Internet based MBA course. *Management Learning, 31*(4), 503-519.

Bolt, M. A., Killough, L. N., & Koh, H. C. (2001). Testing the interaction effects of task complexity in computer training using the social cognitive model. *Decision Sciences, 32*(1), 1-20.

Brown, K. (2001). Using computers to deliver training: Which employees learn and why? *Personnel Psychology, 54*(2), 271-296.

Caputo, R., & Cianni, M. (1997). The job training experiences of black and white women: 1970-1991. *Human Resource Development Quarterly, 8*(3), 197-217.

Compeau, D., Higgins, C., & Huff, S. (1999). Social cognitive theory and individual reactions to computing technology: A longitudinal study. *MIS Quarterly, 23*(2), 145-158.

Davis, F. D. (1989). Perceived usefulness, perceived ease of use, and user acceptance of information technology. *MIS Quarterly, 13*(3), 318-339.

Davis, F. D., Bagozzi, R. P., & Warshaw, P. R. (1998). User acceptance of computer technology: A comparison of two theoretical models. *Management Science, 35*(8), 982-1003.

Gefen, D., & Straub, D. (1997). Gender differences in the perception and use of e-mail: An extension to the technology acceptance model. *MIS Quarterly, 21*(4), 389-400.

Gibson, K. J., Zerbe, W. J., & Franken, R. E. (1993). Employers' perceptions of the re-employment barriers faced by older job hunters. *Relations Industrielles, 48*(2), 321.

Gilroy, F. D., & Desai, H. B. (1986). Computer anxiety: Sex, race, and age. *International Journal of Man-Machine Studies, 25*, 711-719.

Greco, J. (1998). America's changing workforce. *The Journal of Business Strategy, 19*(2), 43-46.

Harrison, A. W., & Rainer, R. K. (1992). The influence of individual differences on skill in end user computing. *Journal of Management Information Systems, 9*(1), 93-111.

Harrison, A. W., & Rainer, R. K. (1995). Gender differences in computing activities. *Journal of Social Behavior and Personality, 12*(4), 849-868.

Igbaria, M., Parasuraman, S., & Baroudi, J. A. (1996). Motivational model of microcomputer usage. *Journal of Management Information Systems, 13*(1), 127-145.

Melone, N. (1990). A theoretical assessment of the user-satisfaction construct in information systems research. *Management Science, 36*(1), 76-91.

Pearson, J. M., Crosby, L., Bahmanziari, T., & Conrad, E. (2003). An empirical investigation into the relationship between organizational culture and computer efficacy as moderated by age and gender. *Journal of Computer Information Systems, 43*(2), 58-70.

Pintrich, P. R., & Schunk, D. H. (1996). *Motivation in education: Theory, research, and applications.* Englewood Cliffs, NJ: Prentice Hall.

Rainer, R. K., Laosethakul, K., & Astone, M. (2003). Are gender perceptions of computing changing over time? *Journal of Computer Information Systems, 43*(4), 108-114.

Robie, C., Ryan, A. M., Schmieder, R. A., Parra, L. F., & Smith, P. C. (1998). The relation between job level and job satisfaction. *Group & Organization Management, 23*(4), 470-495.

Simmers, C., & Anandarajan, M. (2001). User satisfaction in the Internet-anchored workplace: An exploratory study. *Journal of Information Technology Theory and Application (JITTA), 3*(5), 39-61.

Standish Group, The. (1995). *Sample research paper: CHAOS.* The Standish Group International, Inc. Retrieved from *http://www. standishgroup.com*

Statistical abstract of the United States. (1990). Bureau of the Census.

Statistical abstract of the United States. (2001). Bureau of the Census.

Szajna, B. (1996). Empirical evaluation of the revisited technology acceptance model. *Management Science, 42*(1), 85-92.

Thompson, R. L., Higgins, C. A., & Howell, J. M. (1994). Influence of experience on personal computer utilization: Testing a conceptual model. *Journal of Management Information Systems, 11*(1), 167-187.

Truman, G. E., & Baroudi, J. J. (1994). Gender differences in the information systems managerial ranks: An assessment of potential discriminatory practices. *MIS Quarterly, 18*(2), 129-145.

US Census 1970. Retrieved December 3, 2001, from http://www.census.gov/population/www/censusdata/hiscendata.html

US Census 2000. Retrieved December 3, 2001, from http://www.census.gov/main/www/cen2000.html

White, H., McConnell, E., Clipp, E., & Bynum, L. (1999). Surfing the Net in later life: A review of the literature and pilot study of computer use and quality of life. *Journal of Applied Gerontology, 18*(3), 358-378.

Yang, C., & Moore, D. M. (1995). Designing hypermedia systems for instruction. *Journal of Educational Technology Systems, 24*, 3-30.

This article was previously published in the *Journal of Organizational and End User Computing, 17*(4), pp. 49-65, © 2005.

Appendix A

Summary of Key Demographics

Functional Area:	Information Systems	28.70%
	Accounting	21.00%
	Other Areas	25.20%
	Marketing and Sales	13.10%
	Human Resources	6.00%
	Management	6.00%
Position in the Organization:	Executive	3.10%
	Middle Management	17.90%
	First-Line Management	21.60%
	Professional	31.30%
	Technical	12.80%
	Clerical	9.10%
	Other	7.40%
Gender:	Male	50.00%
	Female	50.00%
Educational Level:	Some High School or Completed High School	12.50%
	Some College	10.50%
	College Degree	58.80%
	Some Graduate Work	8.50%
	Graduate Degree	9.70%
Educational Background:	Business	54.00%
	Other	46.00%

Appendix B

Factor Analysis

A confirmatory factor analysis was performed on the two social influence constructs (anxiety and enjoyment). As mentioned within the article, these constructs were derived from work done by Compeau, Higgins, and Huff (1999) and consisted of five questions for the anxiety construct and three questions for the enjoyment construct. A principal component analysis with a varimax rotation was utilized. The Kaiser-Meyer-Olkin (KMO) Measure of Sampling Adequacy was 0.778, which is considered acceptable. Table A1 provides the eigenvalues and explained variance values for both constructs.

Table A1. Total variance explained

Component	Extraction Sums of Squared Loadings		
	Eigenvalues	% of Variance	Cumulative %
1	3.319	41.484	41.484
2	1.768	22.105	63.589
3	0.813	10.167	73.756
4	0.662	8.274	82.029
5	0.505	6.316	88.346
6	0.413	5.159	93.505
7	0.285	3.563	97.068
8	0.235	2.932	100.000

Table A2 provides the results of the confirmatory factor analysis and the corresponding Cronbach's Alpha for each construct.

Table A2. Rotated component matrix

	Component	
	1	2
E1	-0.260	0.846
E2	-0.189	0.863
E3	0.117	0.744
A1	0.569	-0.326
A2	0.698	-0.303
A3	0.818	0.004
A4	0.805	0.002
A5	0.787	-0.008
Cronbach's	0.8014	0.7839

Appendix C

Method Used to Develop Composite Constructs

Composite measures were developed for the anxiety and enjoyment constructs. Each measure was constructed by calculating an average value based on the responses provided.

Anxiety = (QA1 + QA2 + QA3 + QA4 + QA5 + QA6) / 6
Enjoyment = (QE1 + QE2 + QE3) / 3

Chapter X

Users Behaving Badly:
Phenomena and Paradoxes from an Investigation into Information Systems Misfit

Panagiotis Kanellis, Information Society S.A., Greece

Ray J. Paul, Brunel University, UK

Abstract

In its formative years and during the 1990s, Global Energy PLC (GE)[1] went through a series of structural changes precipitated by the deregulation of the electricity industry in the UK. The severity of these changes had a disruptive effect on its enterprise information systems, which were found unable to adapt to the new and constantly emerging organizational realities. GE's experiences illustrate the vulnerability of information systems in turbulent environments, provide for a rich description of the causes of misfit due to contextual change, and establish the ability of a system to flex and adapt as a dependent success variable. In addition, the idiographic details of this interpretive field study raise interesting questions about a number of assumptions we hold regarding the development of information systems and the means by which flexibility can be attained.

Introduction

Avison and Fitzgerald (2003) identified instability as a "notable trap" of the systems development life cycle (SDLC) approach due to the modeling of processes that are unstable because of changing business and markets. Similarly, Lycett and Paul (1999) argue that the methodical approach to system development leads us to design systems that are unable to deal with the challenge of evolutionary complexity and work in a dynamic world. If the future is one in which change will have to be reacted to continually, we understand "disappointment" as a resulting phenomenon due to the destabilization imposed by change on information systems (IS) that have not been designed to provide for it. On the contrary, the post-industrial organization should demonstrate adaptability and therefore must be characterized by frequent and continuous change in structures, domains, goals, and so forth, even in the face of apparently optimal adaptation (Huber, 1984). It is our contention that so should its IS. Flexibility as a success variable for IS — albeit implicitly or with varied placement of emphasis — has also been stressed by Blumenthal (1969), Cotrell and Rapley (1991), Fitzgerald (1990), Gunton (1989), Oei, Proper, and Falkenberg (1994), and Swanson (1982), amongst others.

Needless to say, the myriad of reasons that determine whether an IS is successful or not can be matched by an equal number of explanations. Arguably, one of the prevalent methods of inquiry that characterizes a large body of the empirical IS literature revolves around the concept of "fit" as defined by the contingency approach in organizational theory. In general, such research is grounded on the argument that any determination of information requirements must be based upon the organizational use to which the IS is put. Hence, the success of any IS must be measured in terms of what it accomplishes in the organization. Thus, a direct approach is mostly followed, aiming to define what are the relevant factors affecting the interaction effect or "fit" between a pair of organizational components (structure, culture, tasks, technology) and then develop a measurement instrument with standard metrics (see, for example, Goodhue & Thompson, 1995). This largely positivist stance adopted by the majority of researchers has deprived the IS field from the rich and insightful descriptions that are mainly possible through interpretive field studies. However, providing for rich descriptions of phenomena under investigation, the premise of interpretive research is important as it helps the practitioner to reevaluate his or her mental frames of reference, resulting in more effective implementation strategies of computerized IS in organizations.

Setting epistemology aside, it is surprising to report that flexibility as a determinant of "fit" or as a dependent variable for IS success has achieved little attention. What explains this may be a set of beliefs and assumptions, practitioners and academics alike hold about systems development. One can safely argue that one assumption currently held about systems is that they do indeed need to be maintained, and that after implementation they simply enter the "maintenance-forever" phase. IT/IS managers and personnel accept this as a reality of their profession. Still, as Gibbs (1994) notes, "…Some three quarters of all large systems are 'operating failures' that either do not function as intended or are not used at all" (pp. 72-73).

The case study reported in this chapter aims to challenge this very reality by arguing that maintenance is simply not enough for the contemporary organization of the 21st century. To the best of our knowledge, no research has been reported that tries to address and enhance our understanding of this issue from an interpretive point of view. In our investigation of the effects of privatization on the IS of an industrial organization, the approach allowed us to (a) illustrate the vulnerability of IS to contextual change, (b) understand the possible effects of change on IS and the ensuing repercussions on organizations, and (c) contribute valuable insight on the topic of IS flexibility. Whilst the paper does not purport to offer definitive solutions, the experiences reported herein suggest lessons for organizations faced with the challenge of planning for and developing flexible information systems. Those will incite awareness and help IT managers to anticipate what they will probably experience should they not approach flexibility as a vital "fit" relationship and not cater for the accommodation of change, not only in the design of the IS themselves, but also in the structure and capabilities of the very corporate IS organizations they themselves manage. The following section provides a critical review of the literature on IS "fit," "success," and "failure." In the third section we present our epistemological assumptions and research design. The analysis and interpretation of the case study data are presented in the two sections that follow, while a discussion on key findings concludes the chapter.

Information Systems "Fit," "Success," and "Failure" in the Literature

For more than 30 years the issue of "fit" between an organization and its strategy, structure, processes, technology, and environment has served as a building block for theory construction and research in strategic management. Many different conceptualizations and operational tests of "fit" can be found in the literature (Drazin & Van de Ven, 1985; Galbraith & Nathanson, 1979; Lawrence & Lorsch, 1967; Thompson, 1967; Venkatraman, 1989). Because of the multiplicity of the components covering a range of different types of phenomena in any given environment, research has typically focused on specific fits between specific pairs of components with the central idea as articulated by Nadler and Tushman (1979) being: "Between every pair of [components] there exists a degree of congruence or fit. Specifically, the congruence between two components is defined as follows: the degree to which the needs, demands, goals, objectives, and/or structures of one component are consistent with the needs, demands, structures of the other component" (p. 415).

There have been many attempts to apply this line of reasoning to the IS field (see Daft, Lengel, & Trevino, 1987; Ein-Dor & Segev, 1982; Ewusi-Mensah, 1981; Gordon & Miller, 1976; Leifer, 1988; Raymond, Pare & Bergeron, 1994.). In general, such research is based on the argument that any determination of information requirements must be based upon the organizational use to which the IS is to be put; for example, the work of Goodhue and Thompson (1995) on task-technology "fit." Iivari (1992) undertook an extensive survey of the existing research into the organizational "fit" of IS, which he categorized under three headings: *Contextual Factors* (environment, technology, structure, control systems, others); *Information Systems Characteristics* (database, reports, processing, formalization, applications, architectures); and *Types of "fit"* (selection approach, interaction approach, systems approach). His findings indicate that most research regarding IS "fit" falls under the selection approach. In other words, the objective is a "direct" approach determining what the relevant factors of a pair of components are, and then developing a standard solution with standard metrics. This observation refers largely to causality and its nature; the selection approach implies a unidirectional causal model based on the assumption that the characteristics of an IS are dependent totally on the organizational context. As Iivari (1992) put it, however, "this means that unidirectional causalities expressing the fact that either the organizational context determines the characteristics of an IS, or that, vice versa, information technology and information systems determine organizational technology and structure, may be too simplistic" (p. 5). Indeed, information technology (IT) for contemporary organizations is a rather proactive and not a reactive agent. It influences the context, at least as much as the context determines the ways and the extent to which it can be deployed.

Not surprisingly, if we assume that an IS with a "good 'fit'" is a successful IS, a scan of the literature (see DeLone & McLean, 1992; Lucas, 1975; Markus, 1983; Sauer, 1993) uncovers the same plurality regarding definitions, views, and opinions as to what constitutes success and how it can be assessed. This difficulty in defining "success" as an objective entity existing "independently" of its effects explains why it is often more conveniently discussed in terms of "what it is not." The social nature of such conceptions is emphasized by Lyytinen and Hirschheim (1987), whose extensive survey defined the overriding generic concept of "failure" as that of *expectation.* Their work 'stresses the importance of understanding how various stakeholders comment on the value of the IS: "failure is the embodiment of a *perceived* situation" (p. 264, emphasis added). This highlights the fluidity and inter-penetration between technological and social views and leads us to propose that success (or indeed, failure) is a perspective that emerges from the social and technical interplay within an organization. This interplay results in patterns of emergent social regularities that are not a priori given but are constantly shifting and evolving (Lycett & Paul, 1999).

We posit, therefore, that flexibility is an important "fit" relationship for developing contemporary IS and agree that in such an innovation process, like the development of an IS, there exist a number of variables that may be seen as unavoidable flaws for which eventually they could be accounted. The same cannot be said though about change, which uncovers a fallacious assumption we hold about IS, and more specifically, about certain approaches we follow in developing them. In IS development one works toward establishing what is needed now and using some hindsight toward what might be needed tomorrow. Any approach, methodology, or a group of tools begin with and base their eventual success on one objective: to achieve a "complete" and "correct" set of system requirements. Grindley (1986) termed this stage the "freezing factor" and held it responsible for much disappointment in total integrated systems development. Because of the system's complexity and interdependencies, it is extremely difficult to change the design once programming has commenced. System requirements have to be defined beforehand and also in one go so that all likely future demands can be catered for in its design. As a consequence, "an artificial freeze has to be imposed on the 'getting agreement' exercise after a while, partly to enable a start to be made, but mainly to ensure that no new requirements are introduced while project development is under way" (ibid: p. 5). Paul (1994) illustrates this with the mock fixed-point theorem illustrating how this freeze results in systems that are built for one (hypothetical) point in time — a fallacy — as they must work over some time continuum.

On the basis of this, we postulate that for IS exposed to change, the *perception* of most stakeholders involved with them is that of disappointment. Furthermore, we argue that this occurs primarily because most systems as currently developed are static entities whose purpose is to model a dynamic world. As such, the premise of this paper is that the description of a series of phenomena, and the ensuing interpretations offered, can lead to a reconsideration of assumptions we currently held about the "fit-flexibility" relationship and consequently about the development and management of IS in organizations.

Research Design

Organizations are open systems where, we would propose, invariant empirical regularities do not hold in the sense that they do in the natural sciences (where systems can be experimentally closed and initial conditions controlled). Accordingly, we surmise that there can be no single account of success but only different perceptions influenced by context. As such, an interpretivist position is adopted regarding our epistemology (see Appendix). We believe that no individual account of social reality can ever be proven as more correct that another, since it will be impossible to compare them with any objective knowledge of a "true" reality. Even when two observers experience the same phenomena, the true meaning for each may be different. The answer therefore lies in broadly interpretive research methods (Walsham, 1993) that aim in producing an understanding of the context of IS, together with the process whereby the IS influences and is influenced by such a context.

The study presented herein was carried out over a period of 11 months during which we worked as external advisors at Global Energy's (GE) Information Technology Strategy and Planning Unit (ITSPU). GE was a devolved organization operating within and outside the UK electricity sector with a turnover of over $6 billion. With our initial unit of analysis being the larger intra-organizational context and the IS, we opted for a design that would allow us to obtain data from multiple levels and perspectives throughout the organization. Three data sources were identified: (a) the ITSPU department, which could provide us with a holistic perspective of the organization and its systems, being responsible for the company's IT infrastructure as a whole, (b) the individual business units, and (c) the users of the systems at a number of sites across the company. Triangulated data was thus collected, providing multiple perspectives on an issue allowing for cross-checking, supplying more information on emerging concepts, and yielding stronger substantiation of constructs (Orlikowski, 1993). Data was being collected on a daily basis primarily through documentation review, observations, and informal discussions. Several interviews were also conducted with IT and business unit managers. Our role as external advisors to the ITSPU engaged in a project to evaluate the company's IS ensured to the extent possible, that the narratives collected from the participants across the various business units were objective with minor distortions and possible biases.

Using a questionnaire as a guide, the interviews were mostly semi-structured and were conducted in a way that allowed for a focus on the issues under investigation, whilst permitting the interviewees to expand on areas of personal interest that they thought were important. All interviews were tape-recorded, and verbatim transcripts were made from the recording as soon as possible thereafter. As Hirschheim, Klein, and Newman (1991) noted, "Presenting verbatim extracts of subject's comments is obviously selective, but it does allow the reader to examine the subject's perceptions of the phenomena directly" (p. 591).

Grounded theory, developed by Glaser and Strauss (1967) as a reaction to the failure of quantitative sociology to capture "lived experience," was followed for the collection and analysis of data. Our data was analyzed for each business unit, as well as across the various units to detect similarities and compare differences using *open coding* (Strauss, 1987) as a form of content analysis. Open coding is based on an analytic technique that tends to force the generation of a core category or categories, together with their properties and dimensions. Once the core categories were established, *axial coding* (Strauss, 1987) was performed. As Strauss and Corbin (1991) maintain, it is the data itself that should guide the researcher's interpretation, further coding, and collection of data. Adhering to this rule, we terminated this process when we believed that the collected data was exhausted with respect to providing enough evidence in explaining what have been observed across the various business units. The categories together with the identified concepts are listed in Table 1.

In terms of the relationship between research question and research method, grounded theory starts from a vague initial question and allows the theory to emerge from the data, hence this approach is not about identifying and testing hypotheses. A hermeneutic cycle (Gadamer, 1976) forms its essence, whereby as Klein and Myers (1999) note "…the process of interpretation moves from a precursory understanding of the parts to the whole and from a global understanding of the whole context back to an improved understanding of each part…" (p. 71). They also state that in line with Hans-Georg Gadamer's description of the "hermeneutic cycle," a broad and liberal interpretation should be given to the terms "parts" and "whole." Accordingly, they can be parts of a historical story, with the whole being the proper perspective of the historical context. For this study, the identified "parts" are the seven identified categories depicted in Table 1. Via interaction, our understanding of the categories stemming from the literature review is coupled with the views and understanding of the interviewees, resulting in a synthetic whole, which is presented in the section that follows. Klein and Myers (1999) emphasize that the idiographic details revealed by the data

Table 1. Categories and concepts

Categories	Concepts [2]
Environmental Context	♦ Regulation ♦ Competition ♦ Customers
Organizational Context	♦ Corporate strategies ♦ Structure of company ♦ Culture of company
Information Systems Context	♦ Attitude towards systems and technology ♦ IS policies and practices ♦ IS Structure and operations
Change	♦ Origins of change ♦ Nature of change ♦ Change as a threat to IS
Information Systems 'fit'	♦ Perceptions of IS 'fit' ♦ Types of and causes of IS 'fit'/Misfit'
Information Systems Flexibility	♦ Definition of IS flexibility ♦ Enablers of IS flexibility

interpretation should then be generalized and related to theoretical general concepts and constructions. We adhere to this principle attempting to do so in the form of a discussion in the last section of the paper.

Change and Information Systems at Global Energy PLC

In the beginning of the 1990s, GE was moving from a period of relative certainty during the privatization process, to a much more uncertain time in the UK electricity market. This was coupled with an expansion into new, and unfamiliar, international markets. During the initial period following privatisation (1990-1993) there were clear objectives, which drove a well-defined program of IT projects. After 1993, the outlook was much less certain. The fact that it was only price distinguishing GE's electricity from that produced by any other company or source resulted in the company having to set new and clear objectives, with a focus on generating electricity at the lowest possible cost. This required a rapid and radical reorganization to become more flexible and efficient, streamlining the business and introducing new working practices. GE's IS were put in place in 1990. Upon its establishment, the company was a "green field" with no enterprise IS in operation, and a major consulting firm undertook the task of designing and implementing them. The "classic" methodical approach was adopted for their development using a proprietary methodology. The main systems were:

- **Plant Reliability – Integrated System for Management (PRISM):** A work management system.

- **Energy Management Centre (EMC) systems:** Based on a data warehouse, these were mainly used for optimising the company's trading position.

- **Finance Systems (WALKER):** Catering for all financial and accounting needs, and very complex with lots of interfaces to every other system in operation.

Taking into account the continuing change the organization was experiencing post-privatization, we set to investigate how these systems had fared. The synthesized analytical framework (Figure 1), which is derived directly from the interpretation and analysis of our data, provides the basis by which the categories and key concepts are ordered, and subsequently interpreted, providing an explanation with regards to certain phenomena as we observed them.

The need for IS flexibility has its source in a set of circumstances that originate in the environment in which the organization resides *(arrow 1),* and are basically the result of the actions of the industry's regulator and the organization's customers and competitors. Based on their knowledge and continuous observation of this environment, assumptions are formulated by the management of the company, which are then translated into organizational initiatives for change in response to environmental shifts. These may affect the strategy, structure, and culture of the organizational context.

The outcomes of this stage are: (a) these proposed changes have a direct effect on the "fit" of existing information systems *(arrow 3)* and (b) they have an effect on the information systems context *(arrow 2),* that is, the structure, operations, policies, and practices of the systems department. Being bi-directional, *arrow 2* emphasizes the fact that although "fit" and flexibility are IS states due to externally imposed change, the very same IS should also be seen as capable of causing organizational change themselves.

At the same time, any possible information systems misfit requires corrective action that must be undertaken by the systems department *(arrow 4),* and it is the outcome of the employment of any evaluation practices or mechanisms that are currently in place. The activities that follow allow for an initial perspective on the flexibility of the systems; how easy, for example, was it to provide for this disequilibrium. They also allow for an increased understanding and knowledge regarding flexibility itself and the situational conditions that make it possible, or

Figure 1. Change, information systems "fit," and information systems flexibility: a synthesized analytical framework

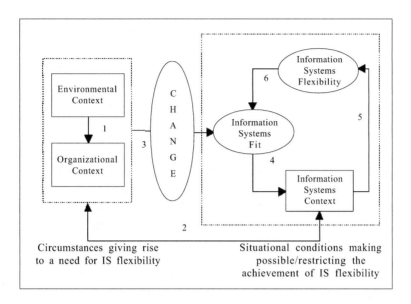

equally restrict its attainment. Possible assumption changes by developers and managers alike may result in pro-activeness *(arrow 5)* with respect to future systems and the ways they should be developed. In turn, such IS with a higher level of flexibility mean an improved ability to cope with unforeseen changes, and hence a better future "fit" with less disruption *(arrow 6)*.

Two points must be raised regarding this framework. Firstly, it should be remembered that it only provides an abstraction of reality, and as such it is necessarily a simplified one. For example, most arrows that illustrate relationships and interactions between contexts and processes should be bi-directional: In some cases, the position of the company within the structure of the industry itself is such that it gives the power to influence the environment *(arrow 1);* the systems department, in an attempt to improve the systems "fit," may employ new policies and practices that could result in severe restructuring and lay-offs *(arrow 2)*. In order not to overcomplicate the framework, such interactions are not depicted. The second point is that we can make no claim that the concepts and interactions that are identified are exhaustive.

The following subsections discuss the framework's categories and their interactions and provide our interpretation of the situational conditions resulting initially in IS misfit at GE, whilst at the same time making possible the emergence of true flexibility in an unorthodox way.

The "Environmental Context" Category

With regard to continuing pressures from the external environment, GE itself was acknowledging that regulatory issues demanded both significant management attention, and represented major continuing uncertainty. The uncertainty regarding the future could best be visualized by reference to generation and the supply of electricity. Competition was flourishing in generation with around 20 generators engaging in tactical battles each year to secure a segment of the market at a certain price. The increasing competition in the production of electricity had seen the market share of GE in England and Wales fall from 46% when it was privatized, to around 30% in 1996. Regarding the supply side, in addition to the 12 RECs, there were more than 20 other suppliers, which together sold electricity to around 23 million customers. Up to 1998 there were in effect two separate markets, the first supplying industry and commerce, and the other covering domestic and smaller users who had the sole right to supply customers in their local area. Regarding the former, GE had "permanent" contracts with customers such as a number of major public coal and transport companies and the Regional Electricity Companies (RECs), which used to buy most of the generated electricity and sell it to the domestic customers. As those were to expire in 1998, GE had to find alternative revenue streams, contributing to (or even defining) the development of new markets.

The "Organizational Context" Category

Upon its formation in the early 1990s, GE started by having a centralized organizational structure. During 1992-1993, a decision was made in favor of devolving the business activities to power stations and giving them the authority to operate as independent business units with minimal centralized control. All business units across five main divisions were given almost total autonomy. This move was another attempt to increase the overall flexibility and competitiveness of the company by enabling decisions to be made closer to the operational level. However, a lack of experience with respect to certain business functions such as planning had delayed the introduction of formal mechanisms, and thus numerous critical functions were performed on an ad hoc basis. As a result, barriers were introduced for basic procedures designed to be common to all business units, as well as for some groups, like Strategy and Planning, which were operating at the corporate level and provided the interface between business units and executive directors.

Additionally, various change initiatives had attempted to make GE a project-oriented organization as opposed to hierarchy-based, by trying to assign groups of people assembled from a number of different business units to the various development efforts. This project-oriented attitude seemed to work, providing the company with a level of flexibility at the unit level, while at the same time this very flexibility was constrained at the organizational level. A manager made the following comment:

There are barriers in our ability to respond to future changes because of the organizational structure. We have ended up with a structure [after privatization] which I believe does not enable us very easily to respond to new slots of business because the new business tends to be allocated to the existing structures.

A look into GE's culture explains to a large extent the disparities that are observed at the unit and organizational levels: Extremely flexible at one end, but at the same time a great lack of trust and territorialism at the other end, which meant that when a change occurred, there was an aggressive/defensive stand rather than a co-operative one — exactly the time when more cooperation was needed.

What explains the above phenomenon was the fact that GE came into being from the old monopoly, which was a hierarchical organization. Team working did not happen at all, and managers referred to it as a "patch-protected" organization, where in a sense no one was allowed to infringe on what one did. The culture promoted in the new organization was a strikingly different one. Innovation was encouraged, and so was individuality and devolution of responsibilities, resulting in intense competition at the individual and business unit levels. These two opposite cultural dimensions have given rise to a deadlock situation that seemed to plague the organization. On the one end, there was almost total autonomy and freedom with respect to performing any task or activities one saw fit with the prospect of adding value to the company. At the other end, the culture of the old monopoly that the people brought into GE with them made them unwilling to take a macro view past the boundaries of their own business units.

The "Information Systems Context" Category

Regarding the information systems in the company, attitudes were formed by two camps: the ITSPU, whose role was to safeguard and oversee the development of the infrastructure, making sure that any development activities at the unit level resulted in compatible outcomes with whatever else was going on in the company, and the individual business units. A level of mistrust and disbelief toward any initiatives proposed, or advice offered by the ITSPU was evident.

The fact that the group did not have the power to veto any business unit activities that were perceived as "harmful" gave rise to a complex and highly political situation, with attitudes fluctuating constantly around a positive/negative axis.

In spite of the above, the company's policy to remain state-of-the-art encouraged the consideration of alternative approaches to the development of systems, and it was constantly assessing the viability of new system approaches. Hence, the company's three main IS — PRISM, EMC, and the Finance Systems — paint only half of the picture with respect to the *IS structure and operations*. Bespoke application development paints the other half. Following the decision to devolve, the emergent autonomous business units had complete freedom regarding the development of bespoke applications that suited their own particular needs. The argument for that form of policy was that certain styles might have been more appropriate in different departments. This liberty given to the business units with respect to developing their own applications had culminated in a highly complex, and hence difficult to manage infrastructure. A senior manager noted:

One of the things that has happened to GE is that we are disintegrating; we are devolving in terms of development, and as a result of that, we lost a lot of coordination, so department A is using one tool, and department B is using another tool. I mean, if you give users a lot of autonomy, you should not be surprised that they use it.

Such was the extent of the issue facing the company, that a new business unit called Business Systems Department (BSD) was established to address this seemingly problematic situation. Its objectives were clear: to scale down and maintain the complexity quotients of the infrastructure as low as possible, and create an integrated high-caliber UK business systems competency. Thus, having started from nothing in 1990, GE went through a period of major IT investments, through a period of devolved budgeting and responsibility for development, and was heading toward one of more coordinated control, having as few products to be used to deliver bespoke applications as possible. This situation that GE was facing could be summed up by the two following IS development scenarios:

- Business requirements are identified, and a system is designed, built, and tested to those requirements (The "classic" methodical approach to development).
- The user, given tools, creates added value to the business in the form of some kind of "informal" application; other users view this and request to use the result, upon where the application is then used as a multi-user system.

The former systems are the ones with the large number of users, where high performance and maintainability are the criteria for success and acceptance, whereas the latter normally suffer from problems of maintainability and performance but are seen as successful by the users who built them to "fit" their needs as they themselves perceive them. But this is not irrational behavior. Out of necessity, the "informal" takes the place of the "formal" when, due to changing requirements, the latter as an organizational model does not provide anymore the service required of it.

The "Change" Category

There was a wide range of forces acting upon GE, which made the need for change inevitable. These forces of change can be broadly taxonomized under two categories with respect to their origins: Those that originate in the interaction of the company with its external environment (externally induced changes), and those that originate in the various organizational components themselves (internally generated changes). The responses of the interviewees indicated that the former was responsible for the majority of changes imposed on the company. The change that GE was experiencing was of an evolutionary nature — steady and permanent, albeit a fast one. A large percentage of it seemed to be predictable, but what the actual effect(s) on the organization could be, were not.

An important issue, which we also needed to discover, was whether or not *change was perceived as a threat to IS*, and if it was what types of IS were most likely to be affected by it. A senior systems developer gave the most fitting remark as to whether change was perceived as a threat for the Generation division. He said:

I don't think anyone knows the true answer to that, but all I can say is since 1988 when all this started, we have never had a single stable period of 12 months in systems terms. Not one!

All the managers that we interviewed agreed without exception that change has serious repercussions on the IS. Change certainly introduced an amount of risk that caused considerable anxiety and stress. It was seen as affecting both current and ongoing development efforts, and equally, existing systems that were already in place. In the framework depicted in Figure 1, change is related to the category of IS "fit." The next section explains how change had affected the IS at GE and what have been the consequences of this.

The "Information Systems 'Fit'" Category

"Perceptions of information systems 'fit'" is the first concept upon which we focused our attention during the analysis of the data regarding the "fit" of systems. Although the perceptions of managers as to what the "fit" of a system was were numerous, mixed, and varied greatly between departments and from individual to individual, a common ground can be found. This revolves around two dimensions: Business and technical, with both relating to a third one—the cost dimension. What our analysis shows, however, is that the most valuable insight regarding this concept is gained by a consideration of the time factor. Looking at "fit" at both micro and macro levels uncovers a dilemma and poses a fundamental question with respect to our attempts to develop systems that will have a good "fit". At the macro level, any IS should "fit" into the overall business strategy of the company. At the micro level, a system has a "fit" if at least replicates faithfully a business process in place, or takes the process to a new dimension in terms of adding value. It must also fit in technological terms with the company's infrastructure. What perspective should be given priority when decisions are being made to develop an IS? Is it possible to develop a system that can satisfy both macro and micro views?

The problem at the macro level is that development is totally dependent on the company's business strategy which itself changes and fluctuates abruptly responding to environmental changes. One manager commented:

I think the problem with the longer term is the business strategy, and how this could be supported by the systems is not clearly communicated through. You should understand that this is not a management problem. It is simply that the problems we are dealing with tend to be 10 minutes away. This is the environment, and you cannot do anything about it. And if you say to me "You cannot sort out the business strategy — I cannot sort out the IS strategy!" you are going to get laughed at. We are all grappling with that problem.

The alternative — if it can be called that — is to disregard the long term and instead concentrate on the short term by putting in place the application that you think will suit the business needs of the moment. However, this approach has its own problems.

I tend to think these days that if you are looking at the long term "fit" at the application level, you are wasting your time because the business is changing. In the short term, the benefits are that you produce something very quickly, very cheaply, and you get reasonable user satisfaction because they get what they want quickly. But you are going to have problems in the long run because these systems run out of date, they are not cohesive, and they are going to loose this "fit", and you will have a much bigger problem in replacing all these diverse elements.

This resembles a "catch-22" situation: You cannot develop systems for the long term that "fit" the organization's strategy simply because there cannot be a definite one, and although possible in the short term, the implications for the long-term may far outweigh the possible benefits. A negative consequence seems, for example, to be the escalating cost. This is very important for a cost-conscious organization such as GE.

This situation has made managers and senior developers at GE come to an illuminating realization: It is not possible to develop an IS with a "perfect fit". The literature and the numerous textbooks on information systems planning and development may like us to think otherwise. Indeed, we do not believe that one could find amongst the plethora of "cookbook" approaches a set of guidelines that could help us to build an "imperfect" system. Ironically however, this is a more precise snapshot of reality, and to our experience many practitioners rarely consider any of the research or books on the market that offer "best practice" or definitive guidelines. The notion of "fit" as it stands is rooted in the fixed-point theorem (Paul, 1994) mentality, and a reconsideration of the concept in more relative terms is clearly needed if it is to be of any practical value (Kanellis, Lycett, & Paul, 1999).

The next concept in our analysis is *"types of and causes for information systems 'fit/misfit,'"* and what follows explains to an extent how perceptions like the above have been formed at GE regarding this concept.

The analysis of data indicated three major types of "misfit" being experienced at GE. For the purpose of clarification, we have termed these as *structural* misfit, *process* misfit, and *technological* misfit. Structural misfit refers to a change in the organizational structure that the IS has not been able to follow. It is differentiated from process misfit because business processes may change whilst the structure remains more or less the same, and vice-versa. Finally, technological misfit is referring to a change in technology itself that makes the existing systems obsolete and cumbersome in the eyes of the users. This type of misfit usually determines the level of systems usability. Before we address each one of these types and seek to provide some evidence for their existence, let us provide two interesting points for consideration. A manager at the Research and Engineering business unit provided the first. He remarked:

There are two points to that question! [How well do you think your information systems "fit" your business now?] How well does the IS "fit" with what we do and how well we have to "fit" with what they do?

This rather cynical comment, we believe, is by itself strong evidence for the existence of misfit. It seems that things have changed whilst systems have not; and people have to adapt to the way the systems work, rather than the other way around. An attempt is made now to describe the three types of identified misfit beginning with structural misfit.

The systems at GE were built around the structure of the company, and either just after they were implemented or at the point that they were implemented, the company changed. A three-month review was carried out by the ITSPU in February 1992 of the suitability of the IS to operate following the devolution of business activities to power stations. The systems in question were mainly WALKER and the PRISM systems. The findings of the review were that the systems available were suitable for devolved use with some maintenance modifications. Those modifications represented only those aspects of the systems that could directly prevent devolution. It was also recognized that as those systems were designed prior to devolution, other changes could be usefully made to enhance effectiveness or efficiency. In the time space of almost three and a half years (February 1992 to May 1995), one would expect that the modifications would have been completed successfully, resulting in no misfit at all. However, evidence shows that this is not the case — the process of devolution made demands on the systems that could not be satisfied by simply maintaining them.

The finance systems [WALKER] we put in, we set up for a particular structure, culture — whatever you want to say, and that changed in the last couple of years tremendously. It was like trying to "fit" a square in a rounded hole, and the numbers of requests for changes to the systems increased and have been coming non-stop ever since.

Procurement, for example, was a central activity that had specialist people dedicated to this task. Devolution meant that this task was now undertaken "part time" by non-specialist personnel, as people were required to be more flexible and to work on different job aspects. This meant that the task was now only four or five hours a week of an employee's time, resulting in a negative perception about the systems as being too complicated and difficult to use.

The very clear division of the organization into distinct business units provides another example of structural misfit. The systems were designed to fit this structure, but in time the business cycle has come to cross all the function areas; the systems now fit the functional breakdown, but they do not fit the organization as one entity. In addition, systems were perceived as being too "big" for what the organization was doing at that time. This type of misfit has serious implications for the ways that development projects will be managed in the future. It indicates a change to the structure of the system's development units themselves and poses a question as to how they will operate in the future. A senior developer explained:

You cannot shrink the business continually and expect those projects of that size to remain unchallenged. So far as the changes concerned, the threat is that if the operation is reduced, we get to a particular financial level where the IS activity becomes disproportionately large in terms of operation. I think that is perhaps the single area where the greatest threat is.

Process misfit refers to the inability of an IS to keep providing the same level of service to a business process. It would not be an exaggeration to say that no process has remained the same since the early stages of privatization; processes have not only changed, but they have kept on changing. For example, the systems at the Energy Management Center (EMC) had to be scrapped altogether, and a new breed of systems based on the concept of data warehousing had to be developed to account for the changed processes. Also, a senior manager at another division commented:

I have seen a couple of instances where management information systems have failed to cope with the pace of change and have caused the organization to make inappropriate decisions as a result, and we then had to run to catch up with the circumstances.

This type of misfit emphasizes the need for a different approach to development. One developer responsible for developing such systems for the Sales and Marketing and Strategy and Financial Planning business units remarked:

If everything is changing, which it does do, then one thing that I have found is that it is actually quite difficult to alter the scope of a system whilst under development. You tend to fix your scope at the beginning, and you refine it into more and more detail, and by that stage it is quite difficult to stick your head above the parapet and see if you are still at the same place. Then you show it to the users for acceptance tests, and they say "Oh! But that was all very well then — we do things differently now!"

Technological misfit, which is caused simply by advancements in technology, seemed to affect all the main systems at GE, as those were character-based and with busy screen representation. In the sense of usability, they were perceived as not being up to the then current practice standards. This meant that in order to use the systems, users had to get familiar with them for some time, and this was not always possible under the current situation — few employees, many tasks, little time. Users simply had to be fairly able to switch from one system to another and perform various tasks at the same time. Technological misfit does not immediately mean that an existing process can be performed more effectively with new technology in terms of the quality of information needed to make a decision. Indeed, managers commented that for many people at GE, that seemed to be secondary, and they drew a parallel with the fashion world. They saw however this desire to work with the most current and "sexy" system as a natural thing — a progression, but at the same time they were also aware of the fact that it might lead to a diversion from what the business actually wants. Most managers, feeling powerless with this technological evolution, have decided to consciously "ride" along with it. What they were discovering, however, is that the line between "going there because it is there" and "going there because you know why you go there" is becoming more blurred, as the rate of this technological progress increases.

The Implications of Information Systems Misfit and the Emergence of True Flexibility

This section presents an interpretation of the data related to the category of information systems flexibility and the associated concepts *"definition of IS flexibility"* and *"enablers of IS flexibility"* (see Table 1). It was at this point in our investigation that we were faced with a paradox. How, on one hand, is it possible for such a level of IS misfit to exist, and yet an organization as heavily dependent on its systems as GE, to be able to flex and adapt successfully to continuous environmental contingencies? Although there was a negative overall perception regarding the "fit" of the systems, with a large percentage of those not being used as they were supposed to, user activities and tasks did not seem to be disrupted in any way. We expected otherwise, but we found that users were not tied down by the systems. What explains this phenomenon is perhaps the simple rule of survival: Threatened by adverse circumstances, one has no choice but to adapt. One manager from Sales and Marketing said:

As changes occur in the business world, if you cannot get to change the system because the money or the project team has gone — they do it with a spreadsheet — they do not bother with the system that you have spend half of your life to develop — that's a hidden problem as well. I mean, we look at systems and say "Oh! We never change the system. It is a bloody success!" But really, what happens is that the buggers put a Lotus spreadsheet there to do their work with it. I mean our Finance systems are crap. If I wanna know how much money I have spend on contracts at the end of this month, I go and get a bloody spreadsheet. WALKER cannot tell me — not in the way I wanna say it. So people do bits and bobs around the edges, don't they?

The same phenomenon was evident at Generation. A manager commented:

Systems have fallen away, and people are not using them as much as they should. And just about everybody, everywhere, is taking data out of the main systems, and either re-keying it in, or use whatever method is available to them to get data into little applications, so that they can then move the data around and use it the way they want to, because they see that the system they access — the PRISM system — is inflexible. What we are trying to do now is to recognize that this is a key requirement, and just deal with the data — not to deliver them any systems.

There were a number of conditions that made possible the development and existence of the above phenomenon. If we consider our discussion thus far, those become clear. GE upon privatisation put in place a number of IS; continuous change since then has practically crippled them with respect to what their initial purpose was; at the same time, the policy of the company was such that it gave users almost complete autonomy and freedom with respect to meeting their own systems and informational needs. People used this freedom and have developed small applications of their own, and along with application packages have cannibalised the over-arching systems to give themselves a system that is working by adapting it to their particular need — a truly flexible IS, but certainly not a planned or intended one.

ITSPU even had a name for this situation. When we were asking for comments, they were referring to it as the "Lotus Cult." An appropriate name we thought — "cult" signifying a kind of underground alliance — for the groups of users who have a disregard for the formal IS imposed on them, and in a way have taken control of their own "fate." We must note, however, that this underground activity has come to be seen as essential, even by the "authorities" themselves. One member of the ITSPU team said that if one ever attempts to take this away, parts of GE would stop operating within a day, and the company would soon collapse. To us, as researchers faced with this phenomenon, there remained an obvious question that we soon asked. We were curious to find out what the plans for future development were in light of this situation. The leader of the ITSPU team gave us an answer:

Why don't we just build them a Lotus system that does all that? Well, the real reason is that they will not use it — they all got a slightly different view of what they want it to be.

Within ITSPU and the various business units, the idea that you should ask people what they do with a system before you impose it on them was perceived as anathema. Users, it seemed, have criticisms about what the systems are not able to do, but when they are actually asked what they like or what they would use a particular system for, then they do not have an answer. What can be postulated from this, however, is that there is a clear need for systems that are able to adapt to unforeseen circumstances. The one described above is a good example, but it was the result of certain conditions giving rise to circumstances that made it possible. Furthermore, it was an informal one.

The challenge we face, therefore, as systems developers is to try and offer the user a flexible IS. Will an old mindset and unchallenged ways of thinking suffice for approaching this task? To that a manager of the systems development team at Finance offered us his view:

Flexibility… I think it is a difficult area, which is why I think the solution does not lie in providing these people with a system. Because you work in a department, you have your own way that you want to produce information. I am not pointing out that there are rights and wrongs with that, but then somebody else comes along in this department and has certain key parameters that he thinks are important to him — there may be valid changes because the business has changed or from a better understanding of information needs. But to actually try and deliver that in a system, you just are prescriptive again, and as soon as you have done that, you take the flexibility away.

In trying to identify what was perceived as necessary prerequisites for the attainment of flexibility, the answers of senior managers and developers focus on people and technology. In general, advancements in technology are seen as highly enabling with respect to both what developers and users themselves can do. For example, new technologies hold the promise of providing the users with more "hands-on" user-friendly tools that allow them to generate their own inquiries and deliver their own development without coming back to the systems department for an implementation of the change they want.

The use of methodologies, on the other hand, was seen as severely limiting any possibility of achieving flexibility. With respect to a number of methodologies that have been used at GE, opinions range from bad to worse than bad. It is because those methodologies were so constraining and inadequate that guaranteed that no one would go near them. This ensured that nothing was done in a disciplined fashion, and instead the development of the systems was driven underground — very paradoxically resulting in unintentional but flexible IS.

People themselves play an important role in achieving a flexible IS. Managers were referring to a new breed of sophisticated users that is needed, calling it an "intelligent population" — users who are technologically competent and never say, "I have always done it this way!" For an IS to flex and adapt, the first and foremost of its components that should be able to do the same is the people themselves. What managers were effectively asking for is a new culture, and the same applies to the developers themselves. They, in addition, must have a strong understanding of the business, be aware of the changing organizational and environmental realities, and furthermore, be prepared to accept this fact even though this realization may result in a paradigm shift with respect to the ways they carry out their work.

Discussion

This research was guided by a number of theoretical preconceptions about "fit," flexibility, IS development, and IS success as presented in the second section. The purpose of this section was to reflect on the actual findings provided by the case study and to relate the idiographic details to those theoretical and general concepts in line with the fundamental principle of the hermeneutic cycle for interpretive field research (Klein & Myers, 1999). The findings emanating from our inquiry on the post-implementation "fit" of systems at GE illustrate that (a) flexibility is a vital "fit" relationship in designing IS for organizations operating in turbulent environments; (b) that development approaches for such systems should cater to the emergent socio-technical regularities that constantly evolve and cannot be a priori given; and (c) that although flexibility can be attained at a micro level (i.e., the application level), the real challenge is how to allow for maximum flexibility at the user and business unit level without the introduction of conflict that could jeopardize the integrity and stability of the corporate IS organization. The prerequisite in order to meet this challenge is for IS departments to be transformed into "emergent" organizations. Next, we discuss those in turn.

Flexibility is a Vital "Fit" Relationship

With the selection approach as the prevailing contingency paradigm for the study of "fit" between an organization and its technology (Iivari, 1992; Knoll & Jarvenpaa, 1994), empirical IS literature has assumed static environments. We argue that for contemporary organizations, the flexibility of a system determines to a large extent how successful this system is, and furthermore, because of the rate of change, the assumption that systems can achieve a long term "fit" at the application level needs to be revisited. The misfit of the systems at GE, which were built by defining a set of requirements with the belief that these require-ments could at least hold true for a long period of time, proved the opposite. A "good fit" or success is a perceived state describing the accomplishment of a set of desirable goals — a "fit" between the IS and its context. Such a "fit" is not permanent but is dependent on external or internal change, which is a product of time. Change affects the context (the organization) within which the IS exists and has direct implications for the capabilities of the IS to satisfy expectation. It follows that a system with a "good fit" is a system that is capable of demonstrat-ing the ability for continuous adaptation and not one that satisfies some requirements at a particular point in time. Truex, Baskerville, and Klein (1999) argue that "…systems should be under constant development, [and] can never be fully specified" (p. 121). Similarly, Lycett and Paul (1999) propose that IS design should be thought of as an ongoing process and not as a predictive or contingent one. This line of thinking has also been followed by Baskerville, Travis, & Truex (1992), Paul (1993), and Kanellis and Paul (1995, 1996). It follows, that the practical relevance of the selection approach as a "fit" model should also be questioned together with the epistemological assumptions that guide such contingency-focused research. Undertaking an assessment of the contingency theory of Management Information Systems (MIS), Weill and Olson (1989) argued that it has too narrow a focus, advocating largely its abandonment. Based on the above discussion, we share their call for more subjectivist, less functional, and less deterministic research approaches.

Emergent Socio-Technical Regularities are Constantly Evolving and Can Never be A Priori Given

An interesting question that should be asked is how a designer would know at the time he is building a system if he is achieving more or less flexibility. It is doubtless that the answer can be found in the methodical approaches to IS development. Generally, methodologies are inflexible, do not allow changes to requirements during and after the development phases, assume stable environments, as well as knowledgeable users and skilled analysts that can reach a consensus as far as requirements are concerned (Avison & Fitzgerald, 2003). But as the authors underline, rarely such conditions exist in practice. At GE, models of producing software or IS, which had the traditional specification design delivered in one big chunk, were stopped being followed. The time horizon for new development projects is now perceived as a very short one with the longest time period an integrated enterprise system having to produce the expected benefits being two years, from five to eight that was before. GE had lost its faith in methodologies, and it is not hard to see why. They were simply unable to cope with the pace of change. As a result, they produced sub-optimal systems that had to be either modified continuously (the PRISM system) or completely re-developed after their implementation (the EMC systems). It is this poor pedigree of the methodical approach to development that has been forcing researchers and practitioners alike to reappraise the concepts and usefulness of the methodologies since the late 1990s (Avison & Fitzgerald, 2003). All new efforts that will define this "post-methodology" era have to be based on the realization that the success (or indeed, failure) of a development effort is a perspective that emerges from the social and technical interplay within an organization resulting in patterns of emergent social regularities that are not a priori given but are constantly shifting and evolving (Lycett & Paul, 1999). The assumption that social structures, mechanisms, and processes can be seen as "invariant regularities" that only have to be revealed to be understood has to be abandoned. Turning back to the question asked in the beginning, we argue that true flexibility in systems development is achievable only at the user level, when and if the axis of system ownership in an organization shifts from the IS department/developer to the user. What is meant by system ownership is to defer the design decisions and transfer the authority to the end user who has the means to manipulate the behavior of the IS. These means in the form of tools and enabling technologies are increasingly being made available to the market (Stamoulis, Kanellis, & Martakos, 2001). Undoubtedly, this will have implications for the ways the actual development teams in organizations are structured and operate. As a consequence, the idea of having systems analysts and designers will fast become obsolete. One manager at GE said that it is not good anymore having a team — getting a piece of paper, putting down the requirements, and saying: "Well, here we are chaps!" For him, the very name "IS Department" was erroneous. He mentioned, with some cynicism, that this should be changed to "data-pointer department". In other words, show the user where the data that he wants resides. The user then starts with what he wants to do, the question he wants to answer, or the decision he wants to understand and make, and then having the means to do it, he or she just builds the application. The application is then used and can be kept or equally can be thrown away. True flexibility at the user end is the ability of the user to develop a system that matches precisely the way he or she views the world at the moment. The "Lotus Cult" as described in the previous section is an illustration of that. It was a mix of certain conditions that allowed the users at GE to transform the formal over-arching and organizationally invalid systems into working ones. Will, therefore, information technology and systems departments as we know them be discarded completely or given a new or different role? We cannot be sure of the outcome, but we strongly believe that things as they are now will not remain the same for very long.

IS Departments Should be Transformed into and Managed as "Emergent" Organizations

It is, we believe, that the battle for IS flexibility will be decided not at the user end (micro level), but at the organizational level (macro level). Flexibility will not be assessed with respect to how well a tool, system, or application allows the user to "get what he or she wants, when he or she wants it". There is a simple reason for this. Users are getting more informed and sophisticated by the day, while at the same time, technology is advancing with great leaps. As a result, flexibility will become a managerial problem at the macro level; users themselves will be able (and increasingly enabled by the technology) to satisfy their changing needs at the micro level. Our case study provides the necessary insight needed to understand this point of view. GE had a flexible IS, and its employees did not need any models or the most advanced technology to achieve that. All they ever used were Lotus spreadsheets to produce systems that were working, by constantly adapting them to their particular needs. By doing so, they achieved maximum flexibility at the micro level, but in the eyes of the company, they created a whole sub-universal system that got out of control. It became difficult to manage and to keep an eye on its evolution. Such was the perceived problem that led to the introduction of a whole new business unit — the Business Systems Department — whose main role was to stop this from continuing to happen. Was this a wrong decision for more formalization and control that could lead back to "dead" systems? Not necessarily, if IS departments as organizational entities reconfigure themselves around a set of principles borrowed from "organizational emergence" — "a theory of social organization that does not assume that stable structures underpin organizations" (Truex et al., 1999, p. 117). Emergence theory emphasizes a continuous redevelopment perspective demanding the creation of an IS development environment that is optimized for high rather than low adaptation. This can be interpreted as an environment where maximum independence and flexibility are allowed at the user and business unit level, but with the necessary culture, policies, and controls in place so as to avoid the introduction of conflict that could jeopardize the integrity and stability of the organization as an entity. According to Truex et al. (1999), the closer to "emergent" the IS development environment gets, the more freedom it gives to each and every end user for participating in an active reality reconstruction. As requirements conflicts rise — as they undoubtedly will — increased negotiation and other service activities are prescribed and provided to support ongoing business processes. Although end user productivity tools, open system architectures, and software components are some of the vehicles that could support an emergent organization, an extended number of organizational capabilities is clearly required that will define the form of the interface between the user end and the organization. These capabilities can be technical, economic, social, cultural, or a mixture of them all. Isolating and paying attention to one level or to one aspect of this interface will be at the expense of the others and ultimately will have negative consequences on the flexibility of any contemporary IS. Further research is urgently needed toward this direction.

References

Avison, D. E., & Fitgerald, G. (2003). Where now for development methodologies? *Communications of the ACM, 46*(1), 79-82.

Baskerville, R., Travis, J., & Truex, D. (1992). Systems without method: The impact of new technologies on information systems development projects. In K. E. Kendall (Ed.), *The impact of computer supported technologies on information systems development* (pp. 241-271). Elsevier Science Publishers BV.

Benbasat, I., Goldstein, D. K., & Mead, M. (1987). The case research strategy in studies of information systems. *MIS Quarterly, 11*(3), 369-386.

Blumenthal, S. C. (1969). *Management information systems: A framework for planning and development.* Englewood Cliffs, NJ: Prentice-Hall.

Boland, R. J. (1985). Phenomenology: A preferred approach to research on information systems. In E. Mumford, R. Hirschheim, G. Fitzgerald, & T. Wood-Harper (Eds.), *Research methods in information systems*. New York: North-Holland.

Cotrell, N., & Rapley, K. (1991). Factors critical to the success of executive information systems at British Airways. *European Journal of Information Systems, 1*(1), 65-71.

Daft, R. L., Lengel, R. H., & Trevino, L. K. (1987). Message equivocality, media selection and manager performance: Implications for information systems. *MIS Quarterly, 11*(3), 355-366.

DeLone, W. H., & McLean, E. R. (1992). Information systems success: The quest for the dependent variable. *Information Systems Research, 3*(1), 60-95.

Drazin, R., & Van De Ven, A. H. (1985). Alternative forms of fit in contongency theory. *Administrative Science Quarterly, 30*(4), 514-539.

Ein-Dor, P., & Segev, E. (1982). Organizational context and MIS structure: Some empirical evidence. *MIS Quarterly, 6*(3), 55-68.

Ewusi-Mensah, K. (1981). The external organizational environment and its impact on management information systems. *Accounting, Organizations and Society, 6*(1), 35-50.

Fetterman, D. M. (1989). *Ethnography step by step.* London: Sage Publications.

Fitzgerald, G. (1990). Achieving flexible information systems: The case for improved analysis. *Journal of Information Technology, 5*(1), 5-11.

Gadamer, H. G. (1976). *Philosophical Hermeneutics.* Berkeley, CA: University of California Press.

Galbraith, J. R., & Nathanson, D. A. (1979). The role of organizational structure and process in strategy implementation and related commentaries. In D.E. Sshendel & C.W. Hoffer (Eds.), *Strategic management: A new view of business policy and planning* (pp. 249-302). Boston: Little Brown.

Galliers, R. D. (1992). Choosing information systems research approaches. In R.D. Galliers (Ed.), *Information systems research: Issues, methods and practical guidelines* (pp. 144-162). Oxford, UK: Blackwell Scientific Publications.

Gibbs, W. W. (1994). Software's chronic crisis. *Scientific American, 271*(3), 72-81.

Glaser, B., & Strauss, A. (1967). *The discovery of grounded theory: Strategies for qualitative research.* Chicago: Aldine.

Goodhue, D. L., & Thompson, R. L. (1995). Task-technology fit and individual performance. *MIS Quarterly, 19*(2), 213-236.

Gordon, L. A., & Miller, D. (1976). A contingency framework for the design of accounting information systems. *Accounting, Organizations and Society, 1*(1), 59-69.

Grindley, K. (1986*). Fourth generation languages: A survey of best practice.* London: IDPM Publications.

Gunton, T. (1989). *Infrastructure — building a framework for corporate information handling.* New York: Prentice-Hall.

Hirschheim, R., Klein, H. K., & Newman, M. (1991). Information systems development as social action: Perspective and practice. *Omega, 19*(6), 587-608.

Hirschheim, R. (1992). Information systems epistemology: A historical perspective. In R.D. Galliers (Ed.), *Information systems research: Issues, methods and practical guidelines*. Oxford, UK: Blackwell Scientific Publications.

Hirschheim, R., Klein, H. K., & Lyytinen, K. (1995). *Information systems development and data modelling: Conceptual and philosophical foundations*. Cambridge, UK: Cambridge University Press.

Huber, G. P. (1984). The nature and design of post: Industrial organizations. *Management Science, 30*(8), 928-951.

Iivari, J. (1992). The organizational "fit" of information systems. *Journal of Information Systems, 2*(3), 3-29.

Kanellis, P., Lycett, M., & Paul, R. J. (1999). Evaluating business information systems "fit": From concept to practical application. *European Journal of Information Systems, 8*(1), 65-76.

Kanellis, P., & Paul, R. J. (1995). Unpredictable change and the effects on information systems development: A case study. In *Proceedings of the 13th Annual International Conference of the Association of Management* (pp. 90-98). Vancouver, BC: Maximillian Press, Virginia.

Kanellis, P., & Paul, R. J. (1996, August 16-18). Will information systems continue to disappoint? In *Proceedings of the 2nd Americas Conference on Information Systems,* Pheonix, AZ (pp. 752-754).

Klein, H. K., & Myers, M. D. (1999). A set of principles for conducting and evaluating interpretive field studies in information systems. *MIS Quarterly, 23*(1), 67-94.

Knoll, K., & Jarvenpaa, S. L. (1994). Information technology alignment or "fit" in highly turbulent environments: The concept of flexibility. In *Proceedings of the 1994 Computer Personnel Research Conference* (pp. 1-13). Alexandria, VA: ACM Press.

Lawrence, P. R., & Lorsch, J. W. (1967). *Organization and environment*. Homewood, IL: Irwin.

Leifer, R. (1988). Matching computer-based information systems with organizational structures. *MIS Quarterly, 12*(1), 63-73.

Lucas, H. C., JR (1975). *Why information systems fail?* New York: Columbia University Press.

Lycett, M., & Paul, R. J. (1999). Information systems development: A perspective on the challenge of evolutionary complexity. *European Journal of Information Systems, 8*(2), 127-135.

Lyytinen, K., & Hirschheim, R. (1987). Information systems failures: A survey and classification of the empirical literature. *Oxford Surveys in Information Technology, 4,* 257-309.

Markus, L. M. (1983). Power, politics, and MIS implementation. *Communications of the ACM, 26*(6), 430-444.

Nadler, D. A., & Tushman, M. (1979). A congruence model for diagnosing organizational behaviour. In D.A. Kolb, I.M. Rubin, & J.M. McIntyre (Eds.), *Organizational psychology* (3rd ed.) (pp. 442-458). Prentice Hall.

Oei, J. L., Proper, H. A. & Falkenberg, E. D. (1994). Evolving information systems: Meeting the ever-changing environment. *Information Systems Journal, 4,* 213-233.

Orlikowski, W. (1993). CASE tools as organizational change: Investigating incremental and radical changes in systems development. *MIS Quarterly, 17*(3), 309-340.

Orlikowski, W. J., & Baroudi, J. J. (1991). Studying IT in organizations: Research approaches and assumptions. *Information Systems Research, 2*(1), 1-28.

Paul, R. J. (1993, March 29-30). Dead paradigms for living systems. In *Proceedings of the First European Conference on Information Systems* (pp. 250-255). Henley-on-Thames.

Paul, R. J. (1994). Why users cannot get "what they want." *International Journal of Manufacturing System Design, 1*(4), 389-394.

Raymond, L., Pare, G., & Bergeron, F. (1994). Matching information technology and organizational structure: An empirical study with implications for performance. *European Journal for Information Systems, 4*(1), 3-16.

Reponen, T. (1994). Organizational information management strategies. *Information Systems Journal, 4,* 27-44.

Sauer, C. (1993). *Why information systems fail? A case study approach.* UK: Alfred Waller, Henley on Thames.

Smith, N. G. (1990). The case study: A useful research method for information management. *Journal of Information Technology, 5,* 123-133.

Stamoulis, D., Kanellis, P., & Martakos, D. (2001). Tailorable information systems: Resolving the deadlock of changing user requirements. *Journal of Applied Systems Studies, 2*(2), 294-311.

Strauss, A. L (1987). *Qualitative analysis for social scientists.* Cambridge, UK: Cambridge University Press.

Strauss, A. L., & Corbin, J. (1991). *Basics of qualitative research.* Newbury Park, CA: Sage Publications.

Swanson, B. E. (1982). A view of information systems evolution. In J. Hawgood (Ed.), *Evolutionary information systems*. Amsterdam, The Netherlands: North-Holland.

Thompson, J. D. (1967). *Organizations in action*. New York: McGraw Hill.

Truex, D., Baskerville, R., & Klein, H. (1999). Growing systems in emergent organizations. *Communications of the ACM, 42*(8), 117-123.

Van Maanen, J. (1995). *Representation in ethnography*. London: Sage Publications.

Venkatraman, N. (1989). The concept of "fit" in strategy research: Toward verbal and statistical correspondence. *Academy of Management Review, 14*(3), 423-444.

Walsham, G. (1993). *Interpreting information systems in organizations*. Chichester, UK: Wiley

Walsham, G. (1995). The emergence of interpetivism in information systems research. *Information Systems Research, 6*(4), 376-394.

Weill, P., & Olson, M. H. (1989). An assessment of the contingency theory of management information systems. *Journal of Management Information Systems, 6*(1), 59-85.

Yin, R. K. (1989). Research design issues in using the case study method to study management information systems. In J. I. a. L. Cash (Ed.), *The information systems research challenge: Qualitative research methods* (pp. 1-6). Boston: Harvard Business School Press.

Endnotes

[1]   For confidentiality reasons, the actual name of the organization has been disclosed.

[2]   In the analysis and interpretation of the data, major concepts appear in the text bold and italicized.

[3]   Positivism postulates that all knowledge can be expressed in statements of laws and facts that are positively corroborated by measurement (Hirschheim et al., 1995).

Appendix

Interpretive Approaches to Information Systems Research

The ontological and epistemological assumptions a researcher makes drive any subsequent scientific inquiry. These assumptions are the outcome of reflections on reality and its nature. For example, it is easy to observe the common thread that runs through any positivist[3] notion. The awareness of the notion of subjectivity that the human element introduces gave rise to the anti-positivist epistemologies and doctrines. The major theme of anti-positivism as introduced by Wilhelm Dilthey (1833-1911) is the view that as individuals do not exist in isolation, they need to be studied and understood in the context of their cultural and social life. In addition, the possibility of positive and observer-independent knowledge is denied. Instead, the emphasis is placed upon sympathetic reason in understanding phenomena and attributing meanings through "understanding" (Verstehen) methods rather than seeking causal connections and universal laws via the employment of "explanation" methods (Hirschheim, 1992; Hirschheim, Klein, & Lyytinen, 1995).

The point that made anti-positivism come of age is therefore an acknowledgement of the fact that it is not viable to understand and explain the nature or the rationale behind the actions for the human element, as it is impossible to collect complete and objective sets of data that cover all the biological, social, and most importantly, psychological drivers that give rise to them.

On the empirical side, interpretive research techniques in information systems include case studies, textual analysis (hermeneutics), participant observation/ action research, and ethnography. Due to their relevance to the empirical side of this paper, case studies as tools for interpretive research are explained in some detail in the following section. For a comprehensive coverage on ethnography, the interested reader should consult Fetterman (1989) and Van Maanen (1995), whilst Orlikowski and Baroudi (1991) and Reponen (1994) cover participant observation/action research. Boland (1985) addresses hermeneutics in information systems research.

Case Studies in Interpretivist Research

The flexibility of the case study as a research approach allows it to be equally promising from a positivist stance (Yin, 1989) or an interpretivist one (Walsham, 1995). Galliers (1992), for example, included it under the scientific (positivist) heading of his taxonomy because the majority of its exponents classify it as such. Ultimately, the utilization of the case study method depends on the philosophical stance of the researcher and the research objective. Benbasat, Goldstein, and Mead (1987), although approaching the issue of case studies from a positivist perspective, provide a useful definition: "A case study examines a phenomenon in its neutral setting, employing multiple methods of data collection to gather information from one or a few entities (people, groups, or organisations). The boundaries of the phenomenon are not clearly evident at the outset of the research and no experimental control or manipulation is used" (p. 370).

Case studies can use either qualitative or quantitative evidence, or even a mixture of both. The case study does not imply a particular type of evidence, nor does it imply the use of a particular data collection method (Yin, 1989, p. 59). The main criticism that is made regarding interpretivist case studies is that they are problematic with respect to generalizability. As their application is restricted to a single organization, generalizations cannot be made easily if at all. But for non-positivist studies, generalizability is not of concern. This is because in interpretive information systems research, the validity of the case study approach, becomes clear once it is realized that one seeks to understand "the context of the information system and the process over time of mutual influence between the system and its context" (Walsham, 1993, p. 14). To this end, the case study is not merely a technique or even a means of obtaining data; for the interpretivist it is a method for organizing data, and the selection of a case for study will not as a consequence rest on how typical (for example) the case may be, but on its explanatory power (Smith, 1990). Epistemology and research methods are interrelated, and a conscious effort must be made by the researcher to establish and communicate the extent of this relationship. Hence, if one adopts a positivist epistemological stance, statistical generalizability is the key goal (Walsham, 1993). For an interpretivist, generalizability is irrelevant; the focus is instead on "the plausibility and cogency of the logical reasoning used in describing the results from the cases, and in drawing conclusions from them" (ibid., p. 15).

Chapter XI

Quality of Use of a Complex Technology: A Learning-Based Model

Marie-Claude Boudreau, The University of Georgia, USA

Larry Seligman, The University of Georgia, USA[1]

Abstract

It has been argued that simple conceptualizations of usage are inadequate for understanding and studying use of complex information technologies. In this paper we contend that quality of use, instead of the dichotomy of use versus non-use, is appropriate for understanding the extent to which a complex information technology is being used. An inductive case study of the implementation of a complex information technology was conducted, which led to the development of a learning-based model of quality of use. This model suggests the inclusion of factors relating to training (either formal or informal), learning, and beliefs, their impact on quality of use, and their change over time. Moreover, it describes how quality of use evolves over time as learning increases and perceptions of the system change. Evidence from the case study, along with relationships from the literature, is provided to support the model. Implications for future research are also discussed.

Introduction

The antecedents to use of an information system (IS) have been extensively explored in the technology adoption and diffusion literatures. Typically, these studies examine the construct of use and its antecedents through models based in diffusion of innovations theory (Rogers, 1995), the theory of reasoned action (Ajzen & Fishbein, 1980), and the theory of planned behavior (Ajzen & Madden, 1986). Studies of these models often measure perceptions, attitudes, intentions, and use at a single point in time, with a dichotomous conceptualization of use, that is, either the system was used or it was not used.

It may be argued that such models are not suited for the study of a complex technology; rather, they are most relevant to simple technologies that can only be used in a limited number of ways. Eveland and Tornatzky (1990) pointed out that, "problems arise when the diffusion model is applied in situations where its basic assumptions are not met — that is to say, virtually every case involving complex, advanced technology" (p. 123). Indeed, many studies of adoption/acceptance models based on the aforementioned theories explore technologies that are relatively simple to use, such as e-mail (e.g., Karahanna & Straub, 1999; Szajna, 1996) and word processors (e.g., Agarwal, Sambamurthy, & Stair, 2000; Chau, 1996). Because simple technologies are easy to conceptualize and operationalize, and because many people use them, researchers have often preferred the study of simple technologies to complex ones for testing their models.

By many accounts, ERP packages qualify as a complex technology (Akkermans & van Helden, 2002; Gill, 1999; Maney, 1999; Ribbers & Schoo, 2002; Umble, Haft, & Umble, 2003). Because they typically involve many processes that are highly integrated, the basic infrastructure of ERP packages fits systems theorist's characterization of complexity: A large number of elements together with a large number of relationships between them (Flood & Carson, 1993). When introduced within organizations, complex information technologies often impose a substantial burden on potential adopters to use them effectively (Attewell, 1992; Fichman & Kemerer, 1997; Robey, Ross, & Boudreau, 2002). Tornatzky and Fleischer (1990) claim that complex technologies tend to be "fragile," because they do not always operate as expected. Moreover, they argue that complex information technologies (IT) often require hand-holding in their appropriation because they are difficult to learn.

Given this complexity, the successful implementation of an ERP package may not always imply that its users exhibit a high quality of use, that is, high levels of satisfaction, efficiency, and effectiveness resulting from users' interaction with the system (Bevan, 1995). This is consistent with past research, which shows that it is common for complex IT to be successfully implemented but unsuccessfully appropriated. For example, organizational members often resist changes induced by technology (Kling & Iacono, 1989). They also use technology in ways that are not expected *a priori* (e.g., Kraut, Dumais & Koch, 1989). As a result, unanticipated (and sometimes contradictory) consequences may result from an implementation that was initially considered successful (Robey & Boudreau, 1999). Indeed, a successful implementation, that is, one that is on time, on target, and on budget (Dennis & Wixom, 2003), does not necessarily result in the attainment of the desired benefits of the implementation.

We purport that a successful implementation must be coupled with high quality of use in order to fully realize the benefits of the ERP package. Therefore, it would be valuable to understand how quality of use develops. Based on this, a case study of a successful ERP implementation was conducted. This inquiry led to the development of a learning-based model identifying relevant factors influencing quality of use.

In this paper, we discuss the literature on the construct of use and its antecedents, along with the literature on quality of use. Specifically, we emphasize the need for a focus on quality of use instead of use itself when considering the utilization of complex ITs, and we discuss the potential role of learning in explaining quality of use. Then we introduce the research approach, a case study conducted with the grounded theory research methodology. Next, we present empirical data supporting a learning-based model of quality of use. Finally, we discuss implications and contributions of the study.

Literature Review

Use and Quality of Use

The literature on the construct of use within the field of information systems reveals that use is one of the most frequently reported measures of system implementation success (DeLone & McLean, 1992; Seddon, 1997). However, IT use has generally been defined narrowly. Indeed, researchers have typically understood use in terms of "usage" and "user satisfaction" (Auer, 1998). When understood in terms of usage, use is further subdivided according to three dimensions (Trice & Treacy, 1988): Time, reliance, and diversity. Although this perspective on use has been valuable in past research, it is not as compelling as when one tries to assess the results of user interactions with the system, that is, how well an end user understands a piece of software and how efficiently and effectively the user can exploit the capabilities of the software.

To date, research efforts directed towards the creation of a richer conceptualization of use are few (Agarwal, 2000). Notable steps in this direction have been taken by Saga and Zmud (1994), who focused on the infusion of technology at an organizational level. Infusion is "the extent to which an innovation's features are used in a complete and sophisticated way" (Fichman, 2000, p. 110). Saga and Zmud distinguished three levels of infusion: extended use, integrative use, and emergent use, with each level being successively more sophisticated. Auer (1998) also suggested a taxonomy of five classes of issues to look holistically at "quality of use." Contributing to a richer operationalization of use, Nambisan, Agarwal, and Tanniru (1999) developed a construct labeled "intentions to explore," which measures one's willingness and purpose to find new ways of applying IT to work tasks. Another perspective was proposed in the framework developed by Lassila and Brancheau (1999), which distinguishes four "equilibrium states" corresponding to increasing levels of use of a software package. Their model, meant to be interpreted at an organizational level of analysis, is based on the relationship between technology and organization change.

It is thus clear that many valuable conceptualizations of use exist. One view that is particularly compelling as it captures how well an end user understands, and later achieves, a certain level of performance with a given technology is proposed by Bevan (1995), who describes "quality of use" as "the effectiveness, efficiency and satisfaction with which specified users can achieve specified goals in specified environments" (p. 118). Effectiveness and efficiency are also understood as the components of "performance." In Bevan's model of antecedents to quality of use, user interactions with the software influence satisfaction and performance, which in turn influence each other.

Bevan (2001) explains that "usability" is a similar term to "quality in use" as both terms are defined in various International Standards Organization (ISO) reports. "Quality in use" is defined essentially as performance, satisfaction, and safety, whereas "usability" is defined as "the extent to which a product can be used by specified users to achieve specified goals with effectiveness, efficiency, and satisfaction in a specified context of use" (p. 537).

Vidgen, Wood-Harper, and Wood (1993) argue against definitions of quality that are created from a purely "logic-based perspective," such as those that are comprised of objectively measurable usage outcomes such as efficiency and effectiveness. They maintain that there is a socially constructed element to "IS use quality" that is culturally influenced and dynamic. Therefore, in order to understand what constitutes quality of use in a given context, one must understand the culture and social aspects of the context of use.

For the purpose of this paper, we also refer to satisfaction and performance as components of quality of use. Like Wood-Harper and Wood (1993), we also acknowledge the importance of understanding what quality of use means in a given context, as opposed to in the absolute.

Training and Use

Studies of technology acceptance typically do not investigate the role of training in acceptance, but rather include only subjects who participate in training and then use the new technology (e.g., Agarwal, Sambamurthy, & Stair, 2000; Davis, 1989; Venkatesh, Morris, Davis, & Davis, 2003) or subjects who were identified (or who identified themselves) as being already familiar with the technology (Agarwal & Prasad 1998; Karahanna & Straub 1999). The reason for this lack of focus on training and use in the IS literature might be because use of technology begins in the "Acceptance" stage, whereas training occurs in the earlier "Adaptation" stage (Cooper & Zmud, 1990). Thus, studies that examine only the acceptance phase would not include training or learning as factors in the acceptance models. Many acceptance studies, including those mentioned above, are based on models with formed perceptions as exogenous variables, implying that at least the initial training or other familiarization activities had already occurred. Some (e.g., Venkatesh et al., 2003) measure these perceptions at different points in time with the understanding that experience affects perceptions. However, training is not typically treated as a factor that leads to acceptance, but rather as a necessary contextual condition for the study of acceptance and usage-related research. Quality of use focuses on outcomes of usage, which are in the domain of the "Infusion" stage. Thus training/learning, initial use, and quality of use all occur in different stages (i.e., adaptation, acceptance, and infusion). However, "...political and learning models may be more useful [than rational decision models] when examining infusion" (Cooper & Zmud, 1990, p. 123). This statement supports the notion that quality of use may have antecedents in learning. A model of learning-based antecedents to quality of use thus implies a model spanning the adaptation, acceptance, and infusion stages.

Training, and the resulting learning, have been integrated into models of use in a variety of ways. Training has been identified as an antecedent to self-efficacy (e.g., Gist, Schwoerer, & Rosen, 1989; Martocchio & Webster, 1992), which has been found to be related to other usage-related perceptions as well as use itself. CASE training availability was found to be related to "CASE adoption behavior," which was measured according to the number of CASE functions being used in a more-than-experimental manner (Rai & Patnayakuni, 1996), although this measurement would correspond more to a diversity of usage than to quality of use. "Learning performance" has been described as influencing attitudes (Bostrom, Olfman, & Sein 1990). Thus there are varying opinions on how to integrate learning and use into a model, and learning effects on perceptions and use are supported by these and other studies. Additionally, training does not always occur as formal, pre-usage instruction. For example, Spitler (2005) found that training occurs on an on-going basis in the form of social interaction with other users (including "master" users who have formal or informal guidance roles), online help, just-in-time training (see also Huang, 2002), and so forth. Thus training and use both occur on an ongoing basis. Therefore, it is possible that quality of use is subject to ongoing change as a result of ongoing learning, so that models of quality of use might need to be cyclical or otherwise longitudinal in order to capture these ongoing effects.

Since the skills necessary for high quality of use of a complex technology will develop over time, a set of perceptions at any single point in time cannot fully capture the influences on quality of use. It is similarly insufficient to measure perceptions and quality of use at multiple points in time if there is no understanding gained as to how these perceptions evolved. Rather, it is necessary to understand how perceptions change, and the results of those changes, in order to understand how quality of use improves. Because learning is a result of training, and learning leads to changes in perceptions, it is necessary to understand quality of use in terms of the training and learning that occur over time. This is what our case study, presented next, illustrates.

Research Approach

The grounded theory research methodology was chosen for the pursuit of this inquiry (Strauss & Corbin, 1990). Grounded theory uses a qualitative approach and techniques of induction, deduction, and verification to develop or elaborate a theory about a phenomenon (Schwandt, 1997). More specifically, the "Straussian" version of the theory was used. This version differs from the "Glaserian" version in that it allows for the use of theory to help researchers gain insight into the data (Boudreau, 2002; Strauss & Corbin, 1994). The grounded theory methodology is not limited to the generation of a new theory, but may include the consideration or elaboration of an existing theory (Strauss & Corbin, 1994). Accordingly, in this research, constructs and relationships from the existing literature were used to inform and help interpret our empirical findings.

Although the "Straussian" version of the grounded theory methodology allows for the use of theory to make sense of the data, it is mainly an inductive approach, and accordingly, the use of a specific theory prior to entering the field is undesirable. In this case, we entered the field with little *a priori* theory, and were initially simply interested in quality of use in the context of a successful implementation.[2] We found such a successful implementation in a medium-size (i.e., 3,000 employees) public organization from the southeastern United States (i.e., PubOrg, a pseudonym), which we studied during a 15-month period spanning 1999-2000. Prior to our arrival in the field, PubOrg had implemented financial modules from a popular ERP vendor (PeopleSoft®). Project leaders considered this implementation to be very successful because it had proceeded on time and on budget, and had also met PubOrg's financial requirements.

Interviewing was the primary means of data collection. From a total of about 700 potential respondents, 74 interviews were conducted with 65 organizational members holding a variety of roles at PubOrg. More specifically, interviewees included clerical workers (mainly in charge of the entering of basic financial transactions, such as purchase requisitions or purchase orders), finance special-ists (in charge of producing and analyzing financial reports, along with making financial entries), and project leaders. Different roles were sought out to reduce the bias toward one type of user versus another. Interviewees were selected based upon their involvement with the system and their willingness to be interviewed by one of the researchers. Accordingly, the interview process included only those who were willing to openly discuss their experience with the ERP. Only two individuals refused to be interviewed, as they were not comfortable in sharing their thoughts about the new system. Interviews lasted on average one hour each. They were semi-structured in their format and were tape-recorded (except for five) and fully transcribed.

In addition to interviewing, we also utilized participant observation and document review as two additional data collection techniques. Participant observation and document review served to inform us in our interpretation of the interviews. Therefore, we were able to develop a better understanding of the context surrounding this implementation, along with a more accurate appreciation of the organizational members' enactment of the new system (Jorgensen, 1989). Participant observation was possible because the first author had access to the implementation team members and the meetings they attended. Over the period of inquiry, 30 such meetings and training sessions were attended. Furthermore, the project leader agreed to send this author to a two-week training program to become more familiar with the ERP system being implemented. This allowed the participant observer not only to get a deeper understanding of the technology, but also to get involved in the development of a few financial reports, giving her a sense of the capabilities of the ERP system. As to the document review, it included training manuals, meeting minutes, newsletters, and some electronic mails.

Data analysis, conducted with the help of a qualitative data analysis tool (i.e., Atlas.ti® Version 4.2), incorporated different types of coding typical of grounded theory: Open, axial, and selective coding. Open coding was the process of breaking down, comparing, conceptualizing, and categorizing data. Such coding was realized by comparing each incident, event, quote, and instance gathered during the data collection for similarities and differences. From the verbatim interviews and field notes, similar textual segments were labeled and grouped to form codes.

Axial coding necessitated that the data be put back together in new ways by making connections between codes to form factors. This was done by grouping codes based on their conceptual similarity. Through the axial coding emerged a model (or "theoretical network" as it is called in grounded theory) revealing factors influencing quality of use of a complex technology. This axial coding procedure led us to an understanding of how end users had learned, through different means, the new software package.

Finally, during selective coding, the most relevant of these factors were selected to establish a stronger and more parsimonious model. To clarify under-developed factors or relationships between factors, more data was collected (data collection and analysis are intertwined in grounded theory). Selective coding was considered completed when theoretical saturation was obtained, that is, when no new or relevant data seemed to emerge regarding a factor, when the factor development was dense, and when the relationships between factors were well established and validated.

Resulting from this analysis was a model (referred to as "learning-based model of quality of use") explaining antecedents to quality of use of a complex technology at PubOrg. Although the model exhibits a variance theory appearance, it uses process logic to explain how some predictors influence certain outcomes. This is consistent with Sambamurthy and Kirsch (2000) and Van de Ven's (1992) categorization of process research, which recognized "process as explanation" as a valid type of process-oriented research. Process as explanation requires one to open the proverbial "black box" between predictors and outcomes, so as to directly observe the process (Van de Ven, 2000), shedding light on *how* outcomes actually happened (Mackenzie, 2000). Empirical support for our proposed learning-based model of quality of use follows.

Results

The results are divided into two sub-sections. First, we illustrate the extent to which users exhibited different levels of quality of use of the new ERP system (i.e., the outcome of interest). Second, we provide empirical support highlighting the process that led to the different levels of quality of use.

Differences in Quality of Use

After the ERP system became live at PubOrg, end users began using the system. At the beginning, the vast majority of them struggled with even the simplest functionalities of the system. Surprisingly, even after a few months of regular use, many end users still considered the interaction with the new system to be a challenging task. Other end users, however, had made remarkable progress and were using the system in a sophisticated way. Project leaders were puzzled by the existing disparity of use among PubOrg's employees.

End users who were deficient in their use of the system appeared to lack appropriate know-how: "They don't know how to use it... they don't understand it," commented one project leader. Instead of directly interacting with the system (i.e., entering the information online), these individuals used it indirectly through the available paper forms. For instance, one would choose the appropriate paper form for a particular transaction, fill it with the required information, obtain the necessary signatures for its approval, and transmit it to the staff in the Finance and Administration department. Those end users who ventured to use the ERP system more directly felt highly intimidated by it. They were hardly successful in interacting with it, and blamed their inadequacy on their lack of understanding of the system's functionalities:

I don't know how to use half of the functions in this system. I don't know if they pertain to me or not. I know enough to get what I need to get in there.

Most of us use the system like monkeys: we are pushing buttons. We have directions in front of us that say "Push this button, push that button"... we don't push other buttons. People are afraid of pushing the wrong buttons... They know the buttons to push for their task, but not necessarily what is around.

Because of their superficial understanding of the system's functionality, end users had difficulty retrieving information. Verifying that a purchase requisition had been approved, for example, was something many of them could not do. Confirming that a check had been cut was often deemed infeasible. Likewise, finding out the free balance of a particular account was problematic. Even though they could enter a basic transaction within the system, users could not, for the most part, track the information; it was "lost in cyberspace."

I don't really know of any way of going back to check and see where things are, or if things went through. If you put a request, you order something, and it never arrives, you don't know if somebody down the line is having a problem with the system, or if the system failed and you didn't put in the order correctly. So, you wonder, did it work?

Nevertheless, other users demonstrated a much better understanding of the system. Instead of using the paper forms, these individuals used the system's computerized interface not only to do their job, but also to experiment:

I enjoy entering the information and digging information out... With [the new system], I am more in control because I am actually entering the information myself, whereas before I would type it and submit it and someone else would put it in. I like to be empowered to put my own stuff in.

These users felt that they benefited from the promised advantages resulting from the use of the new ERP system: It provided real-time information, obsolesced the shadow systems (which were originally necessary to make up for the outdated information of the legacy system), fostered a paperless office, eliminated perfunctory tasks, and allowed for better reporting capabilities. For example, among the accounting assistants who worked at PubOrg, some were raving about how their performance had improved, thanks to the system. One of them illustrated that point:

It makes my job so easy, sometimes I think "what am I missing, what am I forgetting to do?" I pay the utility bills that use to take me, using the old method, an entire day... I can now do this in one hour. Huge is not even the word for it. No shadow system, and it will run its own reports! The only thing I got to do is enter how much they [the utility companies] are going to be paid and an address for record keeping, and that's it!

As these users became even more familiar with the system, they eventually felt capable of "tweaking" the system to better respond to their needs when facing its constraints. Such "tweaking," also called "workarounds," allowed them to use the system in a slightly different way than it was intended to work, so that they would get things processed the way they wanted them. Instances of workarounds included the use of a field (the "statistical code") to capture information of another nature (i.e., credit card payments); the use of multiple referenced records to handle a single vendor that had multiple locations; the use of "header comments" to compensate for a line item too short; and the use of a line item to indicate a particular action to take:

On a purchase order, if you find that you have to add money, you can't just go and change the line amount. It's not going to work; something is going to happen and [the Disbursements Department] won't be able to pay it. So, a workaround we have here is to add an additional line to say "Increase PO by x amount of dollars!" just so the dollar amount equals what you need it to equal.

In summary, whereas some end users interacted with the new ERP system in a very superficial way, others extended its basic capabilities, thus making use more effective. Use greatly differed in terms of quality. One thus wonders: What, exactly, influenced some users to appropriate the new ERP system in a limited way, while others thrived in using it in a more extended fashion? One particular group of factors appeared to be critical to quality of use: The extent to which end users had learned (and thus understood) the system. Given the complexity of ERP packages, it is necessary (but not sufficient) for an individual to first understand a technology quite well before using it in an efficient and effective manner.

Explaining Quality of Use

We were able to suggest a preliminary answer to the aforementioned question through the analysis of our empirical data. Overall, our resulting model seeks to demonstrate that as end users held initial beliefs about the new ERP system, they elected to participate (or not) in its training, and learned about the system's functionalities. This new learning led to a new set of beliefs about the system, which in turn influenced the end users' general satisfaction toward the new technology. This satisfaction affected the extent to which end users attempted to use the new system, which was a prerequisite to reaching higher quality of use. In the following paragraphs, we provide empirical support for the relationships that lay the foundation of our proposed learning-based model of quality of use (see Figure 1).

Training/Learning. Training was one major component that clearly influenced the extent to which some users did not understand the system while others appeared to master it. At PubOrg, formal training sessions were offered a month before the system went live, as well as one month after. It is through these sessions that many end users initially learned about the system and its functionalities. The following quotes are representative of a generally positive relationship between formal training and learning (relationship #1 in the model):

Figure 1. Learning-based model of quality of use

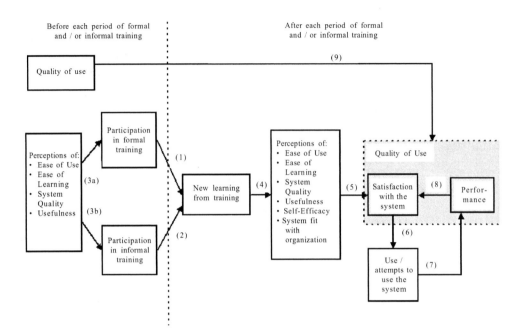

Now, I don't think anybody should try to do this without having gone through the training. I don't think they would even know where to start!

I thought the training was good. The training manuals I think are excellent because in the very beginning, some of the things I had to do... my first instinct was to grab Debbie [a support person] but then I said I'll just get my handout and I'll do it like that. I've already left my frantic message for Debbie to "please call me! I have to do something new!", but then I would look at my handout. It was great because it gave you a frame-by-frame screen; click here, click there, and it took you exactly through every step to the end.... By the time Debbie shows up, I say, "I did it, I followed the manual, and I think I did it perfectly — look at it!", you know. The training manuals are very good. That is how I learned how to do things on my own, and after a while I did stop calling Debbie.

At PubOrg, employees were encouraged (but not required) to attend the numerous formal training sessions. However, to the project leaders' dismay, these sessions had been attended by only a minority of employees. Indeed, most end users had only attended a few sessions or had avoided them entirely. Instead, they elected to increase their knowledge of the system through what we call "informal training," that is, the training that occurred in a very unstructured and unplanned way. For the most part, informal training was continual, that is, it emerged on a "need to know" basis rather than being predetermined (as formal training was). Informal training took multiple forms. It incorporated "water-cooler" conversations, casual questioning of more knowledgeable users, and spontaneous demonstrations of and experimentation with some of the system's functions. At a given time and for a particular system function, a user could either become unofficial trainer or trainee. When a user would discover how to perform a particularly useful task, peers were quickly updated about the tip:

I can't tell you how many things that we learned, not because of [formal] training, not because the trainers knew it, but because somebody figured it out, and it became kind of folk knowledge.

Informal training turned out to be quite widespread at PubOrg. The numerous users who had forgone formal training sessions relied on this type of training to get them started with the new ERP system. In light of the role of informal training in increasing learning, we incorporate relationship #2 into the model.

Initial Beliefs

Many end users had previous experience with basic information technologies, that is, with the previous legacy system and desktop applications such as word processors and spreadsheets. This prior experience with technology gave some users the false confidence that they could learn the system by themselves and did not have to bother with training, formal or informal. Many thought that the ERP package would be generic enough to be self-taught:

I didn't think the training would be that crucial... that sounds terrible, but I thought that maybe it would be something that you could OJT [on job training] a little bit, that you could learn on the job.... Every system we had here, we learned it that way. You sit down, and you learn it by yourself. So, I had the feeling that this is a standard program, a package... I mean, it is not even specific [to our type of institution], so how hard can that be? That's what I thought. It is not like it was written specifically for us, so we thought that it was created with general, pre-assumed code.... I did think I would be able to pick it up on the fly, so to speak.

As this quote illustrates, end users' previous experience with learning new technologies on their own influenced them into thinking that the system would be easy to learn and to use, and that accordingly, training would be unnecessary. Users' initial perceived ease of use and ease of learning, therefore, were posited to influence the undergoing of training.

Users' perceptions of the quality of the system and the usefulness of the system also had an impact on their participation in training. Some users were highly troubled by what they perceived to be a "buggy" system, and therefore, did not consider the system as one ready for use or learning. As the word spread that the system had "a few kinks," many users made the decision to disregard training until the system was fixed. In other words, for the users who perceived the new system as being not yet ready for use, training was considered a waste of time and effort:

I have this kind of German mentality, rigid mentality, where I think that it ought to work. So, I'm waiting for them to straighten that out. I don't feel like, anymore, that I need to go dancing around in circles: I've done enough stuff.

Other users, though, felt that that the system would be very useful after they underwent training:

I think that once it's learned, it will certainly make the job easier. Certainly easier for tracking and lessening the possibility of losing pieces of paper. I think once we've learned it, that's going to be good.

Thus, our model reflects two additional relationships: One between beliefs and participation in formal training (relationship #3a), and the other between beliefs and participation in informal training (relationship #3b).

Revised Beliefs

Once end users learned some of the ERP's functionalities through formal and/ or informal training, they revised their beliefs about the new system. Initial perceptions were thus reassessed in light of earlier expectations (relationship #4 in the model). In most cases, perceptions about the system's user friendliness and ease of learning were revised downward, as suggested by the following quotes from users who had recently undergone training:

And then, having to learn it, it was not easy...it's not user friendly. It's called PeopleSoft, but it's not...it's PeopleHard!

I have never had one [system] where I absolutely could not find the answer for so long. Usually, you just play around, flip enough switches, and something will end up working, but with [the new system], I just didn't have that luck.

Similarly, perceived usefulness was revised, as users reconciled their pre-training perceptions with their new learning. For most users, this belief was also reassessed more negatively, as illustrated in the following quote:

Before we actually saw the system, I was pretty excited about it. I was thinking: "Wow, this is going to be a really great system; it is going to always be in balance; there won't be any problem [...],"so I thought it was going to be much better than [the legacy system]. But for a while, the [legacy system] was better than [the ERP]! [...] I guess I expected it to run smoothly, and it didn't, so that part I was disappointed.

In addition to perceived usefulness, perceived ease of use, and perceived ease of learning, the belief that the system was a misfit to PubOrg became particularly salient. Indeed, most users considered that the system had not been customized enough:

In the training, I learned that PeopleSoft and the people who built [the system] completely failed to address taxation issues!

In our training, we were going through all these fields, and they would say, "This is a useless field; this is a useless field..." they kept repeating..."It would be too expensive to tailor toward our needs, so we have to just deal with what's here."

They didn't want to accommodate a lot of modifications, which I understand why: It costs too much for the next versions. That is something that is bad about this software: It may be fine in industry, but it is not fit for what we need it to do. But you can't modify it because it costs too much money to modify it... Well, then, my god, I'd find another system! There has to be something out there that would be more appropriate.

Another belief that became prominent for the end users who participated in the training was self-efficacy. The training caused some users to doubt that they had the necessary skills to use the new system. The following quote from a user who had just attended formal training sessions exemplifies low self-efficacy:

Like yesterday, I was feeling stupid, inept, inadequate — all of those things!

Satisfaction

Users' revised perceptions affected their overall satisfaction of the new ERP system (relationship #5 in the model). For example, a user's revised belief about the perceived usefulness of the system turned out to be a prime reason for her dissatisfaction with the system. This user shared her frustration about having to redo data entry because the ones she had previously entered had allegedly "disappeared in cyberspace:"

I have orders that I have issued... I had, at one point, 200 or so orders entered in the system. To have a clerk call me and tell me "all of those numbers you gave me, I can't use any of them." That's 200 orders I have to redo. And that's what I'm doing in between the other things that I do... So, I'm very frustrated; I am not a happy camper right now! I was happier a year ago because I had hope. I have no hope left!

Another user's revised belief about the perceived ease of use of the system triggered his dissatisfaction with the system. His struggle seemed to him almost too much to bear:

It is really hard when you are frustrated not to be mad at the whole system. Right now, I'm so frustrated with it... And you know how that makes you feel about your job; you just want to go home and quit.

Another example of how revised perceived beliefs impacted users' satisfaction is in the following quote, which illustrates the situation in the Disbursements Department, whose members strongly perceived that the new system was a misfit for their needs:

All it has done is to create a nightmare over in Disbursement; there are a lot of angry people over there. I know people who worked here many, many years, and they said if they could retire now they would do it. They don't want to deal with this system. People have been complaining so much; they are just not happy about the whole thing.

In turn, satisfaction with the system influenced the extent to which end users would use, or attempt to use, the system (relationship #6 in the model). This is reflected in the following quotes from users:

Some of those [system] weirdnesses have not made me feel real comfortable about getting online and doing it... So I'm just trying to find the quickest way to do something, and for me that's currently filling it out on the screen and printing it off and sticking it in the interoffice mail.

Right now it is very very frustrating and complicated, so we just don't deal with it, which is sad. I hate to admit I do it, but it is true.

Discussion

To summarize, our results show that users held initial perceptions of the ERP system, and that those perceptions influenced their decision to participate in training. Indeed, even prior to participating in any formal or informal training, potential users had opinions about the new system, as was exemplified earlier. Users then elected to participate (or not) in formal and informal training, which impacted their learning of the system and led to a revised set of beliefs and a revised level of satisfaction toward the system. Users who mentioned having a low level of satisfaction showed a minimal desire to use the system, and some sought to use it minimally.

The learning-based model emerging from our results highlights antecedents to a very important concept, quality of use, as represented by satisfaction and performance. In this case study, equating use to any of the three dimensions of use previously discussed (e.g., time, reliance, and diversity) would have misled one to believe that this system was successfully used. Indeed, although some users exhibited low quality of use, they, at the same time, were spending many hours a week on the system (often through indirect interactions); they relied on it to conduct their work, and they interacted with a wide variety of its functions (including the processing of purchase requisitions, travel authorizations, express vouchers, consultant agreements, petty cash advances, reimbursements, and journal entries). In other words, according to the dimensions of time, reliance, or diversity, use was high. Nevertheless, as it was demonstrated, quality of use was limited for some users, while being extended for others. Rather than considering use in a simplistic way, we have proposed to reframe this construct so as to make it more appropriate to the study of complex technologies. Quality of use, in the context of complex information technology, is thus a more valuable way to assess use.

Bevan (1995) includes a two-way relationship between satisfaction and performance in his model. We also included additional relationships to reflect this. Specifically, a relationship from satisfaction to performance was represented indirectly through the relationships #6 and #7. Relationship #6 was supported in the results, but relationship #7 was supported by the literature on quality of use (Bevan 1995). As to the direct relationship from performance to satisfaction, it was represented in the same way as in Bevan's (1995) model.

The quality of use exhibited at any given time is likely to influence future quality of use as an end user's learning accumulates and the learning is applied through using or attempting to use the system. Therefore, a relationship between the quality of use before and after training was represented in our model (relationship #9). We propose that the quality of use after an occurrence of training is a function of quality of use before training, of the revised perceptions resulting from the new learning, and of the users' interactions with the system.

Prior research has provided support to the idea that changes in beliefs, over time, will impact user satisfaction or IT usage (e.g., Bhattacherjee & Premkumar, 2004; Karahanna, Straub, & Chervany, 1999; Khalifa & Liu, 2003). The current research supports previous findings stating that initial expectations are particularly important once the technology has been adopted by the user base, that is, during the "post-adoption" stage (Bhattacherjee & Premkumar, 2004; Khalifa & Liu, 2003). The proposed learning-based model also emphasizes that, even within the post-adoption stage, changes in beliefs are not static; they may change over time, as they did before and after the numerous instances of training that took place at PubOrg. Moreover, the proposed learning-based model suggests that beliefs will not only influence users' satisfaction with the new system, but also the overall quality of use enacted by users.

Prior research also suggests other factors (other than the ones included in the proposed learning-based model) that could impact user satisfaction or IT usage. For instance, managerial interventions, personal characteristics, and image enhancement, have previously been singled out as important factors impacting post-adoption use (Karahanna, Straub, & Chervany, 1999). Although some of these factors did emerge from the analysis of the case study's data, they did not demonstrate direct influence on the intermediary constructs of training and learning, and therefore were not included in the resulting model. Additionally, various studies show that there are asocial means by which usage-related learning occurs, that is, by experimentation (Raelin, 1997; Spitler, 2005). We considered experimentation to be a type of informal learning; however, future research could have as a goal the explicit distinction of experimentation and other asocial means of learning.

Contributions to Research

Our findings show that new beliefs emerge as end users learn and use the system. Specifically, perceptions regarding the fit of the system and self-efficacy can change and become relevant after users have exposure to training and use. Thus, we purport that a model of quality of use of a complex IT should include different sets of beliefs at different points in time if it is to reflect the process undertaken by end users when appropriating a complex technology. These findings address the question about the changes in, and relevance of, usage-related beliefs other than usefulness mentioned by Bhattacherjee and Premkumar (2004) as an issue for future research.

Although longitudinal models representing beliefs at multiple points in time have already been suggested in the literature (e.g., Bhattacherjee & Premkumar, 2004; Khalifa & Liu, 2003), they do not explain the mechanisms through which these beliefs change, other than through expectation and disconfirmation. Our evidence supports the notion that training and learning play important roles in how these cognitions change. The consideration of training and learning is particularly important in the case of complex technologies, as these technologies are likely to demand more time and effort from end users than simple technologies would. Inclusion of constructs related to training, both formal and informal, along with the resulting learning, is thus key to our understanding of how end users appropriate complex technologies over time. We thus agree with Cooper and Zmud (1990) that, at least in the case of quality of use, learning-based models can be useful for understanding infusion-related phenomena. Indeed, as organizations go through the phases of implementation, it is reasonable to think that end users' beliefs at a given stage will evolve, have multi-phased longitudinal impacts, and vary in relevance over time. The model derived from our data constitutes a first attempt to subsume multiple implementation phases into one graphical representation highlighting changes in beliefs over time and their effects on quality of use.

We do not know, and cannot test with an emergent model based on qualitative data, the relative importance of the various beliefs, either initially or on an ongoing basis. It is possible that the usefulness of the system plays a dominant role in determining ongoing participation in training and ongoing usage. Another possibility is that the desire for training is guided primarily by feelings of low or even high self-efficacy. Understanding these relative influences over time in a model based on training and learning is a topic for future research.

Contribution to Practice

Although an implementation may be considered a technological success, it is risky for management to presume how a new information technology will be used, particularly if it is a complex one. Indeed, end users may spend many hours using particular software, while incorrectly exploiting its capabilities. This was observed in our case study, as many end users made use of the new ERP system, but exhibited a very low quality of use. It is true that dips in performance are common after ERP systems become live (Ross and Vitale, 2000); Markus and Tanis (2000) refer to this period as the "shakedown." However, we contend that after 15 months, low quality of use should be the case of a few rather than the majority. Management should make sure that formal and informal training are well facilitated and supported in order to overcome low quality of use.

Managers should also be particularly aware of end users' beliefs, not only before training, but also after training and during end users' early attempts to use a new technology. By doing so, they will stay "in synch" with their users and will be able to promptly adjust (through better training, change management programs, etc.) when these beliefs are overly negative. However, the question of how to conceptualize and measure quality of use in specific circumstances so that specific adjustments can be made is an issue for managers and researchers to explore.

Conclusion

This research has provided a conceptualization and model of quality of use based on training, learning, and their influence on cognitions. The model we inductively derived shows the changes in the end users' beliefs as they appropriated a complex technology. Although these factors are not necessarily the only ones that will have an impact on quality use, they were the most critical for PubOrg's employees.

Efforts toward a better conceptualization of use are supported by many, including Agarwal (2000), who thinks that "greater value would be derived from novel ways of [studying] technology use" (p.102) and Karahanna et al. (1999), who encourage the development of "a more sophisticated conceptualization of usage" (p. 202). The model resulting from this case study suggests that the inclusion of factors relating to learning allows us to better understand why quality of use may vary among individual users. The model was inductively created to represent the factors that appear to have the greatest impact on quality of use of a complex technology. From empirical data collected in a single site, we thus extended theory explaining quality of use. This approach is consistent with the notion of generalizability associated with inductive research and case studies (Lee & Baskerville, 2003; Yin, 1994). Further research calls for empirical validation of this model in various organizational contexts.

References

Agarwal, R. (2000). Individual acceptance of information technologies. In R. Zmud (Ed.), *Framing the domains of IT management. Projecting the future... Through the past* (pp. 85-105). Cincinnati, OH: Pinnaflex Education Resources.

Agarwal, R., & Prasad, J. (1998). The antecedents and consequents of user perceptions in information technology adoption. *Decision Support Systems, 22*(1), 15-29.

Agarwal, R., Sambamurthy, V., & Stair, R. (2000). The evolving relationship between general and specific computer self-efficacy – An empirical assessment. *Information Systems Research, 11*(4), 418-430.

Ajzen, I., & Fishbein, M. (1980). *Understanding attitudes and predicting social behavior.* Englewood Cliffs, NJ: Prentice-Hall.

Ajzen, I., & Madden, T. J. (1986). Prediction of goal-directed behavior: Attitudes, intentions and perceived behavioral control. *Journal of Experimental Social Psychology, 22*(5), 453-474.

Akkermans, H. & van Helden, K. (2002). Vicious and virtuous cycles in ERP implementation: A case study of interrelations between critical success factors. *European Journal of Information Systems, 11*(1), 35-46.

Attewell, P. (1992). Technology diffusion and organizational learning: The case of business computing. *Organization Science, 3*(1), 1-19.

Auer, T. (1998). Quality of IS use. *European Journal of Information Systems, 7*(3), 192-201.

Bevan, N. (1995). Measuring usability as quality of use. *Software Quality Journal, 4*(2), 115-150.

Bevan, N. (2001). International standards for HCI and usability. *International Journal of Human Computer Studies, 55*(4), 533-552.

Bhattacherjee, A., & Premkumar, G. (2004). Understanding changes in belief and attitude toward information technology usage: A theoretical and longitudinal test. *MIS Quarterly, 28*(2), 229-254.

Bostrom, R. P., Olfman, L., & Sein, M. K. (1990). The importance of learning style in end-user training. *MIS Quarterly*, *14*(1), 101-119.

Boudreau, M. C. (2002). Using grounded theory in IS research. In *Proceedings of the 20th Annual Conference of The Association of Management and the International Association of Management*, *20*(2), 383-394.

Chau, P. (1996). An empirical assessment of a modified technology acceptance model. *Journal of Management Information Systems*, *13*(2), 185-204.

Cooper, R. B., & Zmud, R. W. (1990). Information technology implementation research: A technological diffusion approach. *Management Science*, *36*(2), 123-139.

Davis, F. D. (1989). Perceived usefulness, perceived ease of use, and user acceptance of information technology. *MIS Quarterly*, *13*(3), 319-340.

DeLone, W. H., & McLean, E. R. (1992). Information systems success: The quest for the dependent variable. *Information Systems Research*, *3*(1), 60-95.

Dennis, A., & Wixom, B. H. (2003). *Systems analysis and design* (2nd ed.). New York: John Wiley & Sons.

Eveland, J. D., & Tornatsky, L. G. (1990). The deployment of technology. In L. G. Tornatzky & M. Fleischer (Eds.), *The processes of technological innovation*. Lexington, MA: Lexington Books.

Fichman, R. G. (2000). The diffusion and assimilation of information technology innovations. In R. Zmud (Ed.), *Framing the domains of IT management. Projecting the future... Through the past* (pp. 105-128). Cincinnati, OH: Pinnaflex Education Resources.

Fichman, R. G., & Kemerer, C. F. (1997). The assimilation of software process innovations: An organizational learning perspective. *Management Science*, *43*(10), 1345-1363.

Flood, R. L., & Carson, E. R. (1993). *Dealing with complexity: An introduction of systems science* (2nd ed.). New York: Plenum Press.

Gill, P. J. (1999, August 9). ERP: Keep it simple. *Information Week*, 87-92.

Gist, M., Schwoerer, C., & Rosen, B. (1989). Effects of alternative training methods on self-efficacy and performance in computer software training. *Journal of Applied Psychology*, *74*(6), 884-891.

Huang, A. (2002). A three-tier technology training strategy in a dynamic business environment. *Journal of End User Computing*, *14*(2), 30-39.

Jorgensen, D. (1989). *Participant observation: A methodology for human studies*. Newbury Park, CA: Sage Publications.

Karahanna, E., & Straub, D. (1999). The psychological origins of perceived usefulness and ease-of-use. *Information and Management, 35*(4), 237-250.

Karahanna, E., Straub, D. W., & Chervany, N. L. (1999). Information technology adoption across time: A cross-sectional comparison of pre-adoption and post-adoption beliefs. *MIS Quarterly, 23*(2), 183-213.

Khalifa, M., & Liu, V. (2003). Determinants of satisfaction at different adoption stages of internet-based services. *Journal of the AIS, 4*(5), 206-232.

Kling, R., & Iacono, S. (1989). The institutional character of computerized information systems. *Office, Technology and People, 5*(1), 7-28.

Kraut, R., Dumais, S., & Koch, S. (1989). Computerization, productivity, and quality of work-life. *Communications of the ACM, 32*(2), 220-238.

Lassila, K. S., & Brancheau, J. C. (1999). Adoption and utilization of commercial software packages: Exploring utilization equilibria, transitions, triggers, and tracks. *Journal of Management Information Systems, 16*(2), 63-90.

Lee, A. S., & Baskerville, R. L. (2003). Generalizing generalizability in information systems research. *Information Systems Research, 14*(3), 221-243.

Lucas, Jr., H. C., & Spitler, V. K. (1999). Technology use and performance: A field study of broker workstations. *Decision Sciences, 30*(2), 291-311.

Mackenzie, K. D. (2000). Processes and their frameworks. *Management Science, 46*, 110-125.

Maney, K. (1999, June 23). Software so huge and complex — ERP!. *USA Today*, 03B.

Markus, M. L., & Tanis, C. (2000). The enterprise system experience — from adoption to success. In R. W. Zmud (Ed.), *Framing the domains of IT management. Projecting the future... Through the past* (pp. 173-207). Cincinnati, OH: Pinnaflex Education Resources.

Martocchio, J. J., & Webster, J. (1992). Effects of feedback and cognitive playfulness on performance in microcomputer software training. *Personnel Psychology, 45*(2), 553-578.

Nambisan, S., Agarwal, R., & Tanniru, M. (1999). Organizational mechanisms for enhancing user innovation in information technology. *MIS Quarterly, 23*(3), 365-395.

Oliver, R. L. (1980). A cognitive model for the antecedents and consequences of satisfaction. *Journal of Marketing Research, 17*(2), 460-469.

Raelin, J. (1997). A model of work-based learning. *Organization Science, 8*(6), 563-578.

Rai, A., & Patnayakuni, R. (1996). A structural model for case adoption behavior. *Journal of Management Information Systems, 13*(2), 205-234.

Ribbers, P. M. A., & Schoo, K. C. (2002). Program management and complexity of ERP implementations. *Engineering Management Journal, 14*(2), 45-52.

Robey, D., & Boudreau, M. C. (1999). Accounting for the contradictory organizational consequences of information technology: Theoretical directions and methodological implications. *Information Systems Research, 10*(2), 167-185.

Robey, D., Ross, J. W., & Boudreau, M. C. (2002). Learning to implement enterprise systems: An exploratory study of the dialectics of change. *Journal of Management Information Systems. 19*(1), 17-46.

Rogers, E. M. (1995). *Diffusion of innovations* (4th ed.). New York: Free Press.

Ross, J. W. & Vitale, M. R., (2000). The ERP revolution: Surviving vs. thriving. *Information Systems Frontiers, 2*(2), 233-241.

Saga, V., & Zmud, R. W. (1994). The nature and determinants of it acceptance, routinization, and infusion. In L. Levine (Ed.), *Diffusion, transfer, and implementation of information technology* (pp. 67-86). Amsterdam, The Netherlands: Elsevier Science BV.

Sambamurthy, V., & Kirsch, L. J. (2000). An integrative framework of the information systems development process. *Decision Sciences, 31*(2), 391-411.

Schwandt, T. A. (1997). *Qualitative inquiry: A dictionary of terms*. Thousand Oaks, CA: Sage Publications.

Seddon, P. B. (1997). A re-specification and extension of the DeLone and McLean model of IS success. *Information Systems Research, 8*(3), 240-253.

Spitler, V. K. (forthcoming). Learning to use IT in the workplace: Mechanisms and masters. *Journal of Organizational and End User Computing.*

Strauss, A. L., & Corbin, J. (1990). *Basics of qualitative research: Grounded theory procedures and techniques.* Newbury Park: Sage Publications.

Strauss, A. L., & Corbin, J. (1994). Grounded theory methodology: An overview. In N. K. Denzin & Y. S. Lincoln (Eds.), *Handbook of qualitative research*. Thousand Oaks, CA: Sage Publications.

Szajna, B. (1996). Empirical evaluation of the revised technology acceptance model. *Management Science, 42*(1), 85-92.

Tornatzky, L. G., & Fleischer, M. (1990). *The processes of technological innovation*. Lexington, MA: Lexington Books.

Trice, A. W., & Treacy, M. E. (1988). Utilization as a dependent variable in MIS research. *Data Base, 19*(3-4), 33-41.

Umble, E. J., Haft, R. R., & Umble, M. M. (2003). Enterprise resource planning: Implementation procedures and critical success factors. *European Journal of Operational Research, 146*(2), 241-257.

Van de Ven, A. H. (1992, Summer). Suggestions for studying strategy process: A research note. *Strategic Management Journal, 13*, 169-188.

Venkatesh, V., Morris, M., Davis, G., & Davis, F. (2003). User acceptance of information technology: Toward a unified view. *MIS Quarterly, 27*(3), 425-478.

Vidgen, R., Wood-Harper, T., & Wood, R. (1993). A soft systems approach to information systems quality. *Scandinavian Journal of Information Systems, 5*, 97-112.

Yin, R. K. (1994). *Case study research, design and methods* (2nd ed.). Newbury Park: Sage Publications.

Endnotes

[1]   The authors worked equally on this paper and are thus listed alphabetically. They would like to thank Dale Goodhue for his valuable help on this chapter.

[2]   Grounded theory being an inductive approach, the specific literature on use, learning, and quality of use was not reviewed *before* entering the field, but *during* and *after* the data was collected and analyzed. Nevertheless, our chapter follows a typical presentation format, where the literature is discussed prior to the research methodology.

Chapter XII

Learning from Patterns During Information Technology Configuration

Keith S. Horton, Napier University, UK

Rick G. Dewar, Heriot-Watt University, UK

Abstract

This chapter asks how people can be assisted in learning from practice, as a basis for informing future action, when configuring information technology (IT) in organizations. It discusses the use of Alexanderian patterns as a means of aiding such learning. Three patterns are presented that have been derived from a longitudinal empirical study that has focussed upon practices surrounding IT configuration. The paper goes on to argue that Alexanderian Patterns offer a valuable means of learning from past experience. It is argued that learning from experience is an important dimension of deciding "what needs to be done" in configuring IT with organizational context. The three patterns outlined are described in some detail, and the implications of each discussed. Although it is argued that patterns per se provide a valuable tool for learning from experience, some potential dangers in seeking to codify experience with a patterns approach are also discussed.

Introduction

Information Technology (IT) represents something of a paradox for many people with responsibility for managing IT in organizations: On the one hand it is notoriously difficult to predict what may happben during the development and/or application of IT (Williams, 2000), and yet, IT developments are considered important for the survival of many organizations given their dependence in terms of both frequency of use and variety of application (Dierkes, Marz, & Teele, 2001). Those tasked with managing IT developments, particularly those involving non-bespoke systems, address this paradox through a process of configuring IT with organizational context. Configuration refers to the ways in which people work to get technologies to "fit" their organizational settings, that is, configuring non-bespoke technology with institution specific structures, methods, praxis, and requirements (Williams, 1997). The concept of "fit" expressed here reflects elements of mutual shaping of both technology and context. Configuring IT is both fraught with uncertainty, and yet, essential. We see the concept of IT configuration as an intrinsic part of organizational practice, requiring an assessment of what must be done to ensure both that the technology works, and that it is used, that is, incorporating issues of acceptance and adoption.

In this chapter we present an approach that we argue may have value in aiding IT configuration in organizations, specifically by using patterns as a means of learning from what has happened previously. By learning we refer to the various ways in which people extend and/or restructure the body of knowledge, developed cumulatively by individuals and groups (Weick, 1995).

Several authors use the term pattern in relation to the application of IT in organizations (e.g., Adams, Koushik, Vasudeva, & Galambos, 2001), but rarely is the term explored. It appears that for many authors the term *pattern* refers to something that is seen as having a taken-for-granted meaning that requires no further explanation, definition, or exploration. Let us begin, therefore, by introducing a working definition of a "pattern" as a concept. We shall expand on this later in the paper, but for the moment we mean *a recurring metaphor, policy, design, action, instrument, or artefact that is specific to some context and reflects a situation of interest.* We do not, therefore, regard the term *pattern* as being synonymous with either *process* (a series of events and/or actions) or *methodology* (a way of doing something). With this definition in mind, the concept of the pattern provides us with two opportunities. Firstly, we can identify particular areas of activity through looking for recurring aspects of organizational practice utilizing the concept of "pattern." Secondly, having derived patterns we have a perspective on practice that affords reflection — a key element in improving future courses of action (Schon, 1983). The use of patterns encourages groups to confront the paradoxes and ambiguities of interaction in order to engage in double loop learning (Stacey, 1996), a factor distinguishing successful from less successful organizations (Kirton, 1984).

The chapter has the following structure: In the first section we consider patterns in relation to IT configuration and learning. In the second section we discuss the concept of Alexanderian Patterns. We then outline details of a longitudinal study of IT configuration undertaken in several UK Police Forces. Using this data, we identify three patterns as a means of demonstrating the potential value of patterns as an effective IT management device.

Information Technology Configuration and Patterns

The concept of configuring non-bespoke IT with organizational context incorporates a number of areas. These areas include: Making decisions about the introduction of IT, IT strategy formation, IT acquisition, IT requirements gathering, and IT implementation and adoption, amongst others. Therefore, we can see that configuration of IT in this usage means considerably more than just customizing screens or data to fit with a particular organization's processes, as usage of the term configuration implies when installing many Enterprise Resource Planning (ERP) systems, for example. We regard the processes that are part of configuration as constituting a dualistic relationship with the organizational context in that, it is not simply a matter of the technology "fitting" the context, but also of the context being shaped by the technology (Williams, 1997). We have concentrated upon the processes at a strategic level, concerned with what can be termed high-level decisions surrounding decisions to invest, acquire, and implement new large-scale IT based systems — we label these areas as IT planning, and this is a part of configuration.

Within IT planning people actively develop and exploit what they currently know, their current wisdom about their world as they endeavour to shape, and are shaped by, their social, technical, and economic context (Williams, 2000). It is through such interaction that people develop their knowledge, their current wisdom about their world, singularly and collaboratively; and here we are implicitly addressing notions of learning. It is this learning from experience about the usage of IT that means that what happens in the future is grounded in an understanding of the past. However, all too often those people tasked with introducing or applying IT into organizational contexts do not seem to learn from past experience (Currie, 2000) — repeating the errors of the past.

There are means by which opportunities can be provided to identify and learn lessons from the utilization of IT in organizational settings. For example, project review and debriefing sessions during and at the end of projects (de Weerd-Nederhof, Pacitti, Gomes, & Pearson, 2003) can address what went well, or less well, and consider alternative courses of action. Very often, however, despite having formal project management processes in place, these review meetings simply do not take place (ibid.). A less formal approach toward learning is to encourage reflective practice (Schon, 1983) amongst those taking part. This is not without problems, both at the individual level, where it can be hard to identify time and space for reflection to take place, and at the collective level, for the sharing of any lessons that may become apparent.

There is some empirical evidence that patterns may offer a means of identifying and codifying aspects of IT related practice, as well as a means of making such situations of interest available to other groups of people through the provision of a pattern template. For example, such patterns have been considered valuable in assisting an understanding of the configurational processes surrounding the adoption of IT in areas such as air-traffic control and ambulance control rooms (Martin, Rodden, Rouncefield, Sommerville, & Viller, 2001). The opportunity provided by patterns in deriving lessons regarding IT configuration in the workplace has also been noted in relation to the work of organizational consultants (Erikson, 2000).

In arguing that we can learn from the use of patterns, we do not seek to portray patterns as "things" that await the discovery of the observer. Instead, we consider patterns as subjective constructs that may be applied as a way of thinking about a situation — treating some area of organizational practice as though it were a pattern, as opposed to saying that it is a pattern.

Having introduced a working definition of the pattern earlier, let us now expand on this notion. Christopher Alexander (1979) introduced the notion of patterns — hence the prefix Alexanderian. An architect and philosopher, he recognized that certain attributes in the design of buildings and urban spaces frequently recurred. As such, successful solutions to recurring problems in context were identified. He then arrived at a means of communicating these by standardizing the format into what he called a pattern. He also argued that each solution resolved many of the competing forces that the architect faced in building design (e.g. light, comfort, aesthetics, etc.), to a greater or lesser degree. This meant that the solution transformed the initial context in some way and generally had advantages and disadvantages. In addition, by being explicit about the nature of the resulting context, Alexander contended that the patterns were not necessarily prescriptive but could be used in a reflective sense instead, encouraging the pattern user to think for him or herself rather than blindly following a procedure: "You can use this solution a million times over, without ever doing it the same way twice" (Alexander, Ishikawa, & Silverstein, 1977). Nonetheless, many of those using patterns do in fact adhere to a prescriptive view (Salingaros, 2000).

To date, patterns have become a powerful and increasingly popular concept in relation to various aspects of software engineering (Coplien & Schmidt, 1995; Gamma, Helm, Johnson, & Vlissides, 1995). There have also been discussions of patterns taking place in other areas of literature concerned with IT, noted previously. Patterns have been utilized in discussions of IT adoption in the workplace (Erikson, 2000), in relation to the understanding of computer supported co-operative work (Martin et al., 2001), and in planning system architectures (Adams et al., 2001). Patterns are by no means a concept unique to the discussion of IT. We have seen discussion of patterns taking place in literature from mathematics (Steen, 1988), architecture (Salingaros, 2000), and linguistics (Whiteside & Hodgson, 2000). The use of the term pattern in these latter areas is interesting in so far as it tends to be used to refer to a recurring phenomenon in what is perceived to be the physical world — whether that finds expression as a building or as a mathematical equation. The former areas see patterns being applied to the sociotechnical organizational context. Since IT configuration in organizations may be viewed as incorporating social and technical dimensions, this development bodes well for us being able to understand and influence practice through the application of patterns.

Salingaros (2000) describes patterns as empirical rules that represent regularities of behavior, which we derive from the observed world through analysis of cause and effect and documentation of solutions that recur in different contexts. Patterns in this sense are closely linked to the design of something (e.g., in architecture — a building; in computing — a software artefact) with a key facet being the way in which the pattern represents a practical way of solving a recurring problem. These views reflect an orientation toward the use of patterns in an objective and prescriptive sense, a notion that is challenged by others. Erikson (2000), for example, prefers to view the patterns he identifies as descriptive devices of workplace phenomena, which can act as "a lingua franca for creating a common ground among people who lack a shared discipline or theoretical framework" (p.254). This is a situation prevalent, according to Erikson, amongst those involved in the design and use of information technologies in the workplace. This insight introduces patterns as devices that are descriptive of IT phenomena, and which can act as a basis for discussion and reflection. Similarly, Martin et al. (2001), looking at the use of patterns in several ethnographic studies of computer supported cooperative work, state that they can usefully serve as "a means of documenting and describing common interactions, and as vehicle[s] for communicating the results of a specific analysis" (p. 41) to interested parties.

Again, we see patterns describing situated IT related practice to aid communication with others, and it is this promise that affords opportunities for reflection and enhancing knowledge development. We also note that both Erikson and Martin et al. have moved away from a problem/solution orientation in their use of the patterns concept. This addresses one of the potential weaknesses of approaches that focus solely upon problem situations, missing the learning that can come from more positive, opportunity-based situations (Nonaka & Takeuchi, 1995). We too have sought to avoid this problem/solution orientation, enabling us to consider positive and negative instances of workplace practice (still acknowledging the interpretive variation surrounding what is deemed either "positive" or "negative"). Therefore, we see patterns moving away from their often-criticized form of prescriptive recipes to becoming reflective devices. As a result, we would tentatively suggest, patterns are evolving from *solution-oriented* to *phenomenon-oriented*.

In tandem with the concept of a pattern, a pattern language is formed when patterns are collected together and cross-references are provided between those that provide mutual support. Thus, patterns may be conceived as forming a hierarchy, whereby a pattern can be related to larger scale patterns that it supports, whilst being supported in turn by smaller scale patterns (Erikson, 2000). This connectivity creates something akin to a synergistic effect, offering the potential for reflection on possible courses of action that the pattern user may take, given access to a range of solutions comprising a pattern language. Similarly, as referred to above, a pattern language can act as a lingua franca for developing knowledge amongst groups of people about aspects of practice in relation to problem situations or opportunities.

While the form of a pattern is the subject of some debate (Meszaros & Doble, 1997), we have introduced the additional perspective of situation of interest, enabling consideration of either problems, or opportunities, or other phenomena of note, into a typical pattern template as follows:

- A short evocative name (providing a *short cut* for those familiar with the pattern)
- A description of the context in which the pattern has arisen including any prevailing forces (such as time, cost, quality, availability, and risk)
- A situation of interest (e.g., problem or opportunity) that recurs given the context and forces
- The practice that addresses the situation
- The resultant context (or consequences) that describes the action's pros and cons and states how well the forces called up in the context have been resolved

- Related patterns that may work well with, before, after, or instead of this one
- Known uses (see next paragraph)

For patterns to attain a useful level of abstraction and for users to have some faith in them, they should be *validated*. A widely recognized heuristic applied by the patterns community is *the Rule of Three* (Appleton, 1997). The implication of this "rule" is that the pattern can be said to be valid if it has been seen on at least three separate occasions. For this reason, the known uses called up in the pattern provide evidence of its validity, but they can also point the reader to the people, projects, or resources where more information can be found — the so called *know-who* to augment the *know-how*.

However, such validity does not necessarily imply applicability beyond the pattern's wider, implicit context. A pattern may only be valid within one domain, organization, or even project. It may even only be valid for a limited time.

Thus, we now have a *verifiable* (albeit bounded) description of action taken in relation to a specific situation of interest, which has some application in complex, socially constituted domains of knowledge and practice. Such patterns provide opportunities for reflection, and knowledge development, during which people may choose to adopt or ignore aspects described in a pattern specification.

Deriving Patterns: An Empirical Study

We have derived three patterns from an empirical study in which we looked at IT configuration in the UK Police Service. We present brief details only, because our purpose here is to give a flavor of the research context as a background to our discussion of patterns. The case studies themselves are not the focus of this paper.

Method

The research approach was characterised by the belief that it is only through interpretation of social constructions that we can develop our understanding of what happens in institutional settings, and that this should be undertaken through an ongoing dialectic between theory and analysis. We were interested in investigating what took place from the perspective of those people involved. To do this we adopted interpretive in-depth case studies as our research method

(Darke, Shanks, & Broadbent, 1998), acknowledging that people socially construct what is meaningful and what is significant in their environments within and through their interactions with others. We undertook longitudinal, cross-case comparative analysis, in the UK Police Forces reported here between 1994 and 1998 (1994-2003 in one case). Data collection involved a number of methods and included 182 in-depth semi-structured interviews with members of the senior executive, operational senior management, and those involved in the management of IS/IT within the cases. Interviews lasted between one and, on occasion, three hours, with 62 being tape recorded and, subsequently, transcribed. Notes were completed during and immediately after each of the other interviews.

The researchers returned on three or four occasions per year to each case organization, spending several days at each. The detail of informal conversations was recorded as soon after they took place as possible. One of the researchers undertook an intensive three-month period of participation within one of the cases, working on IT implementation and adoption planning. During the research period, a substantial amount of documentation was collected, including minutes of meetings, organization and IT policy documents (where available), as well as collation and analysis of secondary materials. This provided a rich set of data for a cross-case comparative analysis, and it is this data that we have mined for patterns.

The data went through a process of coding undertaken using software package, NUD*IST (Non-numerical Unstructured Data Indexing Searching and Theorising, ver. 4). The software enabled us to undertake both coding and analysis of data, utilizing the coding categories associated with the pattern template. We looked for issues raised by interviewees as being significant from their perspective in relation to the large IT projects with which they were concerned, thus having identified a problem situation, the context, practice, and consequences. This was done on a case-by-case basis, following which a cross-case comparative analysis was undertaken. This process we refer to as "mining" the data, something which we view as being distinct from an attempt to identify patterns in-situ within organizations, perhaps for example through a process akin to action research (Baskerville & Wood-Harper, 1998). Thus, possible patterns were identified across the case studies following an analysis of emerging problem situations, together with associated contexts, practice, and consequences within each of the cases.

Anonymity of each police force, and of the respondents, has been maintained. Details of the six case studies are shown in Tables 1 (1a and 1b) to provide a context to the discussion of patterns.

The discussion of the patterns arising from the six cases will address both the form, and the contribution of such patterns in relation to theory and practice. To theory, they provide a means of codifying a version of events from interpretations of practice. To practice, they provide opportunities for reflection and learning, as well as providing a potential lingua franca across groups who may be drawing upon differing ways of thinking about technology, both in application and implication.

In researching the concept of IT planning within a Police Force, we can recognize the culturally specific nature of so much of what we term "practice." For example, the terminology of strategy is relatively new to many of those working within the Police service, with the quasi-militaristic command structure having traditionally concentrated on undertaking policing through the tried and tested practices developed over decades. Several police officers commented that they had never had to think about the concept of strategy until the early 1990s, but felt that they increasingly had to have "a strategy for everything."

It would be relatively easy to contest from these case extracts that the essence of strategy formation comprises a web of socio-political interactions that are so specific to the context that they are most unlikely to be repeated elsewhere, and

Table 1a. Overview of case studies (Cases A-C)

CASE	A	B	C
Focus of research	1994-98. IT strategy formation, IT acquisition & implementation	1994-98. IT strategy formation, IT acquisition & implementation	1994-03. IT strategy formation, IT acquisition & implementation
Background	History of under-investment through 1980's & early 1990's. Decision taken to acquire new force-wide integrated system in 1993 from preferred supplier. Mostly non-bespoke, although some applications developed with a view to selling on to others. Implemented 1995-98. System not well-accepted. New systems sought from 1999.	Central command and control system dated, but also a history of ad-hoc IT development — people able to develop 'pet' projects. 1994, a new force-wide integrated suite of applications sought off-the-shelf via tender process. Implemented 1996-99. New systems sought from 2001	Central command and control system dated and technology can no longer support application. IT strategy developed 1993-94. Integrated suite of off-the-shelf applications sought from 1995 via tender process. Implemented 1997-2000. Systems well received & adopted.
Key Issues in configuration	IT strategy driven by one senior police officer. Small group (2 people) specified IT requirement, managed relationship with supplier & oversaw implementation. Formal IT group of 6 people set up to 'oversee' IT project — but no responsibility; a façade to satisfy external audit groups. Senior staff excluded from process/input.	IT strategy driven by one senior officer. Small group (3 people) specified IT requirement, managed relationship with supplier & oversaw implementation. Formal IT project group 'oversee' IT developments — but no responsibility; a façade to satisfy external audit groups. Senior staff excluded from process/input.	IT strategy led by IT professional. Senior police managers not interested in IT, but are interested in seeing well-managed process. Formal project boards/groups set up to oversee project — part of role to provide audit trail. Two-way dialogue with end-users about IT to gather requirements & to manage expectations.

Table 1b. Overview of case studies continued (Cases D-F)

CASE	D	E	F
Focus of research	1994-98. IT strategy formation, IT acquisition & implementation	1994-98. IT strategy formation, IT acquisition & implementation	1994-98. IT strategy formation, IT acquisition & implementation
Background	IT systems limited & ad-hoc. IT strategy developed 1992. Integrated suite of off-the-shelf applications sought from preferred supplier 1993/4. IT implemented 1994-1997. Many technical problems, & systems not well received. New IT sought 1998/9.	Central command and control system dated. Limited coordination of IT. IT strategy developed 1994 onwards. Integrated suite of applications sought, and some developed 'internally' but with a view to sharing with others. Implementation 1998 onwards. Systems well received	IT strategy developed 1994 onwards. Integrated suite of applications sought, and some developed 'internally' but with a view to sharing with others. Implementation 1998 onwards. Systems well received.
Key Issues in configuration	IT strategy driven by one fairly senior officer. The most senior police officers not interested in IT. Senior staff excluded from process. Formal IT project group 'oversee' IT developments — but no responsibility; a façade to satisfy external audit groups.	IT strategy led by IT professional. Senior police 'champion' interested in IT, but are interested in seeing well-managed process. Formal project boards/groups set up to oversee project — part of role to provide audit trail. Two-way dialogue with end-users about IT to gather requirements & to manage expectations.	IT strategy led by IT professional. Senior police 'champions' interested in IT. Formal project boards/groups set up to oversee project — part of role to provide audit trail. Two-way dialogue with end-users about IT to gather requirements & to manage expectations

hence have no relevance for other situations. However, patterns provide us with a means of abstracting lessons from practice as a basis for knowledge development and shaping future action. At the same time, the contextually specific nature of such practice does not deny the possibility that these abstractions will not be of use in very different organizational contexts. Bearing this in mind, we have utilized the concept of Alexanderian patterns in analysing the above case material. We have called the patterns that we discuss *Formal Façade, Strategy Team,* and *Manage Expectations.* It should be noted that the patterns are not, in themselves, the cornerstones of our argument. They only serve to show that patterns **can** be mined from the intricate milieu of socio-technical interaction.

Formal Façade Pattern

Shown in Table 2, this pattern reflects the structuring of formal committees and groups that were enacted officially as part of the strategy formation for IT. This pattern exposes a situation that was identified from data concerning cases A, B, and D. The groups acted as rubber stamping committees to proposals put forward in each of the case studies by the Officer leading the IT department, together with the project team. For example in Case A, decision making was

Table 2. Formal façade pattern

Formal Façade

Context: Formal systems and procedures are necessary to placate external auditors and senior officers, however, in reality, these are seldom followed during periods of excessive change since they prevent timely and pragmatic decision making. When the auditors eventually discover the breaches made to procedures, they apply the appropriate censure, but the next crisis will follow the same chaotic path as before, regardless.

Situation: You have to be seen to be doing formal strategy, but how can you when the job needs doing?

Practice: Construct a façade of formality and expect to be caught out.

Consequences: You can now carry on doing what you consider important without having to be constrained by procedure. Since auditors or senior officers will probably catch you out, you may as well admit this to yourself and prepare your defence. In the meantime you have breathing space to have a success that may mitigate your censure. However, the censure may impact your funding so be aware that cutting the formal corner may threaten a project's completion.

Related Patterns: A Strategy Team may help to minimise the negative impacts of such a risky approach.

Known Uses: Researcher A has seen this approach followed in the preceding case extracts.

---

undertaken at informal meetings between the two Officers in the project team, and the Deputy Chief Constable. It was the senior officer in the project team who sought to set up formal decision-making processes for IT planning. Final authorization for decisions in relation to IT strategy took place through the informal structure. This sort of activity was reflected in cases A and B, with strategy formation being dominated by very small groups of people, both in terms of actual decision making and in construction of formal façades. Decision-making was largely informal, although most of the same people participated in formal decision-making structures. However, the management of these processes provided an illusion of formality for the benefit of senior managers, Governmental bodies such as the Audit Commission, and HMIC. The setting up of formal processes demonstrates the importance of affording opportunities for reflecting upon such practices, where the actions of the individuals leading IT strategy formation managed access to the processes, as well as the processes themselves. While this supports a political view of strategic decision-making (Mintzberg, 1978), it also codifies aspects of workplace phenomena that invite further discussion.

Looking beyond this specific context for Formal Façade, we sense resonances in other professions where coercive bureaucratic practice is imposed and "work-arounds" are used by professionals — for instance late adopters of quality assurance procedures in manufacturing and elsewhere. However, a salient consideration here would be the public sector nature of the police versus private sector organizations operating in a competitive environment. In certain contexts greater formality in IT configurational processes may be appropriate, although some means is still required to enable people to ponder the nature of both process and context in order to develop knowledge.

Strategy Team Pattern

The second pattern, shown in Table 3 and alluded to in Table 2, presents a very different aspect of the micro-activity.

This pattern exposes a situation that was identified from data concerning cases C, E, and F. The pattern enables us to think about the periods of time when the "team" most involved in strategy formation were active in developmental practices that resulted in decisions to adopt IT, followed by implementation of working systems. In these instances, the strategy teams worked most effectively when the individuals involved combined authority in an hierarchical sense, interest in IT planning, and knowledge of IT, which normally (but not always) resided with civilian IT professionals. One aspect of this may be characterized

Table 3. Strategy team pattern

Strategy Team

Context: IS strategy has been given a new lease of life in the organisation and there is a sense that something should be done. Senior people could delegate the task of formulating a strategy, but are unsure about who would be suitable. Less senior people would be interested in being involved, but have seen "IT disasters" in the past and are cautious of being associated with another. Others would be willing to volunteer, but do not feel they have enough knowledge. Indeed the culture of the organisation may prevent those with suitable interest and/or authority from admitting that they do not have enough knowledge to make a valuable contribution.

Situation: How can you create a team that will push strategy formation forward in a direction aligned with vested interests?

Practice: Be creative in team selection seeking a balance between people who demonstrate the following: *knowledge, interest, and authority* even if that goes against traditional hierarchically based procedures. More importantly, make sure that those who claim knowledge do get the opportunity to use it, and that authority resides with vested interests.

Consequences: Authority and interest are generally straightforward to assess, but claims of knowledge are more difficult to verify. Authority can allow the team to have a champion who can help push forward ideas. Interested individuals can act as local champions within the user and developer communities. Finally, knowledge of the technical aspects of the strategy is essential in order for proposals to be workable.

Related Patterns: Manage Expectations is something that a team should address

Known Uses: Researcher A has seen this pattern in the preceding case extracts.

in terms of shared relevance structures (Berger & Luckman, 1967). By way of example, for those who wish to be seen as IT specialists, what is viewed as of relevance to that person will be structured differently from what another person needs to know to operate in a different area of organizational practice (Schamber, 1994). In other words, we may assume that people who engage in strategy formation practice, "will need to know whatever is deemed necessary for the fulfilment of a particular task" (Berger & Luckman, 1967, p. 95). Thus, in the Strategy Team pattern, we hypothesize that it is at the intersection of these relevance structures — the point at which people have meaningful things to say to one another (*ibid.*) — that there are opportunities for influencing the ways in which people engage with others. Reflecting on this pattern therefore provides a means of thinking about practice that was evident in the cases C, E, and F. It also provides an opportunity for reflecting upon the future membership of groups of people engaged in the area of IT planning.

Manage Expectations Pattern

The third pattern, shown in Table 4 and alluded to in Table 3, presents a very different aspect of the configurational activity.

This pattern reflects a situation that was identified from data concerning cases C, E, and F. This pattern allows us to think about the way in which the people leading the IT developments addressed the process of communication with end-

Table 4. Manage expectations pattern

Manage Expectations

Context: New IT is to be introduced to the organisation. End-users are sceptical given past IT problems, and wary of claims that IT will help them. Senior management are dubious that the spend on IT will deliver something meaningful, but feel they have no option but to be seen to be investing in IT.

Situation: How can you introduce new IT that is appropriate for the given requirements, while at the same time seeking to ensure that the technology accords with user expectations?

Practice: Make sure that in addition to seeking to gather requirements from potential end-users, that you communicate to them what they can realistically expect from the technology — and maintain that dialogue throughout the project lifespan.

Consequences: While this does require some effort to maintain the dialogue, it avoids the situation of end-users developing unrealistic expectations about the technology. The likelihood of technology acceptance and usage is enhanced through this management of expectations.

Related Patterns: Strategy Team pattern may be necessary to assist this process.

Known Uses: Researcher A has seen this pattern in the preceding case extracts.

users. The pattern was closely allied to the Strategy Team pattern, with the mix of team members led by an IT professional leading the active dialogue. The pattern predominantly reflects one of maintaining a conversation between those tasked at a strategic level with configuring IT with the organizational context, and end-users. It could be argued that the idea of expectation management is akin to the more traditional concept of determining end-user requirements. The latter may be considered to be a form of gauging expectations, although we would suggest that it might often not embody the active, conversational dimensions found in the pattern discussed here. The conversation about IT remained active throughout each of the three projects identified above, and was concerned with both judging and influencing IT expectations. In each of the three cases the resulting systems were widely accepted by end-users, and adopted.

Implications

What value might codified patterns have to practitioners; and how can patterns be incorporated into practice without becoming yet another coercive bureaucratic instrument? A reader of a pattern description may recognize a certain aspect of the context, problem, action, or consequences and sense that fleeting jolt of "revelation" (Falconer, 1999) as they see their own experience articulated for the first time. However, this presents an opportunity for IT planners not only to consider practical activity, but also for reinterpretation of the interactions between actors and their contexts. These may lead to new patterns of activity, or to reconfirm existing modes of practice. Either way, this does not mean that the use of patterns is oriented towards maintaining the status quo, but rather that patterns can provide valuable opportunities to confront contested and contradictory interpretations of practice that may emerge. The act of thinking about whether there are any patterns, as well as reflecting upon the appropriateness of particular patterns that may have been observed previously is a means of learning lessons. These reflections upon practice can serve as mediators for change (Jarzabowski, 2003), while the patterns act as ways of making organizational knowledge explicit as a basis for sharing.

We can now look at the way in which a pattern such as formal façade may be used. In reflecting upon experience, formal façade may be interpreted in a number of ways. For example, one reading by those engaged in IT planning may be that such practices need to be maintained in order to satisfy the expectations of external agencies that are interested in the practices of the institution. A further interpretation of this pattern might lead to a view that dialogue is required between those within the institution engaged in IT planning and external parties to clarify what is required, and why the latter consider formalization of IT strategy to be so important. Alternatively, another reading could be that the expectations of the external agencies that formal strategy processes will be enacted are reasonable, and that more consideration should be given to formalizing strategic practice in a way that moves beyond the superficial — the façade.

This latter interpretation on experience may then link with a reading of the *Strategy Team* pattern, as decisions are taken as to whom should be involved (assuming, perhaps, an ideal world free of power/political relations). The *Manage Expectations* pattern was found in those cases also displaying the *Strategy Team* pattern. With the *Manage Expectations* pattern it reinforces the need to maintain an active dialogue with end-users, not merely to garner viewpoints, but to influence them. While this may appear as common sense to some, it is this sort of cross-cultural dialogue within organizations that can prevent some of the dysfunctional interactions that inhibit effective learning (Schein, 1996). Furthermore, it is also worth noting that this form of active dialogue was not undertaken in three of the cases (cases A, B, & D) we discuss above, each of which ended up with systems that were not well accepted. This begins to hint at some interrelationship between patterns, which has been noted by others (Erikson, 2000). We are not arguing that this use of patterns forms a basis for making decisions in a prescriptive manner, but rather that considering whether there are patterns as well as a reading of patterns that have already been identified can form a basis for reflecting upon experience. In addition, the use of patterns that we have discussed also enables people engaged in the various aspects of IT configuration to consider aspects of practices that may otherwise be ignored, or which may remain the preserve of the tacit understanding of individuals or groups. As we attempt to develop a pattern language in the area of public sector IT configuration, further research opportunities are opened up as we consider whether pattern languages from one context may be applicable in another.

At the same time, however, we do recognize some limitations that will need to be confronted in relation to any development in the use of patterns as suggested here. We are acutely aware of the cultural specificity of the context in which this fieldwork has taken place, as alluded to in Section II. For example, while police organizations are seeking to adopt new technologies, there is not the rapid cycle of technical change that may be found in other sectors, such as in financial services. We may speculate that the use of patterns may be better suited to contexts where the pace of change, particularly technical change, is less pronounced. In such instances, the patterns described may resonate more readily with those for whom the situation and context is both recognizable and still applicable — something that may be less easy where the nature and pace of change is unrelenting.

There is, however, a potential for stifling innovation through the codification of past experience (Levinthal, 1997). Given the way in which patterns are both based on, and are in turn subject to, interpretation, it is possible to develop false beliefs about relationships between action and outcome. An important aspect of the role of the pattern developer/user must not only be to exercise care in interpretation, but also to emphasise patterns as a basis for reflection only — and not a recipe for action. Furthermore, interpretations based upon past experience may not be appropriate to future practice given that contexts change (as noted above). Allied to this, codification of experience in a pattern may result in the description of phenomena resulting in a view of the pattern as *the truth* — "the way things are done round here." The danger is that this may lead to a tendency to follow previous patterns of behavior without giving sufficient attention to ongoing changes in context.

Finally, there are practical considerations that must be addressed if learning is to take place via patterns in IT configuration projects, specifically, issues relating to how we derive patterns, how we disseminate them to relevant stakeholders, and how we motivate people to contribute to an effective patterns culture. Our thinking on these issues is, at this stage, embryonic, but we would suggest there are extremes within which a workable solution lies. Perhaps we could denote these extremes as being informal and formal approaches. Informal would imply that a patterns culture spontaneously emerges and is maintained by an interested, empowered, and knowledgeable community. Formal, on the other hand, may well imply an imposed bureaucracy embodied in a project or knowledge management methodology where pattern derivation and dissemination are mandatory processes. Regardless of the level of formality, we anticipate that the presence of a process will allay the aforementioned concern over accepting a pattern as *the truth*.

Conclusion

We have argued that using patterns in, what we have termed, IT configuration provides us with a means of identifying, evaluating and reflecting on practical activity as a means of developing knowledge. To this end, we have been able to extract patterns from case material. People working in organizational settings can learn from such knowledge, including any less desirable aspects or mistakes (Van de Ven, 1993). We contend that each of the patterns that we have above represent instances of practice that allow those tasked with introducing and configuring IT to confront some of the paradoxes and ambiguities that are a part of organizational life.

Patterns and pattern languages are not a panacea for the problems of introducing IT in organizations; patterns do not necessarily denote exemplary practice. We are not suggesting that our patterns, or those which may follow, provide a lingua franca of IT configuration *per se*. Instead we contend that the concept of Alexanderian patterns and the accompanying pattern language provides us with a potential means of evaluating practices, one that can form a basis for reflection and learning. Another way of viewing this is as a lessons learned process (LLP), a type of knowledge management process (Davenport & Prusak, 1998) that develops from the collecting, analyzing, storing, distributing, and reusing of lessons to support organizational activity. In other words, a pattern can be viewed as a knowledge artefact representing a validated (i.e., factually and technically correct) distillation of experience, in this instance, surrounding the configuring of IT with organizational context.

References

Adams, J., Koushik, S., Vasudeva, G., & Galambos, G. (2001). *Patterns for e-business: A strategy for re-use*. New York: IBM Press.

Alexander, C. (1979). *The timeless way of building*. New York: Oxford University Press.

Alexander, C., Ishikawa, S., & Silverstein, M. (1977). *A pattern language: Towns, buildings, construction*. New York: Oxford University Press.

Appleton, B. (1997). *Patterns and software: Essential concepts and terminology*. Retrieved November 5, 2000, from http://www.enteract.com/~bradapp/docs/patterns-intro.html

Baskerville, R., & Wood-Harper, A. T. (1998). Diversity in information systems action research methods. *European Journal of Information Systems, 7*, 90-107.

Berger, P. L. & Luckman, T. (1967). *The social construction of reality: A treatise in the sociology of knowledge*. London: Penguin Books.

Coplien, J. O. & Schmidt, D. C. (1995). *Pattern languages of program design*. Reading, MA: Addison Wesley Publishing Company.

Currie, W. (2000). *The global information society*. Chichester, UK: Wiley.

Darke, P., Shanks, G., & Broadbent, M. (1998). Successfully completing case study research: Combining rigour, relevance and pragmatism. *Information Systems Journal, 8*, 257-272.

Davenport, T. H., & Prusak, L. (1998). Working knowledge: How organisations manage what they know. Boston: Harvard Business School Press.

de Weerd-Nederhof, P., Pacitti, B., Gomes, J. F., & Pearson, A. (2003). Tools for the improvement of organizational learning processes in innovation. *The Journal of Workplace Learning, 14*(8), 320-331.

Dierkes, M., Marz, L., & Teele, C. (2001). Technological visions, technological development and organisational learning. In M. Dierkes, A. B. Antal, J. Child, & I. Nonaka (Eds.), *Handbook of organisational learning and knowledge* (pp. 282-301). Oxford, UK: Oxford University Press.

Erikson, T. (2000). Supporting interdisciplinary design: Towards pattern languages for the workplace. In P. Luff, J. Hindmarsh, & C. Heath (Eds.), *Workplace studies: Recovering work practice and information system design.* Cambridge: Cambridge University Press.

Falconer, J. (1999). The business pattern: A new tool for organizational knowledge capture and reuse. In *Proceedings of the 62nd ASIS Annual Conference,* WA (pp. 313-330).

Gamma, E., Helm, R., Johnson, R. & Vlissides, J. (1995). *Design patterns: Elements of reusable object-oriented software.* Reading, MA: Addison-Wesley.

Jarzabowski, P. (2003). Strategic practices: An activity theory perspective on continuity and change. *Journal of Management Studies, 40*(1), 23-55.

Kirton, M. J. (1984). Adaptors and innovators: Why new initiatives get blocked. *Long Range Planning, 17*(2), 137-143.

Levinthal, D. (1997). Three faces of organizational learning: Wisdom, inertia, and discovery. In R. Garud P. Nayyar, & Z. Shapira (Eds.), *Technological innovation: Oversights and foresights* (pp. 167-180). Cambridge, UK: Cambridge University Press.

Martin, D., Rodden, T., Rouncefield, M., Sommerville, I. & Viller, S. (2001). Finding patterns in the fieldwork. In W. Prinz, M. Jarke, K. Rogers, K. Schmidt, & V. Wulf (Eds.), *Proceedings of the Seventh European Conference on Computer-Supported Co-operative Work.* The Netherlands: Kluwer Academic Publishers.

Meszaros, G., & Doble, J. (1997). *A pattern language for pattern writing.* Retrieved May 21, 2000, from http://hillside.net/patterns/Writing/pattern_index.html

Nonaka, I., & Takeuchi, H. (1995). *The knowledge-creating company: How Japanese companies create the dynamics of innovation.* New York: Oxford University Press.

Salingaros, N. A. (2000). The structure of pattern languages. *Architectural Research Quarterly, 4,* 149-161.

Schamber, L. (1994). Relevance and information behaviour. *Annual Review of Information Science and Technology, 29*, 3-28.

Schein, E. H. (1996). Three cultures of management: The key to organizational learning. *Sloan Management Review, 38*(1), 9-20.

Schon, D. (1983). *The reflective practitioner: How professionals think in action*. New York: Basic Books.

Stacey, R. D. (1996). The space for creativity in organizations. In *Complexity and creativity in organizations* (pp. 165-191). San Francisco: Berrett-Koehler Publishers.

Steen, L. A. (1988). The science of patterns. *Science, 240*, 611-616.

Van de Ven, A. H. (1993). Managing the process of organizational innovation. In G. P. Huber & W. H. Glick (Eds.), *Organizational change and redesign: Ideas and insights for improving performance* (pp. 269-294). New York: Oxford University Press.

Weick, K. E. (1995). *Sensemaking in organisations*. Thousand Oaks, CA: Sage.

Whiteside, S. P. & Hodgson, C. (2000). Speech patterns of children and adults elicited via a picture-naming task: An acoustic study. *Speech Communication, 32*(4), 267-285.

Williams, R. (1997). The social shaping of information and communication technologies. In H. Kunicek, W. Dutton, & R. Williams (Eds.), *The social shaping of information superhighways: European and American roads to the information society* (pp. 299-338). Frankfurt: Campus.

Williams, R. (2000). Public choices and social learning: The new multimedia technologies in Europe. *The Information Society, 16*, 251-262.

Chapter XIII

Learning to Use IT in the Workplace: Mechanisms and Masters

Valerie K. Spitler, USA

Abstract

Fluency with information technology (IT), defined as "an ability [to use information technology] to express [oneself] creatively, to reformulate knowledge and to synthesize new information" (Committee on Information Technology Literacy, 1999, p. ES1) is an important concern for those who manage workers with jobs that require the use of IT. Training is one mechanism to build fluency, but research about "influential individuals" hints that other mechanisms might also play a role. This article presents an interpretive case study of junior-level knowledge workers at a management consulting firm. To learn to use the IT of their jobs, these workers relied not only on formal training, but also on on-the-job learning through experimentation; reading books, manuals and online help; and social interaction with their peers. The researcher identified different types of "master users" who were indispensable for this learning to take place. The findings of this study suggest that managers and researchers interested in training users also devote attention to these other mechanisms for learning, especially the "master user" phenomenon.

"Fluency with information technology... entails a process of lifelong learning in which individuals continually apply what they know to adapt to change and acquire more knowledge to be more effective at applying information technology to their work and personal lives."

(Committee on Information Technology Literacy, 1999, pp. ES1-2)

Fluency in the Workplace

With the preponderance of information technology in our society and the growing importance of the Digital Divide (Anonymous, 2000), *fluency with IT*, defined as "an ability [to use information technology] to express [oneself] creatively, to reformulate knowledge and to synthesize new information," has become an important concern for our society (Committee on Information Technology Literacy, 1999, p. ES-1). In particular, "[m]any (people) who currently use information technology have only a limited understanding of the tools they use and a (probably correct) belief that they are underutilizing (sic) them" (ibid., p. ES-1). Thus, research directed at how people use information technology (IT) in their work and the process by which they learn to use it is valuable for those who manage workers with jobs that require the use of IT.

The present research examines the use of IT by knowledge workers at one organization to understand how they become fluent with the information technologies of their work. In particular, the purpose of this research, a qualitative case study, is to determine the mechanisms these workers — management consultants at a global, strategic management consulting firm — employ to use fluently the information technologies of their work. These management consultants, recent graduates from elite educational institutions, work in project teams to assist clients, Fortune 500 or Fortune 1000 companies, in determining the strategic direction of their firms.

In comparison with many studies about learning to use IT, this study examines mechanisms for learning that surpass formal, structured training. In particular, this study investigates on-going learning of the information technologies workers have at their disposal, rather than the formal training devoted to use of a particular system. Additionally, this study uses intensive research methods to understand users in their natural work settings. By using intensive methods, the researcher was able to pursue a line of enquiry that has been disregarded in the literature, namely, the reliance of knowledge workers on mechanisms other than training for learning to use IT, that occur on-the-job, especially social interactions with master users. Furthermore, the researcher was able to probe into the "master user" phenomenon at the firm studied to identify categories of master users and to raise additional questions about the phenomenon.

Prior Research

Few studies concerned with an individual's learning to use IT examine the learning that occurs *after* the initial training and implementation period, that is, the learning that occurs during *on-going use*. The literature review below first covers the few studies devoted to learning IT during on-going use, then briefly covers the studies devoted to first-time use.

Social Support and Training for On-Going Use of IT

Some research indicates that users rely on a social support mechanism to improve their fluency with IT over time. For example, in their literature review, Orlikowski, Yates, Okamura, and Fujimoto (1995) identified "influential individuals" who tend to be associated with on-going use of IT: (1) *designated support staff* — those individuals who react to users' problems and requests, and (2) *translators, tailors, and local experts or gurus* — those individuals who do not hold IT positions but who do provide support for other users (Orlikowski et al., 1995, p. 425). Other researchers have found that individuals rely on others in their community to learn about IT. For example, users who developed a community of practice were more effective at integrating a new IT into their work than users who did not develop a community (George, Iacono, & Kling, 1995). Another study shows that workers used a system to a greater degree when they believed that others in their work environment thought they should be using the system (Lucas & Spitler, 1999). In these studies, other people were important influences on the individual as he continued to use and build fluency with information technology after initial training and implementation.

Some users also benefit from training during on-going use. For example, the three-tier IT training strategy used by a firm called SVF Corporation shows how SVF views training (and therefore, users' learning) as a process (Huang, 2002). The process begins at SVF with General Technology Education (Tier 1), then Business Application Training (Tier 2), and finally, Just-in-Time Training (Tier 3). These latter training interventions, often referred to as continuous training and just-in-time (JIT) training, occur some time after the initial training period.

Social Support and Training for Initial Use of IT

Another stream of research acknowledges the influence of certain individuals during the formal training and implementation process. For example, in an experimental study, researchers found that negative comments made by a stranger during an IT training session reduced the trainee's intention to use the software (Galletta, Ahuja, Hartman, Teo, & Peace, 1995). Other researchers showed how interaction between peers in a co-discovery learning mode led to users' developing better (more consistent with designers' objectives) mental models of software (Lim, Ward, & Benbasat, 1997). Orlikowski et al. (1995), in their review of literature, distinguished *champions and trainers* as individuals who "typically intervene in the initial stages of technology implementation, establishing its importance and motivating its initial use" (p. 425). Additionally, Lee used the term "*lead users*" to specify users who assisted their colleagues during implementation of new personal computers (Lee, 1986), and Nelson and Cheney used the term "*resident experts*" to specify a valuable "technique" utilized by managers during training to improve their computer abilities in the early 1980s (Nelson & Cheney, 1987).

Other studies examine the *trainers* conducting the training courses (Compeau, 2002; Fidishun, 2001) or the ideal *format* of these training courses (Simon, 2000; Simon, Grover, Teng, & Whitcomb, 1996). Still others ask what the *content* (focus on procedures or mental models) of these formal training courses should be (Santhanam & Sein, 1994) and what *skills* should be taught (Gattiker, 1992). Other studies are concerned with diagnosing and "treating" the *attitudes and behaviors of the computer users*, that is, the trainees. See, for example, Agarwal and Prasad (1998), Compeau and Higgins (1995), Guimaraes and Igbaria (1997), Hong, Thong, Wong, and Tam (2001-2002), Kernan and Howard (1990), Marakas, Yi, and Johnson (1998), Murphy, Coover, and Owen (1989), Webster and Martocchio (1992), Woszczynski, Roth, and Segars (1998), and Yager, Kappelman, Maples, and Prybutok (1997).

This literature review suggests that research directed at understanding the social mechanism at play during on-going use of IT would contribute to our understanding of building fluency with IT. Thus, the current research is aimed at understanding this social mechanism.

Theoretical Basis for the Research

In order to explore the social mechanism, a situated learning theory, legitimate peripheral participation (LPP), was chosen to guide an empirical study. LPP is

Figure 1. Pre-study view of IT learning over time, based on literature review and theoretical perspective, LPP

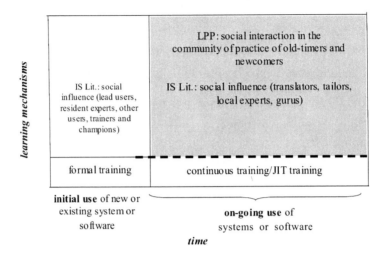

characterized as participation in the social world and has the following main features: learning within a community of practice; learning involving the whole person and the construction of identities; a diverse field of actors including newcomers and old-timers, where newcomers learn from old-timers and peers but where old-timers also continue to learn; and learning in practice, where learning takes place in productive activities (Lave & Wenger, 1991). According to LPP, training is only one mechanism by which learners learn, and not the primary one.

Figure 1 shows the pre-study view of an individual's learning to use IT over time. It incorporates ideas from the IS literature, as well as from LPP. It shows *time* on the horizontal axis and *mechanisms* on the vertical axis. In this view, a user learns IT through formal training interventions, first at initial use, and then possibly with additional training in the form of JIT training or continuous training, after initial use. Learning, both during the initial use period and during the on-going use period, may be supported by a social mechanism. The shaded area represents the area of primary interest in the present research.

Research Methods

The research objective was to understand how workers learn to use IT in their natural work settings. Additionally, the researcher's objective was to understand the workers' lived experience, by capturing their interpretation of events and the world around them (Schwandt, 1998). (Note that the researcher also must interpret the interpretations of participants.) Thus, the researcher chose to conduct an interpretive case study. The research follows approaches outlined by Orlikowski and Baroudi (1991) and Klein and Myers (1999) for conducting interpretive case studies.

The research site was chosen to meet certain criteria that are relevant to the theory underlying the research, a principle known as theoretical sampling (Strauss & Corbin, 1990; Yin, 1994). Two criteria were deemed important for the theory. First, given that LPP emphasizes the relationship between newcomers and old-timers, the group of knowledge workers at the chosen site were required to include a significant number of both newcomers and old-timers. Second, given that LPP claims learning occurs in productive activities, the use of IT for productive work had to be an integral part of the work. The site chosen, Echo Management Consulting (a pseudonym), met these criteria.

Research Site

Echo provides strategic advice to Fortune 500 and Fortune 1000 companies and competes with firms such as McKinsey, Booz Allen Hamilton, and Bain and Company, among others, for client projects. At the time of the study, October 1998 through June 1999, Echo had approximately 1,700 employees in over 15 offices worldwide. Echo recruited two types of new consultants. Those hired with a job title of "analyst" held undergraduate degrees, mainly from Ivy League universities and their equivalents; and those hired with a job title of "associate" held graduate degrees, mainly from top M.B.A. programs in the U.S. and abroad.

Data Collection and Analysis

Data collection and analysis strategies were determined by following the principles proposed by Klein and Myers (1999) and Glaser and Strauss (1967). Using these principles, the researcher compared findings across different respondents, documents, and observations, within the context of the consulting profession and the firm under study, and used the theoretical framework depicted in Figure 1 as a guide. Data collection and analysis were intertwined; analysis occurred as the data was collected and led to further data collection and analysis. The process itself was partially emergent, in that the process of collecting and analyzing data was not planned entirely in advance, as is done in other kinds of research (Myers, 1999).

Data collection methods included interviewing research participants, participating in training events and social events in the firm, collecting documents in the firm, and using the communication and information technologies of the consultants at Echo. These multiple data collection methods allowed the researcher to triangulate findings and to apply the principle of suspicion, that is, "sensitivity to possible 'biases' and systematic 'distortions' in the narratives collected from the participants" (Klein & Myers, 1999, p. 72). For example, although in interviews consultants praised the optional training offered at Echo, when the researcher attended the training sessions, consultants were not in attendance. Thus, had the researcher relied only on interview data, she may not have understood that much of the training was ineffective in this firm, even though consultants praised it in initial interviews.

Data collection proceeded in two stages. During the first stage, roughly from October 1998 until January 1999, the researcher collected data in order to understand the structure and work of the firm, and the terminology particular to consulting and to Echo. In the second stage, from January 1999 until the end of June 1999, the researcher probed research participants and training materials to understand deeper issues in the firm, specifically related to training, use of IT by consultants, and the communities of practice at Echo. Based on data collected during the first phase, the researcher devised a semi-structured interview protocol for interviews conducted during the second phase.

Table 1. Formal interviews conducted at Echo

Position	Number of People Interviewed
New Analysts	10 (12)
Second-year Analysts	10 (16)
Seasoned Analysts	6 (7)
New Associates	5 (7)
Other Associates	5 (10)
Line Partners	3 (14)
Total NY Consulting	39 (66)
IS Staff	3
Other Staff	3
Staff Partners	4
Total Staff	10
Total Number of People Interviewed In-Depth	49

Note: The numbers in parentheses represent the estimated number of people in the position at the NY office. During the researcher's stay at Echo, people left the firm, transferred to or from another office, or were promoted to different positions.

Table 1 shows the breakdown of interviewees by position in Echo. New analysts and new associates were recent graduates and had joined Echo within the past six months. Second-year analysts had been with Echo more than a year, but less than two years. Seasoned analysts were consultants who had been hired as entry-level analysts, and had been with Echo three, four, or five years; they had all been promoted to a new position. New analysts, second-year analysts, and seasoned analysts held bachelor's degrees, while new associates and other associates held MBA degrees. Appendix B shows the documents the researcher collected at Echo, and Table A3.1 in Appendix C shows the training sessions she attended.

The researcher tape-recorded formal interviews, transcribed them, and returned them to interviewees for their review. Interviews were voluntary, confidential, and anonymous. Interviewees had the opportunity to withdraw from the research at any time and had the opportunity to revise interview transcripts. These measures were taken in order to gain the trust of the interviewees, and thereby improve the reliability and validity of the data. Interviews lasted between 30 minutes and two hours.

For this research paper, two specific analyses were conducted. The first consisted of assembling all respondents' comments related to training and learning about IT. These interview comments (see Appendix A and Table A3.2 in Appendix C), combined with the researcher's observations at the site (especially at training sessions) and her perusal of Echo's training materials, provide the evidence for the results of Analysis 1: Mechanisms for Learning about IT.

The second analysis consisted of tabulating the results of interview questions that asked consultants who they thought were the proficient users of IT at Echo. The tabulation consisted of first counting the number of times an individual was mentioned by name for each specific information technology and for IT, in general, then grouping individuals who were mentioned a similar number of times, to arrive at two categories of experts. The results of this analysis appear in the results section under Analysis 2: Master Users of IT.

Results

Analysis 1: Mechanisms for Learning about IT

Consultants at Echo relied on two *types* of mechanisms for learning to use the information technologies required for their work: *training* and *on-the job learning*. The partner in charge of training described Echo's training philosophy as an apprenticeship, where formal training played a limited role:

I think the primary view in consulting is that training is an apprentice thing, and really if we think about the bulk of the training that the people get, it's on-the-job-training, and that we augment that with some formal interventions.... (Lucy, partner in charge of training, Echo)

Because the focus of this paper is on mechanisms other than formal training, training mechanisms are summarized in Appendix C, and other mechanisms are described below.

On-Going Use of IT: Learning on-the-Job

Consultants indicated that while formal training was useful, it was insufficient for doing their jobs; thus, they were required to learn much of their work on-the-job. Analysis of the interview transcripts, combined with observations, allowed the researcher to identify three sources of on-the-job learning: (1) social interaction; (2) experimenting; and (3) reading books, manuals, and online help.

1.   **On-the-job social interaction:** The most common methods for consultants to learn to use information technology with which they were either unfamiliar or not proficient were to ask others, to work with others, or to observe others. See quotes 1 through 9 in Appendix A. They asked the experts, others on their team, those sitting nearby, or occasionally friends or colleagues at other organizations. Interestingly, they did not ask the IS support staff, even though there were three IS support staff on-site in the New York office. One of the IS support staff explained:

We do not train users in Excel. If a user asked me for training in Excel, I would say no. What I meant by saying that is, we the 'help desk' don't train users on Office applications, Excel, Access, etc. Not because we don't want to, we just don't have the time. And if we have the time, sometimes we don't have the knowledge. ...They can ask me a question here and there: how do you do this or how do you do that? If I know the answer, I will tell them. We in IS are not really savvy users of Excel and Access and all those applications. We handle operating systems and configurations. (Yosef, IS support staff, Echo)

Another IS support person explained that his time was spent supporting the partners at Echo, and that the support provided the consultants was minimal.

2. **Experimenting:** Experimenting was an important aspect mentioned by consultants to learn the IT tools and how to use them in their work. Expressions such as 'playing with it,' 'figure it out,' and 'fool around with it' were used to describe how these consultants learned what they needed to do.

    Experimentation and playing, therefore, included (a) actively looking at features and functions of the software, (b) using the software for a specific task, (c) creating dummy data sets for use with the software, (d) anticipating making mistakes, and (e) accidental learning by "bumping into new things." Quotes 10 through 15 in Appendix A are typical comments made by consultants.

3. **Reading books, manuals, and online help:** Some consultants also relied on books, manuals, and online help. These were less often cited as sources for learning. Some consultants reported buying a book and studying it to learn a specific software package.

    When consultants reported reading a book or manual, this was in addition to asking people for tips and advice, and in addition to experimentation. Further, many of the experienced consultants criticized books or manuals as being poorly organized, too lengthy, and too heavy to carry on the road. See quotes 16 through 25 in Appendix A.

Summary of Analysis 1

In sum, learning to use IT at Echo is a rich and complex process that surpasses formal training and requires personal initiative both with respect to experimenting with IT and approaching others for help. The following, complete story, told in the voice of Jessica, relates her experience of learning to use Microsoft Access for a project, where she was working with an Access database specialist, Justin, who was called in from outside of Echo to assist on the project.

I actually designed quite a bit of what Justin would need, because he didn't know anything about the client or how their business worked. I explained what the keys would be. I know some Access, and I learned more through that case. I stayed up all night two nights learning it here once (laughing). I used the online tutorials, and I didn't know anything about it prior to that. I had never looked at a database program, had no idea what a query was, none of that. So I learned all the basic stuff so at least I could talk to Justin, and work him through it, and basically understand what he was looking for. And I wasn't sure, he did all this stuff about the integrity of the database; he knew that sort of thing. I worked side by side with him, so if something was missing or we weren't sure about something, I would go to the client to find out and then come back.

I spent the two nights reading the online tutorials, and a book too. ... If you are just doing basic stuff, [the online tutorials] aren't bad, because as opposed to a textbook, they make you do the stuff while you're on the computer. I just found the book [I read] around the office; it was a Microsoft Access 4-point-whatever, or something. So you learn basic stuff like what's a query and what's a primary key, what you can do, how it works, how to read the file. [Access is] one of those programs that when you open it up, it's not intuitive what you're supposed to do with it, like how you save and what buckets it all falls in, so I started playing with it, making databases of friends, their names and phone numbers. So you figure out what you can do with it, like find your birthday, and everyone's birthday. (Jessica, second-year analyst, Echo)

One of the new analysts had a similar story to recount about learning to use SPSS, the statistics software package. This analyst had a strong computer science and analytical background, but had never used SPSS before. She explained how she relied on the 'expert' to help with specific questions, and that she learned the programming scripts by copying code generated by the program itself, rather than books or manuals.

I had to learn SPSS on the job, but the person I was working with, this associate, Conner, has been working with the client, he's been on the case for about two years. He had already built the model, so he was our expert on SPSS. So any question, we could go up to him and he would know. The CD-ROM contains some manual-type information. The stuff we needed to learn was how to write the scripts, like the programming language. SPSS has those dialogue boxes, and there's a little paste button, and it pastes the code into a different window. That's what we use as a base, and then you learn the code from that. It was very easy. We would use the dialogue box and put one variable because it was easy, and then paste it, take the code, and then just replace all the variable names. (Marie, new analyst, Echo)

Figure 2. Post-study view of IT learning over time

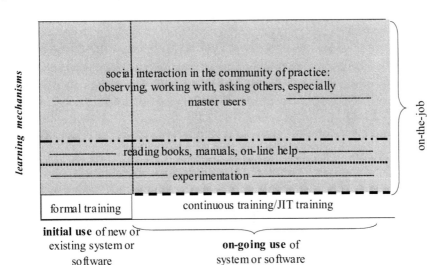

Notes: The shaded area represents on-the-job learning, where no time had been specifically allocated by the organization for the individual to learn or train. Such on-the-job learning occurred for both first-time use and on-going use of systems and software packages at Echo.

These findings, depicted in Figure 2, extend the pre-study view of building fluency with IT over time. This group of knowledge workers relied not only on traditional training, but also on experimentation, on reading, and on the social aspect of work. The social aspect is explored in detail in the next section.

Analysis 2: Master Users of IT

Given the importance of learning from others, the researcher probed interviewees for information about proficient users of IT at Echo. In particular, she asked each interviewee who he or she considered to be the proficient users of IT at Echo. The question was intentionally open-ended, allowing respondents to specify as many individuals and as many different types of IT as they required to answer the question. (All interviews were confidential, and all names have been disguised.) The researcher probed for elaboration if answers were not clear. Within each cell of Table 2 are the names of the people at Echo who were considered to be proficient users by at least one interviewee. The number following the name represents the number of people who considered that person to be proficient. For example, 15 different people named George as a proficient user of IT in general, and four different people named him as a proficient user of Excel.

Several themes emerged in conducting this analysis. First, those named as proficient users were by-and-large other consultants (analysts and associates) in the New York office. In contrast to findings reported in the literature, the experts at Echo were junior members of the organization. For example, the referent users in Lucas' study of a new health information system tended to be older, and more likely than non-referents to be in a management position (Lucas, 1978). In Lee's study, one-third of lead users were managers (Lee, 1986, p. 322). At Echo, analysts, the most junior members of Echo, were named as a generic grouping as the experts 16 times; partners were rarely mentioned as the experts; and the IS support staff was given as a response only two times, and never with respect to using a specific software program. This finding about the IS support staff contrasts with 48% of respondents in Lee's study, who indicated that they relied on the IS support staff for information.

Second, consultants may be recognized as proficient in information technology in general, or as proficient in specific information technologies, for example Excel or Access. Some of those who were viewed as general experts were *not* viewed as particularly proficient in specific applications such as Excel, and someone with a reputation as an Excel expert might not share that title with respect to Access or statistics packages.

Third, the data suggest that some users enjoy an extended reputation for their expertise (the Recognized Experts in Table 2), whereas many users have only a local reputation (the Local Experts in Table 2). The Recognized Experts like George, Robert, and Jonathan are likely called upon regularly by many of their peers for assistance. Local Experts like Ravi, Susan, and Samantha are likely called upon less frequently, and by just a few of their colleagues, for assistance.

One of the new consultants elaborated on the importance of the social network, and on Echo's own deficiency in identifying and documenting the experts:

...I know I've seen people scrambling trying to figure out who knows how to program in VB (Visual Basic) and why things happen. That's tough. We have knowledge in terms of going to the knowledge bank and figuring out who has worked in an industry, but we don't necessarily have a knowledge bank in terms of who has great skill sets in certain things.

Table 2. Master users of IT

	IT in general	Excel	Access	Proprietary Strategy Tool
RECOGNIZED EXPERTS	**George (15)** **Robert (10)** Jonathan (10) Tony (9) Karen (8) **Stuart (7)** Matthew (7)	**Robert (5)** **George (4)** **Stuart (4)**	Matthew (5) Tony (4)	—
LOCAL EXPERTS	Marie (3) Josh (3) Susan (3) Martin (3) Ravi (2) Kurt (2) Jessica (2) Sandeep (2) Arnold (2) Omar (2) Kelly (2) Randy (1) Dianne (1) Katie (1) Samantha (1) Carolyn (1)	Marie (2) Tony (2) Karen (2) Sandeep (2) Susan (1) Martin (1) Samantha (1) Arnold (1) Josh (1) Jonathan (1) Matthew (1) Kurt (1) Ravi (1) Jessica (1)	**Robert (3)** **Stuart (2)** Randy (1) Susan (1)	Arnold (1) **Stuart (1)** Kurt (1)
number of times "analysts" was given as a response	5 times	0 times	11 times	0 times
number of times IS support staff was mentioned	2 times	0 times	0 times	0 times

We have a listing of the cases you've worked on and the skills and knowledge you have, including (foreign) languages, but I'm talking about knowing within the office who the expert is in how to do [a strategy model in Excel], or how to run a regression (in SPSS), so that you have a human resource. It's one thing to call someone on the phone, it's another to go to someone and ask them: what did I do wrong? (Lena, new associate, Echo)

Discussion

The original research question posed was what other mechanisms besides formal training do knowledge workers rely on to learn over time to use the information technologies of their work? Figure 1 represents the pre-study view of learning over time and is based on prior studies reported in the literature, and on the theoretical perspective, legitimate peripheral participation. Two mechanisms, training and social interaction, are indicated in the pre-study model.

The results of the empirical study (Figure 2) indicate that while training plays a role as expected, social interactions play a significant role. Additionally, two other mechanisms were revealed: Experimentation and reading books, manuals, and online help.

The social interaction was foreshadowed by reference in the literature to "influential individuals," lead users, and resident experts. Yet those early studies merely identified the existence of such non-IS personnel in an organization. The results of the present study support the findings of two earlier studies that alluded to the importance of learning from others. Lead users (Lee, 1986) and resident experts (Nelson & Cheney, 1987) were both highly utilized and highly satisfactory mechanisms for users in those studies to improve their fluency during the early years of personal computing. "Recognized experts" and "local experts" at Echo were a primary means for junior consultants to learn to use the IT of their work.

Given the importance of experts, the ability to identify them would be useful to an organization. For example, if personal innovativeness in IT (PIIT), defined as, "the willingness of an individual to try out any new information technology" (Agarwal & Prasad, 1998), were shown to correlate with expertise, the instrument developed to measure that personality trait could be used as a proxy for identifying expertise. Additionally, recent work by Marcolin, Compeau, Munro, and Huff (2000) has attempted to create instruments to measure this type of user expertise, through the construct they call "user competence."

Recent studies of implementation indicate that social factors are important to users. The social norms construct has recently been re-inserted to the Technology Acceptance Model (Lucas & Spitler, 1999; Venkatesh & Morris, 2000). The new Unified Theory of Acceptance and Use of Technology also includes a social component (Venkatesh, Morris, Davis, & Davis, 2003). The findings of the present study suggest that these social elements will play an important role in these and other theories of implementation.

Additionally, the social element has been an issue in the knowledge management literature. For example, in their study of strategic management consulting firms, Hansen and his colleagues found that successful firms who use a personalization competitive strategy follow a person-to-person knowledge management strategy. That is, they, "develop networks for linking people so that tacit knowledge can be shared" (Hansen, Norhia, & Tierney, 1999, p. 109).

With regard to the theory guiding the research, this analysis reinforces the importance of the community of practice, especially with regard to specific IT-use for tasks. Consultants often approached others in their peer group for assistance and advice on using IT for their work.

Directions for Future Research

This study showed that formal and informal training are just two mechanisms by which consultants learned to use information technology. If a knowledge worker has never used a particular software package or feature of the software, formal training may introduce the worker to some of the concepts of the software and its features. However, in knowledge work environments such as the one investigated in this research, workers build their fluency with IT, over time, as they are challenged with new problems and tasks, and as they encounter new or unfamiliar information technologies to help them meet these challenges. This process and organizational view of an individual's learning to use IT could be incorporated into researchers' views, moving the training literature in a new direction. In addition to studies on trainers, training content, and training delivery methods, studies exploring how different individual workers build (or do not build) fluency over time are warranted.

The findings about reliance on and recognition of expertise at Echo raise several questions. Given the rapid turnover in such firms, how does expertise get replenished when master users "walk out the door"? What can organizations do to recognize and reward the master users? Are perceptions about who the master users are consistent with the master user's knowledge?

Understanding the process by which such reputations get built should be important to an organization like Echo. Since so much of learning and performing one's job rests on skills and knowledge of other people, knowing where to go for certain kinds of assistance is important. If the knowledge base is broader than a few people, the organizational members and the organization at large would benefit from knowing who the master users are. It should be noted that some consultants were experts by virtue of what they knew the day they arrived at Echo, and these people often remained experts; others, by reading a book, working with the software on a project, and asking and working with others became recognized experts in the organization. So, while expertise begot expertise, people also *became* experts through their work.

The present study suggests that the importance of expert users can no longer be ignored. Thus, future research could focus on the qualities and characteristics of user expertise and how to identify or measure user expertise. Expert studies have been conducted in many other disciplines, such as music, writing, dance, and medicine (Ericsson & Smith, 1991), and might be called upon to inform research geared toward understanding expertise in using IT for work tasks.

At Echo some questions remain unanswered. For example, do the experts, as perceived by others, also perceive themselves to be experts? If so, do the experts work specifically and intentionally to maintain and improve their expertise? Are there any mechanisms in the firm to nurture their expertise? Future research could address these questions.

Another question to pursue is whether a worker's perceived expertise automatically increases the longer he remains in the firm. To answer such a question would also require a longer time in the field, and probably a different type of study which focuses specifically on identified and perceived expertise; such a study might include administering a survey at several points in time to track perceived expertise of the members of the community of practice.

The findings of this study suggest that future studies could explore the mechanisms workers in other settings use, and to determine the relative weight placed on the mechanisms. Further the relationship between the mechanisms used and the acquisition of fluency with IT should be explored. For example, do the experts rely on certain mechanisms to a greater degree than non-experts?

Limitations of the Study

In this study, no attempt was made to draw statistical generalizations; however, analytical generalizations were sought (Strauss & Corbin, 1990; Yin, 1994). Whether these analytical generalizations hold in other organizations or environments requires further research. For example, do all sorts of knowledge workers in all sorts of organizations use the mechanisms management consultants at Echo used for improving their fluency with IT? Or do some workers rely strictly on formal training, never daring to experiment; read books, manuals, and online help; nor to ask, work with or observe others? Consultants at Echo are among the best educated knowledge workers in the U.S.; thus, they may be naturally more curious than other workers, leading to reliance on these other types of mechanisms. Further, one selection criterion for hiring consultants at Echo is the consultant's social skills; thus, it is possible that the social mechanism that is so strong at Echo is not dominant among workers in other organizations. The research design selected for this study allows analytical generalization to other firms only insofar as other firms are similar in their characteristics to Echo.

Additionally, the finding that junior consultants relied mainly on their peers for answers to their questions about using IT may be an artifact of the time period in which the study was conducted. Many of the partners at Echo belonged to a different generation and did not grow up with IT, as did the junior consultants; thus it is possible that the IT generation gap is partially responsible for the consultants' reluctance to ask partners their IT-related questions. If this speculation is correct, then the same study conducted in ten years' time might have a different outcome. However, since the focus of this study was the junior consultants, and since the researcher was restricted in her access to the partners in the firm, the data cannot answer this question.

Similarly, in a different firm, the IS support staff might be trained and selected differently and the culture may be such that those in the IS support staff are able to, and are expected to, respond to junior workers' questions.

Another limitation of this study is the reliance of the researcher on participants' identification of experts (master users of IT) at Echo. The researcher did not attempt to assess the perceived experts' expertise through standardized instruments, or some other means.

Conclusion

In spite of the study's limitations, the findings presented here have some important implications for practice. If these findings are typical in firms, then end users and organizations need to focus on mechanisms other than formal training to ensure effective use of IT, and to account for the social component in designing formal training interventions. In particular, organizations may want to give greater consideration to issues of staffing for particular skills and experience for work assignments. At Echo, consultants regularly joined new project teams, a typical experience for many types of end users. Since IT is critical to performing certain types of work, organizations may want to consider equipping teams with individuals who have experience with particular types of IT, who are known innovators with IT, and who are likely to share their understanding with others on the team.

In terms of delivery of training programs, this research suggests that on-going training be provided as needed. At Echo, this could be achieved by budgeting time and money to client projects for the express purpose of training the junior people assigned to the project. Further, this research suggests that training be delivered by peers actually engaged in using IT for their tasks, either in conjunction with, or instead of IT people and senior people. At Echo, this could be accomplished by making one-on-one or group peer-training part of consultants' formal job responsibilities, by adding it as an item on consultants' periodic performance reviews, for example.

Another point concerns evaluating and experimenting with new technologies. Given the importance of IT to performing many types of knowledge work, organizations may want to promote evaluation of and experimentation with new information technologies by a few key end users in the organization, who can then share their findings with others.

Organizations could work to identify the expert end users of different information technologies for particular tasks. Without objective diagnostic tools, however, identification may be difficult, and organizations will have to rely on perceptions of others in the organization in order to do so.

This research also has implications for end users. Once on the job, end users should heed their communities of practice. End users new to an organization may expect to use their peers as resources, especially with respect to using and understanding information technologies for their tasks. They may also want to develop their own areas of expertise to share with others. These end users should not necessarily expect the most experienced and longest tenured members of the organization, nor the information technology specialists, to provide assistance with the information technologies they use in their work.

For research, this study identified an important phenomenon that deserves greater attention, that of master users of IT. Researchers can build on this concept to study other organizational phenomena. Additionally, by utilizing intensive research methods, the researcher was able to identify by name and position, the master users at one organization, and to identify some characteristics of those groups. These analytical techniques and associated findings can be used by other researchers interested in similar phenomena.

In summary, this field study has identified the mechanisms a group of junior-level end users at a management consulting firm relied on to learn to use the IT needed for their jobs. The evidence gathered indicates that formal training was only one mechanism, and that other mechanisms, notably social interaction between peers, were also important. In particular, these end users' reliance on master users within their own community was paramount, and the phenomenon deserves further attention in future studies.

References

Agarwal, R., & Prasad, J. (1998). A conceptual and operational definition of personal innovativeness in the domain of information technology. *Information Systems* Research, *9*(2), 204-215.

Anonymous. (2000). *Falling through the Net: Toward digital inclusion.* Washington, DC: U.S. Department of Commerce, Economic and Statistics Administration, National Telecommunications and Information Administration.

Committee on Information Technology Literacy, C. S. a. T. B., Commission of Physical Sciences, Mathematics, and Applications, National Research Council (1999). *Being fluent with information technology.* Washington, DC: National Academy Press.

Compeau, D. (2002). The role of trainer behavior in end user software training. *Journal of End User Computing, 14*(1), 23-32.

Compeau, D. R., & Higgins, C. A. (1995). Computer self-efficacy: Development of a measure and initial test. *MIS Quarterly, 19*(9), 189-211.

Ericsson, K. A., & Smith, J. (Eds.). (1991). *Toward a general theory of expertise.* New York: Cambridge University Press.

Fidishun, D. (2001). People servers vs. information providers: The impact of service orientation on technology training. *Information Technology and Libraries, 20*(1), 29-33.

Galletta, D. F., Ahuja, M., Hartman, A., Teo, T., & Peace, A. G. (1995). Social influence and end-user training. *Communications of the ACM, 38*(7), 70-79.

Gattiker, U. E. (1992). Computer skills acquisition: A review and future directions for research. *Journal of Management, 18*(3), 547-574.

George, J. F., Iacono, S., & Kling, R. (1995). Learning in context: Extensively computerized work groups as communities-of-practice. *Accting., Mgmt. & Info. Tech., 5*(3/4), 185-202.

Glaser, B. G., & Strauss, A. L. (Eds.). (1967). *The discovery of grounded theory.* Hawthorne, NY: Aldine Publishing Company.

Guimaraes, T., & Igbaria, M. (1997). Assessing user computing effectiveness: An integrated model. *Journal of End User Computing, 9*(2), 3-14.

Hansen, M. T., Norhia, N., & Tierney, T. (1999). What's your strategy for managing knowledge? *Harvard Business Review, 77*(2), 106-116.

Hong, W., Thong, J. Y. L., Wong, W. M., & Tam, K. Y. (2001-2002). Determinants of user acceptance of digital libraries: An empirical examination of individual differences and system characteristics. *Journal of Management Information Systems, 18*(3), 97-124.

Huang, A. H. (2002). A three-tier technology training strategy in a dynamic business environment. *Journal of End User Computing, 14*(2), 30-39.

Kernan, M. C., & Howard, G. S. (1990). Computer anxiety and computer attitudes: An investigation of construct and predictive validity issues. *Educational and Psychological Measurement, 50,* 681-690.

Klein, H. K., & Myers, M. D. (1999). A set of principles for conducting and evaluating interpretive field studies in information systems. *MIS Quarterly, 23*(1), 67-93.

Lave, J., & Wenger, E. (Eds.). (1991). *Situated learning: Legitimate peripheral participation.* Cambridge: Cambridge University Press.

Lee, D. M. S. (1986, December). Usage pattern and sources of assistance for personal computer users. *MIS Quarterly,* 313-325.

Lim, K. H., Ward, L. M., & Benbasat, I. (1997). An empirical study of computer system learning: Comparison of co-discovery and self-discovery methods. *Information Systems Research, 8*(3), 245-272.

Lucas, Jr., H. C. (1978). The use of an interactive information storage and retrieval system in medical research. *Communications of the ACM, 21*(3), 197-205.

Lucas, Jr., H. C., & Spitler, V. K. (1999). Technology use and performance: A field study of broker workstations. *Decision Sciences, 30*(2).

Marakas, G. M., Yi, M. Y., & Johnson, R. (1998). The multilevel and multifaceted construct of computer self-efficacy: Toward clarification of the construct and an integrative framework for research. *Information Systems Research, 9*(2), 126-163.

Marcolin, B. L., Compeau, D. R., Munro, M. C., & Huff, S. L. (2000). Assessing user competence: Conceptualization and measurement. *Information Systems Research, 11*(1), 37-60.

Murphy, C. A., Coover, D., & Owen (1989). Development and validation of the computer self-efficacy scale. *Educational and Psychological Measurement, 49*(4), 893-899.

Myers, M. (1999, March 8-11). Ethnographic research methods in information systems. *IS World Net Virtual Meeting Center at Temple University.* Retrieved from http://interact.cis.temple.edu/~vmc

Nelson, R. R., & Cheney, P. H. (1987). Training end users: An exploratory study. *MIS Quarterly, 11*(4), 547-559.

Orlikowski, W. J., & Baroudi, J. J. (1991). Studying information technology in organizations: Research approaches and assumptions. *Information Systems Research, 2*(1), 1-28.

Orlikowski, W. J., Yates, J., Okamura, K., & Fujimoto, M. (1995). Shaping electronic communication: The metastructuring of technology in the context of use. *Organization Science, 6*(4), 423-445.

Santhanam, R., & Sein, M. K. (1994). Improving end-user proficiency: Effects of conceptual training and nature of interaction. *Information Systems Research, 5*(4), 378-399.

Schwandt, T. A. (1998). Constructivist, interpretivist approaches to human inquiry. In N. K. Denzin & Y. S. Lincoln (Eds.), *The landscape of qualitative research* (pp. 221-259). Thousand Oaks, CA: Sage Publications.

Simon, S. J. (2000). The relationship of learning style and training method to end-user computer satisfaction and computer use: A structural equation model. *Information Technology, Learning, and Performance Journal, 18*(1), 41-59.

Simon, S. J., Grover, V., Teng, J. T. C., & Whitcomb, K. (1996). The relationship of information system training methods and cognitive ability to end-user satisfaction, comprehension, and skill transfer: A longitudinal field study. *Information Systems Research, 7*(4), 466-490.

Strauss, A., & Corbin, J. (Eds.). (1990). *Basics of qualitative research.* Newbury Park, CA: Sage Publications.

Venkatesh, V., & Morris, M. G. (2000). Why don't men ever stop to ask for directions? Gender, social influence, and their role in technology acceptance and usage behavior. *MIS Quarterly, 24*(1), 15-139.

Venkatesh, V., Morris, M. G., Davis, G. B., & Davis, F. D. (2003). User acceptance of information technology: Toward a unified view. *MIS Quarterly, 27*(3), 425-478.

Webster, J., & Martocchio, J. J. (1992, June). Microcomputer playfulness: Development of a measure with workplace implications. *MIS Quarterly,* 201-226.

Woszczynski, A. B., Roth, P. L., & Segars, A. H. (Eds.). (1998). *Exploring the theoretical foundations of microcomputer playfulness.* Baltimore: Americas Conference of the Association for Information Systems.

Yager, S. E., Kappelman, L. A., Maples, G. A., & Prybutok, V. R. (1997). Microcomputer playfulness: Stable or dynamic trait? *Data Base for Advances in Information Systems, 28*(2), 43-52.

Yin, R. K. (Ed.). (1994). *Case study research design and methods.* Thousand Oaks, California: Sage Publications.

Appendix A

Excerpts from Interviews

I. Working with Observing and Asking Others

1.	*Earlier when I spoke (to you) about finding these functions in Excel, it happened by working with other people on teams and seeing the way that they would do things. It's amazing how much time you actually spend sharing the keyboard with someone or you sit down with someone and say "I don't know why this isn't working," and they'll say "well, I think it's because you're trying to match these two columns, but that one has capital letters, but you can fix that by using this function.* (Francoise, seasoned analyst Echo)
2.	*Normally I ask people when I get stuck. I have my 10-minute rule that I think most people go by. First you try to figure it out on your own, and if you can't, you ask your neighbor.* (Mary, new analyst, Echo)
3.	*Usually I just try to figure it out, or use the on-line help functions. I don't generally look at books. If it's gotten to that point, I will usually just ask someone.* (Aaron, new analyst, Echo)
4.	*And there are times when I don't know what the right function is to do something, or I have to ask someone to do something.* (Omar, second-year analyst, Echo)
5.	*I think it's general presence of knowledge and an awareness of people that have either used the product, or are more expert in it, so that you can leverage them and ask for their help.* (Robert, second-year, Echo)
6.	*We learn IT mostly on the job. When you have a question, you ask people around you.* (Samantha, second-year analyst, Echo)
7.	*I'm learning PowerPoint lately. In addition to playing or experimenting with the program, I learn a lot by watching what other people are doing with the program. I don't mean watching what keystrokes or computer commands they use; that would be weird. When I'm working with someone (for example, in Production, or someone's model), I ask them "um, how'd you do this?" That is probably the primary way I learn new things, because I often don't even know the features exist. Usually I learn of a new feature because someone shows me a file because we're working together, so then I see what the person has done. No, I never read manuals. I use the on-line help a fair amount. The tricky part is to know the computer or software package can do something. When you know it can do something, that often works, but not always. It sometimes takes a few tries. For instance, I am now learning how to make animated bullets in PowerPoint. That was a big learning. I didn't know how to do that before.* (George, seasoned analyst, Echo)
8.	*... I'll be sitting next to an analyst and we're making a slide and all of a sudden I see how s/he's using a certain set of keystrokes, and I'll ask "what did that do?" For example, it's the coolest thing, Control-Shift-LessThan changes the font size. [laughing] So, it's just like that.* (Fred, sr. associate, Echo)
9.	*For the most part, we learned Excel by being thrown into a case situation. Now, I think there's better training, but for the most part, it's a learn-as-you-go process. I still find that you can learn a lot about functions, but until you're really in a situation where you have to use them, you either forget about them, or you're not sure what is the best function to use in a certain situation. So you're always asking people, understanding what the best way is to set something up is – what the best application is, what the best functions are.* (Amina, new associate, Echo)

II. Experimentation

10.	Even at Wharton I didn't learn much in the class. I learned by playing with it. That's just how I am. I'll test out all the things and see how they work. When I want to do something, I'll search through the function list and see if anything pops up. I'm just very inquisitive about what all the different options do. I'll just try to figure things out. (Robert, seasoned analyst, Echo)
11.	I learn new information technology by using it [laughing]. I look at all the features, like when I first went to use Lotus Notes for [a client project]. I basically opened up the program and looked at each of the menus, and went down each one to look at what it said it could do, to understand what the possibilities were for using them, even if I wouldn't have to, so I knew what it could do. (Barbara, seasoned analyst, Echo)
12.	What I usually like to do is have a glance at a tutorial, or at least have a tutorial handy. If I don't know anything about the specific program, I'll just skim through part of the tutorial and then it's going to be trial-and-error, and I like to have a specific task. For example, I don't like to learn Access for the sake of learning Access, because generally, I'm not able to learn it that way. But if I had something to do in Access, then I will just look at the tutorial a little bit, then start to do my task, then playing with, at the same time, trial-and-error, and also go back to the tutorial if I have some specific questions. If I suppose that I should be able to do something, but I am not able to do it, then I will refer to the on-line help. (Thomas, new analyst, Echo)
13.	...it's just sitting for a day with an analyst and saying, "Walk me through how you are going to do this." And then just playing with data sets more and more, and making mistakes. That's the only way [I] learn. (Pierre, new associate, Echo)
14.	It's one of those programs that when you open it up, it's not intuitive what you're supposed to do with it, like how you save and what buckets it all falls in, so I started playing with it, making databases of friends, their names and phone numbers. So you figure out what you can do with it, like find your birthday, and everyone's birthday. (Jessica, second-year analyst, Echo)
15.	You bump into it. You've got the basic toolkit on Excel, Microsoft Word, PowerPoint, and you fool around with it and pick up things here and there and learn about it. You bump into it basically. You hear from other people around the office, "hey, did you hear that there's this cool function that you can use?" (Fred, sr. associate, Echo)

III. Books, Manuals, Online Help (positive)

16.	I learned SAS from the little red SAS book. (Jonathan, second-year analyst, Echo)
17.	For my [Asian] project, because I knew I would be doing a lot of Excel, I bought a whole Excel book, and on the plane — flight, I literally read it. It was the big, blue Excel book, the super thick one. (Kurt, second-year analyst, Echo)
18.	Most stuff I just pick up a manual and learn how to do it. I don't know if you're familiar with SPSS. It's a statistical software program. I had to use that on a recent project so I learned how to do that from the manual. (Josh, seasoned analyst, Echo)
19.	I know that I can sit with a book and figure out how Access works. I've done this before. I understand the fields and a little bit about how it works, and that made me confident enough to know that if I had to do it, I could do it...I also have the big red Excel book. Since I've been here, I've learned some new functions on Excel, which are kind of neat. Sometimes, when I'm working in Excel, I tell myself that there's got to be an easier way to do what I'm doing, so I use the help function to find an easier way. I find the help function to be very useful. (Elaine, second-year analyst, Echo)

IV. Books, Manuals, Online Help (limitations and criticisms)

20.	*I picked up SPSS and Access by sitting there with people who knew them and asking questions [laughing]. I rely on manuals and books for reference for specific things, but to get going, I've always just stopped and sat there and worked my way through it, usually with someone. I never use the on-line help.* (Paul, sr. associate, Echo)
21.	*I don't tend to read manuals unless I have to. I don't really read them. I would never open them up and then read them before I looked at the program. I usually go to them when I can't figure out what I have to do. It's easier to ask someone than to look it up in a manual.* (Barbara, seasoned analyst, Echo)
22.	*In my case so far, I usually get a couple of initial pointers from people that I know have good experience with it, and then the rest, I just teach myself, from manuals or on-line help, which is generally not as good as it should be.* (Sandeep, seasoned analyst, Echo)
23.	*I don't look at manuals. I'll ask people. For Excel, I knew a couple of people ... who were better than others, so I'd ask them. Sometimes I'll read a manual if it's a manual no one else will know. The problem with reading a manual is, unless I can read a very specific page of a manual on how to do x, it's not useful to me because I won't remember it two days later, because I will not have had to use it. It's more trial by fire.* (Peter, seasoned analyst, Echo)
24.	*I can't stand manuals; I won't even touch them. They're so ridiculous. At [school] I went out and bought some books on Excel, including <u>Excel for Dummies</u>. Each book was in excess of 1000 pages, and they were so poorly organized. I prefer to use the little Clip-It guy. I don't like it that much, but it helps when I need it. It helps with the indexing. When you type in a question, the keywords eventually lead you to the topic you're looking for. Most of the times I need help with programs when I'm on the road. I can't carry around manuals when I'm on the road.* (Pierre, new associate, Echo)
25.	*I would turn first to someone who knows. I know that they can show me in 10 minutes what I can read in 10 hours. Sometimes people are busy and you don't want to impose, or people aren't available or no one is around who knows; then you have to read the manuals. I never use the on-line help. I don't use the manual for Excel, because there are enough people in the office who are good enough to show you.* (Ravi, second-year analyst, Echo)

Appendix B

Documents Collected at Echo

Name of Document(s)	Description of Document	Source
Face Book	provides a brief biography of each person in the NY office, with the following information: portrait photograph, title, hire date, universities attended, name of spouse and children (if applicable), home address and telephone number	Sr. Staff Member
Confidential Client Proposal	a confidential, 20-page document prepared for a prospective client, in the form of a PowerPoint presentation, outlining the products, services and competencies of Echo	Staff Member
Tools of the Trade and Orientation Training Binders	two three-inch thick binders provided to new hires during initial two-week training	Consultant (European version from Director of Training)

Project Simulation Training Binder and other documents	1. a three-inch thick binder providing:
	    (a) schedule of week-long training events
	    (b) "face book" of training participants
	    (c) instruction in and guidance for the analysis,
	        presentation and execution of a mock client project
	2. supporting documents include data for the client
	    project
		Researcher participation in training

Handouts from Informal CCS Training	e.g., "Getting the Most Out of Access and Excel: Becoming 10x More Productive," a 77-page PowerPoint document with many pages of screen shots; prepared by member of CCS *other* than person delivering training	Researcher attendance at workshop
Handouts from IS Training Workshops	short documents, ranging from 3 to 20 pages each, to supplement trainer's instruction, prepared by IS trainers	Researcher attendance at workshop
IS Training Manuals	"Echo Computer Environment -Win 95, Student Manual," a 60-page document covering logging into and using the network, file server contents, intranet contents, printing, security, support, troubleshooting, remote access phone numbers; other manuals on individual topics such as Word, Excel, Access, PowerPoint, Project, Outlook, Windows Operating System, these are generally generic materials prepared by an outside firm specializing in training in information technology. For example, the titles for Excel and Access are: Excel 97 Tips and Keyboarding Shortcuts, 20 pages; Excel 97: Advanced (Windows 95) Student Manual, 1/2 inch thick; Excel 97: Worksheets (Windows 95) Student Manual, 1/4 inch thick; Excel 97: Charting and Organizing Data (Windows 95) Student Manual, 1/2 inch thick; Access 97 Tips and Keyboard Shortcuts, 16 pages; Access 97: Level 1 (Windows 95) Student Manual, 1/2 inch thick; Access 97: Level 2 (Windows 95) Student Manual, 1/2 inch thick; Access 97:Advanced (Windows 95), 1/2 inch thick	IS Trainer
Informal Training Documents	e.g., "Conjoint Analysis for New Product Design and Segmentation," a 52-page PowerPoint document	Consultants and downloaded from server
Miscellaneous Documents	e.g., human resources memos, Echo newsletters, invitations to Echo social events, Echo in the news, staffing survey, "Changing Your Primary Network Logon," status of recruiting efforts, etc.	Inter-office mail at Echo, handouts at meetings, e-mail

Appendix C

Training at Echo

At Echo there were several types of training, including mandatory and optional group training sessions, and optional, individual, self-initiated computer-based training. The group training sessions are summarized in Table A3.1. Formal, mandatory training for consultants consisted of "Orientation and Tools of the Trade" in September, and "Project Simulation" in January. Informal training was optional and consisted of (a) workshops offered by other consultants: "Valuation Models Workshop," "Advanced Excel Workshop," and "Slide-Writing for Presentations Workshop," (b) IT training offered by the IS Department about specific software packages: Microsoft Access, Microsoft Excel, and Microsoft Outlook, and (c) individual, self-initiated computer-based training. Consultants rarely, if ever, used the computer-based training, so the following sections discuss the group training sessions only.

Formal Mandatory Training

Although formal training played a limited role, it played a very important and specific role at Echo. First, it provided a common basis for all new consultants who joined the firm. Because consultants came from a variety of backgrounds and experiences, this training was designed to give exposure to the concepts and terminology new consultants would need when they began their work on client projects. Tools of the Trade training was two weeks long and covered a vast number of topics. The first week was devoted to orienting new consultants to the organization.

The second week covered topics such as accounting, finance, and so forth, and three days were devoted to information technology skills, primarily Excel skills. Tools of the Trade training provided consultants basic and intermediate skills in Excel and exposure to a few other software packages, such as PowerPoint, Access and Outlook. The partner in charge of training described the technology training new consultants received in their first weeks on the job:

So, for example, when you're first coming in, you get literally orientation, and something called [Tools of the Trade] Training, which are designed to give you basic blocking and tackling kinds of skills. That would include, on the information technology side, things like learning Excel, or learning PP, or Access, or Microsoft Word. You basically get blitz-type tutorials in those things over the first two weeks... (Lucy, partner in charge of training, Echo)

The training ensured that all new consultants had a minimum skill set and understanding, and that they were exposed to a wider skill set and concepts which they might need at some point in the future; it also directed them to resources they might need in the future, and set their expectations for using and learning about IT. Most of the new analysts agreed that Excel training provided them a foundation, but for more sophisticated use of the program, they would be required to learn it in the process of doing their work. Quotes 1 through 10 in Table A3.2 corroborate the description and purpose of formal training for consultants.

Informal and Optional Training

In addition to mandatory training, several types of optional training were available to consultants. These included informal training sessions in groups, and computer-based training available from the IS department or training workshops available for download from the server. Although nearly everyone the researcher spoke with lauded the informal training provided at Echo, when she asked them specifically if they partook of this type of training, few people had used the computer-based training, many were unaware of the informal workshops available for download, and many listed the reasons why they had not been able to attend the group training sessions.

As indicated in Table A3.1 consultants generally did not attend the optional training workshops during the time the researcher spent at Echo. The best attended workshops were those offered by one of the junior partners. Workshops offered by other consultants and the IS trainer were very poorly attended. The reasons consultants gave for not attending training were that they were too busy, (this reason was generally linked to an important project deadline), that their manager on their project team did not allow them to attend the training, or that they were out of town on a client project during the training. See quotes 11 through 14 in Table A3.2.

Table A3.1. Training for consultants at New York office of Echo (Sept 1998 - May 1999)

Date and Duration	Name of Training (unless indicated, attendance optional)	Description	Researcher Attended?
September 1998 2 weeks	Orientation and Tools of the Trade Mandatory	2 weeks for new analysts and associates in the New York office	no
Dec. 4, 1998 1- 2 hours	Informal Training Workshop on Valuation Models	taught by jr. partner, attended by about 15 consultants, who drifted away until only about 3 were left at the end of the hour and a half; workshop held in a conference room, very informal, no technology; when consultants went to get their calculators, they did not return	yes
January 1999 one week	Project Simulation Training Mandatory	1 week off-site for new analysts and associates, all offices worldwide	yes
March 24, 1999 1 - 2 hours	IT Training (Access)	given by IS Dept. trainer, only one consultant attended (George, one of experts)	yes
March 24, 1999 1 - 2 hours	IT Training (Excel)	given by IS Dept. trainer, no consultants attended	yes
March 24, 1999 1 - 2 hours	IT Training (Outlook)	given by IS Dept. trainer, no consultants attended	yes
April 2, 1999 1 - 2 hours	Informal Training Workshop on Advanced Excel	taught by consultant four new consultants plus one second-year consultant attended, one left after 15 min., one left after 30 min. content, differences between Excel and Access and how to use them together. Materials developed by someone other than consultant who delivered course	yes
April 14, 1999 1 - 2 hours	IT Training Access '97 Using Queries	taught by IS Dept. trainer, no consultants attended, although two signed up; attended by office support staff	yes
April 14, 1999 1 - 2 hours	IT Training Access '97 Forms and Reports	taught by IS Dept. trainer; no consultants attended, although two signed up; attended by office support staff	yes
May 6, 1999 1 - 2 hours	IT Training (Outlook, Scheduling Meetings)	taught by IS Dept. trainer, no consultants	yes
May 21, 1999 1 - 2 hours, lunch time	Informal Training Workshop: Slide Writing for Presentations	given by jr. partner, attended by 17 consultants (2 left early) PIZZA	yes

Table A3.2. Interview excerpts related to training

I. Formal Training

1.	*I thought the training was phenomenal. Not only do I not have a background in computer skills, but I don't have a background in accounting or finance either. The training did a good job getting me prepared to do all this stuff that I hadn't had experience with before. I felt comfortable saying that I have to start from square one. (Prior to the training), I knew how to turn on Excel, but that's about it. I think they moved at a quick enough pace that people didn't get bored. I was probably one of the people with the most basic skill levels, but I learned it. I learned Excel, some of Access, more PowerPoint, accounting, finance, valuations, etc. Excel training was really good. I had no idea it could do these tricks, that you could make a macro. They told us that anything you want to do more than twice in a program, you should make a macro for. I had no idea what that was. They also said to use the on-line help. They told us that anything you think you might want to do in Excel, the help can do in one keystroke. So they taught us all kinds of shortcuts and tricks. (Jean, new analyst, Echo)*
2.	*Overall, I thought the Tools of the Trade training was good and it did help me. Excel training was fairly good. All the IT training, Excel, PowerPoint, and I think, Access, maybe - yes, there was a little bit of Access as well - it was fairly good, but again I think you learn best by doing it yourself. Even though the training was pretty hands on, it's not after one week of training that I master all the secrets of Excel and Access. (Thomas, new analyst, Echo)*
3.	*I learned Excel at the Tools of the Trade Training. Excel was one thing in the Tools of the Trade Training that we spent a lot of time on. We probably spent a whole day on it. People come to the Tools of the Trade Training with varied backgrounds. Some people come into the training with expertise in Excel, had really used it a lot or had used it in business school. I hadn't used Excel that much, just a little bit in prior summer work, but I think I had seen it enough that when I came into the training, I was able to pick it up quickly. (Aaron, new analyst, Echo)*
4.	*The Excel (training) is more showing some tricks, like how do you do a pivot table, or how do you do a lookup, and that type of thing. ... Of course, some of the more sophisticated applications of Excel, you might need to learn it more on an ad hoc basis, such as regressions and that type of stuff. (Arun, new analyst, Echo)*
5.	*The Excel training was excellent, and it has been very valuable for this project. George was an excellent teacher. Training set the foundation, so that I feel comfortable with Excel and the model. If I have a problem doing something on this [model] I play around a bit first, and if I still have a problem, then I ask Marius (who built the model). He can figure anything out. (Dianne, new analyst, Echo)*
6.	*The technology training is good at teaching basic skills, like the basic Excel skills and the basics of PowerPoint, and how to use Outlook. That's about it. Everything else, you're expected to ask around and pick up on your own, which is interesting because some people went to business school and have been using this stuff forever, know all the command lines. The rest of us had to struggle a bit more, but people are friendly, so it's helpful. (Jonathan, second-year analyst, Echo)*
7.	*The training is helpful; I understood that Excel is a calculation tool, and there are certain things I could use it for. In no way does that training prepare you for what you'll eventually have to do with it. (Sally, second-year analyst, Echo)*
8.	*That (Tools of the Trade) training taught me what Excel does - the concept of having one cell equal to another cell, and being able to change one cell and this number goes here. But that seems so automatic to me now, that I don't really consider that I learned it, but that definitely was a learning experience. In terms of the actual functionalities, learning that this function does that, or this is how you set up this table, I learned that on the cases. (Kurt, second-year analyst, Echo)*
9.	*Over just the past few years, the use of data mining has grown exponentially in the firm. And that was realized, so they decided to spend a little more time in the up-front training, explaining how to use Access given that more and more people are getting exposed to it. It was not extensive; it was just enough that they understand what it is, and that they'll know enough that they have to open a book to teach themselves. (Sandeep, seasoned analyst, Echo)*
10.	*What I've found is that even if I take a class on a program or do some exercises with it, I don't really know it until I sit with it and really use it. (Elaine, second-year analyst, Echo)*

continued on following page

II. Informal Training

11.	I don't attend the informal training sessions as I should. I prefer to learn the information on my own. I'm pretty quick at picking these things up. The ones I attended I found to be useful, but not worth the time. I should go to more of them, but inevitably something comes up, or I decide that any individual one is not worthwhile. (Jonathan, second-year analyst, Echo)
12.	I have not attended the informal training workshops. I would love to go (I think they're having one today, in fact, in New York), but I am so rarely in the New York office, that when I'm there, to go into a training session for two or three hours is difficult. That would be half of my day. I'm never in the office, so when I am, I have a lot to do. It's hard to keep people in a room for more than an hour. (Paul, sr. associate, Echo)
13.	Usually what ends up happening is people say, "Oh, you have time to go to this [training] instead of getting this work done. I didn't realize you had this much free time." (Samira, associate, Echo)
14.	I haven't gone to the informal workshops or the special IT training sessions. I probably should. I think I was on vacation the last time they were offered.... I don't know if I would attend (advanced training). Part of it's the whole culture of it. If you try to start it up, and it's not part of the system and people realize that an hour more of training is an hour more of work, then it doesn't fly. Training is not an institution. It's just here and there. It's not as though there's something every Friday. (Peter, seasoned analyst, Echo)

Appendix D

Klein and Myers' Seven Principles for Conducting and Evaluating Interpretive Field Studies in Information Systems

The main principles guiding the research study of Echo Management Consulting come from Klein and Myers (1999). The following table, adapted from their Table 1, provides a summary of the seven principles. As Klein and Myers indicate, not all studies address all principles to the same degree. The reader is referred to the original paper for a detailed explanation of the principles.

1. The Fundamental Principle of the Hermeneutic Circle This principle suggests that all human understanding is achieved by iterating between considering the interdependent meaning of the parts and the whole that they form. This principle of human understanding is fundamental to all the other principles.
2. Principle of Contextualization Requires critical reflection of the social and historical background of the research setting, so that the intended audience can see how the current situation under investigation emerged.
3. Principle of Interaction between the Researchers and the Subjects Requires critical reflection on how the research materials (or "data") were socially constructed through the interaction between the researchers and participants.

continued on following page

4. Principle of Abstraction and Generalization
Requires relating idiographic details revealed by data interpretation through the application of principles one and two to theoretical, general concepts that describe the nature of human understanding and social action.

5. Principle of Dialogical Reasoning
Requires sensitivity to possible contradictions between the theoretical preconceptions guiding the research design and actual findings ("the story which the data tell") with subsequent cycles of revision.

6. Principle of Multiple Interpretations
Requires sensitivity to possible differences in interpretations among the participants as are typically expressed in multiple narratives or stories of the same sequence of events under study. Similar to multiple witness accounts even if all tell it as they saw it.

7. Principle of Suspicion
Requires sensitivity to possible "biases" and systematic "distortions" in the narratives collected from the participants.

About the Editor

M. Adam Mahmood is a professor of computer information systems in the Department of Information and Decision Sciences at the University of Texas at El Paso, USA. He also holds the Ellis and Susan Mayfield Professorship in the College of Business Administration. He is a visiting faculty at the Helsinki School of Economics and Business Administration, Finland and University of Oulu in Finland and a visiting scholar at the University of Canterbury in New Zealand. He also worked for NASA as a visiting scholar in its Jet Propulsion Laboratory at Pasadena, California. Dr. Mahmood's scholarly and service activities include a number of responsibilities. He is presently serving as the program chair for the 2006 Annual Meeting of the Decision Sciences Institute in San Antonio. He is also presently serving as the editor in chief of the Journal of Organizational and End User Computing. He has also recently served as a guest editor of the *International Journal of Electronic Commerce* and the *Journal of Management Information Systems*. Dr. Mahmood's research interests center on generating business value utilizing information technology including electronic commerce for managerial decision making, strategic and competitive advantage, group decision support systems, and information systems success as it relates to organizational and end user computing. On this topic and others, he has published five edited books and 87 technical research papers in some of the leading journals and conference proceedings in the information technology field including *Management Information Systems Quarterly, De-*

cision Sciences, Journal of Management Information Systems, European Journal of Information Systems, INFOR — Canadian Journal of Operation Research and Information Processing, Journal of Information Systems, Information and Management, Journal of End User Computing, Information Resources Management Journal, Journal of Computer-Based Instruction, Data Base, and others. He has also presented papers in a number of regional, national, and international conferences.

About the Authors

Marie-Claude Boudreau is an assistant professor of MIS at the Terry College of Business, University of Georgia, USA. She received a PhD in computer information systems from Georgia State University. Dr. Boudreau has conducted research on the implementation of integrated software packages and the organizational change induced by information technology. She has authored articles published in many journals, such as *Organization Science, Information Systems Research, MIS Quarterly, Journal of Management Information Systems,* and *The Academy of Management Executive.* Her teaching interests include the design and management of databases, integrated software packages, and globalization of IS.

Bradley R. Brown is a graduate student in the Department of Management Sciences, University of Waterloo, Canada. His research interest is in the development and evaluation of information systems.

Nicole Coviello is a professor of marketing and international entrepreneurship in the Department of Marketing, University of Auckland, New Zealand. Dr Coviello's research interests focus on contemporary marketing practices, international business and entrepreneurship. She is published in the *Journal of Marketing, Journal of the Academy of Marketing Science, Journal of*

International Business Studies, Journal of Business Venturing, Entrepreneurship Theory and Practice, Management International Review, Journal of International Marketing, Journal of Interactive Marketing and numerous other journals.

Rick Dewar is a lecturer in computer science within the School of Mathematical and Computer Sciences at Heriot-Watt University in Edinburgh, Scotland, UK. His current research interests include various issues within software engineering (e.g., semantics, distributed tools, tool integration, metrics, modeling, reengineering, refactoring, round-trip engineering and traceability). He is also interested in understanding the nature of socio-technical ICT development from a social learning perspective; with a particular emphasis on widening the application of Alexanderian (sic) Patterns to encapsulate and communicate reflective solutions to recurring problems in a variety of domains. Previously, Rick has been a Rolls-Royce chief engineer as well as a researcher at Heriot-Watt University and the University of Edinburgh. Directly before taking up his current post, Rick was a lecturer in information management at Napier.

Abbas Foroughi is a professor of computer information systems at the University of Southern Indiana, USA, where he also serves as coordinator for the e-business program and for the eCenter. He has received the USI School of Business Faculty Service and Research Awards and the Sadelle Berger USI Faculty Community Service Award. He holds a PhD in business administration from the Kelley School of Business, Indiana University. His research interests include negotiation support systems, decision support systems, Internet security, XBRL, e-business, electronic supply chain management, electronic procurement, and online distance education. He has published papers in *Decision Support Systems, Group Decision and Negotiation,* and other journals. Dr. Foroughi has served as board member and chair of the Education Committee of the Rotary Club of Evansville, Indiana, which named him a Paul Harris Fellow and Rotarian of the Decade.

Sunil Hazari is an associate professor in the Department of Management and Business Systems, Richards College of Business, University of West Georgia, USA. His teaching and research interests are in the areas of information security, infrastructure design of e-commerce sites, Web usability, and organizational aspects of e-learning. He has authored several peer-reviewed journal publications in information and instructional technology areas, has presented papers at national conferences, and is editorial board member of information system journals.

Keith S. Horton is a senior lecturer in information management within the School of Computing at Napier University, Edinburgh, Scotland, UK. His research centres upon the organisational appropriation and application of computer based information systems, particularly in the public sector. His most recent publications have focused upon: e-government and computerisation movements; IT based processes and service evaluation utilising UML and BSC; processes of innovation and change involving information and communication technologies. Current research includes a focus upon systems implementation and adoption across public sector institutions over time, managed learning environments, knowledge management in distributed settings, and the use of patterns in socio-technical perspectives on IT adoption. Prior to becoming an academic, Dr. Horton worked for eight years in the UK public sector.

Len Jessup is dean of the College of Business and Economics, Washington State University, USA, and the Philip L. Kays distinguished professor in management information systems. While at WSU, he has guided the school through AACSB reaccreditation, developed the Boeing Classroom of the Future, and managed the implementation of a Web-based, online version of the MIS curriculum. Dr. Jessup earned his BA and MBA at California State University, Chico, and his PhD in organization behavior and MIS from the University of Arizona. His research interests include groupware, wireless collaboration, electronic commerce, and technology-supported learning and decision-making. He has authored and co-authored numerous scholarly articles, as well as the MIS textbooks *Information Systems Foundation* and *Information Systems Today* with his colleague Joe Valacich. With his wife, Joy Egbert, he won Zenith Data Systems' Masters of Innovation Award for Education.

Panagiotis Kanellis is currently a program manager with the Information Society S.A. in Athens, Greece. Previous to that he held senior consulting positions with Arthur Andersen and Ernst & Young. He was educated at Western International University in business administration (BSc), at the University of Ulster in computing and information systems (Post-Graduate Diploma), and at Brunel University in data communication systems (MSc) and information systems (PhD). He is a research fellow in the Department of Informatics and Telecommunications at the National and Kapodistrian University of Athens and an adjunct faculty member at the Athens University of Economics and Business, Greece, having published more than 50 papers in international journals and conferences. He serves on the Board of the Hellenic Chapter of the Association of Information Systems (AIS). He is a chartered information technology professional (MBCS CITP) and a certified information systems auditor (CISA).

Michael B. Knight is an assistant professor of computer information systems at Appalachian State University in Boone, NC, USA. He is a candidate for a PhD in MIS, holds a double master's degree in education and public administration, as well as a BS in aviation management from Southern Illinois University. His current research interests include group dynamics and strategic IT adoption, end-user education and training, the use of IT for organizational and group communication, and qualitative managerial consulting. His work has been presented at conferences such as IRMA, AOM, AMCIS, and DSI.

Tor J. Larsen got his PhD in management information systems (MIS) from the University of Minnesota, USA, in 1989. Since then he has worked as associate professor at the Norwegian School of Management, Norway, Department of Leadership and Organizational Management. During 2001-2002 he was visiting professor at the John Cook School of Business, Saint Louis University. In addition to reviewing for many central conferences and journals, he has acted as associate editor for *Journal of Global Information Management*, *Computing Personnel*, and *MIS Quarterly*. Dr. Larsen's publications are found in, for example, *Information & Management*, *Journal of MIS*, and *Information Systems Journal*. In 1999 he co-edited a book on innovation and diffusion theory (Idea Group Publishing). The professional memberships include AIS, IFIP WG8.2, and WG8.6. The present research interests are innovation, diffusion, innovation outcome specification, MIS, and technology mediated learning.

Liping Liu is a professor of management and information systems at the University of Akron, USA. He received his PhD in business from the University of Kansas (1995). His research interests are in the areas of uncertainty reasoning and decision making in artificial intelligence, electronic business, systems analysis and design, technology adoption, and data quality. His articles have appeared in *Decision Support Systems*, *European Journal of Operational Research*, *IEEE Transactions*, *Information and Management*, *Journal of Risk and Uncertainty*, and others. He is known for his theories of coarse utilities and linear belief functions, which have been taught in the nation's top PhD programs in computer science, economics, accounting, management, etc. He is currently serving as a co-editor for *Classic Works on Dempster-Shafer Theory of Belief Functions*, and on editorial boards and program committees of many international journals and conferences. He has strong practical and teaching interests in e-business systems design, development, and integration and has won several teaching awards. His recent consulting experience includes designing and developing a payroll system, a course management system, and an e-travel agent.

Qingxiong Ma is an assistant professor of computer information systems at Central Missouri State University, USA. He received his PhD in management information systems from Southern Illinois University at Carbondale, and MBA from Eastern Illinois University, Charleston, IL. His research interests include information technology adoption/diffusion, electronic commerce, and information security management. His articles have appeared in *International Journal of Healthcare Technology and Management, Journal of Organizational and End User Computing, Information & Management,* and *Database of Advances.* He presented numerous papers at the America's Conference on Information Systems, Decision Sciences Institute Annual Meetings, and Security conference. His teaching interests include systems analysis and design, data communication and networks, management of information systems, database management systems, and client/server application development.

Barbara Marcolin is an associate professor in the management information systems area at the Haskayne School of Business, University of Calgary, Canada. Dr. Marcolin served on the editorial board of *MIS Quarterly*, a top journal in the field of information systems. She has conducted research on electronic commerce, IT outsourcing, user competence with technology, system implementation and user complaint processes. Her current interests bring together functional areas for electronic commerce activities fostering new electronic commerce programs and research. Her published articles have appeared in several journals and books, such as *Information Systems Research, Journal of Interactive Marketing, Information & Management, Journal of Organizational and End User Computing, Journal of Systems Management, IVEY Business Journal* (was *Business Quarterly*), *Journal of Information Technology* and *Strategic Sourcing and Information Systems*.

Ji-Ye Mao is a visiting fellow in the Department of Information Systems, City University of Hong Kong, Hong Kong. He received his PhD in management information systems from the University of British Columbia, and taught at the University of Waterloo, Canada for six years. His research interest is in the area of human-computer interfaces (HCI) and interactions, including the design and evaluation of information systems (i.e., their usefulness and usability and their behavioral and cognitive bases) and user-centered design methodologies.

Roger Milley is an information systems manager at Shell Canada Limited, Canada, with over 16 years of IT experience. Mr. Milley spent six of those years implementing e-business initiatives, at both a Canadian and an international level within Shell. Mr. Milley's MBA is based on a thesis that examined how companies should set up their operations for Web-enabled consumer marketing.

Ray J. Paul is a visiting professor of simulation modeling in the Department of Information Systems and Computing at Brunel University, UK. He holds a BSc in mathematics, and an MSc and PhD in operational research, from Hull University, UK. Professor Paul has over 200 journal, book and conference publications in information systems and operational research. He is director of both the Centre for Living Information Systems Thinking (LIST), and the Centre for Applied Simulation Modelling (CASM), at Brunel. Professor Paul acts as a consultant to various government departments, software companies, and commercial companies in the tobacco and oil industries.

J. Michael Pearson is an associate professor of information systems at Southern Illinois University at Carbondale (SIUC), USA. Before coming to SIUC, Dr. Pearson served as department chair (business computer information systems) at St. Cloud State University. Dr. Pearson has presented several papers at regional, national, and international conferences. He has published articles in *Communications of the ACM, Information & Management, Journal of Strategic Information Systems, Journal of Information Systems, Journal of Computer Information Systems, Decision Support Systems, Review of Business, Journal of Internet Commerce, Information Resources Management Journal*, and *Public Administration Quarterly*. His research interests are in the areas of technology adoption, e-commerce, the management of quality, and IT project management.

William C. Perkins is professor *emeritus* of information systems and decision sciences in the Kelley School of Business, Indiana University, USA. He received his BSCE from Rose Polytechnic Institute and his MBA and DBA from Indiana University. Dr. Perkins has received 11 major teaching awards from Indiana University, and he has published papers in *Decision Sciences*, the *Journal of Political Economy*, and other journals. He has co-authored seven books, including *Managing Information Technology* (5th ed., 2005). At Indiana University, he has served as chair of the undergraduate program of the School of Business, chair of the Operations and Systems Management Department, and director of the Institute for Research on the Management of Information Systems (IRMIS). He has received Distinguished Service Awards from Indiana University, the Kelley School of Business, and the Decision Sciences Institute.

Larry Seligman is an assistant professor of MIS at the Terry College of Business at The University of Georgia, USA. He received his PhD in information systems from the University of Texas at Austin. His research interests are in technology adoption, knowledge management, organizational learning, sense making, and healthcare information systems. He has presented papers at several conferences including DIGIT, ICIS, HICSS, INFORMS, and others. He has served as conference chair/co-chair for the Diffusion Interest Group in Information Technology Workshop since 2001.

Øystein Sørebø is Dr.Oecon from the Norwegian School of Economics and Business Administration, Bergen, Norway, 2000. He is currently an associate professor at the Faculty of Education in Business Administration, Buskerud University College, Hønefoss, Norway. Dr. Sørebø's main research interest is in end-user computing and information systems success.

Valerie K. Spitler received her PhD in information systems from the Stern School of Business of New York University. She also holds an MBA from INSEAD in Fontainebleau, France, and a BSc in decision sciences from the Wharton School of Business, University of Pennsylvania. Her research interests include implementation and use of IT in organizations, communities of practice, virtual communities and qualitative research methods. She has taught hundreds of future knowledge workers, both at NYU and at the University of North Florida, USA, where she was a faculty member in the Coggin College of Business. Her research has been published in *Decision Sciences Journal, Information & Management Journal, Proceedings of the Hawaiian International Conference on System Sciences, Proceedings of IFIP Working Group 8.2, Journal of Organizational and End User Computing* and *Journal of Management Information Systems*.

Gregory E. Truman is an assistant professor of information systems at Babson College in Wellesley, Massachusetts, USA. He earned his PhD from the Stern School of Business at New York University (NYU) in 1994, where he was awarded the Outstanding Teaching Award as a PhD candidate in 1990. In 1992, he was a recipient of the annual Doctoral Dissertation Award in Insurance program, sponsored by the State Farm Companies Foundation. His scholarly work has appeared in *Management Information Systems Quarterly, Journal of Management Information Systems, Communications of the ACM, Information & Management, Journal of End User Computing, International Journal of Electronic Commerce, Journal of Organizational Computing and Electronic Commerce,* and other non-peer reviewed venues. Prior to his PhD studies, Professor Truman worked as a systems analyst in the manufacturing and financial service industries.

Shouhong Wang is a professor of business information systems at the University of Massachusetts Dartmouth, USA. He received his PhD (1990) in information systems from McMaster University, Canada. His research interests include systems analysis and design, artificial intelligence in business, and electronic commerce. He has published over 70 papers in academic journals, including *Information Resources Management Journal, Journal of Organizational and End User Computing, Journal of Management Information Systems, Information & Management, International Journal of Information Management, Human Systems Management, IEEE Transactions on Systems, Man, and Cybernetics, Computers & Operations Research, Management Science, European Journal of Operational Research, OMEGA, Decision Sciences, IEEE Transactions on Patter Analysis and Machine Intelligence, Journal of The Operational Research Society, INFORMS Journal on Computing, Computers & Industrial Engineering, Knowledge and Information Systems, International Journal of Intelligent Systems in Accounting, Finance, and Management, Neural Computing & Applications, Journal of Electronic Commerce Research, Industrial Management and Data Systems*, and others. He has been a biographies of *Canadian Who's Who* since 1995, a biographee of *Marquis Who's Who in America* since 2000, and a biographies of *Marquis Who's Who in American Education since 2004.*

Index

surfing 38
system decomposition 166
system use 31, 82, 179, 256
systems development life cycle 217

T

task support 77
technology acceptance model (TAM) 30, 54, 69, 70, 123, 178, 200
text-formatting 138
theoretical network 255
theory of planned behavior 60, 178, 249
theory of reasoned action 56, 249
training 77, 258, 295

U

Unified Modeling Language (UML) 160
URL 4, 14, 62
usability 251
user acceptance behavior 55
user satisfaction 250
user-computer interface 158, 163
user-defined business rules 165

user-friendly 133, 237
user-perceived input 158, 164
user-perceived output 158, 164
users' perception 261
utilization 31, 133, 134, 247, 250

V

video-conferencing 102, 104, 108
virus 174, 192

W

Web browser 5, 61
Web site address 4
Web site user 1
Web technology 3
Web-enabled interactivity 1, 7, 9, 11, 19, 20, 21
Web-enabled Interactivity Self-Evaluation (WISE) 3, 10, 18, 19, 22
WebQ 182
wizard 79, 81, 84, 86, 94, 95
wizard-based scaffolding 79
workplace 292
World Wide Web (WWW) 30, 46